Deep Mapping the Literary
Lake District

~

Aperçus: Histories Texts Cultures

Editor
Kat Lecky
Loyola University Chicago

Aperçus is a series of books exploring the connections among historiography, culture, and textual representation in various disciplines. Revisionist in intention, Aperçus seeks monographs as well as guest-edited multi-authored volumes that stage critical interventions to open up new possibilities for interrogating how systems of knowledge production operate at the intersections of individual and collective thought.

We are particularly interested in medieval, Renaissance, early modern, and Restoration texts and contexts. Areas of focus include premodern conceptions and theorizations of race, ethnicity, gender, and sexuality in art, literature, historical artefacts, medical and scientific works, political tracts, and religious texts; negotiations between local, national, and imperial intellectual spheres; the cultures, literatures, and politics of the excluded and marginalized; print history and the history of the book; the medical humanities; and the cross-pollination of humanistic and scientific modes of inquiry.

We welcome projects by early-career scholars, but are unable to consider unrevised dissertations. Please send a proposal and letter of inquiry to Professor Katarzyna Lecky at klecky@luc.edu.

Recent titles in the *Aperçus* series:

Deep Mapping the Literary Lake District: A Geographical Text Analysis
Joanna E. Taylor and Ian N. Gregory

Oriental Networks: Culture, Commerce, and Communication in the Long Eighteenth Century
Greg Clingham and Bärbel Czennia, eds.

Writing Lives in the Eighteenth Century
Tanya Caldwell, ed.

For more information about the series, please visit www.bucknelluniversity press.org.

Deep Mapping the Literary Lake District

~

A Geographical Text Analysis

Joanna E. Taylor
Ian N. Gregory

Bucknell | UNIVERSITY
UNIVERSITY | PRESS

LEWISBURG, PENNSYLVANIA

Cataloging-in-Publication data is available from the Library of Congress

ISBN 978-1-68448-376-1 cloth
ISBN 978-1-68448-375-4 paper
ISBN 978-1-68448-377-8 epub

LCCN 2021038288

A British Cataloging-in-Publication record for this book is available from the British Library.

www.bucknelluniversitypress.org

Distributed worldwide by Rutgers University Press

Manufactured in the United States of America

Contents

Figures

Tables

Note on the Data

We hope that the corpus data we use in this book will be helpful for other research too. There is a full list of the corpus texts in the appendix. The files that make up the corpus can be found at https://github.com/UCREL/LakeDistrictCorpus, which provides the metadata and includes a full list of the texts; the corpus files with their original markup; a version of the corpus with automated geoparsing applied; and a gold standard version of parts of the corpus in which place names were identified manually.

Deep Mapping the Literary Lake District

~

CHAPTER 1

Deep Mapping and the Corpus of Lake District Writing

At the turn of the nineteenth century, John Housman (1764–1802), son of the gardener at Corby Castle near Carlisle in North-West England, performed a study of his native region. Housman's *Topographical Description* (1800)—originally published serially in *The Monthly Magazine* between 1797 and 1799 as "Tour through England"—has been recognized as one of the earliest indications of the geological interests that were soon to sweep the country.[1] But Housman's aims went beyond the scientific; he hoped to "convey . . . a General Knowledge of the counties, with their peculiarities, [and] inhabitants."[2] He imagined two kinds of reader for his guidebook: "the distant reader, who has not time or inclination to travel," and "the tourist."[3] For his "distant reader," Housman aimed to convey information "without much trouble" or the requirement of "lots of time."[4] But he also wanted to provide the tourist with a "useful guide" that would draw their attention to "all those objects, more or less noticed, and their situations . . . which are felt worth his attention, in the course of his travels through the district."[5] Housman hoped, in short, to provide a multiscalar study that combined distant with close readings. In doing so, he registered that reading at and with such a location requires a technique that blends interests in general trends and in details.

His ambition speaks to a centuries-old recognition that comprehensively understanding a cultural object—whether that be landscape, text, or artifact—requires the simultaneous deployment of multiple analytical scales.[6] Housman's account responded to contemporary concerns that details were being overlooked in favor of prospects, and there was perhaps no place where these concerns were as concentrated as the area of Cumberland, Westmorland, and Lancashire that we know today as the Lake District. The region inspired the key writings of the picturesque movement, drove some of the nineteenth century's most important advances in geological understandings of Britain's past, and inspired some of the period's most influential authors. William Gilpin, William Wordsworth, Dorothy Wordsworth, Samuel Taylor Coleridge, Felicia Hemans, Matthew Arnold, John Ruskin, and, at the tail end of our period, Beatrix Potter each produced some of their best-known works in the Lake District. The place infiltrated their writing—but, in turn, these authors' works have contributed profoundly toward the shaping of the place too. In 2017, the Lake District was awarded UNESCO World Heritage Site Status as a cultural landscape. This category was originally devised with the Lake District in mind,[7] and makes for a practical acknowledgment of an observation made by Raymond Williams: that "the idea of nature contains . . . an extraordinary amount of human history."[8] The Lake District's UNESCO status formally recognizes the influence of authors, artists, and farmers on the ways the landscape has been managed over the course of the last three centuries.[9]

The issues to which Housman's guide drew attention—in conversation with the national aesthetic, cultural, and scientific debates to which a number of those better-known Lakeland authors contributed—remain familiar for today's literary geographers and digital humanists. His account anticipates anxieties inherent in contemporary humanities scholarship, which worry that applying macroscopic approaches to the large volumes of source material available in digital form is largely to miss the point. Understanding these anxieties as part of a long historical trend offers new perspectives on how to approach humanities scholarship in the digital age. Our aim in this book is to show how historical responses to the Lake District landscape might guide an approach to the modern study of literature that combines macro methods with close analysis.

Throughout this book, we use multidisciplinary approaches taken from literary studies, corpus linguistics, and geographical information science (GISc) to develop spatially focused, multiscalar analyses of a select corpus of Lake District literature from the seventeenth to the nineteenth centuries. In doing so, we follow Housman in advocating for a combination of the close and distant gaze. In this way, the works in our corpus are more than simply the objects of our study: their articulations of, and challenges toward, aesthetic and environmental traditions have guided our development of a digital approach to textual analysis that attempts to unite technology with the careful attention to detail which—rightly, we think—continues to underpin literary studies. Digital methodologies might be the "exoskeleton"[10] of our method here, but attentive reading remains its beating heart.

This introduction outlines the ways in which the book attempts to address what we see as the two major challenges in this kind of interdisciplinary, digitally enhanced literary study. The first challenge—how to incorporate texts within a geographical information system's (GIS) database—is technical in nature. The second is more nuanced: how can we balance the ability of GIS and other digital approaches to generate macro or distant summaries of large amounts of data with the more familiar—and still vitally important—humanities requirement of developing an interpretation of the sources based on a close and detailed understanding? Before we explain the composition of the Corpus of Lake District Writing, as well as the key technologies that have underpinned our analyses of it throughout this book, we want to situate the creation of this corpus in the broader debates about analytical approaches to humanistic data that have become central to twenty-first-century humanities scholarship.

THE DISTANT READER AND THE CLOSE:
TOWARD MULTISCALAR ANALYSIS

The digital humanities—and, relatedly, the spatial humanities with which this study engages—have developed rapidly in the past two decades. They have been driven by one fundamental, yet underacknowledged, phenomenon: that computers are no longer concerned only with quantitative data. In 2013 it was estimated that 90 percent of the data that were then in existence had been created in the previous two years, and that this volume of data would double every two years until at least 2020.[11] It is a trend that shows no sign of slacking. Many of these data are qualitative by nature: they comprise text, images, or video derived from social media, other forms of "born-digital" content, or material derived from the mass digitization of libraries and archives. These datasets differ greatly from the tables of statistics that once dominated computing, and they are more difficult for computers to interpret. Yet developments in digital technologies have created new opportunities for exploring qualitative data. In particular, they allow us to process large quantities of data in ways that can—comparatively easily—summarize their contents and uncover patterns that are not obvious through human interpretation alone. From there, as Ted Underwood has shown, we have begun to learn how to recognize the "longer arcs of change" that actually characterize literary history, as we can now say with confidence that we can analyze "thousands of volumes at a time."[12]

This is not to say that "traditional" approaches to humanities study are irrelevant in the digital age—quite the contrary. Rather, as Katherine Bode eloquently puts it, "Confronting the challenges and possibilities that new digital technologies and resources bring to literary history and to the humanities broadly requires a mutually informative relationship of traditional and digital scholarship. Only such a relationship can enable the emergence and consolidation of the new forms of evidence, analysis, and argumentation required by the contemporary conditions of cultural research."[13] Critical approaches to digital methods continue to be essential for interpreting and analyzing data, of whatever size or type. Indeed, humanistic thinking should be—though often is not—central, even to the way we compile our data. For instance, word frequency counts allow a Google search to identify the pages that are most relevant to a search term from billions of web pages, with similar approaches being applied to searching large digital corpora, such as the British Newspaper Archive. Although these approaches have become part of everyday life, they tend to be used uncritically with little understanding of the algorithms that underlie them.[14] Indeed, recent accounts suggest that even the computer programmers themselves cannot always explain precisely how an algorithm works.[15] Humanities-trained researchers thus have an important part to play in ensuring that data practices are ethical, representative, and appropriate for a given inquiry.[16]

In literary studies especially, these questions about the relationship between computer-based analysis and manual interpretation have been thrown into relief by a perceived bifurcation between distant and close reading. This split became more pronounced following the publication of Franco Moretti's *Atlas of the European Novel* (1997), and again after his *Distant Reading* (2013), but, as Underwood has observed, Moretti's work merely highlighted an existing tension. Underwood points out that book historians and sociologists of literature have been undertaking what we now call "distant reading" for decades.[17] Nevertheless, since Moretti's work, distant reading in literary studies has become increasingly associated with computational techniques.[18] Distant reading, of the kind promoted by Moretti, allows the researcher to stand back from individual sentences, paragraphs, and texts to see a larger view of a corpus through computer-generated visualizations. Such digital approaches continue to worry some groups of scholars as much as they excite others. Tanya Clement neatly summarizes the problem for those who work in literary studies: "A rumor prevails," she writes, "that literary scholars should and do neglect using digital applications that aid interpretation because most of these tools seem too objective or deterministic."[19] Johanna Drucker, meanwhile, thinks that the very term "digital humanities" is dangerously close to being oxymoronic, since the broad scope and focus on big data and macroanalysis that the digital promotes seem to be at odds with the nuance and careful attention to detail that characterize humanities study.[20] For Scott Weingart, the problem is even more serious: he thinks that pitching distant against close reading, and accepting the occlusions to which distant reading inevitably leads, risks "significant ethical breaches in our digital world."[21]

Weingart and Drucker share a similar anxiety that digital approaches, when done badly, risk promoting both the superficial analyses of complex texts and the dehumanization of literary works by effecting a problematic distance between the reader and the social, cultural, or political issues that a text might gloss. For Drucker, doing so would not only change the nature of literary studies as a discipline, but would undermine the very reason for pursuing humanities research at all.[22] Literary scholars have expressed particular anxieties about what is lost when digital approaches are applied to textual analysis; they have worried—not without justification—that when we focus on the corpus rather than the individual text, we lose fundamental understandings of how literature works and, perhaps more seriously, how it feels. Yet, as Andrew Piper observes, digital modes of reading and analyzing texts are "inevitably tied to the norms and practices of the past."[23] Nuance remains crucial for accurate, useful, and principled interpretations of humanities data since, as Weingart puts it, "from too great a distance, everything looks the same."[24] And, in fact, this interplay between distance and closeness, trend and nuance, is what he thinks defines the digital humanities: "What sets [digital humanists] apart," he writes, "is our unwillingness to stray too far from the source," even while we use big data capabilities to develop new forms of interpretation.[25]

As digital approaches to literary study become more advanced, however, understandings of how these technologies might be used to develop innovative methods of textual interpretation have led to increasing calls for a mixed methods approach. Thus, while Michael Tavel Clark and David Wittenberg's collection, *Scale in Literature and Culture* (2017),[26] broadly encourages scholars to reject close reading in favor of the macroanalytic techniques that they see as being more suitable for liter-ary study in the digital age, others see distant reading as one tool in the modern literary scholar's arsenal. In the same year as Moretti was advocating for distant reading, Matthew Jockers was arguing for a combination of macro- with micro-analysis.[27] Since then, calls for approaches that combine these methods have prolif-erated; Adam Hammond, Julian Brooke, and Graeme Hirst, for instance, contend that "computational analysis can thrive only in an ecosystem of close reading."[28] More recently, Martin Paul Eve has demonstrated how digital methodologies can be turned toward new kinds of close reading.[29] Underwood perhaps puts it best. He finds that tensions between distant and close reading are both outdated and unhelpful.[30] Moretti's original work in this space was, after all, over twenty years ago and, as the scholars with whose work we seek to engage throughout this book amply demonstrate, the field has moved on in surprising, innovative, and exciting new directions. Now more than ever there are many "different versions" of distant reading that do not pursue a "singular project."[31] Distant reading, as Underwood concludes, "is simply a new scale of description" that "has the potential to expand the discipline."[32] (And even this is not really new; Catherine Nicholson has traced ten-sions between the specific and the general in reading practices back to 1598.)[33]

Distant reading need not, then, be at odds with close analysis; one can—and, in our view, should—be used in complement with the other. An aim of this book is to demonstrate one way that we might move beyond a debate that pits distant against close reading, and toward something that embraces both in the pursuit of a new kind of literary analysis. Our approach, which we have elsewhere termed "multi-scalar analysis,"[34] differs from a macroscopic approach[35] because it does not attempt to privilege distant techniques. Properly speaking, multiscalar analysis moves back and forth between macro- and micro approaches and engages both scales for the development of nuanced literary analysis.[36] In doing so, it pursues a model adjacent to the one advanced by scholars including Sarah Allison, Piper, and Underwood, the latter of whom explains that: "Since a model defines a relationship between variables, a mode of inquiry founded on models can study relationships rather than isolated facts."[37] As we hope will become clear, relationality underpins our approach. In each chapter, we attempt to uncover new relations between time periods, loca-tions, authors, the various occupiers of a particular location, and, above all, between a place and the people who encounter it.

This approach relies on one more type of relationship: that between disciplines. As such, it may be more readily recognizable as what Bode calls "data-rich literary history,"[38] but, regardless of what we call it, the ambition is the same: to "encode a togetherness" in the way we read.[39] In part, this approach seeks to use digital approaches as a mediator between literary studies and other branches of knowl-edge.[40] But digital methodologies might go further, to challenge literary studies "to move beyond close, or even distant, readings" by embracing more fluid and dia-lectic interpretative approaches.[41] In this way, computer-oriented research can be "liberating" for humanists, since it presents new opportunities "for us to bring the skills we have honed in the close reading of texts and artefacts into service for this new species of text and artefact."[42] In other words, multiscalar analysis should be based on the same skill sets on which we rely for more "traditional" approaches to literary interpretation, but it offers new possibilities too. Specifically, multiscalar analysis should both open up access to new kinds of sources and allow us to ask new kinds of questions of this material.

As we aim to demonstrate throughout this book, visualizations, data mining, and computational text analysis each offer new ways of facilitating cross-disciplinary collaborations that might productively destabilize our assumptions about a literary text, period, or genre. As Clement puts it, these kinds of "computer-assisted methodologies . . . often provide the view the magnifying glass gives the user when he or she turns it upside down." She explains that these approaches "defamiliarize texts, making them unrecognizable in a way (putting them at a distance) that helps scholars identify features they might not otherwise have seen, make hypotheses, generate research questions, and figure out prevalent patterns and how to read them."[43] In fact, these methodologies don't just "defamiliarize" a text; the process of digitally transforming a text—whether for text mining, visualization, or another purpose—translates it into something new. These new artifacts are not designed to answer questions, but rather to pose new ones. Such approaches should facilitate new forms of close reading that, even when based on "big data," consolidate a particular research agenda and develop detailed interpretations of specific research questions.

One of this book's core concerns is to demonstrate how combining analytical approaches from three main disciplines—corpus linguistics, GISc, and literary studies—might effect this kind of "defamiliarization" and translation. The scholarship represented by this book has benefited enormously from work by, and conversations with, scholars from across these areas of study. We hope that this collaborative thinking is evident throughout, and serves to demonstrate how digital methodologies can be integrated with literary interpretation to advance both approaches, without compromising the ambitions of either. In fact, recognizing the "limitations" of each discipline might help us to "improve" them all.[44] If Patrick Svensson remains correct that "digital technologies and methods . . . are not necessarily integrated in [humanities] practice,"[45] then we hope that this study will suggest some new angles for how that kind of integration might work.

As we argue here, combining quantitative methods with a detailed understanding of the historical, cultural, and geographic contexts in which these texts were written can lead to new forms of literary analysis that acknowledge the power of big data analytics, but see it as part of a system of nuanced interpretation. While we do not spend much time investigating each author's personal and political motivations, our approach here allows us to position their Lakeland writing as part of a regional literary geography that also takes into account wider social and cultural influences. Our approach does respond to Matthew Wilkens's recognition that there is a moral and social imperative for digital work that uses quantitative methods on large corpora to challenge the literary canon and foster much greater diversity in the texts we read, think about, and write.[46] The Corpus of Lake District Writing positions canonical authors alongside lesser-known texts in an attempt to indicate the extent to which our best-known authors actually operated as part of an extensive network in which popular literature—especially guidebooks and travel writing—was at least as significant as the works with which, today, we are more familiar.

THE CORPUS OF LAKE DISTRICT WRITING

Since its "discovery" by tourists in the mid-eighteenth century, the Lake District has occupied a distinctive place in British cultural geography. This region's physical features seemed to distinguish it from the rest of the country, making it particularly useful for cartographers; as David Cooper and Ian Gregory put it, "The apparent boundedness of this environment offers a clearly defined and mappable terrain."[47] Elsewhere, Cooper neatly summarizes the cultural effect of this distinctive geography: in the early nineteenth century, he explains, the old counties of Westmorland, Cumberland, and North Lancashire "occupied an almost peninsula status within the geography of Great Britain."[48]

This geological distinctiveness was replicated in its social and cultural life. The Lake District—as it became popularly known after the publication of William Wordsworth's *Guide through the District of the Lakes* as a standalone volume in 1822—not only maintained traditional customs and dialects long after the rest of the country had become increasingly homogenized, but developed its own literary culture that advanced alongside, and often in response to, the robust tourist trade.[49] Indeed, by 1900 M.J.B. Baddeley could justifiably declare it "the most compact tourist resort of Europe."[50] More than that, Baddeley thought that there was "probably not in the whole world a district wherein, in so small a space, such a variety of scenery—rugged mountain, verdant valley, spreading lake and luxuriant wood—is comprehended."[51] This variety encouraged an astonishing breadth of artistic responses that facilitated the Lake District's emergence not only as a distinct geographic region but a literary terrain that combined fact with interpretation. Jenny Holt puts it nicely when she writes that, in places like the Lake District, "our perception of the sites [entwines] the conceptual . . . and the physical experience of being 'in' the landscape."[52]

The best-known expression of this distinctive culture emerged in the Romantic period, when the so-called Lake Poets—William Wordsworth, Samuel Taylor Coleridge, and Robert Southey—settled in Grasmere and Keswick (though Coleridge only resided there properly for a little over three years, between 1800 and 1804). Thomas De Quincey, the English Opium Eater, settled there in 1809, residing at Dove Cottage and, later, Nab Cottage (where Hartley Coleridge—Samuel's son—also lived toward the end of his life). Later in the century, John Ruskin's arrival at Brantwood in Coniston in 1871 established him as central to the new generation of Lakes writers. Figures like these were celebrated as a core part of the Lake District's identity when the National Park's boundaries were being

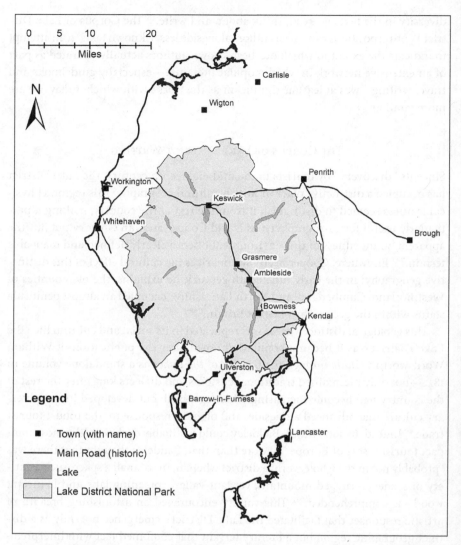

Figure 1.1. The basic geography of the Lake District. For more information, see Figure 1.3.

established (Figure 1.1), although today many more visitors are attracted to the Lakes by the lure of Beatrix Potter's legacy than any of the elder Lake Poets.[53] Potter's significant literary and cultural influence over the Lake District falls beyond the scope of this study, but she—like each of the earlier Lakes writers—contributed to the wider development of important trends in landscape science, aesthetics, and environmental thought to which the Lakeland landscape was integral.[54]

Each of these authors shared a love of the Lake District, but, more than that, they were each profoundly affected by living there. For Tim Fulford, it is this sense of being "marked by living" in the Lake District—rather than "necessarily" writing about the landscape—that defines the Lake Poet.[55] Fulford's work on Southey in particular, alongside Mike Huggins's research on the so-called Cumberland Bard Robert Anderson,[56] has indicated how necessary it is to expand our understanding of the Lake District canon, but the Corpus of Lake District Writing (CLDW) allows us to go further. By combining popular literature of the period with works by canonical Lakeland authors, the CLDW offers a challenge to the very idea of canonicity at this location and throughout this period.

Recent scholarship has shown the need to consider the Lake Poets' works as part of a wider regional tradition, rather than as a distinctive silo; Scott Hess, Saeko Yoshikawa, and Julia S. Carlson have been particularly influential in this regard by revealing the profound effect that tourist guides and travel literature had on Wordsworth's writing about the Lakes.[57] The CLDW allows us to expand on these scholars' studies by positioning authors like William Wordsworth alongside lesser-known contemporaries. The digitally aided approach to analysis we adopt here flattens the distinctions between them; after all, the computer does not know which works are supposed to be canonical.[58] The diverse literary responses to this bounded geographic region make the Lake District a helpful case study for evaluating the role of corpus linguistics and GIS in challenging canonical notions of a place and its literature that—as we hope to show throughout this book—demonstrates the potential of this approach for other regions or nations.

The CLDW comprises eighty texts, which contain accounts or descriptions of the Lake District from the seventeenth century through to the beginning of the twentieth century.[59] By the standards of corpus linguistics, this is not a large collection of texts, although Akiko Inaki and Tomoko Okita have demonstrated how useful a small corpus approach can be even for a discipline that privileges big data.[60] Yet, from a literary studies perspective, this is a sizeable and complex set of texts. The earliest items included in the corpus are extracts from the second installment of Michael Drayton's chorographic poem *Poly-Olbion* (1622), while the most recent is the twenty-second edition of the popular Victorian guidebook *Black's Shilling Guide to the English Lakes* (1900). The texts between the two include well-known works by the Lake Poets, such as Wordsworth's sonnet series *The River Duddon* (1820) and his *Guide through the District of the Lakes* (1822 and 1835). The majority of the corpus, though, comprises nonfictional prose in the form of tourist guides and travel narratives. Canonical examples include Thomas West's *A Guide to the Lakes* (1778) and William Gilpin's *Observations, Relative Chiefly to Picturesque Beauty* (1786).

Crucially, the corpus also contains the writings of lesser-known authors; writers such as the Lancashire journalist and dialect poet Edwin Waugh (1817–1890) and social reformer Harriet Martineau (1802–1876) make important contributions to the corpus that indicate the importance of traditionally marginalized voices for a revised Lake District canon. One of the CLDW's limitations, though, is its comparative homogeneity; notwithstanding the inclusion of authors like Martineau and Waugh, the CLDW is still predominantly composed of works by white, middle-class men. Just six of the texts are by women (and two of those are by Martineau), and there are no works by global majority authors. Although it offers a useful backdrop against which to test our analyses, the CLDW should not be understood as a true sample of writing in the period. As with all literary scholarship, then, these findings are not definitive; rather, they are our interpretations based on a finite set of sources (albeit more than we would feasibly have been able to analyze without this mixed-methods digital approach). Any findings from the corpus have to be interpreted in light of the sources that are, and are not, included in the corpus. Throughout this book, we have used the CLDW as a starting point and have tried to include more diverse works to nuance the broad patterns evidenced by the CLDW.

The combination of quantitative and qualitative approaches adopted from corpus linguistics, GISc, and literary studies that we propose here allows us to construct a detailed account of what is happening in the corpus; we can chart changes over time and across genre, analyzing these alterations as part of the complex literary and cultural milieu that the corpus represents. While this approach starts and ends with the texts—as we would expect from a literary studies methodology—the middle part of the analytical process is underpinned by technologies adopted from corpus linguistics and GISc. By combining approaches from these three disciplines, we are able to ask large-scale questions about the corpus and the region as a whole, alongside more focused questions about specific texts, themes, and localities. The following chapters demonstrate applications of this process, but for the remainder of the introduction we offer an overview of the digital aspects of our workflow and explain the digital technologies on which it is based.

Corpus Linguistics and Geographical Information Science

Corpus linguistics is concerned with using computers as part of a range of quantitative and qualitative approaches to study the way that language is used.[61] Its quantitative methods involve techniques including *frequency counts*, in which the number of times each word occurs in a text is identified; *keyword analysis*, which identifies what words tend to occur more often in one text or corpus compared to another; and *collocation*, which identifies words that occur together and how frequently they *co-occur*.

In its simplest form, collocation involves counting how many times each word occurs within a set number (*span*) of *tokens* of a particular search-term. A word token is either a word or an item of punctuation; thus, the clause "here, there and everywhere." comprises six word tokens because of the comma and the full stop. Simply identifying the most common collocates associated with a given search term can be unhelpful, however, since these are often merely a reflection of the most common words used in general English (such as "the" or "and"). A statistical test is required to identify words that co-occur with the search term more often than would be expected given the word's overall frequency in the corpus. A number of tests are available, including tests that produce Mutual Information (MI) scores or t-scores. MI scores emphasize less common words, while t-scores—which we use throughout this book—provide a measure that favors relatively frequent words.[62] Combining collocation analyses with *concordances*—the words and

phrases that occur around a particular search term—is especially helpful for a multiscalar interdisciplinary approach.[63] There are various software packages available to facilitate this kind of analysis, but we have used the free package AntConc
for this first stage of our quantitative approach.[64]

In order to ask anything meaningful of the corpus's spatial referents, we also
need to be able to examine the location to which a text refers. Corpus linguistics
have traditionally ignored geography as much as GIS researchers have tended to
overlook texts in favor of quantitative sources, such as disease patterns or crime
locations.[65] GIS is a computer technology developed in the late 1960s by computer
scientists, Earth scientists, and the military.[66] GIS has been widely used by geographers and others in the academy since the late 1980s and, by the early 1990s, had
spawned a new field, geographical information science (GISc), which explores the
appropriate uses of geographical information.[67] The political and military origins
of GISc, combined with the perception that it is a quantitative technology, mean
that its use remains (perhaps even should remain) "controversial" in academic
research.[68] More recently, the widespread availability of mapping platforms—such
as Google Earth, ArcGIS Online, or Neatline—has greatly increased the amount
of research in the spatial humanities.[69] These platforms take many of GIS's core
concepts—particularly the combination of spatial and attribute data that we explain
in this chapter—but simplify them in order to make them intuitive to use. But a
GIS offers unique opportunities for spatial humanities study, not least its ability
to integrate different kinds of sources and manage massive data sets; indeed, Anne
Knowles, Levi Westerveld, and Laura Strom go so far as to call GIS "the Mercedes
of geovisualization" thanks to its unrivaled analytical capacity.[70]

At its core, a GIS has a simple data model (shown in Figure 1.2). A table of data,
termed attribute data, is linked to map-based representations of where on Earth's
surface each item is located. The basic unit of storage in a GIS is called a layer.
A layer is to GIS what a table is to a database, so data related to a single theme will
usually be stored together in a layer. A layer differs from a table in that each one
consists of both spatial and attribute data; it can therefore be represented in map
form.[71] These map-based features, known as spatial data, can take one of four
forms: *points*, which, depending on scale, might represent features from individual buildings to entire cities, or geological forms like mountains (Figure 1.3a); *lines*,
which typically represent roads or rivers (Figure 1.3b); *polygons*, which represent
areas such as lakes, cities, or administrative zones (like parishes or districts)
(Figure 1.3c); or *pixels*, which are used to subdivide Earth into a continuous surface to represent, for example, height (Figure 1.3d).[72] Although usually represented
graphically, each of these four forms of spatial data is based on coordinates in a
tabular structure: a point is a single coordinate pair (x, y); a line is made up of two
or more coordinates; a polygon is made up of one or more lines that completely
enclose an area; and each pixel also has a coordinate location.

This data model offers four main opportunities for humanities research.[73] First,
the way it structures the data allows researchers to explore the significance of geography for their research topic. Second, it allows data from different sources—even

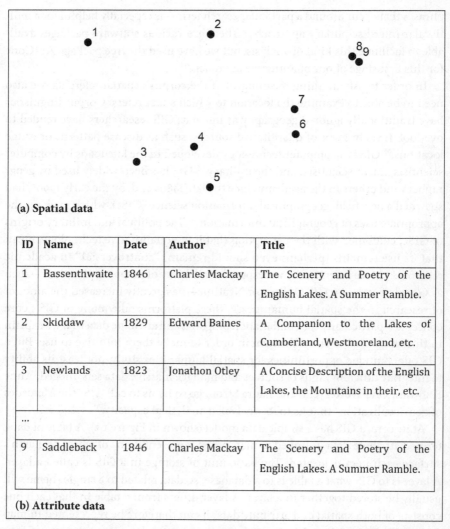

(a) Spatial data

ID	Name	Date	Author	Title
1	Bassenthwaite	1846	Charles Mackay	The Scenery and Poetry of the English Lakes. A Summer Ramble.
2	Skiddaw	1829	Edward Baines	A Companion to the Lakes of Cumberland, Westmoreland, etc.
3	Newlands	1823	Jonathon Otley	A Concise Description of the English Lakes, the Mountains in their, etc.
...				
9	Saddleback	1846	Charles Mackay	The Scenery and Poetry of the English Lakes. A Summer Ramble.

(b) Attribute data

Figure 1.2. A GIS data model based on a hypothetical example of places named in texts about the Lake District, showing (a) spatial data and (b) attribute data. The two are linked by the ID numbers.

different media—to be integrated based on spatial data (usually real-world coordinates or map projections, such as the British National Grid), developing a complex portrait of a location.[74] Third, in making use of the spatial data as well as their attributes, it facilitates more complex spatial analyses that allow us to assess the importance of location in a source, and to explore questions such as whether certain features cluster together or whether one set of features is found close to another.[75] Finally, GIS offers highly effective ways of visualizing data to facilitate spatial analysis. Maps—as well as the digital world animations, fly-throughs, and interactive graphics that are also available in GIS—provide a solid starting point for exploring spatial questions. As William A. Kretzschmar Jr. puts it, maps

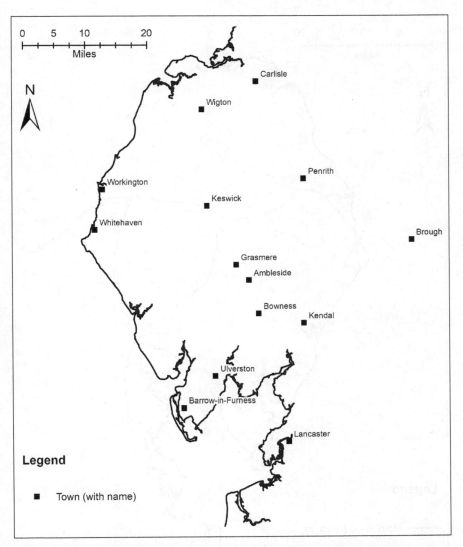

Figure 1.3a–d. The next pages show examples of the four types of spatial data representing features in and around the Lake District. Place names in (a) and (c) are derived from the attribute data, but in (d) are for orientation only. Above, (a) shows a point layer that represents towns.

"provide a graphic means to associate data, texts and more graphics into the complex cultural matrices that we expect to find in our study of the humanities."[76] The map's role is to offer an overview of the data's geographic patterns; it is up to the map reader to interpret and explain them.

Yet the apparent objectivity of a GIS has been a particular problem for literary studies. Sally Bushell, for instance, writes that GIS is often unsuitable for literary research because it resists what she calls the "slipperiness" that she sees as inherent to literary geographies.[77] Literary GIS foregrounds the map as a text to facilitate

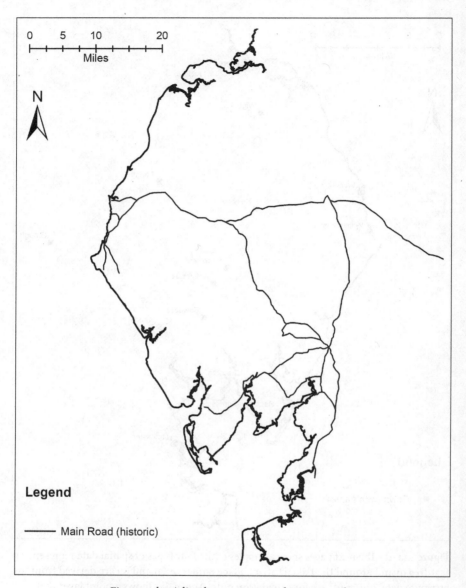

Figure 1.3b. A line layer represents historic roads.

new forms of digitally enhanced spatial interpretation. Projects such as *Emotions of London*, *The Literary Atlas of Europe*, and *Geospatial Innovation in the Digital Humanities* have demonstrated ways in which a literary approach to GIS can be used to draw out diverse textual geographies based on, for example, fiction or aesthetic categories.[78] Such thematic maps, or "distant cartographic readings" as Marko Juvan terms them, can aid scholarly interpretation in a variety of ways.[79] They can assist in the identification of broader patterns that may otherwise be obscured by the reading of only a small selection of works. Moreover, these maps can become what Juvan calls "(meta)texts": cartographic-literary hybrids that

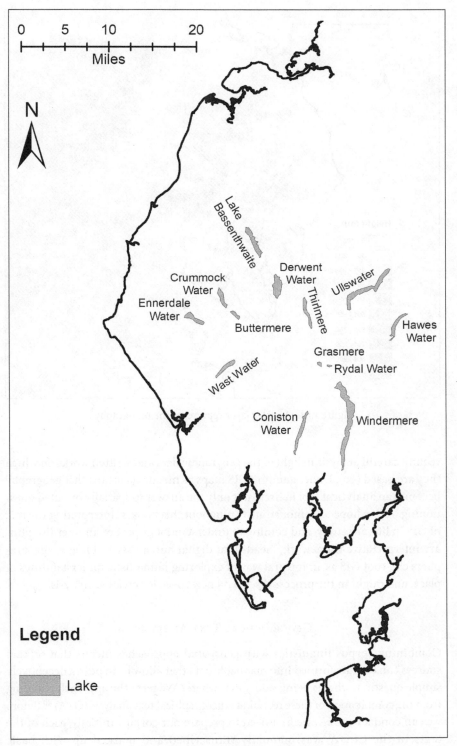

Figure 1.3c. A polygon layer represents major lakes.

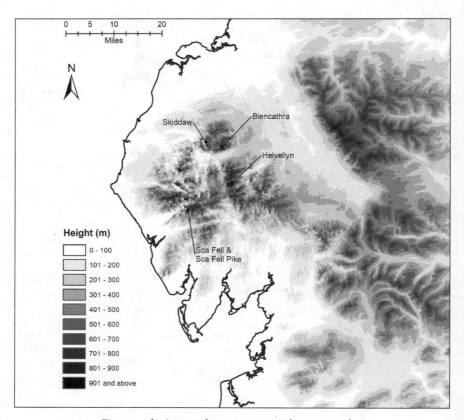

Figure 1.3d. A raster layer represents the topography.

require careful analysis in light of the geographic data and written works on which they are based (90). Understanding GIS maps as metatexts means that geography becomes an analytical tool in itself, not only the answer to spatially oriented questioning. As we hope to demonstrate throughout this book, reinterpreting the role of GIS in literary study, and coming to understand it as part of an interdisciplinary interpretative framework, means that digital humanists and literary geographers can root GIS as an integral way of exploring humanistic understandings of place, and might in the process discover a new space for creative analysis.

Geographical Text Analysis

Combining corpus linguistics with geospatial approaches means that textual sources can be transformed into mappable data that allow us to pose a deceptively simple question: what is being said about where? We term the approach resulting from the combination of these techniques geographical text analysis (GTA).[80] Before we can conduct a GTA, we first need to prepare our corpus. Initially, each of the texts in the CLDW was manually transcribed and marked up with basic

---

(a) Text fragment with XML prior to geoparsing

<p>Went over the Sands to Ulverston by Cartmel & Holker, 22 miles. It is very pleasant Riding...</p>

(b) Text fragment after geoparsing

<p>Went over the Sands to <enamex long='-3.081' lat='54.191' name='Ulverston'>Ulverston</enamex> by <enamex long='-2.943' lat='54.198' name='Cartmel'>Cartmel</enamex> & <enamex long='-2.978' lat='54.183' name='Holker'>Holker</enamex>, 22 miles. It is very pleasant Riding...</p>

Figure 1.4. Simplified example of geoparsing: a text fragment from William Wilberforce's *Journey to the Lake District from Cambridge*. (a) Text fragment with XML prior to geoparsing. (b) Text fragment after geoparsing. Note that an ampersand is often represented by "&" in XML.

XML (eXtensible Markup Language), which encoded formatting as well as key typographical and thematic features.[81] This is a standard early step in creating a corpus. However, to allow the text to be analyzed within a GIS, the text needs to be restructured so that place names can be identified, the locations to which they refer mapped, and, from there, methods devised that allow us to query the significance of place to text.

Identifying place names and the locations to which they refer requires a two-stage process known as geoparsing. The first step attempts to identify words that might be place names (known as *candidate place names*). Once these candidates have been identified, they are matched to a place-name gazetteer, a database table that lists place names along with their coordinates. Most gazetteers provide a single coordinate pair, and therefore indicate a point location.[82] This process was implemented using the Edinburgh Geoparser, a natural language processing (NLP) tool kit, which adds the information on place names and their locations to the text using XML tags.[83] This process is illustrated in Figure 1.4, where the input text (Figure 1.4a) has limited XML identifying basic structural elements (such as the paragraphs delimited using "<p>" and "</p>" tags). In Figure 1.4b, the same text has been geoparsed: the Edinburgh Geoparser has identified the place names and tagged them using the "<enamex>" tag. As well as identifying the place name, these tags include a range of additional information derived from the gazetteer, including the longitude and latitude ("long" and "lat") and a standardized version of the place name ("name").

The difficulty with geoparsing is that place names are complex and ambiguous, and the process thus requires a significant amount of manual intervention. Digital tool kits like the Edinburgh Geoparser cannot—and should not—replace the humanistic process; as Katherine McDonough, Ludovic Moncla, and Matje van de Camp put it, "there is no such thing as context-agnostic tools for GTA."[84] Each tool kit's inbuilt assumptions cause their own problems. As a result, they should be seen as part of an ongoing interplay between digital and manual techniques. Our geoparser encountered issues at both stages. In the place-name identification stage, three main problems arose. First, it can be ambiguous whether or not a word is a place name. "Lancaster" is a good example; it might refer to the place, a person (Stuart Lancaster or the Duke of Lancaster), or a type of airplane. Second, place names change over time; this is a particular problem in our region, where place-name standardization occurred relatively late. Relatedly, variations in place-name spelling—which, in the CLDW, is often thanks either to this lack of standardization or to the author's misinterpretation of the local accent—can make automatic place-name recognition challenging. Several places in the Lake District were known by varying names throughout our period; the waterfall at Lodore, for instance, is referred to in no fewer than nineteen different ways throughout the corpus.[85] The development of a gazetteer that accounts for these differences is complex and time consuming, but necessary.

Allocating the correct coordinates to place names in the second part of the geoparsing process throws up additional issues. Ambiguous place names are a common problem. To return to our previous example, "Lancaster" might mean the city in the North-West of England, or one of several Lancasters throughout the United States, Jamaica, Canada, and elsewhere. Automated techniques can be used to help disambiguate between possible options but, again, are not foolproof. Further problems include spelling variations, where the variant from the text may not appear in the gazetteer, or where the place name itself is not in the gazetteer and thus needs to be located from other sources.

These problems meant that the automated results from the geoparser were by no means perfect, so a considerable amount of manual checking and updating was required. To improve the accuracy of geoparsing, we can take two approaches: accept a large amount of postprocessing to ensure the entire dataset is accurate, or repeatedly test small subsets of the text. We applied this latter method, known as concordance geoparsing, to the CLDW. Each time we performed a search, we checked the results and recorded corrections; each subsequent search would apply these corrections. This iterative process means that the geoparsed text becomes increasingly accurate the more a corpus is worked with, and the more its users input.[86]

This cyclical relationship between digital and human processes is necessary for our wider intellectual goal.[87] As Wilkens observes, the compromises digital literary scholars must make in terms of processing quality are necessary sacrifices for the broader goals of disrupting the existing canon, and developing innovative new means of reading the vastly expanded collection of global literature to which these kinds of digitally based disruptions can lead.[88] While we must remain mindful of the limitations of this way of working, this automated process allowed us to uncover previously overlooked texts about the Lake District that both offer new ways of reading the landscape and disrupt established notions about the development of key aesthetic, environmental, and literary trends.

Pl_name	Longitude	Latitude	St_Name	L_Cotext	R_Cotext
Ulverston	-3.081	54.191	Ulverston	Went over the sands to	by Cartmel & Holker,
Cartmel	-2.943	54.198	Cartmel	the Sands to Ulverston by	& Holker, 22 miles
Holker	-2.978	54.183	Holker	to Ulverston by Cartmel &	, 22 miles. It

Figure 1.5. Simplified representation of a text suitable for reading into a GIS. Pl_Name refers to the original spelling as found in the text; St_Name provides the standardized version; L_ and R_Cotext give five tokens of co-text to the left and right of the place name, with a token being either a word or an item of punctuation. The text is taken from Figure 1.4.

To enable such analysis, the newly marked-up texts need to be converted into a format that is mappable within a GIS. Extracting the required information from the geoparsed texts is an easy task for a computer program; it identifies the "<enamex>" tags added by the geoparser—including the information about the original spelling in the text, the standardized spelling from the gazetteer, and coordinates—and converts these into a tabular form. The latitude and longitude provide the spatial data required to convert this information into a GIS point layer that represents every geoparsed place name. We can also see additional context about how the place name is used in the text by including a set number of words to the left and right of the place name (termed the *co-text*) as part of the attribute data. Figure 1.5 shows what this output looks like, based on the text used in Figure 1.4.

Once the texts have been geoparsed in this way, we can begin to ask more complex questions of the data. A core concept in GTA is the place name co-occurrence (PNC), or a place name that occurs within a set span of a search term. Using PNCs allows us to identify more complex relationships between text and place than has previously been possible; no longer restricted only to a text's "geographic investment,"[89] or the intensity of place names mentioned in a corpus,[90] now we can curate our geographic outputs according to literary interests. Corpus linguistics studies often use spans of four or five tokens in their definition of what connotes a "co-occurrence," but the choice is somewhat arbitrary.[91] Because the sentences in our historical corpus are rather longer than are more commonly found in corpus linguistics work, we have also used a longer span; the average sentence length in the CLDW is 29.8 tokens, and so we have tended to use a span of ten tokens in our work with PNCs.[92] For instance, if we want to ascertain place names in the Lake District that are associated with the Wordsworths in our corpus texts, we find all of the instances where the word "Wordsworth" occurs within ten tokens of a place name.

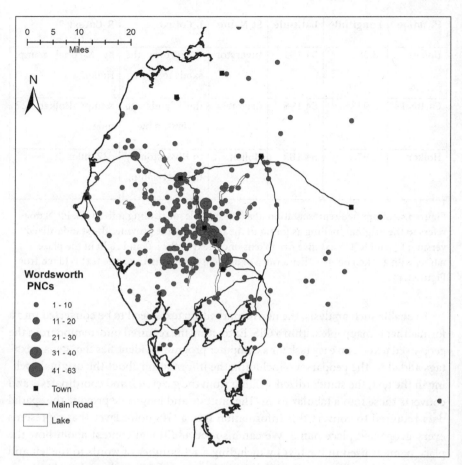

Figure 1.6. Proportion symbol map showing the locations of "Wordsworth" PNCs—the locations of place names that occur within ten tokens of "Wordsworth."

Once the PNCs have been created, they can be mapped in a number of ways. The most straightforward option is a point map (Figure 1.6), which plots each PNC as a single location corresponding to the coordinate assigned to it; in the case of Figure 1.6, we have used proportional symbols to indicate where a PNC occurs multiple times. The map shows that references to "Wordsworth" are widely spread across the region but appear particularly concentrated between Ambleside and Grasmere in the central Lakes, and around Keswick in the north. However, this method also highlights one of this technique's most obvious limitations: that places are usually not contained within a single coordinate. This failing is particularly evident in the case of large features, such as lakes. In the Lake District, it is complicated further by the fact that two of the major lakes (Coniston and Windermere) share their name with the adjacent town. The geoparser is unable to disambiguate the lakes from the settlements, and so mentions of "Coniston" or "Windermere" default to being plotted at the locations of the towns. In the case of Figure 1.6, the

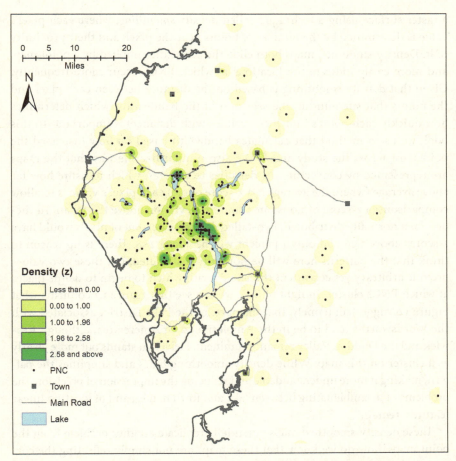

Figure 1.7. Density smoothed map showing the locations of "Wordsworth" PNCs—the locations of place names that occur within ten tokens of "Wordsworth."

large circle just north of Bowness on the east shore of (Lake) Windermere is the point that represents Windermere without distinguishing whether this is the lake or the town (see Figures 1.1 and 1.2 for the locations of commonly named places). Similarly, the large point at the north-west end of Coniston Water represents the town of Coniston. A further problem is the large circle roughly halfway between Coniston Water and Wastwater, which represents the Duddon Valley. In this case, a point is being used to represent a valley, a feature that would be better represented as either a line or a polygon. Issues such as these do not make the map useless; rather, they highlight the degree to which we must treat such visualizations with caution, and continue to foreground the role of humanistic interpretation—and the individual researcher—in analyzing them.

A second problem that is obvious from Figure 1.6 is simply that, where a lot of points occur close together, the map becomes overly crowded and hard to interpret. Alternate ways of representing the data can help to resolve some of these issues. In Figure 1.7, the same data as shown in Figure 1.6 has been converted into a raster surface using a technique called *density smoothing*, where each pixel's value is determined by the number of points near the pixel, and their proximity to it. Density-smoothed maps both elide the certainties implied by a point map, and more easily indicate the locations at which PNCs occur more frequently. Given that density smoothing is based on the distance between each pixel and the points that surround it, the selection of the bandwidth (which determines how quickly each point's influence declines with distance) is important. In this book we use a method that calculates bandwidth based on how dispersed the points are across the study area.[93] We also standardize the way that the maps are represented by converting the densities to *z-scores*, which measure how far above average (where the average is a z-score of 0.0) each pixel's value is to allow comparisons; a z-score of 1.0 is one standard deviation above the mean. In theory, for a normally distributed, two-tailed dataset, 5 percent of pixels would have z-scores above 1.96 and only 1 percent will be above 2.58. There is no reason to think that the patterns here will be normally distributed, but these two values provide arbitrary yet consistent thresholds with which to begin to define places at which PNCs cluster. In light of this, we can see that Figure 1.7 confirms what Figure 1.6 suggested: namely, that the parts of the Lake District associated with the Wordsworths tend to be in the Ambleside to Grasmere area, although Keswick and the Duddon Valley remain prominent. Helvellyn stands out more clearly as a cluster on this map. While density smoothing blurs and simplifies the pattern, making it more understandable and reducing the impression of precision, the problems of disambiguating between lake and town names, and of locating linear features, remain.

These density-smoothed maps potentially replicate another problem from the point maps: how do we know that these maps are not simply reflecting the corpus's background geography? Places such as Windermere, Ambleside, Grasmere, and Keswick—being the most significant settlements along the main trunk road through the region—were the most accessible parts of the Lake District, and so it is not surprising that they are the most frequently named locations in the corpus. It is, therefore, possible that the patterns shown in Figure 1.7 are largely a result of more people having written about these places than have written about locations that were not as accessible, like the western fells. We need a method by which we can take the corpus's inherent bias toward these locations into account.

We have adopted a technique originally inspired by the need for epidemiologists to identify clusters of cancer cases among variable background populations, known as the Kulldorff spatial scan statistic.[94] Coincidentally, much of this research was inspired by the debate in the 1980s and 1990s about whether there was a cluster of childhood cancers near the Sellafield nuclear site on the west coast of Cumbria, which is clearly visible from the western Lake District fells.[95] The central issue for this research was that, on a simple map showing the locations of cases of a disease, it is difficult to identify whether higher numbers of cases indicate a higher rate of cases per head of population or are simply a result of population density. To resolve this problem, techniques such as Kulldorff's statistic identify places that

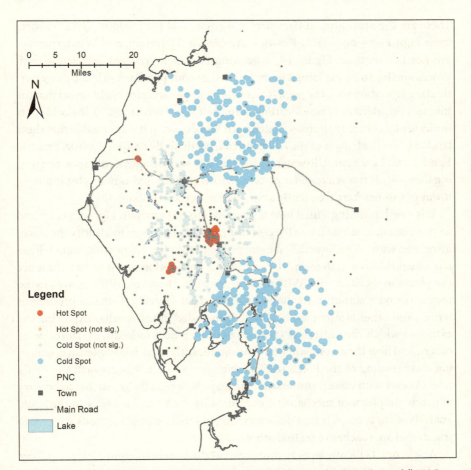

Figure 1.8. Kulldorff clusters map showing hot and cold spots for "Wordsworth" PNCs when compared to all place names in the corpus.

have more cases than would be expected given the underlying population, and those that have fewer than would be expected. These are termed *hot spots* and *cold spots*, respectively. Where hot and cold spots are statistically significant, it provides strong evidence that the underlying population is more or less at risk of the disease in question. Other hot (and cold) spots are not statistically significant, meaning that there still appears to be either a cluster or a lack of cases, but that these may have occurred randomly as a result of the distribution of the disease through the population.

We have applied this approach to the distribution's PNCs, wherein the PNCs for a search term become the cases, while all place name instances throughout the corpus become the underlying population. Areas identified as hot spots have more PNCs than would be expected given the underlying distribution of place names, while cold spots have fewer. Thus, in Figure 1.8, we can see that there are two major hot spots where the interest in the Wordsworths is over and above what we would expect given the popularity of these places in the corpus as a whole.

These are the areas around Grasmere and Rydal, and the Duddon. Other clusters from Figure 1.7—noticeably Keswick, Ambleside, Helvellyn, and Windermere—are not hot spots on Figure 1.8, suggesting that their frequent association with Wordsworth can be explained more by their overall popularity than by any particular association with the poet. (Of course, a deeper analysis might reveal that the inherent popularity of these locations is in itself Wordsworthian.[96]) The cold spots indicate places that are not associated with Wordsworth. It is noticeable that these tend to be on the fringes of the Lake District, particularly around Carlisle, Penrith, Kendal, and Lancaster. Ullswater is also, perhaps surprisingly, a cold spot, suggesting that—while it was a popular place, and its famous daffodils notwithstanding—it was not somewhere frequently associated with the Wordsworths.

It is worth injecting a final note of caution into this analysis. Figures 1.6, 1.7, and 1.8 present a distant reading of the corpus in ways that allow us to identify the places associated with "Wordsworth" or, more precisely, the place names that occur within ten tokens of this search term. The convenient assumption might be that these are the places associated with William Wordsworth. However, William was by no means the only author in the household; his sister Dorothy, herself a prodigious writer, and other family members will be included in the results. Exploring the extent to which the pattern is created from references to William, Dorothy, or others, and how these compare would be significantly more labor intensive, requiring close reading of the PNCs to disambiguate to which Wordsworth the PNCs refer. As ever with distant summaries, the map challenges the researcher to be wary of overly simplistic or mechanistic explanations. As we will see later in the book, analysis of these maps is best done by marrying these digital methods with more traditional approaches to textual scholarship.

At its core, GTA attempts to unite several disciplines—linguistics, geography, and literary studies—that have traditionally functioned in opposition to each other. It rejects the narrative, which Tania Rossetto rightly identifies as being problematically dominant, that continues to posit cartographic and technical competences as in competition with literary skills.[97] Throughout this study, we build on GTA by using a literary approach to GIS as a form of deep mapping. As we now want to explain, this method channels the interpretation inherent to literary scholarship, alongside the technologies that are fundamental to deep mapping, in order to align the map's ability to facilitate the analysis of large amounts of data with the literary scholar's interest in detailed understandings of individual accounts. It attempts to foreground the multiplicities of human spatial experiences, the diverse ways of representing them, and the creative uses to which digital technologies might be put for analyzing—as well as visualizing—qualitative sources.

Deep Mapping as Literary Practice

It is hopefully clear from the foregoing that the data model used by GIS and the analytic methods that it enables offer exciting possibilities for new forms of research into humanities sources. However, the kinds of data on which the humanities depend also emphasize the limitations inherent to the GIS data model.[98] Indeed, GIS's major strength is also its fundamental weakness: the highly quantitative structure that allows us to undertake spatial analysis also depends on translating complex, ambiguous sources into more definite numerical data (such as specific coordinates). This approach also risks stripping the map of its affective meaning; the "mingl[ing]" of the "contours of the land with the human imagination" that Tom Lynch, Cheryll Glotfelty, and Karla Armbruster see as fundamental to a map's "power."[99] A map's ability to partake productively in interpretative endeavors is overshadowed in a GIS map by apparent objectivity. At its most extreme, GIS has been accused of promoting "the very worst sort of positivism."[100] Serious consequences can result from this approach; as Mei-Po Kwan, Marianna Pavlovskaya, and Kevin St. Martin have argued, GIS fundamentally risks perpetuating narratives of underrepresentation—especially of women and nonwhite communities— since the coordinate systems on which it is based are not politically neutral.[101]

For these reasons, Knowles, Westerveld, and Strom conclude that GIS research in the humanities needs to comprehend both GIS's "digital architecture" and its implications for "symbolic communication" in these disciplines.[102] Knowles and her coauthors argue that one way we can productively maintain an awareness of GIS's inherent political biases and structural limitations is by rethinking the terms we use in reference to it. They note that disciplines which are new to GIS have "typically viewed it . . . as a tool in the simple sense of a kind of computer software that enables them to do new kinds of work."[103] By changing our terms, they suggest, we can change the way we understand—and so use—GIS in the humanities.

They advocate instead for calling GIS a "technology," a term that "acknowledges that it was created during a certain period of time to solve particular problems." More than this, they believe that this relabeling also highlights the creative potential of GIS. They continue: "Whereas tool is singular, technology can be plural. As a technology, GIS is not a single tool, but a bundle of techniques with many capabilities; not a hammer, but a workbench, or more than a workbench—a workshop."[104] In referring to GIS as a simple tool, literary scholars—like other digital humanists—have risked limiting the uses to which GIS might be put in analyzing qualitative data. Conversely, when we think of GIS as an entire workshop, myriads of new possibilities emerge. If a tool simply gives us what we need to complete a specific, predetermined task, a workshop encourages play and experimentation. Amy Wells is even more specific; she sees the inclusion of GIS into literary analysis as a way of "transform[ing] a battlefield into a cooperative interdisciplinary laboratory."[105]

In the spatial humanities, the idea of deep mapping has gone some way toward channeling the kinds of interdisciplinarity for which Rossetto, Knowles, and Wells have argued. Based on eighteenth- and nineteenth-century antiquarian approaches to map making—which included history, folklore, local traditions, and natural history alongside geographic and geological data—the deep map attempts to communicate a sense of a place's identity beyond its name and its status as a plottable Cartesian point. As David Bodenhamer, John Corrigan, and Trevor Harris explain, a deep map is "a finely detailed, multimedia depiction of a place and the people, animals, and objects that exist within it and are thus inseparable from the contours and rhythms of everyday life."[106] It aspires to return the map to its role as what Jess Edwards calls a "meeting point for a wide range of knowledges and cultural practices," making it an important vehicle for multidisciplinary, holistic studies of space and place.[107]

The deep map recognizes that human geographic experiences are not based, as Stephen S. Hall puts it, on "the limits of the compass"; rather, the mind interprets space "by association." For Hall, the map should "testify to our belief in the value of exploration, whether the compass is pointed inward or out."[108] A deep map seeks to foreground, often in creative and playful ways, precisely this relationship between personal experience and geographic fact. By emphasizing the human elements of a place, the deep map expresses the extent to which geography always, to some extent at least, combines objective and subjective factors. In this way, a deep map addresses some of the more significant limitations that humanities scholars have discovered in GIS-based approaches.[109] For Bodenhamer, Corrigan, and Harris, the deep map is "the essential next step for humanists who are eager to take full advantage of the spatial turn that has already begun to shape our disciplines."[110]

However, many of the recent debates around deep mapping have been limited to discussions about the integrated use of multiple digital sources, technologies, and methods.[111] The problem with this approach is that it sees the depth in deep mapping as being primarily in the range of technologies and digital content employed, rather than also in the deep map's creative, imaginative, and interpretative opportunities. We argue throughout this book that, in order to implement the kinds of multiscalar analysis that combines digital capabilities with humanistic interpretation, deep mapping must be seen as a practice as well as a product. Our approach recognizes the maps of literary sources produced in GIS as having an analytical character in themselves. In other words, a deep mapping methodology understands the works in the CLDW and the GIS maps we produce from them as interlinked texts, each of which needs to be interpreted carefully in light of the complex social, cultural, and literary data that underpins humanities research. As we demonstrate, this practice uses the maps to help define questions, and to distinguish aspects of the sources to answer those queries more satisfactorily. More than that, it recognizes digital maps as reactive—rather than, as is the case with analogue maps, static—media that can offer gateways into new interpretations of the underlying source material. In this way, the digital provides the framework through which humanities research can be conducted and enhanced.

In this approach, then, digital maps become the basis of a new form of close reading; even when based on "big data," these technologies can facilitate further analysis of specific texts. More than that, by recognizing that the texts offer a guide to reading the map at least as much as the map can help us interpret the text, a deep mapping methodology confronts a central problem with GIS: its inability to register personal or phenomenological responses to landscape. Reading the map in light of the texts, as well as the other way around, transforms the geographic certainties implied by the quantitative nature of GIS into networks of conceptual possibilities that intertwine experience with topography, and technology with interpretation.

This far into the digital turn in the humanities, we might identify three phases in digital humanities scholarship. In the first, databases, corpora, and/or techniques are developed to explore the potential of digital methods in advancing knowledge about a particular kind of source. In the second, method- or data-led research starts to be conducted using these new resources, with the aim of exploring, explaining, and critiquing these new opportunities. A third stage involves moving the humanities back to the foreground by using the technology to develop nuanced responses to applied research questions on topics that are derived primarily from the sources rather than the technology. While the use of the technology is of interest at this stage, and should be critically reflected on, real success is demonstrated by the applied contribution to knowledge. This stage is hardest—but also the most important. While the results from the second stage are likely to offer genuinely field-changing contributions to knowledge, the digital's ultimate contribution to humanities study is made in the third stage: because we return to building on a large existing body of scholarship, the findings—while they will develop the field—are likely to be evolutionary not revolutionary.

This book attempts to move deep mapping firmly into this third stage by exploring a range of themes derived from one basic question: what can our sources and approaches tell us about life and literature in the pre-twentieth-century Lake District? Each of the following chapters addresses this question through different foci, and varying uses of the technologies we have described here. Chapter 2 explores the affinities between the digital humanities and the picturesque gaze that informed the development of the Lake District as a cultural landscape. Both approaches, it argues, adopt technology-driven curatorial methods and stimulate similar concerns about the relationship between interpretation and reality. Our interest in chapter 2 is not to offer another theory of the picturesque but to explore the synergies between this aesthetic and the digital methodologies that we seek to exploit throughout this book. Developing from this, chapter 3 interrogates William Wordsworth's three main categories of Lakeland user: tourists, travelers, and inhabitants. These categories form the basis of our investigation into the uses of deep mapping for revealing the complex sociocultural and geographic interactions that were taking place throughout this period. More than that, it argues that these categories indicate how important it is to interpret the apparently objective data displayed in GIS through a subjective lens.

The remaining chapters each focus more closely on a particular site or concept, and seek to demonstrate how a deep-mapping approach can reveal new things about well-known places and texts. Chapter 4 is interested in the connections between three elements: place, the peripatetic body, and literary form. In particular, it is interested in the implications of the various terms used for a similar movement: walking, rambling, and wandering, for instance, are traditionally taken as being very nearly synonymous. In fact, as the chapter demonstrates, mapping references to these movements across the Lake District using GIS reveals that each term constructed a particular writing and walking identity, one that brought much to bear on the individual's relationship, and cultural or physical engagement, with the landscape. Chapter 5 explores a hitherto underrecognized—yet, as we argue, central—element of the historical Lakeland experience: the ways that visitors to the region used sound as a place-making practice. Visitors to and inhabitants of the region deliberately disrupted this natural soundscape with hyperbolic noises: they blew hunting horns, set off cannon, and shouted into the valleys. These sounds revealed something about the place, the listener, and the relationships between the two. Chapter 6 develops the themes of the previous two in relation to a feature that became prominent in the minds of Lakeland travelers: that is, Scafell, the massif containing England's two highest peaks. In contrast to the previous chapters, this chapter demonstrates how a literary approach to GIS can be used to read specific locations, and how such geographic meanings contribute to—even transform— how we read literary works written at and about that place. The chapter concludes by exploring some possibilities for the future development of deep mapping in humanities scholarship.

Throughout, we have tried to be clear about one fundamental point: computer technology cannot, in or of itself, answer our questions. What a computer can do far better than a human is objectively and accurately summarize a large quantity of material, and present these summaries to a researcher in understandable ways. But there are at least two things a computer cannot do. First, it cannot frame the research questions that justify producing the map, or other summary, in the first place. Second, it cannot interpret the patterns revealed in such visualizations. This second issue in particular is why we think that multiscalar analysis is so important, especially in a deep mapping environment: the human mind cannot interpret very large volumes of material, but it can be guided by the computer in developing deeper understandings of both the map and the texts that created it.

~

CHAPTER 2

Picturesque Technologies
and the Digital Humanities

In 1857, the anonymous author of the popular *Nelson's Handbooks for Tourists: The English Lakes* thought that there was "perhaps, no part of Great Britain" that was "more varied in its scenery, or more calculated to afford intense gratification to the tourist . . . than the Lake District of England."[1] As this writer recognized, the Lake District had displayed an unprecedented commitment to touristic ideals over the course of the previous century, during which the region had been carefully manipulated to reflect the aesthetic fashions of the day. As a result, the Lakes are widely recognized as the birthplace of the picturesque movement, a form of aesthetic calculation that transformed the landscape into a "brand" that comprised an iconic series of picture-like views.[2] Since then, the picturesque has come to define the treatment of wild places around the world, particularly underpinning their transformation into national parks where tourists might safely experience a redacted kind of "wilderness."[3] From the 1770s onward, this landscape—perhaps more than any other—came to embody what Raymond Williams calls "a Romantic structure of feeling," which saw "the assertion of nature against industry, and of poetry against trade; the isolation of humanity and community into the idea of culture, against the real social pressures of the time."[4] The consequences, as we will see in this chapter and the next, were aesthetic, social, and geographic.

There was more to the picturesque than simply looking at the landscape. Our anonymous guide was of the opinion that a visitor on the hunt for the picturesque needed to be actively engaged with the place. This author advised about the various occupations that would keep the nineteenth-century picturesque tourist's mind "constantly on the *qui vive*": the "man of science" will discover much from the "flowers, rare plants and luxuriant undergrowth"; the mountains present the geologist with "a tempting field of investigation"; the "ruins and several very curious Roman and Druidical remains" will "furnish points of interest to the antiquarian"; the painter will be challenged by the "variety of landscape" and the "picturesque effects of light and shade"; and, finally, the literary tourist will find much to fascinate in the "woods and streams . . . associated with the names of many of our greatest poets."[5] To undertake these various occupations, visitors to the Lake District might equip themselves with lenses and mirrors (particularly the Claude glass), sketchbooks, magnifiers, a tape measure, barometers, geological hammers, and, from the mid-nineteenth century, photographic technologies like the camera lucida, panorama, and daguerreotype.[6] Other inventions, including the solar microscope and magic lantern, also fed into the development of the picturesque by making such technology-driven ways of viewing and interpreting the world part of everyday practice.[7] Understanding the deep history of a place, it seems, required modern tools. Equipment like this acted, in Ron Broglio's words, as "computational prosthes[es]" that attempted to "make sense of things in nature."[8] It was an extension of a Romantic stance that sought to make "Nature" both "subjectively particularized and objectively generalized."[9] The technologies that underpinned the picturesque gaze aided the rendering of the region's complex geographical, political, and cultural histories into something that appeared transparently objective.[10]

In Broglio's view, artists used picturesque technologies to critique the aesthetic's limitations and to find ways of "bending" picturesque methodologies to "create new access to the landscape."[11] In doing so, they risked creating a critical distance between observation and location that privileged sentimentalized responses above inconvenient social and political histories. Yet these technologies also offered new means by which to explore subjective responses to a landscape that combined the tourist's personal experiences with a sense of its long and complex histories.[12] As the picturesque developed over the course of the eighteenth and nineteenth centuries, it offered opportunities for considering the relationship between person, place, and the media through which they were represented.

Recent technologies have not discarded a sense of discomfort with what we might continue to recognize as the picturesque gaze. An advertisement for the Samsung Galaxy S8 mobile phone, for instance, encourages the prospective user to "unbox your phone," promising "less to hold—and much more to see."[13] This advertisement signifies a twenty-first-century attempt to move away from a picturesque aesthetic that continues to influence the way we interact with the world in the digital age. Indeed, we might say that with the ubiquity of smartphones and the prevalence of video and photography in everyday Western culture, the picturesque has attained a prominence in today's daily life similar to that in the late eighteenth and nineteenth centuries.

The digital humanities share a number of traits with the picturesque gaze, not least that they adopt technology-driven curatorial methods and stimulate similar concerns about the relationship between interpretation and reality. Johanna Drucker sees methods adopted from empirical sciences—especially data visualizations like the graphs, charts, and maps that flow from digital projects—as being particular culprits in encouraging an assumption that "the phenomenal world [is] self-evident and the apprehension of it a mere mechanical task." She considers such strategies to be "fundamentally at odds with approaches to humanities scholarship premised on constructivist principles." The "sheer power" of graphical displays, she thinks, "seems to have produced a momentary blindness among practitioners who would never tolerate such literal assumptions in textual work."[14] The fundamental problem that Drucker identifies is a picturesque issue: "Rendering observation (the act of creating a statistical, empirical, or subjective account or image) as if it were the same as the phenomena observed collapses the critical distance between the phenomenal world and its interpretation, undoing the basis of interpretation on which humanistic knowledge production is based. We know this. But we seem ready and eager to suspend critical judgment in a rush to visualization."[15] The "collapse" Drucker identifies is comparable to the one initiated by a picturesque view of the landscape, which closes the gap between the "phenomenal world" and interpretations of it by using the literature and artwork it inspires to guide conservation and preservation. A similar "rush to visualization" effects both the uncritical approach that Drucker worries can inform digital humanities research and the transformation of a landscape into a picturesque artifact that risks becoming little more than a Baudrillardian "simulacrum" of itself.

In the digital humanities, data take the place of landscape as the object to be interpreted in light of a particular intellectual mode that, in its careful curation of a "scene," shares close affinities with the picturesque gaze. In line with Trevor Owen's advice about data generally, and Marko Juvan's on maps and other visualizations produced by geospatial technologies in particular, we treat both our digital and our written materials as interpretable texts.[16] We suggest that the ways our corpus data can be, as Christof Schöch neatly summarizes, "transformed, analyzed and acted upon," offer invaluable viewing stations from which to interpret the field from the perspective of both "traditional" and digital humanities.[17] Nevertheless, as we indicate here, the cautions utilized in respect to the applications of and research into the picturesque gaze might be applied with equal felicity to digital humanities practices.

The affinities between the picturesque gaze and the digital humanities inform our approaches throughout this book. Our interest in this chapter is not in offering another theory of the picturesque, but rather to explore synergies between this aesthetic and digital methodologies. Our aim here is both to expand on the historical role of the picturesque in the Lake District and to use that mode to critique the practices and forms of visualization that underpin the methods of both the picturesque and contemporary digital humanities. In this, we want to explore a question that Jessica Pressman and Lisa Swanstrom proposed in their introduction to a special issue of *Digital Humanities Quarterly*: "What kind of scholarly endeavors are possible," they ask, "when we think of the digital humanities as not just supplying the archives and data-sets for literary interpretation but also as promoting literary practices with an emphasis on aesthetics, on intertextuality, and writerly processes?"[18]

This chapter examines both what a digital approach to literary studies can reveal about the picturesque, and how reading the digital in light of that aesthetic can offer productive critiques of the methodologies we apply here. Deep mapping inherits from the picturesque a tendency toward multimedia representations that situate multiple, complex narratives in the same space. It also shares with the picturesque an inherent tension between the examination of histories and the (sometimes hyper-) modernity of the tools it applies. We suggest that digital visualizations—typically maps, graphs, diagrams, or summary statistics—should help to guide the reader's interpretation of the sources on which they are based. These outputs should also offer a space in which quantitative and qualitative features can coexist and be assessed alongside each other.[19] Before we turn to the affinities between the visualizations the guidebooks employ and the technologies we use here, we want to offer an overview of the picturesque's development in the Lake District, and to outline how its insistence on multiscalar readings of the landscape influence our deep mapping practice.

Specifying in General: Deep Mapping and the Gilpinian Picturesque

The picturesque as a named aesthetic was unknown in the seventeenth century; Robert Southey's damning evaluation that Celia Fiennes's manuscript account of her Lakeland tour (gifted to him by her descendants) contained "a good deal of *picture*, though nothing of the *picturesque*" suffices as a summary for general responses to the Lake District's scenery before the mid-eighteenth century.[20] Until then, as Walter John Hipple reminds us, the picturesque usually meant one of two things: either "vivid" or "graphic" when it related to literary style, or something "eminently suitable for pictorial representation."[21] Since, the picturesque has inspired a vast range of interpretations and definitions; indeed, John Ruskin thought that "probably no word in the language, (exclusive of theological expressions), has been the subject of so frequent or so prolonged dispute."[22]

The groundwork for the picturesque was laid in what Ruskin impatiently called "the blundering, pseudo-picturesque, pseudo-classical minds of Claude [Lorrain] and the Renaissance landscape painters," including Rubens and Salvator Rosa.[23] These painters, along with the humanist philosophies of Thomas Hobbes and John Locke, promoted a connection between sense stimuli and the imagination. In John Dixon Hunt's words, establishing this link between body and mind gave the "mental exchanges between figures and painted or real landscapes . . . a proper vocabulary and thus considerable status."[24] In combining what the viewer saw with how they saw it, the picturesque was the aesthetic that most comprehensively followed Lockean principles. It constituted a profound social shift that witnessed an intensification of perspective techniques, complicated understandings about visual perception, and the development of rhetorical strategies for communicating the relationship between the body, the mind, and the landscape.[25] To borrow Paul Carter's succinct phrase, the true picturesque should "[entice] the eye (and the mind) to wander."[26] As we will see, though, that was often not how the picturesque was utilized.

The proliferation of picturesque theories after 1770 communicated this aesthetic evolution to a receptive public whose attitudes toward travel were rapidly evolving. At this time, the impetus for travel was changing from being a quest for culture to a hunt for certain prescribed scenes and objects. After the Cumberland-born curate William Gilpin published his *Observations, Relative Chiefly to Picturesque Beauty* in 1786, the picturesque came to represent "an elitist appropriation" of the environment.[27] It privileged the visual over other senses,[28] and eyewitness reports became travel's principal mode (with long-lasting consequences for the visually impaired, as Hannah Macpherson has shown).[29] As a result, experiences of this landscape were broken down into a series of carefully packaged views. According to Jeffrey Auerbach and Elizabeth Bohls, the resultant homogenization of the landscape suited the logic of a rapidly expanding empire that sought to unite heterogeneous cultures under one geopolitical banner.[30] Through this union, the picturesque created what Pfau calls "an imagined (or virtual) community or class" on a global scale.[31] The Lake District's visitors represented an important enclave of that community, and the picturesque tourists' group identity was reinforced by the guidebooks that began to flood the market from the mid-eighteenth century.

More specifically, what we might recognize as these guidebooks' deep mapping methodologies were crucial for the dramatic rise in the Lake District's popularity in these years. Indeed, Tim Fulford attributes the picturesque's democratization, and subsequent popularization, to its embracing of multimedia modes of communication that combined words with images.[32] The rise in popularity of tours to the Lake District and Scotland allowed what Fulford calls the "new, middle-class reading public" to put into practice the aesthetic theories they learned from their books.[33] Eventually, these tourists became the experts in the picturesque: because of the sheer amount of picturesque scenes they consumed, they became "more reliable source[s] of aesthetic judgement than the landed gentleman."[34]

Gilpin's *Observations* were instrumental in popularizing this mode of reading the landscape. It was Gilpin who encouraged tourists in increasing numbers to visit Britain's uplands; his *Observations* helped to establish a British version of the European Grand Tour even before the Napoleonic Wars rendered the equivalent necessary.[35] His work helped to transform the working uplands of Wales, Scotland, and the Lake District into commodified representations of rural idylls inherited from Claude and Rosa. His influence was astonishingly wide reaching in both fiction and reality; Rosemary Hill writes that it was Gilpin who "sent Elizabeth Bennet to Derbyshire" and "Keats to Scotland, Cumbria, and the Isle of Wight."[36] To do as Gilpin advocated, and judge a natural scene by the rules of artistic composition, became what Ernest de Selincourt calls an "instinct"[37] for writers from Wordsworth to Ruskin (even if it underwent significant changes throughout these authors' works).[38]

It is important to bear in mind that Gilpin's picturesque was a methodology, not simply a category.[39] In his preface, Gilpin explained that—notwithstanding the fact that his work had "received considerable improvements" from both his own revisions and editorial interventions from "several of his ingenious friends"—he still "offer[ed] it to the public with apprehension."[40] His concern was that the methodology that underpinned his *Observations* was far from perfect:

[The author's] apprehension is first grounded on the inadequate time he had to employ in making observations on the several landscapes he has described. No one can paint a country properly, unless he has seen it in various lights . . . he, who should see any one scene, as it is differently affected by a lowering sky, or a bright one, might probably see two very different landscapes. He might not only see distances blotted out; or splendidly exhibited: but he might even see variations produced in the very objects themselves; and that merely from the different times of the day, in which they were examined.[41]

Mountain landscapes exaggerated this concern; in such scenes, Gilpin thought, "local variations cannot be too much attended to by all lovers of landscape." His solution to this dilemma was striking: he aimed "only to specify in general, under what kind of light and weather, the several landscapes he saw were exhibited." This approach was more straightforward near the lakes, where—since he had "spent near a week among them" and so had witnessed "so much of their varieties"—he felt able to provide more detail. He concluded that, at a lake, he could "make allowances for the effects of light and weather," and could "speak of them, in general, with more precision."[42] In both cases, what Gilpin aims for is a multiscalar deep map. He does not simply want to combine the distant with the detailed; rather, he aims to merge the two, so that he may "specify in general." Doing so, he reckoned, would allow him to offer his readers a way of familiarizing themselves with a particular location, while situating themselves within a much larger landscape.

   Gilpin provided practical advice for generating these kinds of subjective interpretations of the landscape that combined what the viewer could, and wished they could, see. His aim was not to improve nature—for that idea was "absurd, and [could] only be adopted by men of false taste,"[43] but to bring "beauties" from various areas into a single scene to compensate for a place's natural "deformities."[44] The onus was on the reader and the viewer to take responsibility for the improving effect of place on a person, and vice-versa.[45] But Gilpin did advocate for a "picturesque eye"[46] that took the natural topography as the starting point for curating a quasi-theatrical scene; indeed, McGillivray suggests that the Gilpinian picturesque eye might be equated with the "theatrical eye"—to which we might add the digital humanist's gaze—since both depended on the careful staging of some kind of fantasy.[47] Through this gaze, a lake transformed into a living Claude glass, and mountains were requisitioned into monumental frames. These objects formed the backdrop to narratives of quotidian fantasy populated by the rural working poor and their animals. It was a mode of storytelling that proved irresistible to generations of Lakeland visitors.

THE PICTURESQUE IN THE CLDW

The earliest mention of the picturesque in our corpus is in Arthur Young's *Six Months' Tour Through the North of England*, but the Corpus of Lake District Writing (CLDW) overall verifies Carl Barbier's claim that it was Gilpin who stimulated

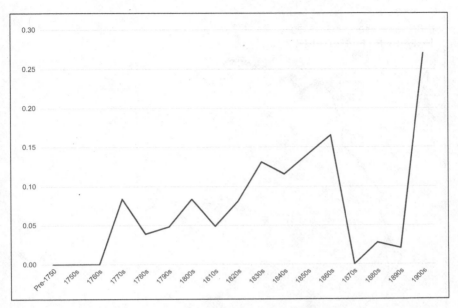

Figure 2.1. Instances of "picturesque" in the corpus over time as a percentage of the total word count.

increased interest in the picturesque: "The journals and diaries written from 1780 onwards by travelers in Great Britain," Barbier writes, "show that the accounts of the tours of William Gilpin had become an aesthetic *vade mecum*."[48] This was not a consistent development:[49] uses of the picturesque were affected by cyclical fashions, and there is a spike in the term's usage at thirty-year intervals from the 1770s to the 1860s that suggests a generational element to the picturesque's popularity (Figure 2.1). Nevertheless, overall mentions of the picturesque in our corpus continued to rise steadily for the century following the publication of Gilpin's *Observations*. But these visitors altered the Gilpinian picturesque in one crucial way: they made it a geographical mode, rather than a spatial one.

Gilpin did not associate the picturesque with named places to any great extent. In his *Observations*, the word "picturesque" occurs on seventy-five occasions, but just 5.33 percent of these instances co-occur with place names. Close inspection of these PNCs (Figure 2.2) indicates that even this low percentage overstates the relationship, and also reveals how simplistic reading of the maps without referring to the underlying texts can result in flawed understandings. One of the PNCs only refers by association to the Lake District (and thus is not shown). Gilpin also compares the Vale of St. John to the Vale of Tempe (a standard point of reference for the picturesque). Another instance co-occurs with three place names at once, and results in the area around Brough being the most pronounced cluster in Figure 2.2b. However, instances like this indicate how important it is to mimic Gilpin, and attend to the specifics in the general: "The entrance into Cumberland presents us with a scene very strongly marked with the sublime; grander, tho less picturesque,

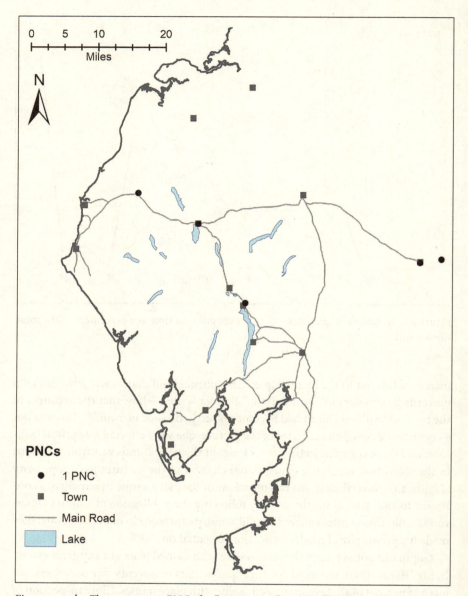

Figure 2.2a–b. These maps are PNCs for "picturesque" in Gilpin's *Observations*. (a) shows proportional symbols.

than the amphitheater we had passed. It is a vista of mountains pursuing each other, if I may so phrase it, through an easy descent of not less than six, or seven miles; and closed at the distant end by Wyburn Lake, a considerable piece of water."[50] A footnote explains that there "are three passages over this chain of mountains, into Cumberland. This by Ambleside, is the wildest, and most picturesque. A second by Brough over Stainmore, is dreary, rather than wild: and a third by Shap, is both."[51] This example indicates the not insignificant limitations in digitally framing data.

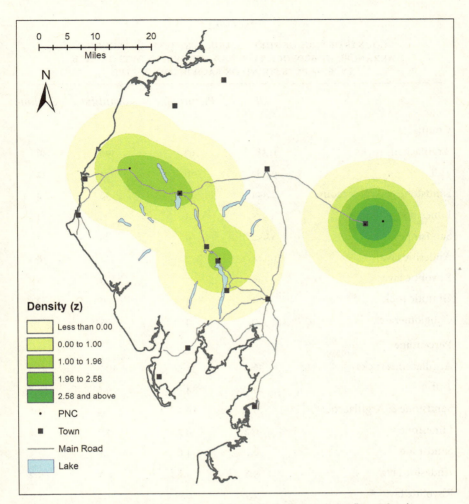

Figure 2.2b. A density-smoothed map of the PNCs for "picturesque" in Gilpin's *Observations*.

Here, Gilpin's point is actually that the view is, on the whole, *not* picturesque: Ambleside is the "most picturesque," but even that is by comparison with the other "wild" and "dreary" places in view. Nevertheless, because the term co-occurs within ten words of Ambleside, Brough, and Stainmore, on the density-smoothed map in Figure 2.2b these areas appear to be the most intensely associated with the picturesque. Still, Gilpin's opinion of this view does indicate the extent to which he was using the picturesque as a method of evaluation, against which he measured the various sights he encountered.

By contrast, in the corpus as a whole, the most significant characteristic of the picturesque is its frequent association with named places: the t-score for the collocation between "picturesque" and all place names is 11.67, indicating a high degree of significance. The only words that co-occur more frequently with "picturesque" are prepositions and conjunctions. The picturesque's geography was

TABLE 2.1

COUNTS OF PNCS OF THREE MAJOR AESTHETIC CATEGORIES
ARRANGED BY BEDROCK TYPE AND THE PERCENTAGE OF EACH
TYPE OF PNCS FOUND ON EACH BEDROCK TYPE

	All	Picturesque	Beautiful	Sublime
Count				
Argillaceous rocks	11,581	63	198	36
Tuff	9,282	66	141	32
Sandstone & Argillaceous	2,354	18	36	1
Limestone	1,975	13	35	1
Sandstone	1,952	9	15	2
Andesitic lava	1,844	7	21	8
Rhyolitic lava	798	1	5	4
Granitic rock	770	4	9	2
Conglomerate	539	1	15	1
Percentage				
Argillaceous rocks	36.2	32.5	40.7	41.4
Tuff	29.0	34.0	29.0	36.8
Sandstone & Argillaceous	7.4	9.3	7.4	1.1
Limestone	6.2	6.7	7.2	1.1
Sandstone	6.1	4.6	3.1	2.3
Andesitic lava	5.8	3.6	4.3	9.2
Rhyolitic lava	2.5	0.5	1.0	4.6
Granitic rock	2.4	2.1	1.9	2.3
Conglomerate	1.7	0.5	3.1	1.1

Source: Modified from Donaldson, Gregory, and Taylor 2017.

affected by the Lake District's physical topography. When J. E. Marr claimed in 1916 that the Lake District's picturesqueness was a product of its geology, he was following a well-established tradition from guidebooks to the region.[52] Our corpus indicates that certain geological categories produced particularly picturesque terrain; for instance, 34 percent of the picturesque PNCs occur in regions on Tuff bedrock, while 33 percent lie in Argillaceous regions.[53] Yet the picturesque is more evenly spread than other aesthetic categories, such as beautiful or sublime (the two categories between which the picturesque was commonly understood to mediate)[54] (Table 2.1). These geological data suggest that, in popular uses, the picturesque occupied a space between the sublime and beautiful, a middle ground

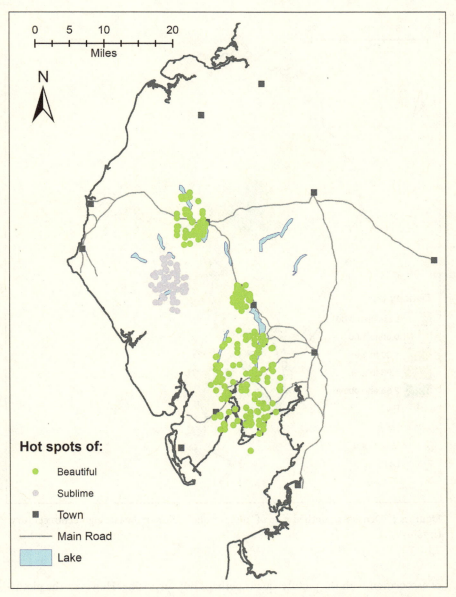

Figure 2.3. Kulldorff hot spots for PNCs of "beautiful" and "sublime." "Picturesque" does not give any hot spots.

for which Uvedale Price and Richard Payne Knight in the eighteenth century, and Ruskin in the nineteenth, argued.[55]

Unlike "sublime" or "beautiful," there are no hot spots for the picturesque, suggesting that this category was not associated to an unusual degree with any particular locations (Figure 2.3). The cold spots display a similar pattern: the only picturesque cold spot is in the area in the north of the Lakes between Keswick and Penrith. Given the fact that this region was beyond the tourists' usual routes, its lack

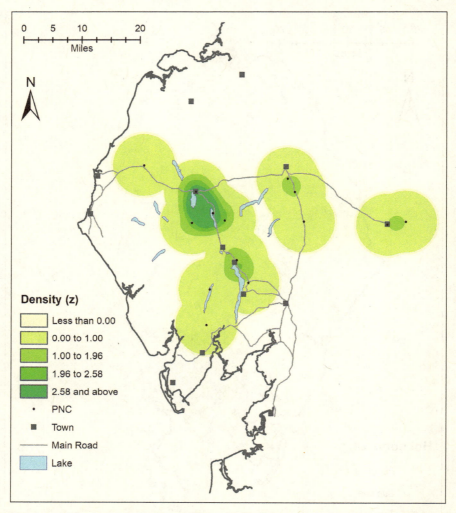

Figure 2.4. Density-smoothed map of "picturesque" PNCs in the late eighteenth century (1770–1795).

of association with the picturesque is perhaps not surprising. However, the picturesque's geography did change significantly throughout our period in ways that reflect alterations over time to how the term was being used and understood. In our eighteenth-century texts (those from 1770 to 1795), mentions of the picturesque are closely focused on Borrowdale and the southern end of Derwentwater (Figure 2.4), which Gilpin had identified as the lake that "seem[ed] to be most generally admired."[56] It was from this region that Gilpin had advised the most distinctive picturesque view was to be gained; the mountains around this lake and toward the Gates of Borrowdale afforded plenty of opportunity for locating natural picturesque frames.[57] It is only in the eighteenth-century texts, though, that the picturesque is so closely associated with the region that Gilpin himself recommended.

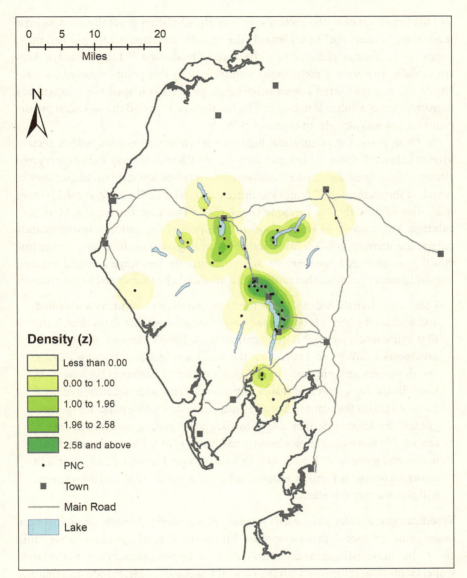

Figure 2.5. Density-smoothed map of "picturesque" PNCs in the Romantic era (1796–1837).

By the Romantic period (for our purposes, the years between 1796 and 1837), Gilpin's picturesque was ubiquitous in topographical writing. In this era, the picturesque's geography became much more concentrated. It is mentioned most frequently in connection with the area around Grasmere, Ambleside, and Bowness (Figure 2.5) and, indeed, it occurs almost nowhere beyond the main transport route between Bowness and Keswick. Its prevalence in this area is thanks to the detailed descriptions of the road in two guidebooks: Edward Baines's *A Companion to the Lakes* (1829) and Samuel Leigh's *Guide to the Lakes and Mountains* (1830).

By this time, however, the picturesque was already being generally used as little more than "a short cut" that allowed "the visually educated reader [to] call upon his own associations with a certain character of landscape."[58] Linda Marilyn Austin explains that uses of picturesque terminology by this point "signaled the paucity of the average tourist's descriptive language even as it aped the spontaneous consumption of a cultural nobility."[59] By the Romantic period the so-called picturesque tourist was already an object of ridicule.

In these years, the picturesque became particularly associated with a certain kind of Lakeland visitor. Although later texts like Charles Mackay's *The Scenery and Poetry of the English Lakes* (1846) addressed themselves seriously to "the traveler in search of the picturesque," James Plumptre's satirical play *The Lakers* (1798) is more indicative of how the "picturesque traveler"—in this case the hapless Miss Beccabunga Veronica—was understood in this period. Veronica misunderstands Gilpin; she attempts to follow his guidance in creating what she believes is "a very fine effect" by suggesting improvements that emphasize the landscape's natural features, but she ignores his advice that nothing "alien" should be introduced to the scene:[60]

> I have only given the hills an Alpine form, and put some wood where it is wanted, and omitted it where it is not wanted: and who could put that sham church and that house into a picture? It quite antipathizes. I don't like such meretricious ornaments. . . . Well—so, I have made the church an old abbey, the house a castle, and the battery an hermitage: I have broken the smooth surface of the water with water-lillies, flags, flowering rushes, water-docks, and other aquatics, making it more of a plashy inundation than a basin of water: then I have put in for the foreground the single tree they ought to have left standing, an ancient tree of remarkable size and venerable beauty; and have sprinkled some ferns, and burdocks, and gorse, and thistles, over this turfy slope. I must, I think, do this in colors: an orange sky, yellow water, a blue bank, a green castle, and brown trees, will give it a very fine effect.[61]

Veronica's garish color palette threatens to transform this hyperbolic picturesque fantasy into an apocalyptic vision; her "brown trees" might produce "a very fine effect," but in realistic terms they also indicate a deep-rooted sickness in the landscape. Her lack of sympathy with the natural Lakeland ecologies indicates that she has fundamentally misinterpreted Gilpin's method.

Other authors despaired over these kinds of misunderstanding. For instance, we find Robert Southey's fictional tourist Espriella musing at Aira Force about a passing chaise: "There were three picturesque tourists in it," he records, but notes wryly that "one of them was fast asleep."[62] The picturesque tourist, whose principle aim was supposed to be to witness the Lake District's most famous sights, misses one of the most renowned beauty spots by napping on the journey. This tourist's dedication to the rules of the picturesque aesthetic is discovered to be no more than a poorly executed performance. Similarly, the American traveler Nathaniel Carter recalls an anecdote about another picturesque tourist's adventures:

A cart, without springs, and drawn by one horse, the only carriage to be had, was chartered to take us to Penrith. A pretty daughter of the landlord, standing in the mud and holding the horse till the cart was laden, said with a significant smile, that we should find it *shaky*. The full import of the epithet was not understood, till the driver set out upon a smart trot, and we began to tremble in every limb. He hushed our complaints, by relating how he once drove in the same vehicle a Frenchman, who came over one summer to see John Bull, and visit the lakes. As soon as the horse started, Monsieur le voyageur, being bounced from side to side, began to swear. This threw the driver into a fit of laughter, which added to the vexation of his passenger, who gave peremptory orders to stop. But the wag pretending not to understand, only drove the faster, till the poor tourist, in search of "the picturesque," was obliged to rise from his seat, turn his back to the horse, and hold up by the stern braces. In this attitude he was carted into Penrith, where all the sashes flew up, to see what was coming.[63]

This tourist's search for the picturesque transports him from the sublime to the ridiculous—although the victimization of the tourist in this particular story is perhaps more indicative of widespread Francophobia. Nevertheless, "Monsieur le voyageur" is symptomatic of the tourist who seemed to consider the picturesque as a particular place that could be tracked down and marked on a map. Like Veronica, such visitors misinterpreted the Gilpinian picturesque; in misconstruing it as a specific location, rather than a methodology by which to read a place, the picturesque tourist emerged as an object of fun for the locals and more canny (by their own reckoning, at least) visitors.

Some later tourists were self-aware enough to mock themselves for their dedication to picturesque scenery. Eliza Johnson's journal recording her travels in "Wordsworthshire" in 1844, for instance, ridicules her and her family's quest for this kind of scenery. When the family's young people set out for their day's activity on September 5, 1844, the journal recalls how they "sallied forth in search of the picturesque & soon found it, at a place called Nook End."[64] Eliza's claim that they have located "the picturesque" is a pastiche of the tourist guides and accounts that had become so common by this period, and indicates the extent to which this kind of picturesque practice had become a joke by the mid-nineteenth century. Twenty years later, by the 1860s, the picturesque was firmly linked with what Austin calls "hackneyed scenes and middlebrow consumption," as well as "reflexive reactions, in which the tourist was nothing more than a consuming machine programmed by the tourist industry."[65]

Perhaps unsurprisingly, then, the popularity of picturesque terminology seems to have declined in the late nineteenth century, especially after 1870 (Figure 2.1). However, "picturesque" occurs more frequently in terms of a percentage of the word count in the mid-nineteenth century than in the eighteenth-century or Romantic era texts. The final steep increase in 1900 is thanks to the only text in the corpus from that year: M.J.B. Baddeley's twenty-second edition of *Black's Shilling Guide*

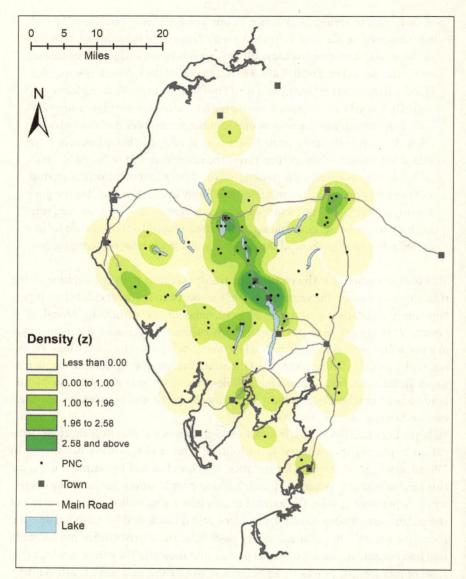

Figure 2.6. Density-smoothed map of "picturesque" PNCs in the Victorian era (1838–1900).

to the English Lakes, which continued to successfully promote picturesque tourism to a receptive readership. Texts like Baddeley's indicated how far the picturesque had changed since Gilpin; no longer associated with a particular set of landscape painters and aesthetic theorists, the picturesque had become something of a catchall for a pleasant, apparently natural scene.[66]

This diffuse definition is reflected in the places associated with the picturesque in the Victorian period (1838–1900 in the CLDW) (Figure 2.6). The only region in the central Lake District not described in any Victorian-era text as picturesque is the Scafell massif at the northern tip of Wastwater. Like in the Romantic period, the picturesque co-occurs most frequently with locations near Ambleside and Grasmere, although the main road between Bowness and Keswick continued as a whole to be closely associated with the term. Still, the geographical spread evident in these later years indicates both the effect of improved transportation links on tourists' routes and the fact that the term was now used as an adjective that was increasingly removed from Gilpin's specific meaning.

This problem was one of interpretation. Gilpin's picturesque gaze relied on the viewer beholding a scene from a distance in ways that would allow them to curate the most pleasing view. By the second half of the nineteenth century, this physical distance seemed to have resulted in an intellectual vacuum that divorced popular understandings of the picturesque from its specific early usage. More seriously, it also appeared to have augmented an emotional distance between spectator and location. While this distance allowed the viewer to survey the scene (with varying degrees of empiricism), it also facilitated responses to it that prioritized the generic over the specific—the opposite of Gilpin's original intent. In doing so, it generated a debate about the imaginative and social roles of objectivity and subjectivity that we can usefully revisit as we negotiate the relationship between digital and "traditional" humanities methodologies.

Protest against the Wrong: The Problem with Picturesque Data

The journalist and novelist Eliza Lynn Linton understood both the problems of and the potential in the distant picturesque gaze. The daughter of the vicar of Crosthwaite, Lynn Linton was born and raised in the northern Lake District. She moved to London at age twenty-two to pursue her writing career—becoming the first salaried female journalist in Britain—but returned to the Lake District in 1858, following her marriage to the artist William Linton. From their home at Brantwood on the shores of lake Coniston (where Ruskin later lived), Lynn Linton wrote her only Lakeland novel, *Lizzie Lorton of Greyrigg* (1866), a work that anticipated one of the key criticisms of Victorian femininity advanced by her infamous "Girl of the Period" essays. In one of the early essays, "Feminine Affectations," published in the *Saturday Review* in 1868, Lynn Linton identified a form of picturesque femininity in which a girl or woman performs an "affectation of being something she is not."[67] It was a criticism that she had been formulating in *Lizzie Lorton*, where picturesque responses to the landscape become metaphorical for relations with the eponymous antiheroine.

The novel's fictional landscape immediately captivates the wealthy landowner, Margaret Elcombe. When she arrives at the fictional village of Langthwaite, "in the wonderful stillness of a calm June evening," to take up residence in her new property, she is instantly enchanted by the view from the mountain road:

She did not know what to look at most—the quiet lake absolutely black in the shadow save when a leaping fish shot up a jet of light or a skimming swallow flashed its wing upon the surface; Green Coom and the Langthwaite fells standing out clear and distinct in the westering light; or Styebarrow with its purple shadows, the white thread of Sour Milk Ghyll, the gloomy pass, the blackened rent of Mickledore . . . and the burnished edges of each crag and knoll, as the parting sunlight caught them aslant and washed them in with ruddy gold; all was so beautiful she did not know what to think worthiest, overpowered as she was with the excess of her emotion.[68]

Margaret's response epitomizes the central problem with the picturesque gaze: without intimate knowledge of the village and its inhabitants, her distant reading of it is fundamentally flawed. When she has lived there a few months, Margaret still enjoys the views from the mountains, but she recognizes her naivety in assuming that picturesque beauty translated to social simplicity:

"What a lovely view!" cried Margaret with a kind of ecstasy on her face, as she looked down into the valley and the mere, which a struggling ray just then caught, and touched with a long line of pale gold. "How quiet every thing is! One might almost believe in the stories of enchantment when one looks at a mountain village from a distance—it is all so still! so happy!"

"To look at," said Ainslie, thinking of the despair that had so lately shadowed Dale Head.

"Yes, I know it is only to look at.["][69]

While the village is enchanting "from a distance," when witnessed up close it is revealed to be a turbulent environment. The view created by the distant picturesque becomes little more than a thin facade over complex socioeconomic narratives.

Lynn Linton's critique, via Margaret, of the Gilpinian picturesque indicates the extent to which later readers of Gilpin were more critical of the political implications of combining the general with the specific. The Gilpinian picturesque prioritized the wide view over the detail in order to provide an outlook that portrayed the most pleasing elements of a given landscape. This methodology risked reducing the landscape to an object by overlooking—or explicitly denying—the environment's agency as a living entity in its own right. More than that, the picturesque frame threatened to effect a disjunction between human subjects and the natural world in ways that had—and have—potentially serious consequences for both human well-being and the ongoing protection of the environment. For Scott Hess, this division between human subject and natural object "subtly reinforces many of the epistemological and ontological categories of modernity: the separation of the perceiving mind or subject from its object; the corresponding separation of mind and body; and the more general division between humans and nature."[70] The consequences were social as well as environmental, resulting in the disenfranchisement of women and the rural working poor.[71]

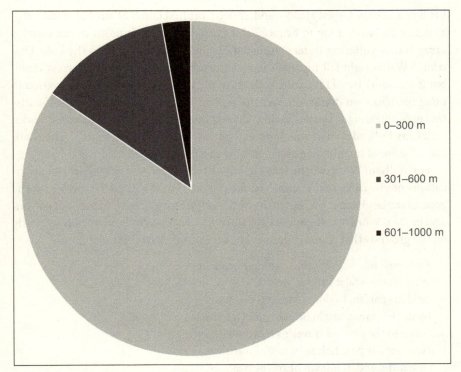

Figure 2.7. Heights in meters (m) of "picturesque" PNCs.

This division was reinforced by the picturesque tourist's or artist's physical position. To discover a picturesque scene, a spectator needed a specific vantage point. One anonymous writer, in a guidebook to Keswick published by John Garnett, explained in 1852 that the "Picturesque Point is always . . . low in all prospects."[72] Other authors evidently agreed that the picturesque was a sea-level aesthetic; 85 percent of the PNCs for picturesque occur below 300 meters, and a mere 3 percent at elevations above 600 meters (Figure 2.7). However, while the picturesque scene was usually discovered at a low elevation, the picturesque gaze needed some height, and a certain kind of distance. Otherwise, as Garnett's author thought, "a foreground would be wanting" in the artist's work.[73] Moreover, the distance achieved by elevation was required to allow the tourist or painter to impose picturesque order on the landscape.[74]

One such platform was Orrest Head, the fell that rises above Windermere. As early as 1792, Adam Walker recommended Orrest Head as "a very good station . . . either for the Painter or Tourist." It was a gentle uphill walk that offered extensive views across the lake and to the nearby fells.[75] Famously, Orrest Head was also one of the walks recommended by Alfred Wainwright for those walkers who could "no longer climb high fells but can still, within reason, potter about on the short and easy slopes and summits of the foothills."[76] Like Walker, he enjoyed its accessible views. For Wainwright, the view from Orrest Head was life changing. He described

his first ascent of Orrest Head—and, indeed, his first climb of any Lakeland fell—
as being an "awakening to beauty"; this "first sight of mountains in tumultuous
array across glittering waters" initiated his lifelong attachment to the Lake District.[77] Wainwright felt himself to be claimed by the mountains at Orrest Head,
but it was more usual for earlier walkers to use the view from such an elevation to
imagine their own dominion over the region. The proprietary nature of the distant gaze encouraged by stations like Orrest Head was typical of picturesque works,
which, as Fulford writes, sought to extend "the rules of polite taste."[78] The result
was a "sense of imaginative ownership" over a picturesque scene.[79]

For William Wordsworth, this kind of distant picturesque gaze, with its implications of vicarious ownership, had the potential to mobilize the viewer for the
good of the landscape over which they felt—at least temporarily—a sense of patron-
age. In 1844, Wordsworth protested against the Kendal–Windermere railway partly
on the grounds that it would destroy the scene from Orrest Head:

> And must he too the ruthless change bemoan
> Who scorns a false utilitarian lure
> 'Mid his paternal fields at random thrown?
> Baffle the threat, bright Scene, from Orrest-head
> Given to the pausing traveler's rapturous glance:
> Plead for thy peace, thou beautiful romance
> Of nature; and, if human hearts be dead,
> Speak, passing winds; ye torrents, with your strong
> And constant voice, protest against the wrong ("Sonnet on the Projected
>   Kendal and Windermere Railway" ll.6–14).[80]

An earlier manuscript is more specific, where the sestet's final line reads, "And must
He too his old delights disown."[81] This speaker worries that the changes to the view
from Orrest Head will require him to "disown" the joys he has discovered in this
iconic view. Wordsworth here figures an imaginative response as a material relationship; that is, the sonnet records one of the countless individual claims that
make it part of what Wordsworth elsewhere famously called a "national property."[82]
It is an example of what Jonathan Bate recognizes as a Wordsworthian "medita-
tion on the *networks* which link mental and environmental space".[83] the picturesque traveler's "rapturous glance" here might offer the impetus for the landscape's
protection, if the traveler can be moved to "plead" on its behalf. If humanity abides
by picturesque rules, though, nature will have to speak for itself.

At its most extreme, this distant picturesque gaze—however "rapturous"—
became an almost cartographic tool that decoupled the tourist, artist, and landscape from what Denis Cosgrove calls the "suffocating embrace of ecology" in favor
of the self-interested liberalism he thinks defined early modern Europe.[84] The physical distance from a scene attained by climbing to a vantage point above it resulted
in an emotional distance that, as Wordsworth knew, could have serious consequences for the place and its inhabitants. Aaron M. Ellison inherits a Wordsworthian concern that such picturesque devotion to distant readings of a landscape

necessarily results in fundamental misunderstandings about the way a place works, and the interactions—human and otherwise—that occur within it. Just as Wordsworth recognized that the distant, picturesque gaze needed to be combined with an intimate connection to a place in order for the viewer to be part of it, so does Ellison argue, expanding on Cosgrove's sense of suffocation, that multiscalar analyses are essential for maintaining ecological world orders: "The roots of splitting trees are like rock-climber's toes, grasping for an ephemeral perch, and an observer similarly grasps for a fixed frame of reference, but finds none. At any scale—from the daily rhythms of growing and dying plants to the eons of soil formation interspersed by volcanism, landslides, and germinating trees—this is nature in all its unbalanced glory!"[85] Ellison demands that ecologists acknowledge tiny details alongside—even within—grand narratives; as he implies, the pebbles loosened by a tree's roots might hold the key for understanding ecological forces on a millennial scale. Like Wordsworth, he believes that it is only when attention to detail is incorporated into the distant picturesque gaze that humans can integrate alongside nature into a place.

John Ruskin would have concurred: he worried that focusing on a distant view allowed the spectator to overlook the human natures contained within a landscape. As John Macarthur succinctly puts it, for Ruskin the Gilpinian picturesque gaze was "nothing to be proud of."[86] Ruskin discovered serious moral failings in the type of Gilpinian picturesque promoted by popular responses to the Lakeland landscape (although, as Lindsay Smith and John Dixon Hunt point out, Ruskin remained indebted to other elements of Gilpin's thinking).[87] As Smith explains, Ruskin viewed the Romantic picturesque that Gilpin inspired as "a minor form of delight by means of exploitative travesty or disguise."[88] For him, the distant picturesque gaze depended on the acceptance of "*suffering*," "*poverty*," and "*decay*."[89] In Ruskin's view, the picturesque tourist was partly responsible for prolonging human suffering around popular viewing stations. Although he clarified that he did not think the "lover of the lower picturesque is a monster in human form," he did believe them to be selfish and fundamentally "incapable of acute sympathy with others."[90]

Ruskin had realized the social dangers inherent in the picturesque gaze on a trip to Amiens. Expecting the picturesque scenes depicted in Samuel Prout's work, he had been dismayed to discover instead persistent signs of hardship: "We delight in seeing the figures in these boats pushing them about the bits of blue water, in Prout's drawings; but as I looked today at the unhealthy face and melancholy mien of the man in the boat pushing his load of peats along the ditch, and of the people, men as well as women, who sat spinning gloomily at the cottage doors, I could not help feeling how many suffering persons must pay for my picturesque subject and happy walk."[91] Ruskin shares humanist concerns that technologies—whether picturesque or digital—might, as Clement puts it, "seem to take the 'human' (e.g., the significance of gender, race, class, religion, sexuality, and history)" out of the picture.[92] In Ruskin's view, the picturesque frame offered by Prout's drawings conceals severe social inequalities; the distance assumed by the artwork—and, implicitly, by those who view it—in capturing the scene leads to a callous overlooking of real human hardship in pursuit of the picturesque scene. Prout becomes, here, emblematic of the moral implications of using picturesque technologies to divorce the aesthetics of ruin or decay from their social consequences. For Ruskin, reflecting on a century of picturesque tourism, the tourist or artist who utilized a distant picturesque gaze was a morally vacuous, artistically vacant, and peculiarly pernicious form of parasite whose presence might uplift some parts of the economy, but did so at the expense of irreparable damage to decent social feeling. Instead, Ruskin offered a different model for combining the general with the specific. What Ruskin termed the "Turnerian picturesque" revised Gilpin's method.

The Turnerian picturesque emphasized the spectator's agency over their visual perception and promoted empathy alongside the "effusive sensibility" that, as Dahlia Porter notes, was a key characteristic of the Victorian picturesque.[93] Ruskin discovered in Turner's paintings a multiscalar combination of distance and closeness that foregrounded the viewer's cultural, social, and environmental responsibilities. He took these works as a model for a new picturesque approach. At first glance, Turner's landscapes appear to represent a distant view of the scene, which offer impressions of storm clouds rolling in over a mountain, waves on a turbulent sea, or a tantalizingly obscured glimpse into Queen Mab's kingdom. Turner called the effect of this distant gaze a kind of "atmosphere" that involved painter, viewer, and scene in a moment of collective feeling. But Ruskin went further, finding in Turner's paintings a specificity of detail that developed socially and environmentally engaged narratives. In Ruskin's readings, the distant "atmospheres" in Turner's works were composed of a series of intricate, carefully rendered details that required a painstakingly attentive gaze to recognize.

John Gage has observed that indistinctness has long been recognized as one of Turner's defining traits. Although Turner viewed indistinctness as a "fault," many of his admirers understood it as a particular "*forte.*"[94] Paintings such as Turner's early work, *Morning Amongst the Coniston Fells* (1798), experiment with the interplay between the distinct and indistinct for which Turner would become well known. *Morning Amongst the Coniston Fells* presents a view across Coniston Old Man and over the lake. The mountains blur into the clouds above in the background, while in the foreground dark vegetation merges into the rock face. The painting anticipates that sense of "atmosphere" that Turner recognized in his later style; the indistinct forms of mountain and cloud indicate a distant view that witnesses these natural elements as conglomerate features. Yet there is a tension at the heart of the painting. What Gage writes of the later work, *Staffa, Fingal's Cave* (1831–32) is true of this portrayal of the Coniston fells; that is, that the canvas's indistinctness has been "manipulated with a sculpturesque precision."[95] When attended to closely, the painting reveals the flecks of water that spray from the waterfall onto a mountainside composed of a series of individualized rock forms. More obviously, the carefully rendered shepherd and flock of sheep, who occupy the space immediately to the right of the painting's center, reveal this to be a working landscape, inhabited by particular people, rather than the generalized types familiar in picturesque portrayals. This early example of the Turnerian picturesque indicates how a distant view can uncover specific details, if the artist and spectator both adopt a multiscalar approach to the landscape.

The picturesque experimented with such interplays between distance and detail in other ways too. In fact, its very popularity is attributable to the success with which it deployed multimedia approaches to the landscape. Fulford attributes the picturesque's popularity to the willingness of its key authors and publishers to combine text with visualizations that communicated to a wide readership.[96] At its worst, this kind of multimedia picturesque reduced a place into a two-dimensional landscape to be viewed from a distance and read in light of the sketches, tables, and descriptions in popular view books.[97] At its best, though, it could uncover hitherto obscured details that lay—often literally—beneath the surface.

VIRTUAL PLAYGROUNDS IN TEXT AND ON SCREEN

"Questions of perspective might be the last place we would expect to encounter math," Ted Underwood writes,[98] a pronouncement that might have come as a surprise to the picturesque practitioners of the eighteenth and nineteenth centuries: after all, the picturesque "perspective" was, from early on in its development, characterized by attempts to mathematically—or at least scientifically—objectify it. Much like the practices that underpin digital humanities scholarship, picturesque endeavors in recording, quantifying, and inscribing the landscape relied on technologically well-informed readers' abilities to transform the phenomenal world into a series of signs on flat surfaces. The page of the sketchbook, journal, guidebook, or map anticipated the camera and, later, the computer, tablet, or mobile phone screen in turning the "things" of the material world into culturally inscribed objects that were, as Broglio puts it, imbued "with a halo of social meaning."[99] Commentators worried that guidebooks were eroding the quality of personal experiences of place in ways that anticipated similar worries about the potential disconnect from nature encouraged by digital media and technologies.[100] Ruskin's concern that "many people go to real places, and never see them" was indicative of a wider Victorian concern that the guidebook encouraged the prioritization of the simulacra over the actual place.[101] The guidebook's maps, engravings, and descriptions seemed to endanger authentic experience in ways that anticipated contemporary paranoia over the loss of mindful presence in real locations in favor of virtual realities.

The maps and tables in eighteenth- and nineteenth-century guidebooks anticipated the means of displaying information that are the mainstay of spatial humanities research: databases, tables, and maps. In these texts, they offered a stratification of the picturesque landscape that combined the aesthetic with what Pfau designates the "quasi-scientific."[102] The picturesque "proposed a reciprocal relationship between material reality and subjective experience" that, Hill suggests, was mediated primarily through landscape painting.[103] But that relationship was also figured through a range of multimedia and multidisciplinary records, includ-ing lists of demographic or topographic data, maps, and tables. Margaret Linley observes that instances of "statistical and cartographic mapping" made the Lake District "into a virtual playground."[104] The information graphics and maps Linley describes from the Lake District Online collection function, she writes, "in often contradictory, contested, and provisional ways to describe, analyze, produce, and perform space as a naturalized, familiar place—but one that is never wholly know-able."[105] In this way, picturesque technologies translated the landscape into a series of virtual scenes. As we saw with Gilpin, though, these scenes meant little unless the viewer could critically assess the models they were creating through the picturesque gaze. In a similar way—and as we maintain throughout this book—the graphs, maps, and tables that communicate elements of our deep-mapping methodology are insufficient by themselves: they need to be interpreted carefully in light of both the data they contain and that which they exclude.

The picturesque's reliance on quantifiable data began, perhaps predictably, with Gilpin. Rachel Hewitt suggests that Gilpin's language of the picturesque was "a form of aesthetic mapping or 'cultural cartography'" that encouraged tourists to view the landscape as a phenomenological creation.[106] Gilpin proposed that a description of a scene might be made more "intelligible" by taking what he called "a sort of analytical view of the materials" from which the scene was composed: he indicated that the "mountains—lakes—broken grounds—woods—rocks—cascades—vallies—and rivers" should be understood as material objects as well as artistic backdrops.[107] Gilpin himself did not make use of tables or charts to docu-ment these materials; instead, as Porter notes, he "forgoes the historical record alto-gether," preferring instead to analyze the scene based on literary predecessors like Gray, Reynolds, and Pope rather than on what he considers the theoretical writ-ings of more scientifically minded authors.[108] As evidence for his readers of his ana-lytical conclusions, Gilpin provided sketches of key scenes. In his preface, he explained that he had included two kinds of drawings. One, he wrote, was "meant to *illustrate and explain picturesque ideas.*"[109] Indeed, he considered this endeavor to be "one of the most useful aids of the pencil," since drawing was the ideal medium for explaining the "*bodily forms*" of his "*picturesque ideas.*"[110] But it was not suffi-cient for communicating what Gilpin called "*intellectual ideas*":[111] only careful reading of the accompanying text could do that.

If this first kind of drawing attempted to illustrate how the reader should view the landscape, the second aimed to show what they would find there. In this approach, Gilpin hoped to "*characterize the countries,* through which the reader is carried." He explained that "the ideas are taken from the *general face of the country*; not from any *particular scene.* And indeed this may perhaps be the most useful way of conveying local ideas. For a *portrait* characterizes only a *single spot.* The idea must be relinquished, as soon as the place is passed. But such imaginary views as give *a general idea of a country,* spread themselves more diffusely; and are carried, in the reader's imagination, [through] the whole description."[112] This way of model-ing the specific through the abstract might sound familiar to digital humanists: it is what scholars from Moretti (2005) to Piper (2018) have suggested graphs, maps, models, and trees might contribute to literary study. Like Gilpin, Moretti suggested that these kinds of "artificial constructs" might align the general—or what Moretti calls "distance"—with the specific: "fewer elements, hence a sharper sense of their overall interconnection."[113] In both cases, the aim is to emphasize interactions between discrete elements, and to highlight alternate means of interpretation.

Moretti's work has been—not unjustly—criticized for focusing overmuch on distant approaches at the expense of human elements in individual texts,[114] and, as we have seen with Ruskin's response to Gilpin, the same might be said of picturesque methodologies. Porter argues, though, that Gilpin's preference for antiquarian analysis and representative drawings over scientific discourses does not mean that he was less "empirically inclined" than his contemporaries.[115] Rather, he believed that observations informed by the literary record and based on direct personal observation "have the better chance of being founded in truth" since they are "not the offspring of theory; but are taken immediately from the scenes of nature."[116] Truth, here, does not necessarily correlate with quantifiable, or even replicatable, results. Instead, the important "truth" is a personal one, found in the representation of what the viewer perceives and feels. Gilpin introduced subjective aesthetic taste as a legitimate basis for the analysis of a landscape, and his desire to catalog what he saw as phenomenological experience informed the development of what Porter terms picturesque topography's "empiricist ethos."[117]

Using forward-looking technologies to capture data, even if that enterprise seems at odds with an approach characterized by its attention to the past, is not, then, unique to the digital humanities. By the mid-nineteenth century, the picturesque's comforting nostalgia—its imagining of a forgotten golden age populated by happy and innocent country folk and seemingly preserved in the remaining ruins[118]—had largely given way to "a deep and melancholy consciousness of change and loss."[119] But that backward glance had also succumbed to empirical attempts to encode the landscape. The Victorian picturesque developed what Pfau calls an "elaborate, focused, technical 'grammar'" that sought to categorize and classify the landscape and its histories, as far as possible, into a series of data.[120] Yet these data had been a part of the picturesque tradition from its inception. From the 1770s onward, guidebooks began including paratextual apparatus, including tables of rainfall, depths of the lakes or heights of the mountains, glossaries of flora and fauna, timetables for trains and coaches, maps, and suggested itineraries to aid the tourist in making the most out of their trip.

Thomas West was the first writer in our corpus to begin introducing these kinds of paratexts. From the first edition, he included an appendix detailing the comparative heights of the mountains in Britain with significant peaks globally (particularly those around the Mediterranean). These heights were, West wrote, "taken from the latest surveys,"[121] including Thomas Pennant's travel account *A Tour in Scotland* (1769) and Marc-Théodore Bourrit's *Description des glacières de Savoye* (1773). West implies that he considers all of the British mountains mentioned in his guide—including Helvellyn, Skiddaw, Cross Fell, and Saddleback—to be accessible: "No mountain in South Britain," he notes, "touches the region of barrenness, that intervenes between the limits of vegetation and perpetual snow."[122] West also includes a list of the roads from Lancaster to the Lakes, along with their respective lengths. These paratexts, which remained in place throughout the seven editions published before 1800, served to elucidate for the reader how to travel around the region with the expediency required by the tourist.

By the Victorian period, such appendixes had become standard practice, and the most popular guidebooks prided themselves on the quality and quantity of their empirical appendixes. Such paratexts were designed to enhance the guides' authority in an age that increasingly valued objective content.[123] In 1855, for instance, Harriet Martineau anticipated great success for her guidebook thanks to the addition of several appendixes designed to be of use to the tourist. Having moved to Ambleside in the 1840s, following a long illness that had rendered her unable to walk, Martineau had been eager to make up for lost time.[124] Using the mountains to develop an intimate knowledge of the Lake District's terrain, she set out thoroughly to "learn" the landscape. She remembered in her autobiography that "by the close of a year from the purchase of my field, I knew every lake (I think) but two, and almost every mountain pass. . . . Of these joyous labours, none has been sweeter than that of my first recovered health, when Lakeland became gradually disclosed before my exploration, till it lay before me, map-like, as if seen from a mountain top."[125] Martineau found that a map was "essential" to explain to the viewer what could be seen from the summits of the mountains. With the map in hand, the viewer could mimic the cartographer in surveying the area to construct a detailed plan that was based on the map but which, crucially, adapted it to suit the individual's perspective.

The map included in Martineau's *Complete Guide* (1855) seemed to prove her qualifications. The *Guide* included a strikingly detailed, beautifully hand-colored geological map of the region by the Kendal-based cartographer John Ruthven (Figure 2.8). This piece showed the natural features of the Lake District in astonishing detail. The map facilitates Martineau's construction of a sort of feedback loop between map, walk, and text: she seems to have considered maps as integral to a cyclical process whereby maps are needed to climb mountains and to identify what can be seen from their summits, but the text is based on the walker's personal interpretation of the cartographic view. That, in turn, leads to the creation of a different version of the map being described in the text, which combines the (apparently) objective data gleaned from the map with the viewer's on-site interpretation.

Martineau was delighted with the "accessories and embellishments" acquired by her publisher. She commends Garnett's "zeal and spirit" in organizing the compilation of the work, and, in particular, she acknowledges his collaborative efforts. The "admirable cooperation he has been so fortunate as to secure" means, Martineau thinks, that "my humble work is elevated to a quality of real importance. When I look at Mr. Ruthven's valuable geological map, Mr. Aspland's

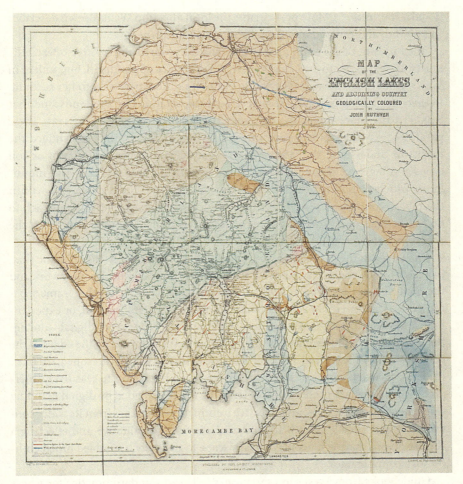

Figure 2.8. John Ruthven's geological map, which was included in Martineau's *Complete Guide* (1855). Reproduced by permission of the Geological Society of London.

beautiful illustrative Views, so finely engraved by Mr. Banks; and, again, the Botanical contributions, so essential to the perfect understanding of the Lake District, it seems to me that the book has become, by all this aid, one which may not only be in every tourist's hands, but find a place on the library shelves of those who have never visited, and may not contemplate visiting, this district of England."[126] Additionally, the Directories—a unique feature that listed the postal addresses of aristocracy, gentry, and tradespeople in the District—sought to make the guide "valuable to residents" as well as to visitors.[127] Her care towards the locals was characteristic of her relationship with them; when William Wells-Brown visited her in 1851, he observed that she was "loved with a sort of idolatry by the people of Ambleside."[128] Wells-Brown seems to have felt a similar kind of affection for her; he had been born into slavery in Kentucky, and he felt that Martineau's involvement in antislavery movements made her worthy of international admiration.[129] More parochially, the local affection Wells-Brown describes was a solid, and rare, qualification for a guidebook writer.

The kinds of tables and glossaries included in Martineau's *Guide* offered the tourist the expertise to do a close reading of the landscape in detail, but, unlike in West's guide, Martineau does not attempt to link these paratexts to her account. Rather, the tables appeared as objective interpretations of the landscape that balanced the more subjective representation of it developed in the text. These paratexts drew the picturesque tourist's attention to details; they encouraged the tourist to understand the landscape as a complex arrangement of rock or soil types and heterogeneous flora and fauna positioned around lakes and mountains, which could be measured and knowledge about them contained within the table's columns. They offered, in short, a quantifiable way through which to do a close reading of the distant representations of the landscape found on the accompanying maps.

The tables in the guidebooks share with digital spreadsheets an aesthetic that, in a picturesque context, is fundamental for understanding the way they work and the implications they express: both are framed, and in both cases that frame separates the data from other content (whether material, environmental, or experiential). Like the picturesque sketch, the picturesque table—analog or digital—divides the landscape up into legible sections that are carefully framed by the edges of the columns. The table, spreadsheet, or database transfers the picturesque gaze from the landscape to the page or screen, and encourages the viewer to selectively interpret the data that are presented. Similarly, the frame provided by digital mapping software isolates a region—and selective information about it—from its wider context. The quantifiable risks being elevated above the qualitative and effecting a similar divorce between people and landscape to that which troubled nineteenth-century commentators.

Guidebooks from West's to Martineau's followed standard practice for where to include quasi-scientific paratexts, such as tables, glossaries, or itineraries. These paratexts tended to be contained in appendixes at the end of the guidebook. In this way, they remained physically part of the book, yet intellectually separated from it. Their position at the end of the books served a rational purpose as much as a practical one: it implied that to understand the data contained in the tables, a reader should have read the preceding pages. In other words, the data are not presented as being fully "transcendental"[130]; their material relationship to the rest of the text implies a need to combine the human experiences described in the guidebook with the data exhibited in the tables. Similarly, in digital humanities research, careful interpretation of the human output—text, sound, or image—is essential for assessing the usefulness of the quantitative sources it inspires.

This chapter has explored the role of the picturesque in the formation of the Lake District as a particular kind of cultural landscape, which was instrumental in perpetuating certain kinds of analysis that combined the quantitative with the qualitative. We have shown that the picturesque gaze was crucial for the curation of both text and landscape, and demonstrated how both digital and picturesque technologies might communicate ways of reading that align aesthetic discourses with quasi-scientific agendas. We have also indicated that the technologies underpinning digital humanities scholarship should be treated with a caution similar to that used in reading picturesque texts; that is, we should understand them as ways of curating data, rather than generators of empirical evidence. But in order to develop fuller understandings of both text and landscape, we—like our eighteenth- and nineteenth-century precursors—need to be willing to learn new strategies that stimulate new forms of critical interpretation.

~

CHAPTER 3

Tourists, Travelers, Inhabitants

VARIANT DIGITAL LITERARY GEOGRAPHIES

Leaving the picturesque behind came with its own risks. After searching for Watendlath with a group of tourists in 1772, Gilpin noted how tricky navigating the landscape could be. When one of his companions stopped a local to ask for directions, they found the response less than helpful:

> "Which way to Watenlath [*sic*]?" said one of our company to a peasant, as we left the vale of Borrowdale. "That way" said he, pointing up a lofty mountain steeper than the tiling of a house. . . . The question we asked . . . we found was a very improper one. We should have asked, in what direction we were to seek it. For way there was none; except here and there a blind path; which being itself often bewildered, served only to bewilder us. The inhabitants pay little attention to paths; they steer along these wilds by landmarks, which to us were unknown.[1]

The picturesque offered one way of navigating the region and its residents, but Gilpin here makes an early discovery of the difference between the picturesque tourist's aims and the inhabitants'—sometimes willful—misunderstandings of them. The carefully curated picturesque gaze evidently overlooked much more than it noticed. But there was a question of pride here too. "There is something unmanly," Gilpin worried, "in conceiving a difficulty in traversing a path which, we were told, the women of the country would ascend on horseback, with their panniers of eggs, and butter, and return in the night."[2] Not to be outdone by the Lake District's working classes—and its women, at that—the group set off up the incline and eventually, with "many a breathing pause," reached the top.

Gilpin's account indicates that it was not only visitors' physical condition that inhibited their responses to the landscape. To understand the Lake District properly, the visitor required training; after all, if "the wild regions of mountain and forest were for the most part objects of conspicuous aesthetic consumption,"[3] then the consumer needed to be well versed in the terms of purchase.

William Wordsworth was among the most prominent in seeking to provide just that. His *Guide through the District of the Lakes*, though never a "runaway best-seller," did become "entrenched as the go-to guidebook for nineteenth-century Lake District tourists."[4] The *Guide* actually identified three main groups of people who engaged with the Lake District landscape: tourists, travelers, and inhabitants. Although the *Guide* did not challenge picturesque appropriations of the region, it did aim to assist visitors both in navigating the landscape and in working through these categories toward a fuller appreciation of it. The *Guide* aimed to teach travelers "who may not have been accustomed to pay attention to things so inobtrusive" *how* to pay attention, rather than merely to what.[5] In short, the text was not so much a guide to the scenery as an advice manual that would enable the tourist to become a traveler, and the traveler to develop the intimately detailed gaze that Wordsworth associates with the Lake District's inhabitants.

This chapter uses Wordsworth's labels as starting points for investigating the uses of deep mapping in revealing the complex sociocultural and geographical interactions that were taking place throughout this period. As we aim to demonstrate, these categories indicate how important it is that the apparently objective data displayed in geographical information systems (GIS) be interpreted through a subjective lens. The Lake District's most significant locations emerge in this approach as multifaceted places that elicited complicatedly plural responses, which were dependent on individual relationships to the region. As John Wilson (publishing in *Blackwood's Edinburgh Magazine* as a fictional German traveler named Philip Kempferhausen) recognized, each category responded to the landscape in very different ways: "Things so familiar to the natives as not even to be seen by them," he writes, "touch a stranger with an inquiring emotion."[6] The landscape itself seemed to adopt a very different character depending on the nature of those inquiries.

In this chapter, we explore each of these categories—tourist, traveler, and inhabitant—to reveal how they operated, both temporally and spatially, in distinctive ways. In doing so, we develop the work of previous critics—most notably James Buzard—to demonstrate that differences between tourists, travelers, and inhabitants were not only based on socioeconomic distinctions.[7] Suzanne Stewart has suggested that visualizing the journeys of tourists and travelers can aid understandings of their spatial identity.[8] In fact, as we demonstrate here, mapping Lake District literature reveals that these categories were intrinsically geographical, creating a dynamic landscape where past and present were seen to interact with extraordinary fluidity. More than this, we reveal that the tourists and travelers who predominate in our corpus ascribed spatial identities to the region's inhabitants in ways that had important consequences for the area's sociocultural—perhaps even economic—development. These three spatial identities contributed to the creation of the Lake District as a multilayered space that was both aesthetically and culturally constructed from the overlaying paths of multiple types of user.

The "Discovery" of the Lake District

The Lake District emerged as a fashionable destination at a moment of significant national and international upheaval. Leanne White and Elspeth Frew summarize that "aspects of tourism and national identity intersect, overlap and traverse," and this connection was particularly visible in the late eighteenth-century Lakes.[9] The mass production of novels and rapid increases in newspaper circulation, as well as educational reform, meant that imaginative and literary landscapes at home were altering radically.[10] At the same time, people across Europe were thinking actively about what a national identity might look like. The Seven Years' War (1756–1763), the French Revolution (1789–1794), and the Napoleonic Wars (1798–1816) in Europe, not to mention the formal ratification of the United States' Constitution in 1787, had encouraged the consolidation of national borders.[11] As Keith Hanley and John K. Walton note, once these political convolutions had "cut [Britain] off from the Continent, cultural travel turned inward to explore the native beauty and history of mainland Britain."[12]

The domestic tourist trade—and heritage landscapes in particular—was an important means by which the idea of the nation was formed and expressed.[13] As a heritage landscape that was already becoming recognized for its ancient history, literary culture, and artistic merits, in the final years of the eighteenth century the Lake District emerged as an icon for the exhibition of national pride. The rise in popularity of the guidebook in the eighteenth and nineteenth centuries was central to these corroborations of national identity because, as Hanley and Walton explain, they "assisted in creating a national travelling culture" that encouraged "the spread of a middle-class national identity which . . . served to highlight the communion of England, Scotland and Wales."[14] This increase in middle-class mobility established the Lake District as fertile ground for the re-evaluation of British landscape as a source of national expression and international fascination.

From the mid-eighteenth century, the Lakeland landscape began to be acknowledged as a palimpsest that contained evidence of deep time on both human and geological scales. In the two hundred years after the publication of Thomas Burnet's *Telluris Theoria Sacra, or Sacred Theory of the Earth* in 1681–1690, thinkers including Georges-Louis Leclerc, Charles Lyell, and Adam Sedgwick revealed that the earth was far, far older than biblical thinking allowed, and the effect on the popular and literary imaginations was dramatic.[15] The Romantic period in particular witnessed an unprecedented fascination with historical objects and, more than that, in what such objects might reveal about contemporary humanity. The expansion of The Society of Antiquaries in London from fewer than three hundred members in 1770 to nearly eight hundred by 1820 is indicative of the dramatic rise in interest toward the past that occurred throughout this period.[16] This new fascination with deep time affected the treatment of the Lake District in important and long-lasting ways.

The recognition of the Lake District mountains as the worn-down relics of ancient geological convulsions revolutionized understandings of the landscape,

and its connection with its human inhabitants. The remains of long-forgotten settlements and ruined buildings found throughout the region confirmed that the
Lakes provided rare evidence of human and environmental histories that could
be traced back over millennia.[17] For early theorists of the picturesque, the sight of
a ruin on a mountainside was evocative of vast epochs of time in one spatial
moment; Charles Kostelnick explains that ruins became "dynamic visual texts
undergoing the universal changes of aging and decay," while for Matthew Wickman, ruins were "concealment made manifest, a vivid rendering of gloom."[18] A ruin
highlighted the interplay between past and present, time and space.[19] They survived
as ongoing reminders of the long-standing, mutually beneficial—and mutually
destructive—relationship between humanity and nature; as Sabrina Ferri dramatically puts it, ruins are reminders of how "works of man [are] slowly overcome by
nature," so that "monumental and architectonic remains testify to the ultimate fate
of manmade things."[20] In the Lake District, they were testament to the ways in
which a location's physical and human geographies might be conceived as a deep
reality consisting of innumerable, overlapping spatial and temporal layers.

In William Wordsworth's view, a major problem with the burgeoning tourist
industry was the fact that the majority of visitors—and Wordsworth had a particular issue with uneducated working-class tourists[21]—did not reflect on these connections between geological and human histories. He thought that the tourist who
expected to witness deep time at hyperspeed missed the point of visiting the region.
Developing reflective responses to the Lake District's ecological narratives required
careful training, and his *Guide through the District of the Lakes* offered a manual
for how to develop more nuanced understandings of this cultural landscape. The
Guide's detailed naturalistic descriptions, environmental and geological histories,
advice as to the right times to undertake certain types of journeys, and the kinds
of details that should be attended to along the route distinguished Wordsworth's
Guide from its competitors.[22] Whether or not the so-called Lakers, as these mobile
and pleasure-seeking tourists became known, paid attention to it was another
matter entirely.

KEEP MOVING: TOURISM IN THE LAKES

In a sense, the Lake District was the birthplace of modern tourism. Although Paul
Fussell thinks that tourism only began making "inroads on travel" with the foun-
dation of Thomas Cook in the mid-nineteenth century,[23] in fact this phenomenon
happened much earlier in the Lakes. The OED (*Oxford English Dictionary*) records
that the first published use of the word "tourist" was in William Cockin's "innocent amusement," *Ode to the Genius of the Lakes in the North of England* (1780),
a poem addressed to "actual tourists," which described in eighteen stanzas the most
popular Lakeland sites. The OED defines the kind of traveler Cockin addresses as
a person who "makes a tour or tours" for "recreation," "pleasure," and "culture." It
emphasizes that the tourist's goal is to witness "objects of interest" and "scenery."[24]
The Lake District tour that developed in the late eighteenth century was descended

from the Grand Tour, but it had decidedly different aims: where the Grand Tour aspired to develop the traveler's worldly knowledge, the Lakers' approach valued expediency and promoted superficial encounters with certain objects or scenes in order to stimulate broader knowledge of, and pride in, the British landscape.[25]

Then, as now, many resisted being labeled a mere tourist. Dean MacCannell argues that the tourist was always an "Other": "other people are tourists, while I am a traveler."[26] An Edwardian skit expressed a similar sentiment: "It's funny, isn't it, how every traveler is a tourist except one's self?"[27] As tourists became ubiquitous presences at the country's landmarks, not to mention in the towns that expanded to accommodate them, they became an increasingly visible, and increasingly vilified, part of nineteenth-century culture. Leslie Stephen's furious despair over the sight of tourists, who he called "an offensive variety of the species of primates," at St. Moritz was an extreme but not unusual response. Stephen was particularly upset at a group of gentlemen who were more interested in their brandy than in the sun setting over the glaciers. "There are persons," he spat, "who *do* the Alps; who look upon the Lake of Lucerne as one more task ticked off from their memorandum book."[28] Stephen's ire at Switzerland's tourists was an echo of Wordsworth's fury at the Lakeland tourist industry.

For early commentators, though, the distinction between tourists and travelers was not always clear-cut. In 1800, when the term "tourist" was still in its infancy, the antiquarian and lexicographer Samuel Pegge the Younger recorded that "a Traveller is now-a-days called a Tourist."[29] Yet, by the second decade of the nineteenth century, when continental peace had been—precariously, at least—restored, important nuances were being imposed on the two terms. For Samuel Taylor Coleridge, both the tourist and traveler seemed to be gripped by the same mania for movement. A few years after the conclusion of the Napoleonic Wars, he commented sardonically that "Peace has set John Bull agadding" ("The Delinquent Travellers," l.10).[30] A renewed enthusiasm for touring appeared to be gripping the country now that continental travel was once more a realistic possibility:

> Keep moving! Steam, or Gas, or Stage,
> Hold, cabin, steerage, hencoop's cage—
> Tour, Journey, Voyage, Lounge, Ride, Walk,
> Skim, Sketch, Excursion, Travel-talk—
> For move you must! 'Tis now the rage,
> The law and fashion of the Age ("The Delinquent Travellers," ll.16–21).[31]

What Coleridge elides here is that the mode of movement was as important as the imperative to obey the "fashion of the Age." In the Romantic period, tourists were ridiculed for their reliance on the stagecoach or carriage, and by the Victorian period trains appeared to be degrading the experience of travel even further.[32] Ruskin's (in)famous comparison of the railway passenger with a parcel reflected his exasperation with the imaginative effects of speedier transportation on the general population.[33] The true traveler eschewed these modern modes of transportation where possible in order to prioritize a connection—which we explore in more detail in chapter 4—between the body, the mind, and the landscape. But for the tourist, "move you must" was a command to be taken literally. The hierarchy that emerged between tourists', travelers', and, to a lesser extent, inhabitants' preferred modes of transport reflected an attitude that simultaneously valued knowledge of the landscape's details and demanded speed. A distinction had already emerged between the traveler—an adventurer who sought to know the landscapes through which they traveled—and the tourist whose "gaze" never quite penetrated beyond the surface of things.[34]

In an early manuscript for her unfinished novel "Catharine, or the Bower" (1792), Jane Austen prefigured Wordsworth's *Guide* by indicating that the inattentive reader equates to the superficial tourist. In a perverse anticipation of Lizzy Bennet's proposed trip to the Lakes, in "Catharine" the vacuous Camilla Stanley personifies what Hanley and Walton describe as the "bovine behavior of English tourists."[35] When the heroine, Kitty, asks Camilla's opinion of Charlotte Smith's novels, she is dismayed to find that Camilla has paid little attention to the crafting that underpins the plot: "'But did not you find the story of Ethelinde very interesting? And the Descriptions of Grasmere, are not they Beautiful?' 'Oh! I missed them all, because I was in such a hurry to know the end of it—.' Then from an easy transition she added, 'We are going to the Lakes this Autumn, and I am quite Mad with Joy.'"[36] The irony is that in attempting to "know the end," Camilla entirely misses the substance of the novel, and her hyperbolically quick reading foreshadows the quick viewing she expects to undertake in the Lake District. Once there, we can confidently expect that she will follow the routes around the main Lakeland sites that, even at this early stage in the region's tourist industry, had already become established to the point of cliché.

The most fashionable Lakeland destinations were—and, indeed, still are—located in the center of the district, and their popularity was attributable to their repeated appearances in the region's literature. Thomas Gray was especially influential in securing Keswick's reputation; as he left the town via Castle Rigg one sunny October day in 1769, he turned back to take in the view. The sight of "the whole valley . . . , the two lakes [Derwentwater and Bassenthwaite], the river, & all the mountains [all in their glory]" almost convinced him to go back again.[37] This tale was repeated by subsequent accounts, including by Thomas West and John Robinson, as proof of Keswick's attractions. As Figure 3.1 indicates, throughout the eighteenth and nineteenth centuries Keswick and Ambleside were the principal locations for accommodating increasing numbers of Lakers. Excursions from these towns did take tourists slightly farther afield; the most popular trip from Keswick, for instance, was a round trip to Buttermere and Crummock Water, which accounts for an isolated hot spot for tourists in the otherwise comparatively unvisited west of the region (Figure 3.2). In the main, though, tourists rarely ventured beyond the beaten track; 76 percent of references to "tour" or "tourist(s)" occur within one mile of a main road or settlement (Figure 3.3). Locations that were not close to main roads remained largely overlooked; Ullswater, for instance, was rarely included in the tourist's route, and as late as 1855 Harriet Martineau

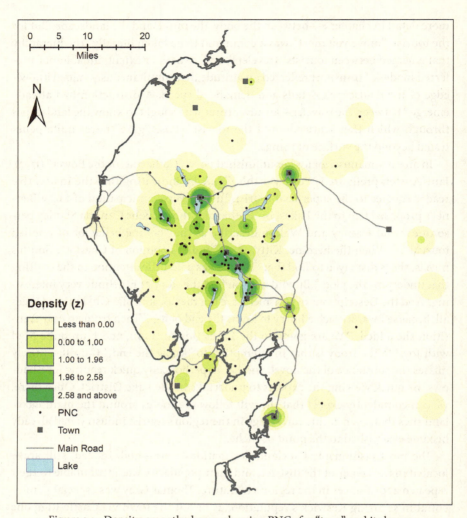

Figure 3.1. Density-smoothed map, showing PNCs for "tour" and its lexeme.

noted that Bassenthwaite could be grouped alongside "the foot of Coniston or Windermere" as being too remote to be of much interest to tourists.[38]

Thanks to its transport links—both to Ambleside in the south and Penrith in the north—Keswick was the north half of the region's principal tourist hub. In 1792, Adam Walker noted that it had "been more considerable formerly than now," but that as "the general head-quarters of numerous Tourists, it improves fast."[39] The proliferation of inns and other types of accommodation indicated how rapidly the town was changing. The local economy altered dramatically as, in Walker's words, "the inhabitants [began] to feel (as at Watering Places) that it is very convenient to make the Summer provide for the Winter" (1792, 100). These changes were not without consequences for Keswick's character; in 1808, Robert Southey joked to the poet and artist Matilda Betham that it was a good thing that "the white sheet has been disused,—for otherwise clean sheets would be sometimes wanting in

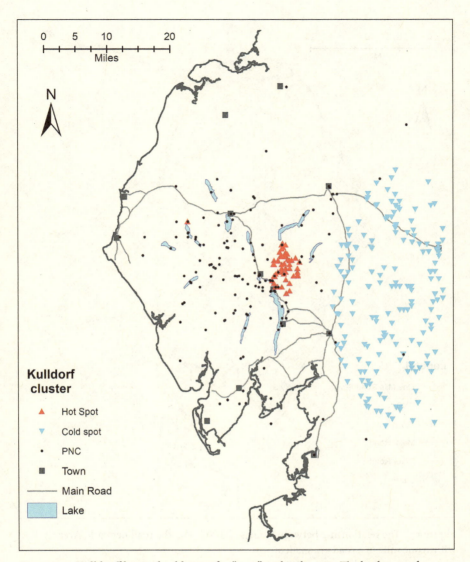

Figure 3.2. Kulldorff hot and cold spots for "tour" and its lexeme. The background population is all place-name instances. Only statistically significant clusters are shown.

Keswick."[40] Keswick began to seem like one of the southern spa towns: its economy, and its population, became increasingly seasonal, mobile, and focused on recreation.[41] By the end of the Victorian period, Keswick, Ambleside, and the new town at Windermere, which grew up around the train station, had become established as "pleasure towns" that offered the kinds of cheap and accessible amusements that attracted tourists.[42]

The popularity of these locations with tourists was cemented by their almost ubiquitous inclusion on tourist itineraries; Table 3.1 indicates the extent to which Keswick and Ambleside outstripped other main settlements and features in attracting tourists. It became a self-fulfilling prophecy: new generations of tourists

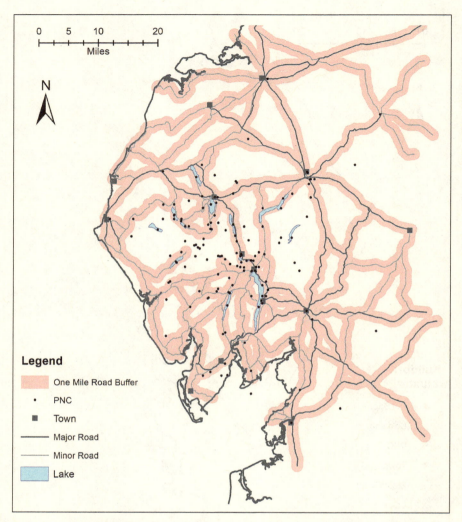

Figure 3.3. The relationship between "tourist*" PNCs and the road network. Areas within one mile of a road are shaded.

followed in the footsteps of those who had come before. Most guidebooks followed a similar agenda: as John Robinson put it, the best guidebooks "notice[d] every object deserving the attention of the tourist, and [furnished] such accurate information as may enable him to visit the Lakes, and survey their beauties, with the least expense of time."[43]

Some authors understood this objective to require the inclusion of quotidian details that would enable the tourist to plan the most effective and enjoyable route; Harriet Martineau, for instance, recommended visiting either in May, June, September, or October, since at any other time of year the incessant rain would impede picturesque viewing.[44] On the other hand, shortly after Martineau first published her *Complete Guide*, an anonymous guidebook writer saw little point in providing

TABLE 3.1

T-SCORES FOR "TOUR*" (WHICH INCLUDES "TOURIST")
FOR THE MOST SIGNIFICANT LOCATIONS

Place	T-score	No. of co-occurrences with "tour*"
Keswick	3.36603	12
Ambleside	2.92889	9
Seathwaite	1.97021	4
Buttermere	1.93982	4
Langdale	1.93757	4
Penrith	1.91518	4
Grange	1.71735	3
Wastwater	1.41019	2
Carnforth	1.40986	2
Patterdale	1.34612	2
Helvellyn	1.33070	2
Grasmere	1.32258	2
Coniston	1.29921	2

"minute detail[s]" about the tourist's route: such minutiae would "only prove per-plexing," they opined.[45] Instead, they sought to offer efficient advice that would enable the tourist quickly and competently to navigate around the main sites in the Lake District: "We conceive that the mere mention of all the places and objects of interest, with one good route to the most of them, and a slight indication of others, is all that is required. This we have attempted to give in these pages, and we trust that the traveler will find the volume sufficiently explicit, while the beau-tiful engravings with which it is embellished will enable him in some degree to anticipate the scenery he is about to visit."[46] This guidebook conceives its aim as being to enable the tourist to collect as many sites as possible, and it aims to mini-mize any surprises by telling the reader in advance what they should expect to see at each location. What this kind of expedient tourist needed was a reliable, pre-planned itinerary.

The itineraries were an early articulation of the problems with mass tourism that Urry and Larson have identified; that is, that the mass tourist is "isolated from the host environment and local people" since they travel "in guided groups and find pleasure in inauthentic contrived attractions."[47] These attractions draw what Urry famously termed the "tourist gaze,"[48] a way of looking which Aaron Santesso glosses as a mode that "does not permit of surprise. It is not oriented towards

TABLE 3.2

T-SCORES FOR "TOUR*" AND "TOURIST*" WITH THE
MOST SIGNIFICANT TYPES OF PLACE

Place type	T-score with "tour*"	T-score with "tourist*"
Bridge	2.09637	1.5517
Hill	2.11359	1.86306
House	2.12768	1.87882
Inn	3.28805	2.79492
Inns	N/A	1.7222
Lake	3.84947	2.79929
Lakes	6.91006	1.93923
Mountains	N/A	1.54274
Road	3.21226	3.21226
Tarn	N/A	1.32794
Town	N/A	1.62864

discovery, but rather towards 'recognition' . . . of what is already known."[49] Fussell puts a similar reading more succinctly when he writes that tourism "requires that you see conventional things, and that you see them in a conventional way."[50] The itineraries promoted tours that tended to follow almost identical geographical patterns, even where the routes to or through the key locations might differ.

In effect, the guidebook itinerary offered regional checklists for tourists to work through. By the 1820s, these itineraries—part of the "technical information" tourists found necessary—were an established part of guidebook culture.[51] Authors like Edward Baines took great pride in the routes they had planned. In his 1829 guidebook *A Companion to the Lakes of Cumberland, Westmoreland, etc.*, Baines assured his reader that his "original" itinerary would "be found of great utility," since it provided the tourist with all the information they needed to conduct a successful and enjoyable tour of the Lakes: "It gives numerous statistical details concerning the towns, villages, lakes, and mountains,—the distances of all the places in every stage,—the names of the noblemen's and gentlemen's seats, with those of their owners or occupiers, (a species of information always desired by the Tourist,)—and many other particulars concerning inns and accommodations."[52] Baines acknowledged the tourist as a specific kind of character who demands a vicarious intimacy with the places through which they pass; here, the tourist is a collector of information about people and, particularly, place. In our corpus, the most significant collocates for "tour" and its lexeme highlight place types that are either low-lying natural landmarks, such as lakes, or man-made elements of the region's infrastructure: roads, inns, or bridges, for instance (Table 3.2). These collocations corroborate what we saw of the picturesque's geographies, and affirm Baines's assessment that tourists were primarily interested in details that would make following their itineraries easy; they were keen to know the distances they would travel, the roads they would take, and the scenes or views they would witness on the way. The fewer surprises they faced, the better.

Other writers resisted including itineraries, seeing them as evidence of the tourist's laziness and incapacity to appreciate the Lake District as it deserved. In his *Guide*, Wordsworth expressed a palpable irritation at the "humble and tedious" task of "supplying the Tourist with directions [for] how to approach the several scenes in their best, or most convenient, order."[53] The *Guide* resisted referring to tourists at all until the third edition in 1822. By 1835, this reticence had been expanded to eight direct addresses to the tourist, an increase that indicates a change in the target market for Wordsworth's publication (Figure 3.4). When the publishers Hudson and Nicholson took the project over from Longman after 1835, they reoriented the *Guide* to become a more commercial tool for Lakeland tourists. After 1842, they expanded Wordsworth's text with railway timetables, a letter on the Lakeland rocks by the renowned geologist Adam Sedgwick, and information on the Lake District's plant life.[54] As Cecilia Powell notes, notwithstanding the academic focus on the *Guide*'s development between 1810 and 1835, the book actually gained a much wider readership in its new form: for more than sixty years from 1842, the *Guide* had "successive print-runs in thousands," meaning it was this version with which Victorian visitors to the Lakes were most familiar.[55]

After 1842, then, the *Guide* contained the "tourist-friendly . . . practical information" to which Wordsworth had earlier been opposed, including detailed itineraries for suggested trips around the region.[56] These had been taken from Ambleside resident William Green's *The Tourist's New Guide* (1819), and suggested some popular excursions with which the tourists might amuse themselves.[57] The shape of these routes is significant: the tourist's itineraries were circular, starting and ending at the same point, and reinscribing particular scenes onto the popular imagination. The traveler, on the other hand, moved differently: their routes were linear, writing new journeys, and new interpretations, into both landscape and literature.

It was to these more adventurous visitors that Wordsworth addressed himself; he declared that he wrote for the "minds of Persons of taste, and feeling for Landscape, who might be inclined to explore the District of the Lakes with that degree of attention to which its beauty may fairly lay claim."[58] Wordsworth's ideal reader was the person who would attempt to understand the landscape's history, as well as their personal place within it. The reader who paid close attention to the right kind of text has the foundations of the traveler who will take their time in exploring and coming to know the region. This traveler would leave the beaten track to discover a Lakeland that is unique to them, but even the traveler who stays on a fixed route might, if they are immersed in the landscape, notice details that can lead to new self-discoveries.

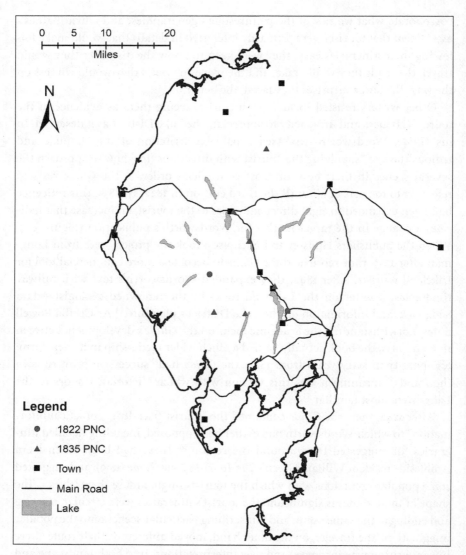

Figure 3.4. PNCs for "tourist(s)" in the 1822 and 1835 editions of Wordsworth's *Guide to the Lakes*.

PROCEEDING AT LEISURE: TRAVELING IN THE LAKE DISTRICT

As travel became more accessible over the course of the eighteenth and nineteenth centuries, distinctions emerged between "genuine" and "spurious" cultural engagements.[59] This tension underwrote nineteenth-century travel narratives.[60] To call oneself a traveler was what Buzard calls an "anti-touristic" strategy; it was necessary for the self-appointed traveler continually to separate themselves from the tourists, in spite of the fact that their practices—perhaps inevitably—were closely related.

Like tourists, a traveler's identity was predicated on the fact that they would have to return home.[61] Unlike the tourist, however, a traveler often left domestic comforts behind in order to access a deeper, more genuine connection to new landscapes, people, and experiences. Proper travel, as opposed to mere touring, necessarily involved a destabilizing of the distinction between self and landscape. It is a critical commonplace to recall the etymological link between "travel" and "travail,"[62] but this history does neatly point to the fact that the traveler's work was both physical, in traversing often difficult terrain, and imaginative. To travel was to enter into an intimacy with the landscape that was risky, that might even be dangerous, and that would certainly have a long-term effect on the traveler's mind.[63]

Edward Baines described the kinds of accommodation and activities that might appeal to different kinds of Lakeland travelers:

> The inns and all the accommodations for travelers have been materially improved, so that now neither comfort nor luxury is wanting; and the tourist may travel through this mountainous region, either in his own carriage or in vehicles found on the spot, with nothing of discomfort to interrupt his enjoyment, except what may occasionally arise from the crowd of travelers. The musing sentimentalist, or the fastidious traveler who is nice about best rooms and constant attention, might wish that the number of tourists were diminished. But such, I am persuaded, is not the general desire of the visitors, any more than of the inhabitants. There is ample space among these mountains and valleys for the rovings of those who love seclusion; and even in the height of the season the rambler will meet with very few parties in any excursion he may make, except in the immediate neighborhood of the towns.[64]

The "fastidious traveler" is concerned with the quality of their accommodation; they desire the "luxury of home" within the wildest mountains. And yet, even this traveler distinguishes himself from the tourist, whom he "might wish" were fewer in number. This traveler is eager to explore the mountains while, as we have already seen, the tourists remain "in the immediate neighborhood of the towns." Baines's implication is that travelers are distinguished from tourists by their willingness to leave the main routes and to head off—alone—to rove around the mountains.

The sum of the difference between tourists and travelers was what Hayden Lorimer terms "embodied acts of landscaping."[65] Through these "acts," as phenomenologists have also demonstrated, understanding place becomes a perceptual experience that necessitates paying close attention to smell, touch, and (as we will discover in chapter 5) hearing, as well as to visual impressions.[66] The best travelers employed all their senses, as well as the movement of their bodies through space, in order to comprehend the landscape. Such embodiment amounted to a form of reading. Michel de Certeau makes this comparison; like the traveler, he finds that the reader must pay attention to the "pathways" through a space, and in reading those pre-existing routes they inevitably construct new, unique paths of their own.[67] Similarly, the traveler proper pays attention to the details and nuances of the terrain, and performs an embodied type of close reading on it in order to unveil the nuances of a place's character that are hidden to the tourist gaze.

Wordsworth's vision of the ideal traveler is predicated on this principle. In Wordsworth's view, the "end of travelling" was to communicate "ideas to enlarge the mind" (Letter to Dorothy Wordsworth, September 6, 1790).[68] Conversely, however, that enlargement depended on a form of contraction; the mind expanded in proportion to the traveler's sensitivity to minute details. In his *Guide*, Wordsworth revealed the landscape to be implicitly textual, but only a true traveler, trained in the Wordsworthian art of reading the landscape, would be able to locate the writing: "The soil is laid bare by torrents and burstings of water from the sides of the mountains in heavy rains; and not unfrequently their perpendicular sides are seamed by ravines (formed also by ruins and torrents) which, meeting in angular points, entrench and scar the surface with numerous figures like the letters W and Y."[69] The landscape here becomes text; the waters form, like ink, the letters W and Y. But only the attentive traveler will find these letters, and only a close reading of them in light of their situation and the reader-traveler's personal perceptions will unveil anything meaningful about them.

It was also important to Wordsworth that the traveler—like the inhabitant but unlike the tourist—recognizes the *entire* region as a scene of interest. In tourist literature, destination tended to be emphasized over the process of travel, and the tourist's ideal forms of transport offered the quickest and easiest ways of reaching the desired location.[70] Conversely, for the traveler the journey was an important part of the experience; while the tourist went from site to site (and sight to sight), the Wordsworthian traveler was attuned enough to discover meaning everywhere. The traveler who "proceed[s]," as Wordsworth advises, "at leisure" should deviate away from the main road. Wordsworth opines, for instance, that the "direct road from Grasmere to Keswick does not (as has been observed of Rydal Mere) show to advantage Thirlmere, or Wythburn Lake, with its surrounding mountains."[71] To secure the best view, the traveler must do what the tourist will not; leave the road and explore what appears, on a conventional tourist's map, to be blank spaces between mapped places. Ian Whyte suggests that the improvement of maps at this time made travelers more adventurous,[72] but in fact it was a two-way process: maps improved as travelers ventured farther from the main routes, and thereby encouraged others to follow in their footsteps.

There are significantly more mentions of "traveler(s)" than "tourist(s)" in the corpus; the words "tourist" or "tourists" are found on 405 occasions, while "traveler" or "travelers" occur 608 times—a little over 50 percent more frequently. In part, that appears to be because of a resistance—understandable given their reputation—toward being labeled a "tourist," meaning that self-identification as a "traveler" was more common. However, as Figure 3.5b indicates, these frequencies are not reflected by the PNCs. When we compare these data to those for "tourist(s)" (Figure 3.5a), a dramatic difference in these terms" relationships to place emerges. Whereas "tourist(s)" co-occurs within ten words of a place name in 82 percent of cases, "traveler(s)" does so just 14 percent of the time.

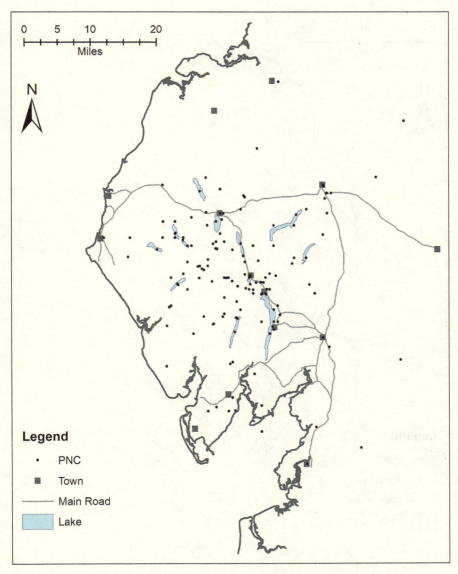

Figure 3.5a–b. Point maps showing PNCs for "tourist(s)" and "traveler(s)." Above, (a) shows PNCs for "tourist(s)."

Notwithstanding the apparent unhelpfulness of mapping this term, given this low level of PNCs, paying attention to the map's blank spaces, as much as to its patterns, tells us a lot about the traveler's relationship with geography. Indeed, Matthew K. Gold has argued that this kind of focus on "deformance" is central to a digital humanist's ability to "undermin[e] assumptions" and expose "the social, political, historical, computational, and literary constructs that underlie digital texts."[73] In this instance, the word "traveler" is used much less frequently in relation to place names—but the resultant ambiguity in the maps still reveals something crucial about the traveler's spatial identity. These lower levels of co-occurrence

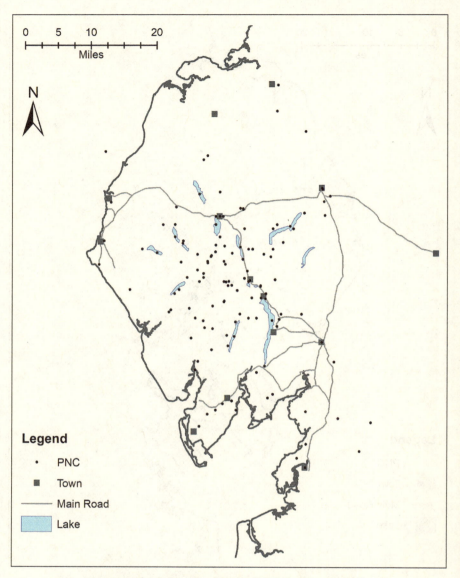

Figure 3.5b. Point map showing PNCs for "traveler(s)."

imply that a greater freedom was entrusted to the traveler about precisely where in the Lakes to explore. The traveler's focus was on the way place was experienced, rather than necessarily the site itself.

Nevertheless, certain places did emerge as particular haunts for the traveler. Density smoothing the data from Figure 3.5b (Figure 3.6b) implies that the traveler and the tourist were drawn to a very similar region (Figure 3.6a): travelers are also found predominantly around the most frequently visited locations near Ambleside and Keswick. Unlike the tourist, however, the traveler appears to fre-quent the mountains around these settlements, rather than the towns. Applying

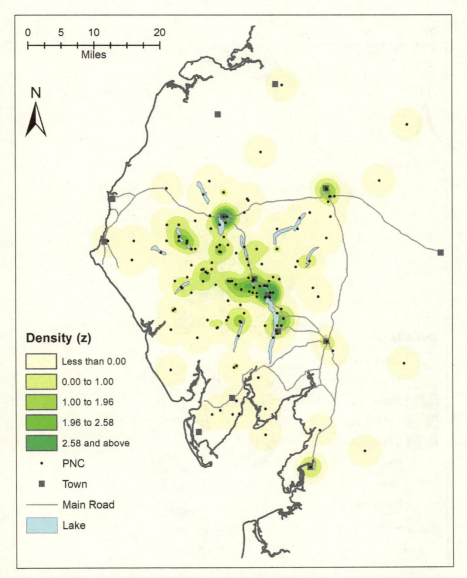

Figure 3.6a–b. Density-smoothed maps showing PNCs for "tourist(s)" and "traveller(s)." Above, (a) shows PNCs for "tourist(s)."

Kulldorff's spatial scan statistic (see chapter 1) allows us to read these data more carefully (Figure 3.7). The data indicate that travelers were particularly associated with the mountains in the Langdale region, as well as, to a less significant degree, the more remote valleys of Wasdale and Eskdale. Travelers appear to have been especially interested in the mountainous regions that required a more adventurous spirit to traverse; these are regions where the road network is much barer. The traveler who intended to explore these areas would have to walk or (where the terrain permitted) go on horseback.

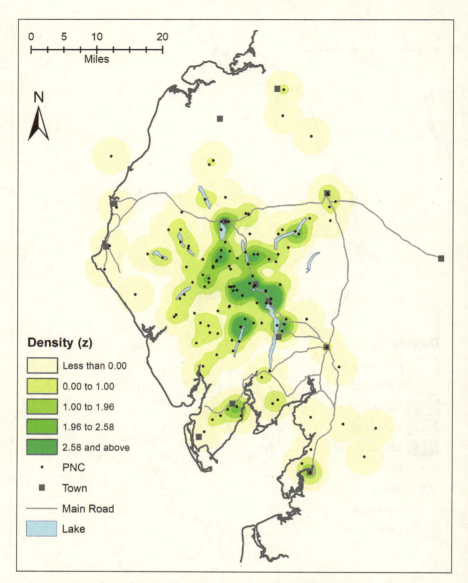

Figure 3.6b. A density-smoothed map showing the PNCs for "traveler(s)."

In short, what defines the traveler against the tourist is the sophistication of their "embodied acts of landscaping." The tourist, as we have already seen, gazes at the views, often from the window of their carriage or coach. The traveler, on the other hand, rambles away to less popular, and less populous, locations. The traveler's habit of venturing into the less well charted regions of the map had an imaginative function too: it allowed them to generate a personal version of Lakeland that was based on the interaction between their body and unfamiliar terrain, and to develop a much more thorough impression of the region. In Wordsworth's view, travelers should aspire to develop the inhabitants' intimacy

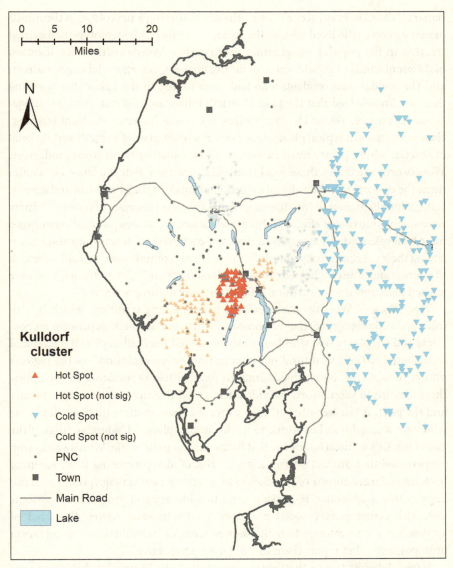

Figure 3.7. Kulldorff hot and cold spots for PNCs of "traveler(s)."

with and care for the landscape. Yet, in his *Guide*, Wordsworth shared with many of his literary forebears and successors a greater interest in the imaginative or aesthetic effects of interacting with the region's inhabitants, rather than the people themselves.

AWAY FROM THE SHOW PLACE: THE INHABITANTS' LAKELAND

Early visitors to the Lake District were not especially interested in the harshness of day-to-day life in the region. By the 1830s, as J. D. Marshall and John K. Walton remark, "the Cumbrian scene . . . was already becoming a stereotype in the minds of many people who lived outside the region."[74] In fact, this stereotype had gained traction in the popular imagination much earlier. Wordsworth's identification of different kinds of inhabitant—including farmers, cottagers, laborers, natives, and the middle-class residents who had often moved to the Lakes after traveling there—acknowledged that the Lake District's inhabitants did not share a homogeneous experience. Yet, as Hess recognizes, the *Guide* "presents the local laboring-class inhabitants in typical picturesque fashion as exemplars of a traditional national character, whose purity must be preserved by isolating them from modernity. Wordsworth celebrates these local freeholders for their independence but denies them the opportunity for cultural evolution or modern social and cultural agency, subsuming them instead into the supposedly timeless processes of nature."[75] There were some positive side effects of this preservation. A picturesque ideal encouraged more benevolent estate management that, in theory, went some way toward acknowledging the local community's needs.[76] This aesthetic commitment, as well as the lack of many grand houses,[77] helped protect the land from the "improvements" that were applied to locations whose natural utilities were not anthropocentric.[78]

Nevertheless, Wordsworth's *Guide* is part of a long tradition, which it both inherited and propagated, that promoted a picturesque aesthetic dependent on nostalgia and simplicity that simultaneously preserved the landscape's character and contributed to the geocultural marginalization—even exclusion—of the region's poorer inhabitants. Notwithstanding his nearly lifelong residence in the Lakes, there remains in Wordsworth's *Guide* a discernible distinction between the farmer and the poet. It is a "separation" that, as we shall see, matters intensely for those who have worked—and continue to work—in this place.[79] Understandings of the Lake District's cultural landscape that focus only on writers, like Wordsworth, who perpetuated that distinction run a higher risk of also promoting it. By stepping back into a larger corpus of works, and by adopting new vantage points on it, we hope in this final section to indicate ways that literary and geographical patterns link with contemporary social pressures. As Underwood writes, this kind of approach is not an attempt to make shorter-term, or individualized, trends seem unimportant—"but it puts them in a different perspective."[80]

James Rebanks thinks that a bias against the Lake District's inhabitants continues in favor of a Wordsworthian response to the region even today, in a dream for "a wider society that was full of people disconnected from the land." But that Wordsworthian vision "was never for us": the people who worked on the land were frequently disenfranchised in this dream.[81] Rebanks acknowledges that William Wordsworth did value the Lake District as "a place peopled with its own culture and history."[82] Yet it was Dorothy Wordsworth who believed most evidently that the history of the landscape was also the history of the people who had lived there for generations:

It is, when any unusual event happens, affecting to listen to the fireside talk in our Cottages; you then find how faithfully the inner histories of Families, their

lesser and greater cares, their peculiar habits, and ways of life are recorded in
the breasts of their Fellow-inhabitants of the Vale; much more faithfully than it
is possible that the lives of those, who have moved in higher stations and had
numerous Friends in the busy world, can be preserved in remembrance, even
when their doings and sufferings have been watched for the express purpose of
recording them in written narratives.[83]

Dorothy discovered that the inhabitants recorded their histories not on paper but
within each other's bodies. This embodied memory seemed to Dorothy to be more
reliable than the paper used by the higher classes. However, these "native" family
histories remained hidden from those who did not join the cottagers around the
fireside. For some writers, like the Victorians Edwin Waugh and William Dickinson, taking these stories and the characters who told them away from the fireside
and onto paper was one of the traveler's most important roles.

It was not an opinion held by many of Waugh's or Dickinson's contemporaries.
Jane Renouf and Rob David's complaint that "the everyday stories of those born
and brought up among the fells and valleys have gone largely unnoticed and
unsung" is evidenced by our corpus.[84] The new cultures that developed as the
region became better known, and which were promoted by tourist guides, travel
narratives, and the most widely read Lakeland literature, were primarily produced
from the perspective of the middle- or upper-class man. As Hess has argued, scholarship has tended to assume that this social position—and the "ecological consciousness" it develops—can be "taken as universal in ways that laboring-class or
female subjectivity cannot."[85] Lakeland literature from throughout this period frequently failed to recognize that local communities were not uncultured backwa-
ters; rather, they operated through regional countercultures that were shaped by
communal responses to the terrain and the opportunities for work and leisure it
provided.[86] This cultural exclusion was reflected in geographical marginalization.

Comparing the mentions of inhabitants with those for tourists and travelers
in our corpus reveals that two cultural versions of the Lake District existed in
parallel with each other. The eastern half—including Bowness, Ambleside, and
Keswick—was claimed by the tourist guides for containing the primary places of
interest for visitors to the Lakes; Eliza Lynn Linton repeatedly called this area the
"show place."[87] To the west were what she called the "wild" places which, throughout our period, seemed to belong to the inhabitants.[88] Her novel *Lizzie Lorton of
Greyrigg*, written at Brantwood in 1865 and published the following year, explores
these "wilds," and the effect this geography might have on the people who live there.
It is set in the fictional village of Langthwaite in the Western Lakes, among some
of the region's most dangerous fells, and that setting suits the eponymous heroine
very well; she, too, is tempestuous and "wild."[89] She is even named for "sweet Lorton valley"[90] to the west of Keswick—although Nancy Fix Anderson believes that
Lizzie's surname is a play on "Linton" to highlight the novel's autobiographical
interests.[91] Herbert Van Thal takes the novel at its word that it is set in the Lake
District,[92] but actually its geography is more complex than that. In fact, Lynn

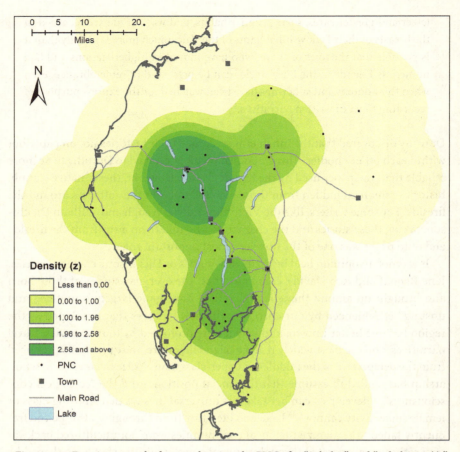

Figure 3.8. Density-smoothed maps showing the PNCs for "inhabit" and "inhabitant(s)."

Linton imagined a fictional version of the "wilds," composed of the real area's most distinctive features: Styebarrow, Mickledore, Sour Milk Ghyll, and Dale Head. These locations enclose the fictional lake, Langmere, and the fictional village. Acknowledging the novel's fictional geography indicates the extent to which these places—so closely associated in the popular imagination with the region's inhabitants—signified a certain kind of Lakeland character.

Lynn Linton's novel reflects a real cultural-geographical perception: that the main line of Lake District mountains—from Skiddaw in the north, over the Langdales toward Loughrigg, and on to Coniston—formed a boundary between the region's tourist and inhabitant zones. The tourist industry's disinterest in the places away from the standard routes meant that tourist guides and travel narratives scarcely took any notice of inhabitants beyond the main road between Kendal and Keswick (Figure 3.8). In fact, when we apply Kulldorff's spatial scan statistic to these data (Figure 3.9), we discover that inhabitants are mentioned less frequently than we would statistically expect throughout the majority of the Lake District. The only major exception to this is the cluster and hot spot located on the

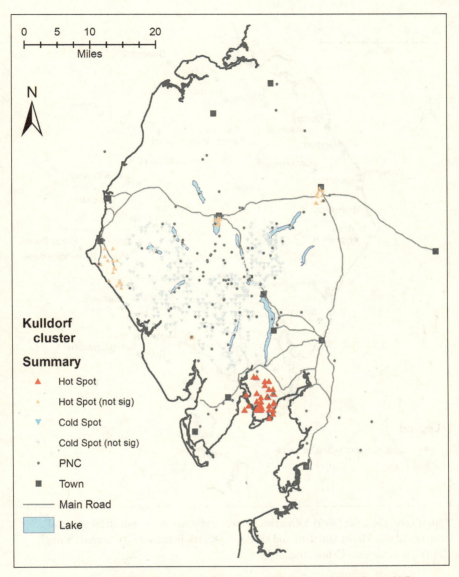

Figure 3.9. Kulldorff hot and cold spots for "inhabit" and "inhabitant(s)."

Cartmel Peninsula, and that is thanks to one author: Edwin Waugh, the journalist, poet, and dialect writer known locally as "Lancashire's Burns." Two of Waugh's works are included in the corpus: *Over Sands to the Lakes* (1860) and *Rambles in the Lake Country and Its Borders* (1864). This second text includes the first as a chapter, meaning that identical material is duplicated, although set in a slightly different geographical context; the later publication situates the Lake District in close relation with its neighbor, Lancashire, and makes clear the geographical and cultural connections between the counties. Waugh's wider interests in the lives and experiences of working people are reflected in these travel guides: he actively sought

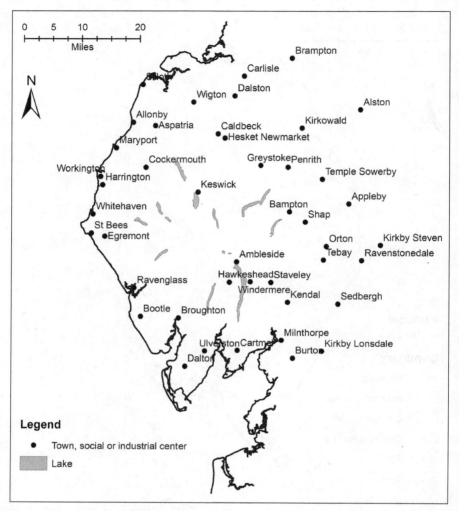

Figure 3.10. The Lake District's market centers and other main industrial or social centers. Adapted from Marshall and Walton (1981, 12). Permission conveyed through Copyright Clearance Center, Inc.

out the regions that were more densely populated by Lakeland residents. As a result, he spent some time in Ulverston—by this point a bustling agricultural market town on the border between Lancashire and Westmorland—and it is his account that emphasizes this place's significance for the Lake District's residents.

An alternative geography, based on the practices and needs of the Lake District's inhabitants, emphasizes the region's industrial and trade centers over the locations famous for picturesque scenery. Marshall and Walton demonstrate how settlements and townships grew up in the first half of the nineteenth century as loci for various industrial and social activities. Of the thirty-five market centers in the region, twenty-six fulfilled a number of key services, including shops, workshops, attorneys, doctors, blacksmiths, schools, and coach, carrier, or canal services (Figure 3.10).[93]

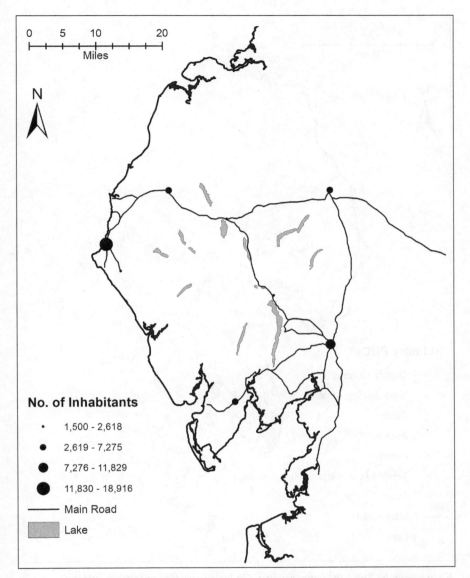

Figure 3.11. The most significant Lake District towns as indicated by *Black's Shilling Guide* of 1853.

But the settlements that mattered to the tourists were not necessarily the same as those that mattered to the inhabitants. In 1853, when the eastern and central Lake District was firmly established as a "show place," the population figures recorded by *Black's Shilling Guide* indicate that the most significant settlements were not the destinations associated with the tourist industry. Figure 3.11 demonstrates that Whitehaven was easily the largest town and, from the inhabitants' point of view, the most significant thanks to its opportunities for trade and employment. The tourist

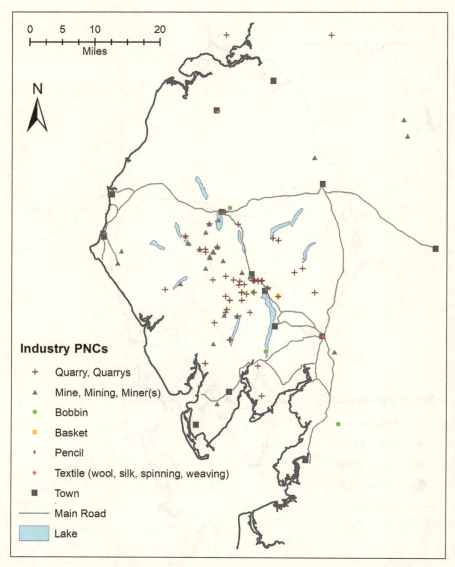

Figure 3.12a–b. PNCs for nonagricultural industries such as quarrying, mining, bobbin-making, basket-weaving, pencil-making, and silk or woolen manufacture (spinning and weaving). Above, (a) shows points distinguishing between industries.

centers of Keswick and Ambleside, based on these figures, played far fewer dominant roles in quotidian Lakeland life than they did in touristic experiences of it.

These other settlements grew up around the Lake District's diverse industrial outputs. As Barry Reay and, in particular, Marshall and Walton have shown, the Cumbrian landscape was marked both literally and culturally by a wide range of industries.[94] The "major industry," as Reay observes, may have been agriculture, but mining, quarrying, charcoal-burning, hoop-making, basket-making, metal-

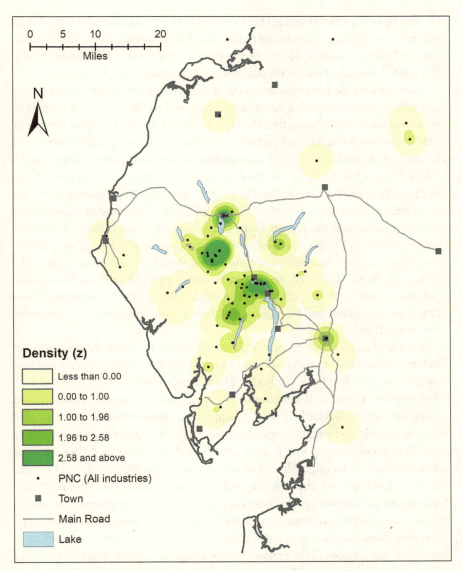

Figure 3.12b. Density-smoothed map showing all industries.

working, nail- and tool-making, silk, woolen and flax manufacture, paper- and pencil-making all played their part in sustaining the economy throughout the Lake District.[95] As Figure 3.12a indicates, the Lake District was riven with quarries and mines, although these unsightly disturbances to the picturesque scene were largely ignored by Lakeland literature. One notable exception was the black lead mine in Seatoller (Figure 3.12b), which continued to provide significant local employment throughout our period, and is frequently mentioned in the corpus by tourists and travelers keen to witness the ores being blasted from the mountainside. In addition, Lakeland bobbin makers were a major supplier for the national cotton, wool, silk, and linen factories. Pamela Horn records that, in 1844, demand was so high that "not enough hands [could] be got for the orders coming in."[96] These manufacturing industries, alongside the burgeoning tourist trade, swiftly and dramatically altered the Lake District's landscape and the society who dwelt in it.

As the tourist industry expanded, it inevitably brought sociocultural change and industrial advancements that unsettled visitors and residents alike: it seemed to contemporary commentators that the region paid for greater financial prosperity in the erosion of its traditional customs and values. This interpretation reverses a Humean assumption that "moral and economic improvement advanced together."[97] In fact, writers like Lynn Linton find the opposite to be true. In *Lizzie Lorton*, Langthwaite finds its character fundamentally altered through immigration: the vicar comes from Oxford; Margaret and Aunt Harriet from London, Ainslie from a mystery place, and the miners from Cornwall and Ireland. Better transport, industry, and social ambitions overcome the area's hostile geography, but with detrimental effects to its character and indigenous population. The novel reflects the fact that, in the real Lakeland, wealthy merchants—particularly from Liverpool—made new additions to the gentry, and the rapid building of villas along the shores of the major lakes indicated the region's shift from a rural backwater to a fashionable holiday location.[98]

Less grand residences were also built to cater to the tourist trade; Joseph Pocklington's installation of an old woman in a hut at the Bowder Stone became a particularly popular spectacle. Catherine Hutton's epistolary novel *Oakwood Hall* (1819) recounts a visit to the landmark: "You would scarcely suppose that a woman wanted to show us Bolder [*sic*] Stone, a stupendous mass of rock which we could not avoid seeing, and which astonished us so much, that we could look at nothing else! "Pray, good woman," said I, "what could you shew us that we do not see?" She could shew us how we might shake hands under the stone. "Very well," said I; "then we will look at the stone where we are, and shake hands when we get home."[99] Hutton imagines a resistance to the more overtly commercial trappings of the tourist industry that reveals two important characteristics of the Romantic-era Lake District: first, that tourists had become sufficiently populous to alter the traditional habits and occupations of the region's inhabitants; and, second, that these tourists could be—and often were—blind to the economic deprivations that facilitated their recreational experiences.

As William Rollinson observes, the Lake District had in common with other British uplands that it was a place where "the pace of life was slow, where changes and innovations were greeted with suspicion and where tradition and folklore died hard."[100] Yet, as early as 1792 the effects of tourism on local cultures were remarkable. Among the earliest traditions to be replaced were the uplands' place names. Joseph Budworth recalled asking a guide for the names of the various fells: "In this valley," the guide replied, they were called "so and so," but "other guides have gi'en' um seck fine neames, we do naw recollect um, but we mun naw contradict um, as they thinken umselves cleverer folks than we are."[101] That Budworth could not remember the fells' original names indicates how unimportant such local toponyms were deemed to be. Two decades in to the next century, John Wilson (alias Philip Kempferhausen) indicates that learning the names of the mountains and streams was one means by which the traveler began to feel naturalized; his lack of knowledge of these names makes him feel like "a stranger—a foreigner—in this heavenly land."[102] Yet an anonymous guidebook in 1857 demonstrated a similar erosion of local onomastic customs as Budworth had noticed; this guide advised that, among the "many delightful short walks about Keswick," is the one to "Castle Head, or, as the inhabitants call it, Castlet."[103] In both instances, the local names—which registered dialect as well as local histories and folklore—gave way to the guides' and visitors less historically rich designations.

Budworth's contemporary, Adam Walker, observed that these erasures of local tradition were particularly noticeable at settlements along the main routes through the Lake District. Of the road from Penrith to Keswick that ran through Patterdale, he observed that "solitude and Peace reign here undisturbed," with one important exception: "The rattling Tourist . . . excites envy and false ideas of happiness among the peaceful inhabitants; for now it ceases to excite laughter or contempt, when the ruddy lass forgets her dialect, and appears at church in a tall bonnet fluttering with ribbands. Turnpike Roads have destroyed provincial manners and provincial dialects; for, as Goldsmith says, 'Fashions now not only travel to the exteriors of the kingdom in stage-coaches, but in the very basket.' Every place in this Island is now only London out of town."[104] Walker describes a compression of national geography, whereby the capital's influence is witnessed in unprecedented ways on what had been, prior to the expansion of the tourist industry, remote northern uplands. John Keats called this malign influence "the miasma of London," and he deplored the "hat-band ignorance" that seemed, to him, to have infected the region's inhabitants. He was dismayed to find that even "Lord Wordsworth" welcomed such degenerate tourists: "instead of being in retirement," as Keats expected, he found Wordsworth and his home at Rydal Mount "full in the thick of fashionable visitors quite convenient to be pointed at all the summer long."[105] This revelation about Wordsworth's private life, so antithetical to what Keats had imagined, changed the younger poet's opinion of the elder: as Carol Kyros Walker summarizes, "Affecting a lordship and courting the fashionable, Wordsworth appeared a poet of another color to Keats."[106] Notwithstanding Wordsworth's resistance in print to the tourist trade, it seemed to Keats that the Bard of Rydal Mount was quite willing to trade the Lake District's integrity to advance his own fame.

These changes to local habits and traditions did not happen at a uniform rate throughout the region; James Plumptre, for instance, implored travelers to Wasdale in 1795 to "put off and forget the dissipated world" before approaching these valleys where "difficulty of access" had protected them from acquiring urban vices.[107] As late as 1936, the so-called Chinese Traveler, Chiang Yee, found Wasdale barren, lonely to the point of animosity—even the trees and mountains seemed to be "running away" as he drove toward them—and so quiet that the 'sound of pines blown by the wind and of water running under a bridge" mingled with the "clear isolated sound" of the motor-car "in a way this traveler had never before experienced."[108]

Other visitors were remarkably obtuse about the effects that encroaching metropolitan values would have on Lakeland habits. Even in 1892, Samuel Barber anticipated that, although the extension of Thirlmere into a reservoir would change the scenery of Wythburn valley—construction had begun on the dam in 1890 and was completed in 1894[109]—it would not affect the "social customs" of the people who lived there. As evidence, Barber reprinted a "true relic of the ancient days," a local shepherd's song which was sung at the shepherds' Merry Nights. At these events, Barber recorded, the shepherds would enjoy a "good supper," a "good talk on the day's proceedings," and ample beer. "No doubt," Barber concludes, "a brisk flirtation takes place here in many meetings." Once the beer had loosened the spirits, a violin or melodeon was produced, and then "the fun commences in earnest" with a song:

> The shepherd's health—and it shall go round—
> And it shall go round—and it shall go round!
> The shepherd's health—and it shall go round!
>   Heigh O! Heigh O! Heigh O!
>   And he that doth this health deny,
>   Before his fact I him defy.
>   He's fit for no good company.
>   So let this health go round![110]

Barber confidently predicted that, since such traditions had survived the onslaught of the eighteenth- and nineteenth-century tourist industries, they would withstand this new threat: "It does not seem probable," he wrote, "that Manchester will have much influence in modernizing the native mind, when we reflect that the shepherd's song given above is still sung with great gusto and continual repetitions at sheep-clipping feasts" (1892, 15). Ironically, whether or not the song survived in Lakeland customs, most of Wythburn village was drowned by the extended reservoir.

Apart from such drastic changes to the topography, remote villages and valleys like Wythburn and Wasdale were relatively protected from modern advances by their comparative inaccessibility. But Keswick, the focal point of the tourist industry, indicated how extensive the erosion of local traditions could be in response to an influx of visitors. We have seen already that the town underwent rapid and radical change from the end of the eighteenth century. An anonymous guidebook published by John Garnett in 1852 recorded that, three hundred years earlier, John Leland had found "a little poor market-town called Keswike, a mile from St Herberte's Isle, that Bede speaketh of."[111] Garnett's author regrets that it is not possible to provide an estimate of the population from this period, but speculates that the "number of inhabitants would necessarily fluctuate with the state of mining operations in the neighborhood, at one period increasing, at others decreasing."[112] The late sixteenth and early seventeenth centuries witnessed a boom period for the local mining industry; William Camden, who authored the first chorographical survey of Britain in the late sixteenth century (the first edition of *Britannia* was published in 1586), had "found Keswick inhabited by miners."[113]

The nearby "extensive swamps and undrained marsh lands" seemed—to Garnett's author, at least—to control the population by breeding disease.[114] Keswick's population had been culled through infectious illnesses at regular points throughout its recent history; this author notes that in 1623, for instance, the number of deaths from the plague recorded in Crosthwaite churchyard was no fewer than 258. As this author observes, the modern advances that had eroded some of the local customs had, at least, improved the health of the population. Still, general health in this region remained seriously behind national trends. In 1850, the engineer and sanitarian Robert Rawlinson offered a damning portrayal of the realities of Cumbrian life in his "Report to the General Board of Health" on sewers, drainage, water supply, and sanitary conditions. Rawlinson declared of Braithwaite, a village in the Derwent valley near Keswick, that, "in proportion to its population," it contained "more dirt, disease, and death than any decent town." It was, he concluded, "one of the most romantic and filthy villages in England."[115] That this village was so close to the tourists' headquarters indicates the real and damaging effects of the self-interestedness for which the tourist was infamous.

As we began to see in chapter 2, tourist and travel literature from throughout this period re-appropriated the region's deprivation into a picturesque narrative that saw its poverty as morally improving, and the inhabitants as contented in their simplicity. This response began early in Lake District literature. In 1769, Thomas Gray recorded a picturesque portrait of Lakeland village life, writing of Grasmere that it was:

> a white village with the parish-church rising in the midst of it, hanging enclosures, corn-fields, & meadows green as an emerald with their trees & hedges & cattle fill up the whole space from the edge of the water & just opposite to you is a large farm-house at the bottom of a steep smooth lawn embosom'd in old woods, wch climb half way up the mountain's side, & discover above them a broken line of crags, that crown the scene. Not a single red tile, no flaring Gentleman's house, or garden-walls, break in upon the repose of this little unsuspected paradise, but all is peace, rusticity, & happy poverty in its neatest most becoming attire.[116]

The pure whites and natural stones that form the buildings look to Gray like they are at one with a paradisial landscape characterized by opulent greenery and luxuriant growth. This land of plenty appears to protect its residents from the elements; they seem to be "embosom[ed]" against the excesses of the Lakeland climate. At this distance, taking a picturesque view of the village from the lake's other shore, the village seems to be the archetype of pastoral calm, home to a population who are "happy" in a life of necessary simplicity. But, as Paul Westover recognizes, visitors frequently "tended to avoid—or greet with discomfort—realities that would disturb their romance."[117] John Wilson's alter ego was so reluctant to disrupt his

fantasy that he feels "afraid to enter into conversation with the shepherds and peas-
ants in whose cottages [he] slept," since he "wished them to be what they seemed
to my imagination."[118] He worried that talking with the inhabitants would destroy
his picturesque notions of them, and their role in creating the "Paradise" (1819, 396)
in which he finds himself. The myth persisted: almost a century after Gray's tour,
William Wells Brown—who, given his own biography, we might expect to be more
suspicious of the narrative—marveled at the "happiness" he witnessed, "even
among the poorer classes."[119]

The material aspects of daily Lakeland life seemed to supplement these visions
of healthy simplicity, a view that was not always restricted to the region's visitors.
Gilpin, concluding his first volume of *Observations*, recorded a "luxurious" meal
of eggs and milk near Buttermere, fare that he was convinced contributed to the
"chearful and healthy looks of the inhabitants." He discovered in these villagers'
appearance "new proofs of the narrow limits, in which all the real wants of life are
comprized."[120] For the so-called Muse of Cumberland, Susanna Blamire (1747–1794),
the Cumberland village of Stocklewath—now Stockdalewath—provided ample
material for a northern pastoral:

> Sweet Row, flow on, and be thy little vale
> The future glory of the happy tale;
> Long be thy banks bespread as they are now
> With nibbling sheep, or richer feeding cow;
> With rock, and scar, and cottage on the hill,
> With curling smoke, and busy useful mill;
> Long may yon trees afford their leafy screen,
> And long from winter save the fading green;
> In every season in their speckled pride,
> Safe may the trout through all thy windings glide;
> Safe may the fowl adown thy waters swim,
> Bathe the webb'd foot, or o'er thy mirror skim,
> Nor yet the schoolboy cast the deadly stone,
> And take that life, no frailer than his own;
> For peace and plenty, and the cheerful tale,
> For happy wives, for mirth, and honest ale,
> For maidens fair, and swains of matchless truth,
> And all the openness of artless youth,
> Whene'er a Cumbrian Village shall be fam'd,
> Let Stoklewath be not the last that's nam'd![121]

Like Gray and Gilpin, Blamire describes a "happy" region: the village's "cheerful
tale" reveals a productive, utopic society in which the "happy wives," "maidens fair,
and swains of matchless truth," keep the butter churning, wool spinning, fields
growing, and the mill "busy" and "useful." As Mike Huggins demonstrates of "The
Cumberland Bard," Robert Anderson, Blamire's view on Cumberland village life
celebrates locality, sociability, and industry.[122] Such celebrations contrast with the

Wordsworthian Lakes, which, as Hess argues, privileged "solitude and reverie and walking." Hess asks why "hard physical work and festive outdoor picnics and community gardening and the act of setting the thermostat" should not also be included in an egalitarian ecopoetics (2012, 5). Blamire's poem offers an insight into quotidian Lakeland life in which the everyday worker enjoyed a productive symbiosis with the landscape.

Works like these, which promoted a form of picturesque pastoral, inspired an ongoing supposition in the region's guidebooks that, in Marshall and Walton's words, "Lakeland, and Cumbrian, society consisted wholly of the inhabitants of limewashed farmhouses at the foot of the bracken-covered steeps."[123] Wordsworth's *Guide* advanced this stereotype. The *Guide* develops Gray's vision of the Lake District's "happy poverty" by indicating how the inhabitants' practical choices confirmed their symbiotic relationship with the Lakeland landscape. Wordsworth noted that the "bracken-covered steeps" were a practical choice for building cottages, since they offered "dryness and shelter" from wind and floods.[124] But more importantly in Wordsworth's view—and in that of the visitors whose readings he inspired—these simple dwellings elevated the mountains' natural "beauty" by revealing the closeness of the connection between the land and the people it supported. John Wilson's fictional alter ego puts it succinctly when he declares that "the very houses seem to grow out of the rocks—they are not so much on the earth, as of the earth."[125] Wordsworth went even further in "Home at Grasmere," the manuscript of which he quoted in the *Guide*. He imagined the fell-side cottages:

> Clustered like stars some few, but single most,
> And lurking dimly in their shy retreats,
> Or glancing on each other cheerful looks,
> Like separated stars with clouds between.[126]

The buildings form constellations that allow the visitor to read the mountains as human spaces; what initially seems to the speaker to be an isolated "lurking" cottage becomes a "cheerful" reminder of human connectivity within a natural ecology when viewed as part of the wider scene. In assimilating the Lake District's rural working poor with the environment on which they depended, this speaker undertakes a similarly artful "act of exclusion" to that which Marjorie Levinson uncovered in "Tintern Abbey."[127] Like in that earlier poem, "Home at Grasmere" offers a form of idyll that willfully overlooks the frequently harsh realities of living with a challenging climate in a remote area.

A guide by Wordsworth's friend and contemporary, Robert Southey, was more perceptive. Imagining his narrator, Espriella, traveling over the Kirkstone Pass above Ullswater, he recorded the "scattered cottages built of loose stones and covered with slates, both roof and sides so rudely built, so tinged by weather, and clothed with ferns and mosses, as to blend with the colors of the natural scenery, almost as if they had been things of nature themselves, and not the work of man."[128] However, when seen up close—and not from the distance that both Gray and

Wordsworth assume—this symbiosis between "man" and nature does not generate the healthful vibrancy that writing in the traditions of Gray, Gilpin, and Wordsworth promoted. Instead, Southey discovered that these dwellings were distressingly unsatisfactory: "They are the rudest cottages which I have seen in England," Espriella records, surmising that they "indicate either great laziness in the inhabitants, or dismal poverty."[129]

In recognizing that the state of these cottages was not (necessarily, at least) attributable to the inhabitants' moral failings, Southey reflected a shift in attitude toward the poor that emerged at the end of the eighteenth century, and which was to have extensive consequences for the laboring classes in the Lake District and elsewhere. Sarah Lloyd has shown how changes to industrial and agricultural practices in this period initiated alterations to public opinion toward poor relief that led—as Southey's account indicates—to a heightened discrimination between the "deserving" and "undeserving poor." Social commentators began to recognize that the increases in short-term contract work in this period often meant that even the most frugal families could not support themselves on their wages.[130] The Lake Counties were among the more inhospitable parts of England, both in terms of weather and social welfare. Cumberland and Westmorland were both non-Speenhamland counties, meaning that they did not benefit from social care reforms established to counter economic hardship brought about by the demands of the Napoleonic Wars. According to Pamela Horn, social conservatives considered the Speenhamland counties to be extravagant, and reformers welcomed the significant decreases in welfare rates in the 1840s that brought the rest of the country's welfare contributions more in line with the sparser contributions of counties like Cumberland and Westmorland.[131] Yet, when Benjamin Seebohm Rowntree and May Kendall surveyed forty-two laborers' families in the early twentieth century, they found that Westmorland was one of five northern counties—along with Northumberland, Durham, Lancashire, and Derbyshire—where the wage paid by farmers was sufficient to maintain an average-sized family in what they called a state of "merely physical efficiency."[132]

Wordsworth, living through the moment of regular enclosure legislations and a complexity of simultaneous changes,[133] witnessed first-hand the development of a new group of prosperous "gentleman farmers." These developments perhaps underlie his belief that the Lake District housed "a perfect Republic of Shepherds and Agriculturalists," consisting of the "humble sons of the hills" whose eco-consciousness both maintained the land and supported each man's family. References to such farms were scattered throughout the district (Figures 3.13 and 3.14). The statesmen who ran them usually worked as part of a feudal system; large landowners continued to own huge swaths of land well into the nineteenth century. By the eighteenth century, Williams suggests that "four hundred families, in a population of some seven or eight million people, owned nearly a quarter of the cultivated land."[134] By the 1870s, Reay estimates, there were a little over 4000 families in England and Wales with over a thousand acres: "together," he concludes, "they owned just over half of England."[135] The Second Earl of Lonsdale (1787–1872) was

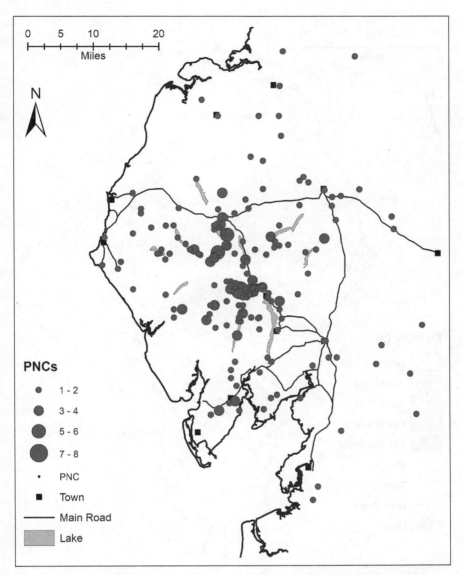

Figure 3.13. PNCs for agricultural search terms as proportional symbols. The search terms are: "farm(ed)," "farmer(s)," "statesman," and "statesmen."

one such landowner; he owned 67,000 acres in Cumberland and Westmorland (slightly less than 5 percent of the two counties' total area).

These landowners rented small parcels of land to tenant farmers, who Wordsworth called "statesmen." These statesmen held small, self-sufficient family farms worth between £10 and £50. In the middle of the nineteenth century, there were almost 7,000 statesmen throughout Cumbria. These family farmers have been largely neglected by historians, who have tended to consider such small-scale enterprises as irrelevant in a market-orientated society.[136] This reticence is reflected in

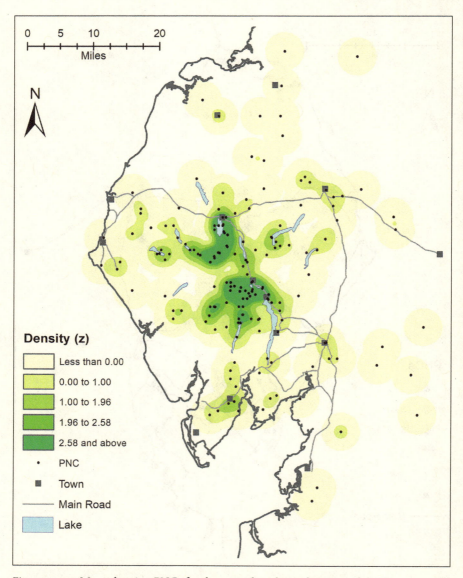

Figure 3.14a. Maps showing PNCs for the agricultural search terms. Above,
(a) density-smoothed map.

our corpus, where Westmorland and Cumberland remain largely the preserve of
tourists and travelers. References to agriculture mostly occur in what was then Lancashire (Figure 3.14). Nevertheless, statesmen farmers were crucial for both the
local and national economies. More than that, these statesmen were at the heart
of local village life in the Lakes. In the 1830s, between 50 and 60 percent of all Westmorland farms were family run on the statesman model.[137] By the end of the nineteenth century, some locations maintained even denser farming populations; in

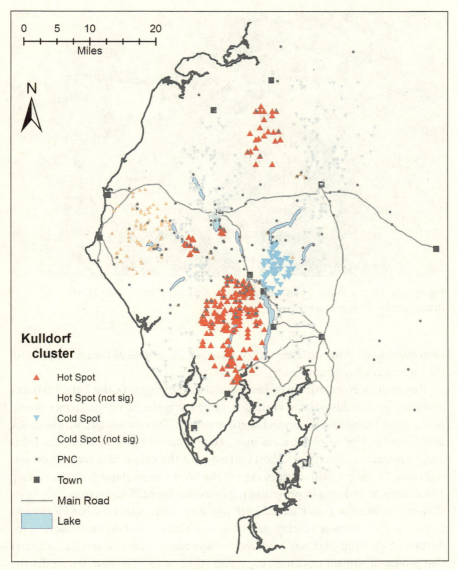

Figure 3.14b. Kulldorff hot and cold spots for the agricultural search terms.

Ravenstonedale in Westmorland, for instance, 50 percent of all households declared themselves to be headed by farmers in 1891.[138]

The main period covered by our corpus—1750 to 1900—witnessed what Horn recognizes as the most momentous changes "in the history of the English countryside." She explains that in this period the trades that had dominated the British economy "from time immemorial" were replaced by industrial activities. In 1811, forestry, farming, and fishing accounted for more than a third of England's gross national product; by 1851, they contributed a fifth. In the interim, they had been overtaken by manufacturing, mining, and building.[139] By 1871, agriculture had

Figure 3.15. Beatrix Potter (right) with sheep. © National Trust/Robert Thrift. Reproduced with permission.

been overtaken by domestic service, commerce, and finance as the industries with the highest employment rates.[140]

This shift in economic focus had necessitated changes in the Lake District's economy too, but this is not to say that farming was replaced; rather, farmers found new ways of fitting into a more industrial economy. The now-ubiquitous Herdwick sheep was bred for wool as well as meat, and by the mid-nineteenth century this hardy animal was identified almost entirely with the Lakes. This connection was cemented by the establishment in 1844 of the West Cumberland Fell Dales Sheep Association, founded to improve and publicize this breed.[141] It was from this Association that Beatrix Potter would later win numerous prizes for her Herdwicks (Figure 3.15). Wool-based cottage industries—which focused on the domestic production of clothing, blankets, and linen—expanded into commercial enterprises that produced woolen stockings, caps, and other items.[142] Arthur Young discovered "about five hundred weavers" and "from a thousand to thirteen hundred spinners in town and country" in the Kendal area alone.[143] Wool was also shipped further afield; it was bought by worsted makers as far south as Norfolk.[144] So well had Lakeland agriculture adapted to meet the needs of a rapidly expanding industrial population elsewhere in the country that, by 1868, one commentator confidently predicted that "so long as the tall chimneys of Yorkshire and Lancashire smoke, so long will the Westmorland farmer have a never-failing demand for all his produce—beef, mutton, cheese, and wool."[145]

Yet, the area was subject to economic downturns similar to those of other agricultural centers, meaning that the Westmorland statesmen experienced particular financial struggles after the conclusion of the Napoleonic Wars. Cumberland farmers joined in the national Corn Law riots between 1815 and 1846; Cumberland supplied the industrial south of Lancashire with corn, just as later—after the damming of Thirlmere in 1890 and Haweswater in 1929—the two Lakeland counties would supply much of Lancashire's water.[146] Conversely, small family farms in the Lake District continued to thrive because of their engagement with industry.[147] Not only did such farms sell their wares to industrial centers, the farmers themselves often worked in the mines and quarries as well as on their farms. Indeed, such was the diverse nature of these rural workers' employments that one observer in the 1860s suggested that "this class of men can scarcely be called farmers, although they are occupiers of land."[148] These industrial interactions operated alongside the tourist industry to bring the hitherto isolated Lake District into national and international sociocultural and economic agendas.

Wordsworth's account of statesman farmers offered an idealistic vision of what Horn calls "pastoral serenity."[149] Wordsworth recognized in the statesman the same dignity that Adam Smith had ascribed to the "common ploughman" in *The Wealth of Nations* (1776). Smith wrote that, although the plowman was "generally regarded as the pattern of stupidity and ignorance," he was

> seldom defective in . . . judgment and discretion. He is less accustomed, indeed, to social intercourse than the mechanic who lives in a town. His voice and language are more uncouth and more difficult to be understood by those who are not used to them. His understanding, however, being accustomed to consider a greater variety of objects, is generally much superior to that of the other, whose whole attention from morning til night is commonly occupied in performing one or two very simple operations.[150]

Wordsworth maintained that the statesman, like Smith's plowman, was uniquely qualified to assess a "greater variety of objects" than the general populace, and this skill was essential for sustaining both the landscape and their lifestyle within it. But an anecdote recorded by Baines indicates that this opinion was not necessarily widely held. One of Baines's companions, Annabella, indicated a sense of irony that the title "statesman" should be given to a "dull-looking farmer-like man." Another companion, William, believes that their hard work—far from being admirable—equates the men with their horses.[151] It seems that a statesman only appeared ennobled to avid readers of Wordsworth.

However, even Wordsworth's writing rarely acknowledged the extent of the hardships faced in the daily grind of maintaining the Lake District as an agricultural landscape. As Roger Sales observes, Wordsworth's writing gave "no indication of the long hours of drudging labor expected from most peasant cultivators or the feudal dues exacted from them by many landowners in Wordsworth's native Cumbria."[152] Wordsworth did acknowledge that the statesman was successful when he had "a twofold support": "first, the produce of his lands and flocks; and, secondly, the profit drawn from the employment of the women and children, as manufacturers; spinning their own wool in their own houses (work chiefly done in the winter season), and carrying it to market for sale. Hence, however numerous the children, the income of the family kept pace with its increase."[153] Farmers' families were brought into the family business at an early age; one Westmorland farmer expected his children to begin contributing to the farm work "as soon as they [could] crawl."[154] Many women also undertook agricultural work, especially after the decline of the hand-loom-weaving industry; according to Reay, Westmorland and Cumberland ranked third and fourth, respectively, in terms of national female agricultural employment until the practice declined after the 1860s.[155]

The robustness of the farming industry as it assimilated industrial strategies did little to allay Wordsworthian worries that mechanization—and the resultant loss of agricultural knowledge among the local populations—would destroy this lifestyle. At stake was a close connection to the Lakeland landscape that Wordsworth thought the statesman shared only with the poet. Anne Wallace has argued that Wordsworth engaged with a version of the Georgic in which he replaced the farmer with the walker to present an eco-aware pastoral vision.[156] The statesmen seemed to Wordsworth to be peculiarly, and intimately, connected with the terrain; the members of the utopian "Commonwealth" he projects had their constitution "imposed and regulated by the mountains." In return, generations of this community had, for "more than five hundred years," cared for the uplands.[157] But there is more to this Wordsworthian Georgic than a straightforward pastoral vision. Wordsworth's *Guide* offers a hierarchy of connectivity between human and environment. If, as we have seen throughout this chapter, the tourist looks at and the traveler reads the landscape, then it is the inhabitant and the poet who write it. The farmers' plow lines, the cottagers' homes, and the shepherds' tracks all remind Wordsworth of the myriad possible methods for reading this complex landscape.

These different representations and interpretations of the landscape did not exist in isolation; rather, as this chapter has explored, the Lake District became the product of a cultural-geographical palimpsest that offered different characters for the different attitudes its visitors and residents brought to it. Geographical text analysis helps us to unveil these differences, and to ascertain the extent to which they were expressed spatially as well as representationally. Moreover, visualizing this form of analysis on a map highlights those locations that are not frequently discussed. But paying attention to these kinds of blank spaces or apparent lack of data is, in some ways, more crucial than focusing on what is present: only when we question these silences can we use digital humanities approaches to investigate the experiences of marginalized or overlooked groups.[158] The blank spaces on our maps in this chapter emphasized the silences in our corpus—particularly, in this case, toward the people who actually lived in the Lake District. We must remain as sensitive to these absences—particularly the lack of women, people of color, and the economically deprived—in our corpus, and consider the extent to which these absences are a by-product of the curation of our data, rather than necessarily a reflection of the reality.

The same is true of moments in our dataset where the patterns are diffuse. A visualization that seems to have little significance from a quantitative or computational point of view can still offer valuable insights when read with humanistic interpretation. We have shown throughout this chapter that the categories of Lakeland user were slippery: a tourist might be trained into a traveler's habits, and a traveler could learn to mimic an inhabitant's embodied attention to the landscape. Walking became a key strategy for the kind of embodied close reading that was considered necessary for a true understanding of this complex region. Channeling this kind of mobility in our own interpretative practices can transform the ways we understand, evaluate, and utilize data in the humanities.

CHAPTER 4

Walking in the Literary Lakes

For Philip Kempferhausen, John Wilson's fictional alter ego, walking was the central means by which he transcended his tourist status. After a few days exploring on foot, he says, he "soon felt like a native." Indeed, so effective was this strategy that his very body seemed to be adapting to the landscape: "I . . . have acquired something of the springing step and forward-leaning attitude of the shepherds and herdsmen."[1] Walking did not just advance an individual's knowledge of the terrain; it seemed as though the terrain transformed the walker's body in ways that matched the imaginative conversion that pedestrian travelers were often searching for.[2]

By 1903, William T. Palmer could ascertain that two distinct walking practices had emerged in the Lake District in the previous hundred years. The first "include[d] attempts to pass a specified number of points in the shortest possible time." This was the tourist's strategy. The second referred to "long walks" on which "time only is approximately fixed."[3] The title of his next chapter, "The Complete Rambler," indicates Palmer's self-identification as belonging to the second group: the "rambler," we are to understand, pays more attention to the landscape through which he moves and develops a deeper understanding of the place than the mere tourist. As we aim to show in this chapter, deep mapping helps us to understand the ways in which these types of walking mattered as much as where a person walked. It reveals how different terms for walking were connected with specific locations throughout the Lakes and, more than this, how certain kinds of walking were cultivated in the search for particular imaginative and literary experiences.

Physical movement is, of course, contingent on the terrain being navigated, but the imaginative effects of specifically located embodied encounters found written expression in the region's travel literature. We will see that the imaginative effects of particular kinds of movement were reflected in a text's form, as well as in the language used to describe the experience. We aim here to develop previous scholarly accounts of walking's roles as aesthetic and literary practices to demonstrate how it was also a central activity in our writers' conceptions of Lakeland ecologies. These issues, we argue, have important implications for historical under-standings about and constructions of the Lake District as a cultural space that continue to implicate our responses to the region today.

The Lake District was not subject to the same level of enclosure as was visited upon the rest of the country in the late eighteenth and nineteenth centuries.[4] Partly, that was because large parts of it had been "effectively enclosed" much earlier.[5] Nevertheless, the comparative lack of private land in the tourist regions meant that the Lakes became one of the most popular destinations for walkers in Britain throughout our period. At this moment, when unrestricted access to landscape became a scarcity, the Lake District offered a welcome respite from the increasingly industrial trappings of modern life.[6] By the late nineteenth century, organizations such as the Cooperative Holiday Association and the Holiday Fellowship had begun organizing walking holidays for working people.[7] Walking remains one of the most popular reasons for visiting the Lake District; the report for the region's nomination to UNESCO World Heritage Site status notes that walks are among the top eight reasons visitors give for choosing this destination.[8] Walking is thus a significant means through which today's tourists—whether knowingly or not—partake in the region's literary heritage. In fact, walking might be the most literary of modern Lakeland practices; as the Lake District National Park Partnership's, *Nomination of the English Lake District* observes, "Wordsworth and his contemporaries were able to roam the English Lake District and derive inspiration just as walkers, ramblers and climbers can today."[9] Today's walkers follow—often literally—in the footsteps of artists and writers who used pedestrian activities to closely read the landscape.

Walking as a literary trope is particularly well trodden ground in scholarship about the Romantic period. Partly, this phenomenon is due to the fact that walking as a recreational activity was a Romantic-era development. Walking seems to minimize the distance between two locations with which Romantic writing is fascinated: a person's subjective experiences and the landscape they perceive. Eric J. Leed, for instance, argues that the motion of this form of travel conflates the distinction between the traveler's mind and body.[10] For Robin Jarvis, walking works poetically to "make possible an intense and concentrated inwardness."[11] Anne D. Wallace, on the other hand, claims that the peripatetic reaches toward a "reconnection with nature and so with the divine, continuity of sense, mind and spirit, community and connection with a communal past."[12] Similarly, in *Imagining the Earth* John Elder suggests that walking "becomes an emblem of wholeness, comprehending both the person's conscious steps and pauses and the path beneath his rising and falling feet."[13] Elder, like Wallace, describes a connection between the body and the landscape that is both physical and imaginative. In fact, walking as a literary device in the eighteenth and nineteenth centuries lies somewhere between Jarvis's focus on "inwardness" and Wallace's on external experiences; as we will see, looking outward is discovered to be a necessity for interpreting the results unveiled in turning inward. Frédéric Gros moves along this middle road in *A Philosophy of Walking*, where he establishes connections between the walker's speed and their imaginative or intellectual responses to place.[14]

These critics' works have been fundamental for the recognition of walking as a central Romantic (and post-Romantic) theme, but the major limitation in all of these studies has been an assumption that walking was a predominantly male activity, and that "he" may be read as a gender-neutral pronoun. This use of "he" as the go-to term has meant that, until very recently, scholarship has largely ignored the role of women in the development of recreational walking in general, and fell-walking in particular.[15] Gros's book is a case in point: in his exploration of the links between walking and thinking, there is only one passing reference to a woman walker on the penultimate page (Carole Cadwalladr remarks of it that it's "unclear if women don't walk or don't think").[16] Aaron Sussman and Ruth Goode go further than most in linking women's walking with sexual politics; their self-described "peripatetic ramble through the literature of walking" includes Edna St. Vincent Millay, Fiona Macleod, and Madge Jenison, but they opine that a woman "may be potentially beautiful, but if she does not believe she is attractive she shows it in her walk."[17] (They also believe that a man's performance of self-confidence is undermined if the style of his walk is not appropriately extroverted.) Rebecca Solnit's feminist intervention *Wanderlust: A History of Walking* (2001) is a rare instance in which women are afforded a place in the history of the peripatetic. Solnit's particular importance is in acknowledging that social restraints, including gender-specific anxieties, affect our freedom to walk in both urban and isolated environments.[18] More recently, Robert MacFarlane's re-reading of Nan Shepherd's *The Living Mountain* (1977) and, especially, Kerri Andrews' *Wanderers: A History of Women Walking* (2020) has encouraged greater recognition of women's place in the history of fell-walking.[19]

This critical neglect is reflected by the relative absence of women in our corpus as authors, and prefigured by their absences in the texts. Where feminine pronouns do appear, they often refer to the landscape itself—to a "mother nature" that can be conquered and tamed by what Kathleen Jamie has called the "Lone Enraptured Male."[20] Marlon Ross and Anne K. Mellor have both argued that this gendering of walking in the Romantic period—although their arguments can justly be applied to post-Romantic texts as well—is central to this "appropriation" of feminine authority.[21] We will see shortly with Charlotte Brontë how such restrictions were felt to be imaginative as well as practical. Nevertheless, many women kept pace beside their male contemporaries—and many outstripped them. Dorothy Wordsworth was a noted pedestrian; Ellen Weeton delighted in traveling around the Lakes by foot on her own;[22] later in the century, Beatrix Potter's love of the Lake District was fostered, in part, by her solitary walks. We will see later in this chapter that both Brontë and Harriet Martineau found different kinds of physical and imaginative fortification in their Lakeland walks.

This chapter seeks to go beyond previous criticism in its recognition of the gendered experience of walking, as well as the precise terms used to describe this activity. It demonstrates how these terms developed highly specific meanings— both for physical practice and for literary endeavors—throughout our period. More than that, though, it departs from previous work on literary representations of walking by exploring how location and the details of the landscape itself were paramount to the type of walking undertaken and, thus, to the imaginative experience sought. Deep mapping our Corpus of Lake District Writing reveals new information about how these terms emerged and evolved, as well as where, and why, these various walking practices were undertaken.

Mapping walking is not straightforward, however. Mike Pearson and Michael Shanks argue that conventional maps of walking routes erase the embodied, and time-dependent, practices of "meandering, stopping and starting, window-shopping, passing-by."[23] Inspired by Michel de Certeau's claim that pathways operate as lines through space that are both interpretative and interpretable,[24] Pearson and Shanks suggest that walking is itself a form of "inscription" of a personal narrative onto a landscape, but they see time as being the most important factor in a walker's experience. Jo Vergunst, by contrast, believes that walking is experienced as a flow that prioritizes experiences of spatiality over an awareness of temporality.[25] In this approach, a line map might uniquely capture a sense of mobility through the landscape.

But even a line map is not very satisfactory. In *Imagined Landscapes: Geovisualizing Australian Spatial Narratives*, Jane Stadler, Peta Mitchell, and Stephen Carelton suggest that attempts to map a walking route in GIS run the risk of rendering movement static by "subordinating the journey to its locations and foregrounding space at the expense of temporal passage."[26] We might, of course, add time stamps to the map—yet, while that would tell us something about how long a walk might take in measured time, it reveals little about the way an individual experiences time in a given location. The challenge is to find a way to represent the experience of movement alongside the phenomenon of personal time. Deep mapping can help us toward combining these elements by positioning the map's spatial narrative alongside the text's representation of individual experience. As Stadler, Mitchell, and Carelton conclude, a collaboration between narrative and visual representations might highlight "epistemological and ontological insights about the cultural and political geography of a place,"[27] as well as its spatial politics.

We push that conclusion further in this chapter to explore how deep mapping can be used to place walking in the Lake District's landscape and literature. John Wylie opines that the written narration of a landscape emerges from, and constitutes, "ongoing, refracting visual cultures."[28] What we want to demonstrate here is that, in fact, visual cartographic media like the maps produced by GIS can both act as new forms of visual representation and allow us to comment in new ways on historical written accounts. Geographical Text Analysis (GTA) allows us to uncover the significance of linguistic responses to embodied place that operate on the level of both the corpus and the individual text.[29] We hope to demonstrate that, when used as part of an approach that combines close attention to detail with recognition of larger geographical and literary trends, deep mapping can reveal a mobile geopoetics that is based on a grammar of physical movement in a particular place. In other words, this approach can be used to investigate the development of the relationship between a specific way of moving, a particular place, and written expression, whereby the mode of peripatetic movement over certain terrain can be read in the text's formal and linguistic choices. As we will now see, different terms for walking signified a diverse range of physical interactions with, and imaginative responses to, particular places in the Lake District.

TYPES OF LAKE DISTRICT WALKING

Throughout the eighteenth and nineteenth centuries, walking in both urban and rural locations became a popular pastime for both men and women. Virginia Woolf's essay "Street Haunting" (1927) captures in evocative terms what walking through a city could do to a person. Walking, Woolf found, eroded "the shell-like covering which our souls have excreted to house themselves . . . and there is left of all these wrinkles and roughness a central oyster of perceptiveness, an enormous eye" through which to view the pedestrian's location.[30] While flaneurs and strollers and haunters explored the city streets,[31] walkers and ramblers and wanderers were taking possession of rural spaces.

Walking emerged as a central theme in Lake District literature from the 1770s, when Thomas West, Thomas Gray, and Arthur Young all published their influential accounts of traveling through the region. It took until the 1790s, though, before walking began to be seen as a recreational activity rather than a symbol of poverty.[32] From the late eighteenth century onward, walking increasingly became what Nicholas Roe has called "an expression of democratic mobility";[33] in the revolutionary years, there was a distinctly rebellious element to walking tours,[34] particularly given the role of pedestrian protests in the French Revolution. By the 1880s, walking was an established form of political protest, and the Lake District played an important role in that development in Britain. Half a century before the more famous trespass on Kinder Scout, walkers in Keswick—including Canon Hardwicke Rawnsley, later cofounder of the National Trust—trespassed on Latrigg Fell in protest at the closing of some of its footpaths.[35] A series of protests culminated with 2,000 people ascending the mountain on October 1, 1887. One letter writer to the *Manchester Guardian*, published on October 7, 1887, predicted that "the Latrigg case will affect the right of ascent to almost every mountain in Great Britain."[36] But by this time, walking was also recognized as the proper mode of travel for those who, more simply, wished to partake in an authentic version of Lakeland, one that deviated from the routes made popular by the burgeoning tourist trade. Foot travelers to the Lake District discovered in walking a uniquely affective means of embodying a symbiotic relationship between self and landscape.

"Walking," for our purposes, is a category that includes a range of bipedal movements. The terms listed in Table 4.1 are synonyms or near-synonyms for walking as a form of travel taken from *The Historical Thesaurus of English* from between 1622 and 1900 (the years covered by the texts in our corpus). They all indicate slow onward progression by foot, but they also imply a range of emotional, intellectual, and physical responses to the landscape. In contrast to previous scholarship on

TABLE 4.1

INSTANCES OF "WALK," ITS SYNONYMS, AND THEIR LEXEMES IN EACH PERIOD

	Instances			Instances per 100,000 words		
	Early Modern & Long C18	Romantic	Victorian	Early Modern & Long C18	Romantic	Victorian
walk*	193	361	421	52.01	61.62	74.37
wend*	1	3	6	0.27	0.51	1.06
hik*	0	0	0	0.00	0.00	0.00
haul*	0	1	0	0.00	0.17	0.00
vagabond*	0	1	1	0.00	0.17	0.18
tramp*	0	4	16	0.00	0.68	2.83
wander*	23	91	69	6.20	15.53	12.19
roam*	4	21	4	1.08	3.58	0.71
rov*	8	26	6	2.16	4.44	1.06
rambl*	14	60	42	3.77	10.24	7.42
vagra*	7	7	4	1.89	1.19	0.71
scamand*	0	0	0	0.00	0.00	0.00
Total	**250**	**575**	**568**	**67.37**	**98.14**	**100.34**

Note: Synonyms determined by *The Historical Thesaurus of English* (http://historicalthesaurus
.arts.gla.ac.uk).

walking in literature, mapping these words uncovers what reading the texts alone
obscures: that some terms connoted a particularly intense imaginative response
to place, and that certain locations in the Lake District were sought out for their
capacity to generate particular feelings.

As might be expected, "walk" and its lexeme are the most popular ways of
describing peripatetic movement throughout the corpus. When we plot the uses
of these terms (Figure 4.1)—random variation due to the different amount of
texts in each decade notwithstanding—uses of "walk" tended to increase steadily
throughout our period, although there are some exceptions. In the 1780s, for
instance, the number of mentions of walking in the corpus texts drops significantly.
Conversely, in the 1840s walking increases sharply in popularity, despite the fact
that there are fewer texts in the corpus for this decade than for either the decade
preceding or following it. We will see in more detail shortly that this particular
anomaly is attributable to the rise in popularity of walking as a tribute to William
Wordsworth. It was a local symptom of the national trend that saw literary tourism become, as Nicola J. Watson writes, a "commercially significant phenomenon"
over the course of the nineteenth century.[37] By the Victorian period, walking

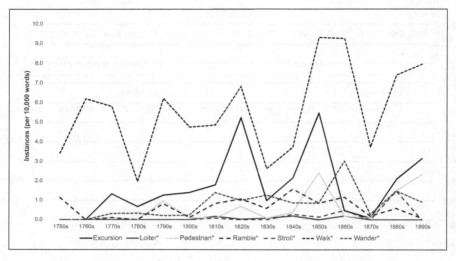

Figure 4.1. Time series of instances of "walk," its synonyms, and their lexemes.

was securely established as a consistent presence in Lakeland literature, and, if William T. Palmer's assessment of the new kind of "fell-walker" is to be believed,[38] in the landscape itself. Our corpus also documents additional terms for movements that form part of a walk, including "trudging" (used by Edward Baines in 1829 and Herbert Rix, the Royal Society's assistant secretary, in 1893), "skipping" and "jumping" (taken from Samuel Taylor Coleridge's notebook entries [1802]), "sliding," "wading," "running," "scratching," and "tumbling" (all from Edwin Waugh's *Rambles in the Lake Country* [1861]).[39] Similarly, Keats's account of his "tramping" around the Lakes in 1818 is indicative both of the heavy-footed nature of Keats's movement across difficult terrain and of an elision between pedestrian travel and vagrancy.[40]

There are also some surprising omissions. The absence of "scamander," a short-lived synonym in use very briefly in the mid-Victorian period (between 1864 and 1873) that connoted walking without an aim, might be expected.[41] But the absence of "hike," particularly given the Lake District's mountainous nature, is notable. The noun "hike" emerged as recreational walking grew in popularity; the OED identifies the first use of it as early as 1809;[42] in 1825 the dialectologist James Jennings observed that it meant "to go away" or "to go off," and was "[u]sed generally in a bad sense."[43] Given the associations between walking, vagrancy, and criminality in the first two centuries covered by the corpus, it is also notable that "vagabond"—and its lexeme "vagabonds" and "vagabondage"—only appears twice in the corpus. In both cases it is used lightheartedly: Thomas Wilkinson recalls chasing after a "runaway vagabond" of a hat blown off his companion's head by a strong wind;[44] and Edwin Waugh records a misadventure of the Lancaster postman: "He was telling about going with letters to the mansion of some old gentleman who was deaf. The gentleman was walking about the lawn when, seeing Joe come up, all travel-soiled and strange, he called out, 'Who are you?' 'Postman, sir!'

'Be off, you vagabond; we've nothing for you!' 'Postman, sir!' cried Joe, still speeding on."[45] In both of these instances, the humor arises from this misapplication of the epithet, "vagabond," to an undeserving recipient. In both cases, too, the term seems to have left behind its sociopolitical connotations. During the Romantic period, the association between walking and vagrancy had been replaced by one between walking and thinking; as Nancy Forgione has demonstrated, over the course of the nineteenth century this development meant that walking was increasingly privileged as a stimulant for the imagination, rather than as a sign of socioeconomic distress.[46] By the time Waugh records this story, the assumption that the postman is a criminal vagabond has become comically outdated.

Meanwhile, "wend" and "wended," archaisms that survive throughout these years, appear with surprising regularity to denote a form of pathless walking. Similarly, "roam" and "rove," along with their lexemes, maintained a subdued yet resilient hold throughout the corpus. Although these synonyms for "walk" were less commonly used, they nevertheless hold an important place in the Lake District literature of this period. "Roaming" and "roving" in particular are both related to the two terms, besides "walk," that emerge as being particularly significant to the peripatetic imagination in the Lake District: "ramble" and "wander." We saw at the beginning of the chapter that rambling indicated a particular type of long walk during which the walker paid close attention to the details of the landscape. Wandering indicated something similar; both ramblers and wanderers prioritized spatial narratives over temporal ones. As we will see later, the differences between these two terms were, predominantly, literary.

As walking—in all these varieties—increased in popularity throughout the nineteenth century, these different ways of referring to walking maintained the cultural hierarchy between tourists and travelers. Two main categories of peripatetic activity emerge through the corpus, into which all of the foregoing terms might be placed: excursionists and pedestrians. The excursionist tended to move from point to point on walks that were carefully planned. The pedestrian, on the other hand, was more adventurous and more willing to depart from the paths established by the tourist industry. We now turn to these two categories. We suggest that both kinds of walkers sought a connection with the landscape through which they moved, but that they prioritized different sorts of peripatetic practice in order to access it. In so doing, both kinds of walkers radically altered the cultural composition of the Lake District in ways that remain evident today.

WALKING ALONG A GOOD ROAD: TAKING A LAKELAND EXCURSION

By the 1790s, a frequent recommendation from Lake District guidebooks was that the best way to experience the region's picturesque scenery was by walking through it. Adam Walker, who punningly styled himself "A. Walker" on his title page, thought that there was "but one way of Travelling more pleasant than riding on horseback, and that is on foot; for then I can turn to the right and to the left."[47] As we will see in the final section, that freedom of movement was important for certain kinds of walkers, and we will also see that more adventurous pedestrians developed a specific language that privileged long, exploratory walks over short trips to well-known sites. The excursionist, on the other hand, was implicitly unadventurous. An excursion took place along pre-existing paths toward well-established, oft-visited destinations. This section demonstrates that those who called themselves, simply, "walkers" and their activity a "walk" were most likely to be describing an excursion that confined itself to existing pathways. The texts that these excursions produced deliberately—and often literally as well as literarily—followed in the footsteps of previous publications, so that the excursion resulted in particular kinds of travel narratives that ratified existing routes, outlined the specific views to be enjoyed, and the correct—if clichéd—responses to particular parts of the walk.

In his long poem *The Excursion*, William Wordsworth toys with the tourist's understanding of this kind of walk. The journey he describes emphasizes the connection between place and person, and the poem displays the excursion as an imaginative, poetic, and physical experience that depended on an escape from, but subsequent return to, confinement.[48] Wordsworth's *Excursion* formulates a sense of community achieved, in part, through walking. Sally Bushell argues that the central figure in *The Excursion*, the Wanderer, maps his way "from person to person." She suggests that the Wanderer is guided through the landscape by what we would term a deep map of it that follows the "lines of human narrative" rather than geographical features.[49] In contrast to the narrator, the Wanderer is characterized by his consistent peripatetic action; while the Wanderer's focus is on his journey, the Poet's is on his destination. The Poet, Bushell continues, possesses a "touristic eagerness . . . to provide us with views and panoramas" from the sites toward which he is directed by the Wanderer.[50] But the Poet misunderstands the imaginative importance of wandering—and that miscommunication is repeated in touristic literature. We will return to *The Excursion* shortly, but for now it is enough to note that walking tourists mimicked this poetic eagerness to seek out key sights and landmarks, and to record their personal responses to them. These locations, and the texts that advocated visiting them, were central to the sense of a walking community that existed between writers, readers, and the inhabitants who acted as their guides.

Elissa Rosenberg's remark that walking "is the central commemorative experience" applies specifically to the excursion.[51] In the parlance of tourist literature, the excursion was a short trip undertaken by a short-term visitor to the region. It was a form of pilgrimage; in the Lake District, religious sites were usurped by the "implicitly religious" experience of attending to picturesque sights or sites of literary interest.[52] Like the pilgrim, the excursionist followed in the footsteps of previous visitors to well-established locations. In the Lakes, that usually meant going to those places that were particularly notable for their picturesque or sublime views. The excursionist's focus on going *to* somewhere is reflected in the number of place names with which these terms co-occur; instances of "excursion(s)" and "excursionist" occur within ten words of a place name 173 percent of the time (meaning

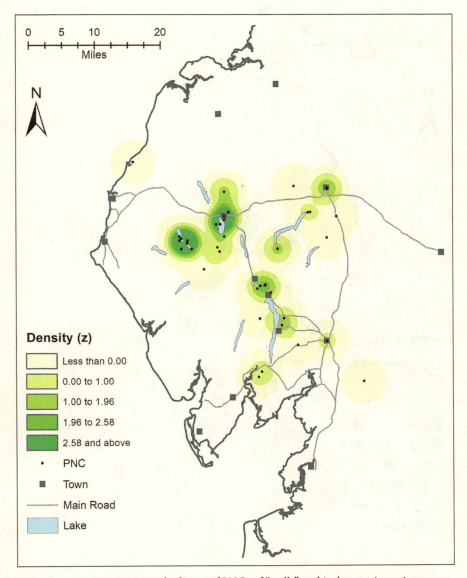

Figure 4.2a–c. Density smoothed map of PNCs of "walk" and its lexeme in various periods. Above, (a) shows the long eighteenth century.

that individual uses of these terms ordinarily co-occur with multiple place names). The excursion, then, was both a form of peripatetic movement and a journey with a specific, sometimes quasi-spiritual, focus.

We have seen already that "walk" and its lexeme are the most frequently used terms for peripatetic action in our corpus, and it is true that these words have a reasonably flexible definition; "walking" can, and frequently did, suggest the freedom of movement that so excited Adam Walker. Nevertheless, the definition of "walk" as a noun influenced in important ways its use as a verb, so that to "walk"

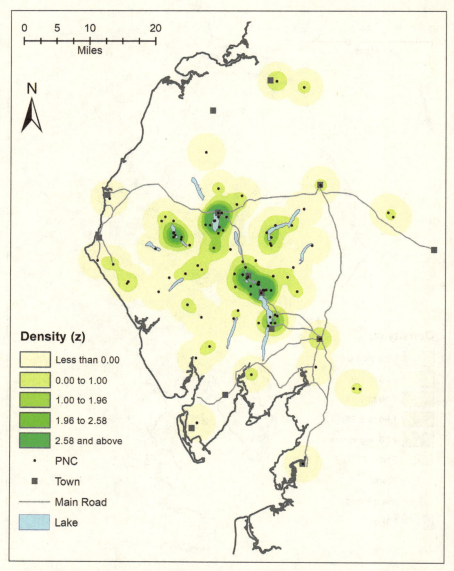

Figure 4.2b. Density smoothed map of PNCs of "walk" and its lexeme in the Romantic period.

in the Lake District most often meant to keep to an existing path and a circum-scribed route. Although self-proclaimed walkers did begin to venture increasingly away from the main tourist centers in the latter half of the nineteenth century, in the main walkers were a circumspect group who tended to stay close to the Lake District's most popular features. Yi Fu Tuan observes of twentieth-century North American tourists that they "are known to drive hundreds of miles to a National Park and yet not explore it beyond what can be seen, and captured in a snapshot, a half mile from the road."[53] In a similar way, eighteenth- and nineteenth-century visitors to the Lake District tended not to explore far by foot. The area around the

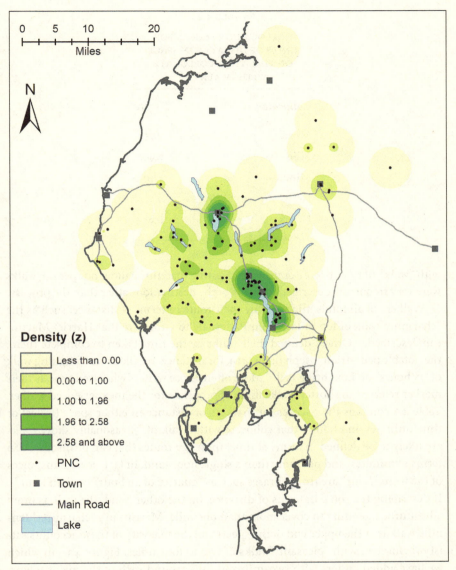

Figure 4.2c. Density smoothed map of PNCs of "walk" and its lexeme in the Victorian period.

tourist centers at Grasmere and Ambleside remained a focal point for walkers in every decade throughout the corpus, as the density-smoothed maps of "walk" and its lexeme for each decade (after 1770, when the terms begin to co-occur with place names) that constitute Figure 4.2 illustrate. These maps suggest that throughout the entire period covered by the corpus the majority of self-proclaimed walkers used the towns and villages popular with tourists as bases from which to go on excursions to the local views. The pattern does change over time, with Buttermere becoming less important while the areas around Grasmere, Ambleside, and Windermere become more so. What is consistent, though, is that "to" strongly co-occurs

TABLE 4.2

COLLOCATION SCORES FOR
UNITS OF DISTANCE IN SPACE
OR TIME THAT COLLOCATE
WITH "WALK OF"

Collocate	T-score
Miles	3.75
Mile	2.90
Minutes	1.40
Hour	1.37
Hours	0.95

with "walk" (it has a t-score of 16.06), suggesting that, throughout our period, walks were very frequently described in terms of the destination rather than the process.

Walkers of all kinds might define their route in terms of distance, such as the "charming walk of ten miles" from Patterdale to Grasmere that Harriet Martineau described.[54] Others defined their walks by the time taken to complete them: the notable pedestrian Joseph Budworth, for instance, recalled one "fatiguing walk of six hours" on Loughrigg Fell.[55] More often, those writers who used time as their marker referred to shorter walks more appropriate for the inexperienced walker. Table 4.2 contains the t-scores for markers of distance in either space (miles) or time (minutes and hours) that collocate with "walk of." Reasonably short walks are likely to be defined in terms of time; these are routes that can be discussed in terms of minutes, and not more than a single hour (and, in fact, several instances of the word "hour" are from phrases such as "quarter of an hour" or "half hour"). If describing the route in terms of distance, on the other hand, the walk is more adventurous, tending to cover more than one mile. Martineau's "charming" ten-mile walk is at the upper end of the spectrum; the majority of these accounts satisfy themselves with "pleasant" walks of two to four miles. Figure 4.3—in which we have added buffers with two-mile radiuses around each of the major towns, roads, and lakes—suggests that most walkers kept the important locations within their excursions well within two miles of the places with the most developed tourist infrastructures. Only 19.7 percent of PNCs for walk or one of its derivatives are located outside these buffers (compared to 32.9 percent for the corpus as a whole). This preference remains true today; the *Nomination for World Heritage Site Status* notes that visitors to the region between 2009 and 2012 were more likely to undertake walks of under two miles.[56]

William Palmer makes the point, though, that a mile along a level road is a very different experience than a mile of fell-walking: "miles walked on the road may be classed as units," he writes, but "the fatigue of each mile over mountain-land varies considerably."[57] The majority of walkers in the Lake District throughout our period

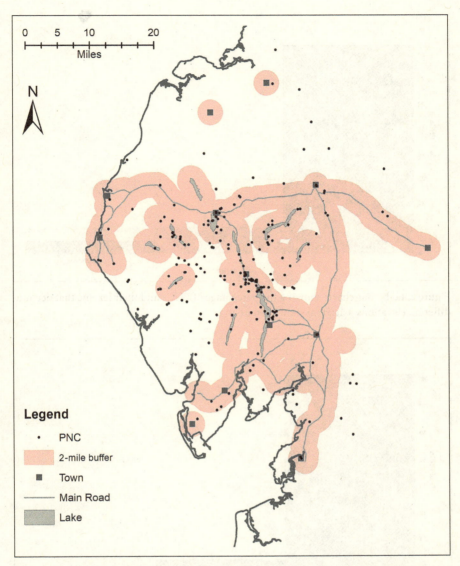

Figure 4.3. The relationship between PNCs for "walk" and its lexeme, with proximity to the major towns, roads, and lakes indicated by the two-mile buffer.

seem to have been reluctant to experience this kind of tiredness: they tended not to go up into the fells. By combining the textual information with a raster that documents the elevation data for the Lake District, we discover that most walkers remained on what Murrieta-Flores, Donaldson, and Gregory would define as a low "cost" route;[58] just 16 percent of places associated with excursions, and 18 percent of places associated with walks, are recorded at elevations above 300 meters (see Figures 4.4a and 4.4b). That just over 82 percent of places named in association with walks are at elevations below 300 meters (Figure 4.4b) suggests that the majority of excursionists did not experience the "fatigue mileage" about which Palmer writes.

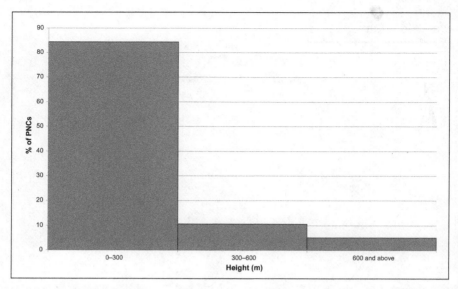

Figure 4.4a–b. Bar charts showing the percentage of PNCs and their lexeme that occur at different elevations. Chart (a) shows "excursion."

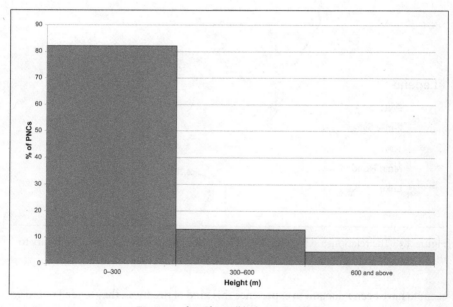

Figure 4.4b. Chart (b) shows "walk."

Excursion narratives, then, tend to be contained within small geographical areas—yet that doesn't mean that texts in this tradition describe identical experiences. A sensitive appreciation of how even these less adventurous walks were characterized in the travel literature throughout this period leads to a more nuanced understanding of how this genre operated in relation to popular travel destinations.

Specifically, paying attention to the prepositions used in relation to walking uncovers new understandings about the eighteenth- and nineteenth-century excursion as a form of aesthetic pilgrimage. Although destinations were fixed in ways that have seemed to make this genre as unadventurous as the routes it advocated, a deep mapping approach that combines close reading alongside GTA reveals that while the areas in which people walked were certainly circumscribed, they were encouraged to explore different routes within these limited zones.

Thomas West was the first author to outline a series of precise routes for this kind of peripatetic pilgrimage in the Lakes; he advocated the excursion's spiritual benefits as early as 1778. In his *Guide to the Lakes*, West recommended walking as the pastime that would best facilitate a long-lasting, spiritual connection with the Lake District: "Whoever takes a walk into these scenes," he wrote, "will return penetrated with a sense of the creator's power and unsearchable wisdom, in heaping mountains upon mountains, and enthroning rocks upon rocks."[59] For West, the reward of these pilgrimages was the discovery of the divine in the landscape. His viewing stations—some of which, like Claife Station on the shore of Windermere, remain popular tourist attractions today[60]—were the locations at which West suggested that godly power might be best accessed. After West, excursions to these viewing stations encouraged a type of recreational walking that prioritized the walk's end point over the journey itself.

We will see in the next section that it was characteristic of wanderers and ramblers not to follow an existing route; as Palmer observes of fell-walkers, "No two parties take precisely the same routes in their walks, each avoiding some particular variety of fell-land" according to their aims or tastes.[61] Yet excursionists were also offered a limited freedom in choosing which route to take to their destination. Rather than direct their readers along specific pathways, travel writers tended to suggest sites to which their readers might take "a walk." Jerome McGann suggests that "a" and "the" are "the two most ambiguous and meaning-flexible words in the English language,"[62] and the ambiguity created by the indefinite article allows these accounts of walks to resist identification as factual topographical narratives. "A walk" is the more commonly used phrase in the corpus; it occurs eighty times in the corpus, and "the walk" only forty-three. That "the walk" occurs almost half as frequently suggests that most writers were more concerned to direct their reader toward a form of movement that actively engaged them with an area, rather than to guide them along a specific path. Yet both of these clusters are heavily concerned with guiding readers toward a particular point. "The walk" co-occurs within ten words of a place name 48.84 percent of the time—that is, in almost every other instance. For "a walk," however, that figure is much higher: this word cluster co-occurs with a place name in 70 percent of cases. Figure 4.5 suggests that the two had broadly similar geographies, concentrated on Grasmere/Ambleside, Ullswater, Keswick/Derwentwater, and Buttermere. Notwithstanding the sense of limited freedom in the indefinite article, then, a lack of specificity as to route did not mean additional agency in the general shape of the excursion.

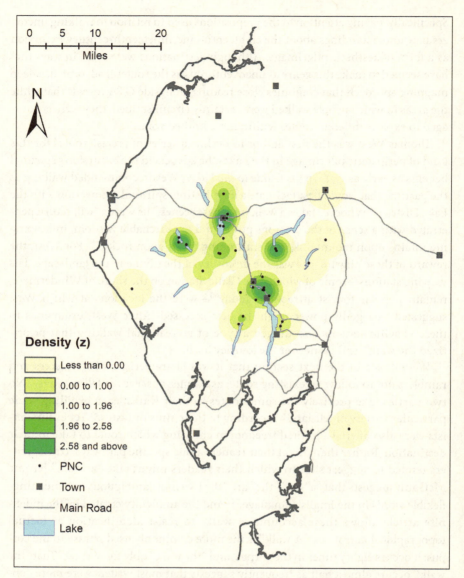

Figure 4.5a–b. PNCs of "a walk" and "the walk." Above, (a) shows PNCs of "a walk."

Nevertheless, there is an implicit creativity even in the most apparently banal touristic acts; the reader is never quite following in the writer's footsteps. The writers in the corpus tend to acknowledge that the reader can *only* take "a walk." That indefinite article is an important indicator of the potential for responsiveness to the landscape that is both physical and creative; while the narrative suggests destinations, merely suggesting "a walk" leaves the details of the journey to the reader's imagination. Thomas Newte, for instance, advises a ferry crossing over Windermere from Bowness, and then "a walk to Hawkshead, about four miles distant."[63] In a similar way, Budworth instructs his reader to "take a walk" to Troutbeck, "and if you meet the

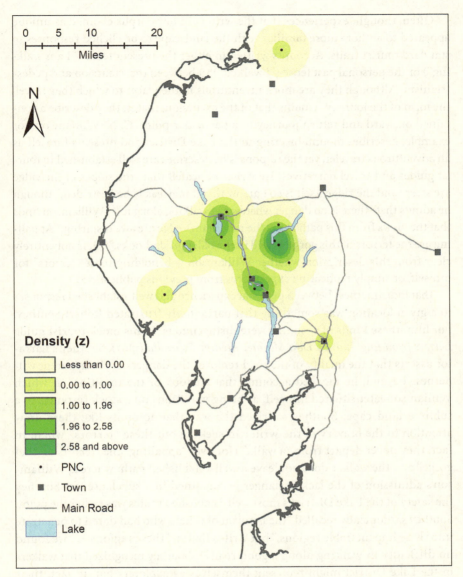

Figure 4.5b. PNCs of "the walk."

same pretty Girl and obliging Person we did, so much the better."[64] Budworth's walk
is based on an established route, and the reader is encouraged to follow in his footsteps. But "a walk" in Budworth's wake does not equate to "the walk" undertaken by
Budworth unless the "same pretty Girl" is encountered again. In other words, it is
only possible to follow "the walk" if an identical experience can be created. Each path-
way, then, becomes a site of innumerable walks, each of which is highly personal to
the walker. In short, the route might be set, but the experience of walking depends on
imaginative and circumstantial contingencies, and the excursionist will experience
something unique as they traverse even well-trodden ground by foot.

Often, though, experiences that the writers in our corpus claimed as unique appeared to authors more familiar with the landscape to be clichéd responses to standard tourist trails. Accounts written in either the present tense ("I am walking") or the personal past tense ("I walked") sit between the excursion and pedestrianism. Although they are more adventurous in the places to which they travel, the form of the journey remains that of the excursion; that is, they describe a contained outward and return journey to a particular point. C. N. Williamson, for example, describes mountaineering in the Lake District and presents himself as an adventurous traveler, yet the responses he describes are well established in tourist guides and travel narratives. He writes of Scafell that "the slopes of the ridge are steep, and the ridge itself is so narrow that it may easily be bestrided," though he admits that "there is no danger whatever in walking along it."[65] Williamson finds that the views from this path along the mountain's edge are awe inspiring: "Appalling are the terrors of this gorge as told in the older guide-books."[66] It is not entirely clear from this description whether Williamson is beholding these "terrors" for himself, or simply replicating experiences from previous publications.

That indistinctness between personal experience and well-established responses to a given location was something that particularly frustrated Robert Southey. For him, these kinds of accounts were disingenuous. In his mock-tourist guide *Letters from England, by Don Manuel Alvarez Espriella* (1807), Southey's narrator asserts that the quality of the road removes the dangers of the apparent wilderness beyond; he mocked accounts that partook of the tradition, in which Williamson later situated himself, as being variations on a stock response to a sublime landscape. Southey satirized the way that accounts like these drew attention to the bravery of the writer in seeking out these "terrors" when, in fact, they never depart from "a walk." However "appalling" the "terrors of [the] gorge" are, the walker does not leave a well-established path; whereas Williamson's admission of the lack of danger is contained in a subclause, for Southey the safety of the Lake District's most well established routes was rather the point. Southey sardonically recalled "the heroism of others who had dared to penetrate into these impenetrable regions," but writes that in "these regions . . . we found no difficulty in walking along a good road."[67] Southey recognized that walkers in the Lake District might represent themselves as explorers but, in fact, their sense of adventure was limited. In Southey's opinion, most walkers were at best tourists fooling themselves into believing they were travelers. Certainly the excursionist, while they aped the peripatetic practices of the traveler, did not discover an embodied landscape to the same degree as those kinds of walkers who did explore away from the beaten track.

Southey mocks the excursionist's preference for staying on an already established path that, he thinks, limits their ability to discover new places and unique experiences. But the choice of where to travel was not equally available to all Lakeland walkers. When Charlotte Brontë visited the Lake District for the first time in July 1850 she was frustrated by the necessity of keeping to existing routes. She regretted the lack of freedom she was afforded to wander alone over the moun-

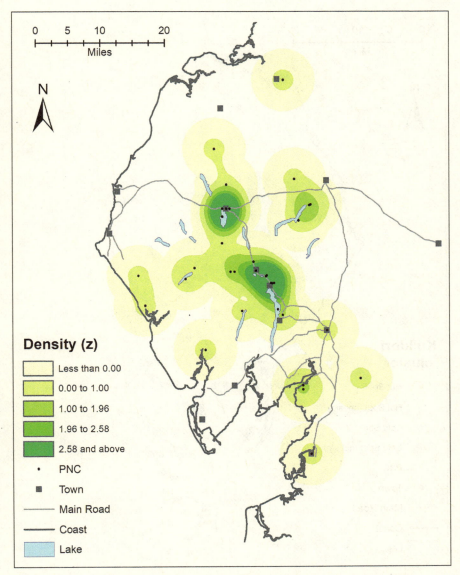

Figure 4.6a–b. PNCs of "we walk," its synonyms, and their lexeme. Above, (a) uses density smoothing.

tains: "The scenery is, of course, grand; could I have wandered about amongst those hills *alone*, I could have drunk in all their beauty; even in a carriage with company, it was very well."[68] There is a tension here between enjoying her companions' company and experiencing the Lake District's full majesty; she continued that if she could have "gone away by [herself] in amongst those grand hills and sweet dales, [she] should have drank in the full power of this glorious scenery. In company this can hardly be."[69] Immersing oneself in the mountains' "beauty" is, so Brontë implies, an experience that can be accessed satisfactorily only when

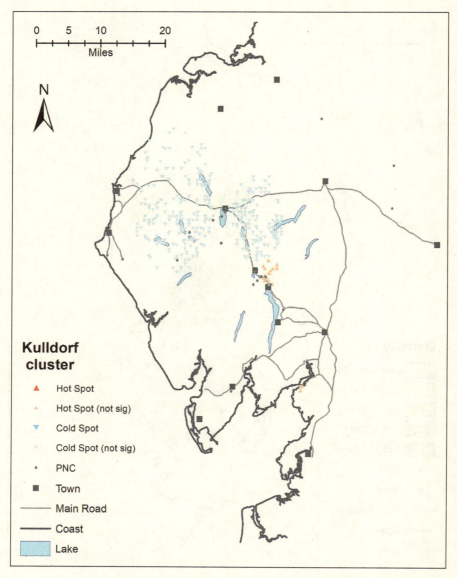

Figure 4.6b Kulldorff hot and cold spots for "we walk."

one is alone. Comparing the PNCs for feminine pronouns with data for those pronouns that denote companionship (we, our, and us)—in other words, pronouns that indicate that a walker was not alone—indicates how rare a solitary walk in the mountains was for women in this period. Almost inevitably, this restriction resulted in a more limited ability to explore the less well known parts of the Lake District. The overall distribution of collective pronouns that co-occur with walking remains very close to the background geography, concentrating on the popular places. Upland areas in particular tend to be cold spots, although not significant ones (Figure 4.6a and b). Solitary travelers, by contrast, tended to either

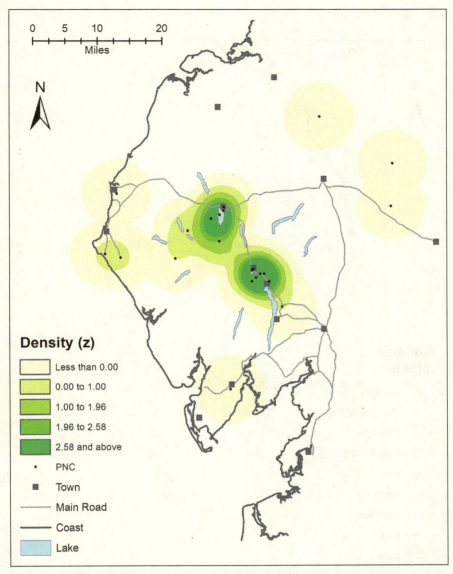

Figure 4.7a–b. PNCs of "I walk," its synonyms and their lexeme. Above, (a) uses density smoothing.

concentrate on the Grasmere/Ambleside area or head away from the main tourist destinations and into the mountains (Figure 4.7a and b). Since, as Brontë found to her frustration, women were very strongly encouraged to travel in company, they were not afforded the opportunities to develop the same degree of physical or imaginative intimacy with the landscape as their male contemporaries.

These geographical relations were also gendered, thanks to women's comparably limited freedom: while men could explore on their own, women were often (though not always, as Dorothy Wordsworth's biography amply shows) restricted by their

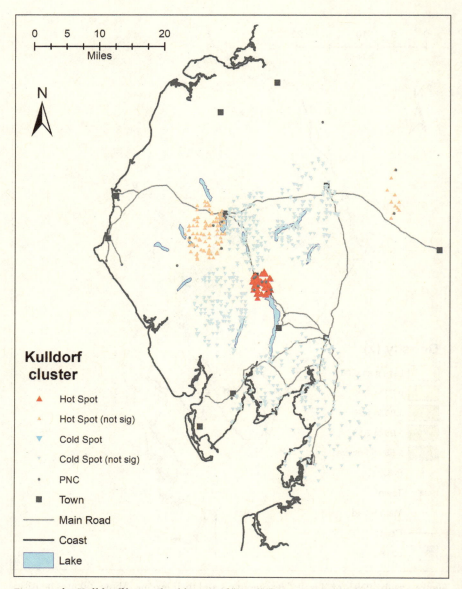

Figure 4.7b. Kulldorff hot and cold spots of "I walk," its synonyms, and their lexeme.

companions. James Buzard observes that women traveling either unaccompanied or in groups without men were "referred to as 'unprotected' and looked at askance; young women travelling any distance alone were almost never to be encountered."[70] In our corpus, feminine pronouns in general are associated with a place much less often than their masculine counterparts: feminine pronouns (her, hers, and she) co-occur with place names 81 percent less frequently than masculine pronouns (him, his, and he) do. However, Figure 4.8a illustrates that men were referred to in relation to places all over the Lakeland region, whereas Figure 4.8b

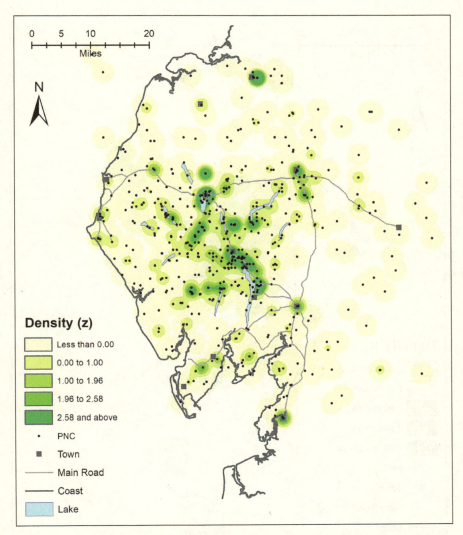

Figure 4.8a–b. PNCs of masculine and feminine pronouns. Above, (a) shows masculine pronouns.

shows that feminine pronouns are much more likely to occur around the towns. Even taking into account the fact that both masculine and feminine pronouns were used in generic ways, it is clear that the two genders had very different spatial profiles. In both cases, the Kulldorff hot spots tend to be away from the modern national park area. However, for masculine pronouns there are a number of relatively localized hot spots within the Lake District's boundaries (Figure 4.9a). Women were much less likely than men to be described as exploring in the areas of the Lake District that lay away from the main tourist routes, meaning that they were largely excluded from pedestrian narratives. An exception appears to exist around the Duddon Valley; the same location also appears as a rare, though not statistically significant, hot spot when Kulldorff's spatial scan statistic is applied to the feminine data

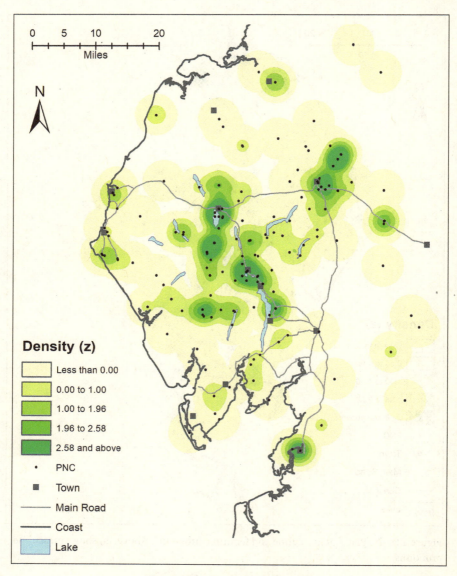

Figure 4.8b. Feminine pronouns.

(Figure 4.9b). In fact, though, that hot spot is attributable to the practice of referring to "Mother Nature" in general, and the river Duddon in particular, using feminine pronouns. Excursions seem to have been considered more appropriate for women in this period, thanks to the fact that they stuck to well-established, populous routes.

Brontë yearned to explore where she pleased; it would only be then, she thought, that she would be able to appreciate the "full power" of the Lakeland mountains. She longed, in short, to be a pedestrian. The pedestrian eschewed popular paths in order to prioritize a more personal embodied and imaginative response to the Lake District. As we have seen already, the traveler was a midpoint in the trajectory

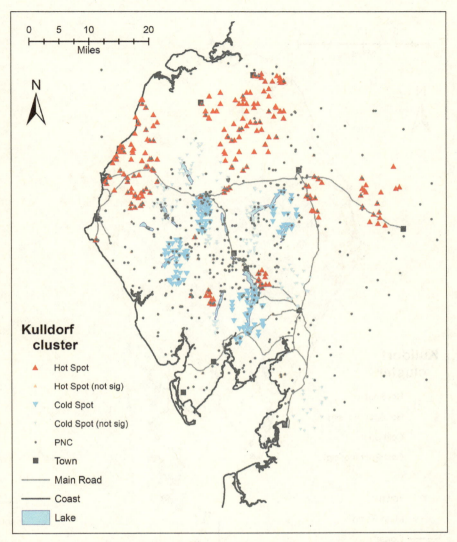

Figure 4.9a–b. Kulldorff hot and cold spots for PNCs. Above, (a) masculine pronouns.

between tourist and inhabitant, and exploring the region beyond the existing pathways was an important means by which the self-identified pedestrian traveler could experience, even if only temporarily, a sense of dwelling in the region.

"Linger There a Breathing While": Being a Pedestrian in the Lakes

The term "pedestrian" has been a persistent source of contention for critics of the literature of walking. Wallace rejects it as being unfit for purpose; for her, it connotes the "boring, commonplace, [and] unimportant," and she believes that the term is used so often that it elides the importance of physical movement in literature of the

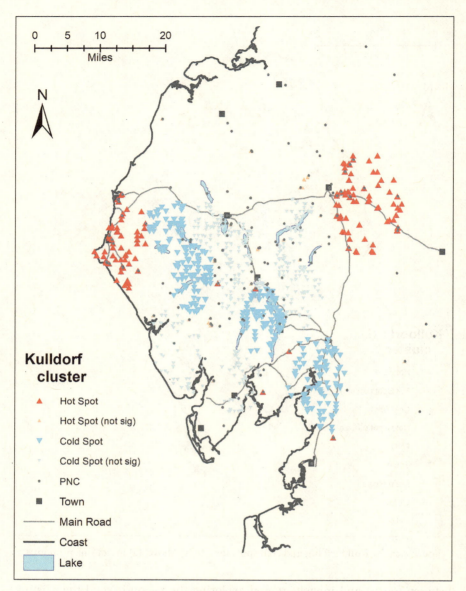

Figure 4.9b. Feminine pronouns.

peripatetic.[71] Jarvis, on the other hand, uses the term in a way more appropriate to contemporary understandings of it. He finds that it recalls the "noted pedestrian[s]" of the age, like "Walking" Stewart or Foster Powell, and suggests that such epithets existed because of the "general emergence of pedestrianism as a cultural phenom-enon" during the Romantic period.[72] Our corpus demonstrates that, far from being a "boring," "commonplace," or even safe type of walking, pedestrianism functioned as a form of semiprofessional identity. The adjectives that collocate most commonly with "pedestrian" are "hardy," "stout," and "sturdy," indicating

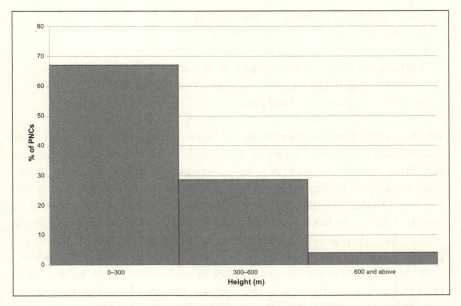

Figure 4.10. Bar charts showing the percentage of PNCs of "pedestrian" and its lexeme that occur at different elevations.

that the pedestrian's routes were somewhat more advanced than those of the "walker." The pedestrian also climbs to higher elevations than the walker or excursionist: 33 percent of pedestrians are recorded at locations above 300 meters (Figure 4.10). Jenny Holt thinks that fell walking "seemed to connect the practice of the hill-farmer and the experience of the tourist,"[73] and pedestrians in particular sought to blur the distinction between inhabitant and traveler.

The early Lakeland pedestrians documented in our corpus prioritize the "independence and freedom of movement" that Jarvis identifies as being key features of this semiprofessional walking class.[74] Over the course of the nineteenth century, two main subsets of the pedestrian emerged in the Lake District: the rambler and the wanderer. These figures were both characterized by their propensity to walk in unplanned ways, and by their deliberate attempts to be absorbed into the landscape. The freedom to explore was a trait central to both ramblers and wanderers, as the young John Ruskin knew. In *Iteriad*, the poem he wrote between 1830 and 1832 (when he was between eleven and thirteen) after a holiday to the Lakes with his parents, Ruskin described one after-dinner ramble:

Now when we somewhat had our hunger allayed,
Our knife and our fork war for some moments we stayed,
Then looked at the sky, and consid'ring the weather,
Determined to take a short ramble together.
And first to the back of the house we went round
Where a huge dirty dunghill, full quickly we found . . .
Oh, then how we, scampering, stumbled along.

Old Virgil himself could not tell how we flew,
With his *Quadrupedante putrem sonitu.*
But scarcely again had we got to the door
'Ere the sun and the sky became bright as before!
So we turned round about and clear 'scaping their wrath,
Again trotted on, by a different path.[75]

Ruskin's ramble incorporates a number of different kinds of movement: he and his cousin Mary Richardson "scamper," "stumble," "fly," and "trot" around the area, suggesting the variety of types of ground over which they move. The meter mimics their movements; as they scamper and stumble, the poem, too, falls over its own feet. What Ruskin describes here is a spontaneous exploration that proves that the rambler need not be lost in the Lakeland wilds; what characterizes the rambler is, instead, their propensity to leave existing paths and explore into the details of a place. Indeed, the limited data for "ramble" and its lexeme suggests that ramblers were more likely than wanderers to explore the well-visited region between Grasmere and Ambleside (Figure 4.11). In either case, though, where these walkers were mattered less than how they walked; as Henry Frith declared of the wanderer, for these kinds of walkers it "did not matter whither [they] directed [their] steps."[76]

Like "walk" and its lexeme, both "wander" and "ramble" feature consistently in our corpus. Like "walk," they were used increasingly often as the nineteenth century progressed, and as walking became an increasingly intellectual activity during the Victorian period. So well understood were the implications of these terms that they were used in the titles of several Lakeland guides, including Joseph Budworth's *A Fortnight's Ramble to the Lakes in Westmorland, Lancashire, and Cumberland* (1792), Alexander Craig Gibson's *The Old Man; or Ravings and Ramblings round Conistone* (1849), James Thorne's *Rambles by Rivers* (1844), and the anonymous *Gleanings of a Wanderer* (1805).[77] The lack of structure implicit in rambles and wanders is indicated by these terms' low levels of collocation with place names: "ramble(s)" or "rambling" occurs within ten words of a place name in 33 percent of cases, and "wander(s)" or "wandering" in just 10 percent.

The lack of specificity inherent in both of these terms means that they are difficult to map; as Figure 4.12 shows, when the data are density smoothed the patterns are indistinct at best. But a failure in a cartographic sense is rich in an interpretative one. These maps do not perform the traditional role of such visualizations, which, as Stephen Ramsay explains, ordinarily "are there to demonstrate the facts of the case—to prove to the reader that things cluster this way or that, that there are indeed more instances of this feature than of that feature." This is, he continues, "odd," given that "the kinds of texts that interest humanists" are "less concerned with proving a point, and far more concerned with allowing the reader the intellectual latitude to see something new."[78] These maps, on the other hand, do emphasize the kinds of interpretative opportunities more familiar in literary scholarship. They are revealing about the literary role of ramblers and wanderers; like the texts on which they are based, the maps mimic the cultivated randomness of the rambler's or wan-

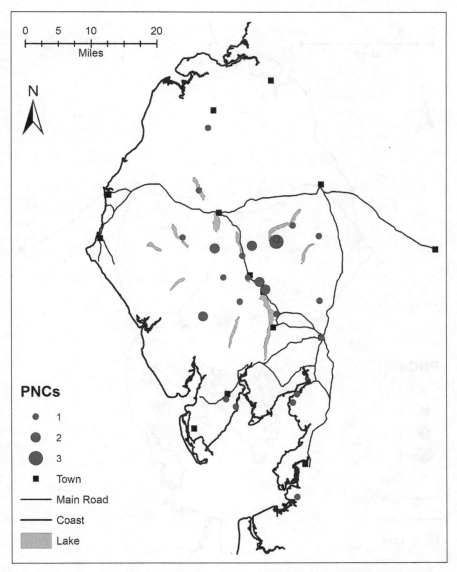

Figure 4.11a–b. Proportional circle maps of PNCs of "ramble" and "wander." Above, (a) "ramble" and its lexeme.

derer's physical movements. Still, in spite of the similarities in their peripatetic practices, there were important differences between the ways these two types of walker imaginatively responded to the scenery through which they passed: ramblers focused outward, whereas wanderers concentrated their attention inward. These foci were expressed, in part, as literary differences.

The principle difference in these terms is in the way they distinguish between subjectivity and objectivity. While the ramble hearkened back to a Johnsonian form of digression, to wander was to partake in a Wordsworthian form of communion

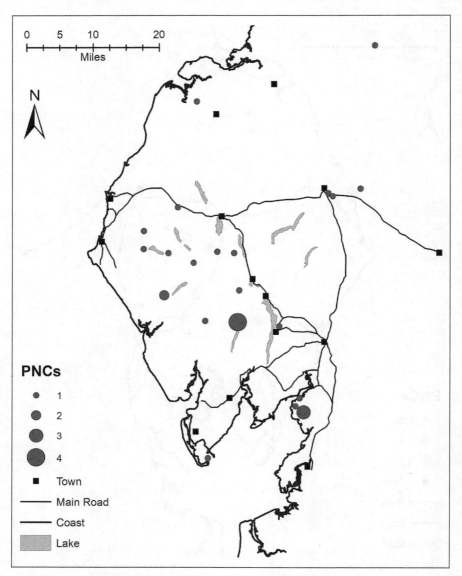

Figure 4.11b. PNCs of "wander" and its lexeme.

with the natural world. Critics such as Sarah Houghton Walker have drawn explicit connections between Wordsworthian wandering and poetic form;[79] for such scholars, wandering is a formal device that enables the poet to move from line to line in blank verse without the constraints of a rhyme scheme. While it has clear connections to the Wandering Jew—a figure with which Romanticism was fascinated and which inspired one of Wordsworth's additions to the 1800 edition of *Lyrical Ballads*[80]—wandering is also a methodology for reading Wordsworth's poetry; Houghton Walker suggests that, to successfully navigate meaning in Wordsworth's poetry, the reader must be prepared to wander through it without a perceptible

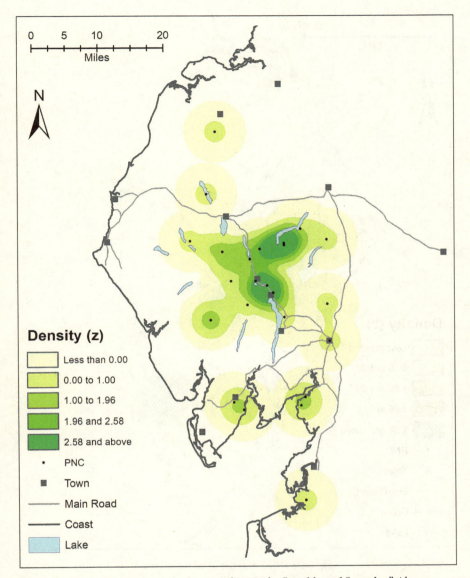

Figure 4.12a–b. Density-smoothed maps of PNCs for "ramble and "wander." Above, (a) "ramble" and its lexeme.

aim.[81] Rambling, on the other hand, was a more prosaic enterprise. We can see from Figure 4.13 that "ramble" first appears in the corpus between 1750 and 1759, making it one of the earliest terms for walking to emerge with consistency. It is no coincidence that Samuel Johnson's periodical *The Rambler* was published between 1750 and 1752; Johnson established rambling as a literary and physical form of movement that situated digression as a means of forward motion.

The vacillations and inconsistencies of Johnson's *Rambler* have seemed confusing, and even alarming, to critics. Manushag N. Powell writes of the evident

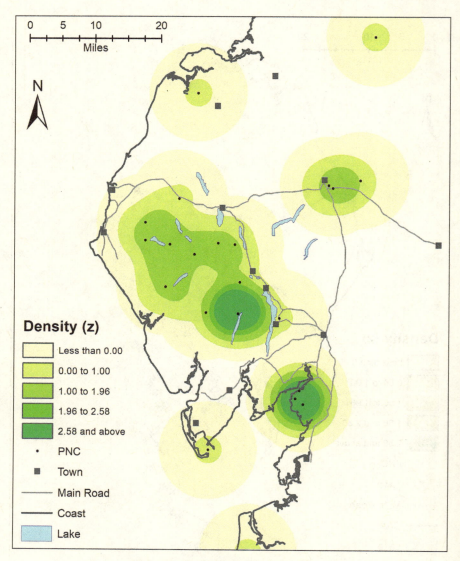

Figure 4.12b. "Wander" and its lexeme.

scholarly ambivalence toward the *Rambler* essays that they have "been to modern readers a sort of ugly baby whom critics feel they really ought to love, but, although they try nobly, cannot quite manage to do so."[82] Some have attributed these digressions to Johnson writing quickly to meet a tight deadline;[83] for others, the apparently ad hoc nature of the essays operates as a form of concealed logic that is understood only by the careful reader.[84] Bruce Robbins and Patrick O'Flaherty are in a surprising minority of scholars who have engaged with the spatiality of this digressive form; O'Flaherty specifically notes the connections between this essay form and the dictionary definition for "ramble," and Robbins draws an explicit con-

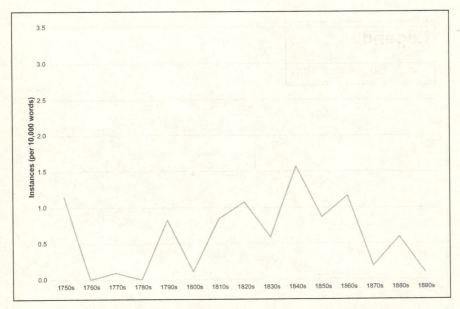

Figure 4.13. Time series graph for instances of "ramble" and its lexeme.

nection between the "rambling mind" and "physical ramblings" in the Johnsonian character Brooke in George Eliot's *Middlemarch*.[85] In order to follow the *Rambler*'s broad range of references, its reader must be what Mary M. Van Tassel calls a "highly social being."[86] That is an important difference between the wanderer and the rambler; the wanderer—and particularly the Wordsworthian wanderer—is a lonely figure, but the rambler actively engaged with the human elements of their surroundings.

Edwin Waugh was one such sociable rambler. Waugh possessed an impressive peripatetic vocabulary; uniquely among the corpus writers, Waugh makes use of every walking synonym we identified in the corpus earlier. He also challenges distinctions between tourists and travelers; in his works, he exhibits how a touristic activity can be transformed by a traveler's attention to detail. Waugh demonstrated that an excursion could become a rambling adventure. The two publications of Waugh's included in our corpus, *Over Sands to the Lakes* (1860) and *Rambles in the Lake Country* (1861) (in which *Over Sands* was reprinted as a chapter) are largely responsible for the concentrated area of data for "ramble" in the southern Lake District peninsulas (Figures 4.11a and 4.12a). For a short time, Waugh made the Sun Hotel in Ulverston his base, from which he set out on trips that slipped between being excursions and rambles. "I made daily excursions into the neighborhood," he reported, "and one of my first rambles was to Swarthmoor, about a mile from town."[87] If anything, here the definition of the two terms implied by the charts and maps is reversed: the "daily excursions" are vague and unattached to any specific destination, whereas he "rambles . . . to" Swarthmoor Hall. Waugh, in an unfamiliar region, made tourist-like excursions to various sites in the neighborhood—but

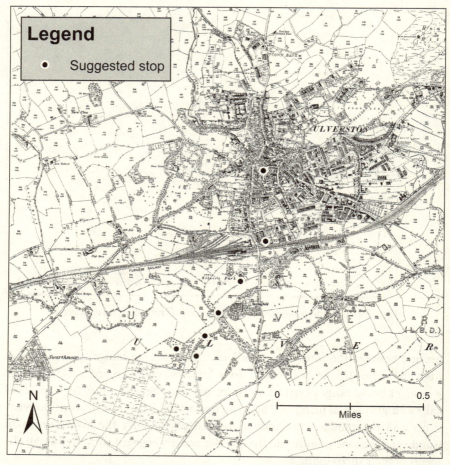

Figure 4.14. Edwin Waugh's suggested journey to Swarthmoor Hall, overlaid onto the Ordnance Survey First Edition (1891). Background map: 1:2500 County Series 1st Edition [TIFF geospatial data], scale 1:2500, tiles: lanc-01603-1, lanc-01607-1, updated: 30 November 2010, historic. Downloaded from EDINA Historic Digimap Service, https://digimap.edina.ac.uk, (2021-04-30 11:08:24.462).

he experienced the traveler's participation in the landscape: his preposition "into" indicates his absorption in the local area.

Rambling—and, as we will see shortly, wandering—indicated a leisurely form of movement that involved spending time exploring in detail the local landscape. Throughout his *Rambles in the Lake Country*, Waugh drew attention to his willingness to loiter. His relaxed attitude toward time allowed him to participate more meaningfully in the landscape—to begin, in fact, becoming a part of it. When he writes, here, that he "rambles" to Swarthmoor Hall, it is indicative of the fact that he did not head straight there, but rather took his time meandering to it. He mentions several stops along the way (Figure 4.14), and he used his journey to Swarthmoor Hall to advise the potential rambler on how to begin that process of inhabiting the Lakes: "The road may be miry, but whoever he be that goes that way, in rain or fair weather, let him linger there a breathing while, for the old house in front of these buildings is Swarthmoor Hall, the residence of George Fox. On my first visit, I wandered about some time before I could find any human creature astir. A contemplative charm seemed to lie upon all around."[88] Digression is an integral element to Waugh's account, and it is characteristic of Romantic and post-Romantic writing on rambling.[89] Waugh's sentence structure here embeds deviation into the heart of the writing project. His language draws out the moment; the long syllables of "miry," "breathing," "astir," and "charm" linger like the rambler himself. Waugh does not slow down simply to take in the view, but the atmosphere; he breathes in the landscape so that it becomes a part of his body. The Hall itself is complicit in the moment; it seems to cast a spell on the visitor to encourage deep thought. It is under the influence of that "charm" that the rambler—a walker interested in the details of the objective landscape—becomes a wanderer, whose thoughts turn inward. "Wander" here is phonetically linked to "wonder," and by wandering slowly through the place, and lingering to allow its charm to enter into his body and imagination, Waugh seems to discover a hidden magic that is only available to those who take their time.

Points or lines on a map, though, eradicate the sense of "linger[ing]" that Waugh is so careful to communicate in his account. Visualizations like Figure 4.14 indicate the markers Waugh used along his way, but they do not suggest anything of the time he spent exploring around each location, away from the straightforward path that visualizations like these imply. One way we might begin to imply the fact that these locations are not precise and that they are contingent on the time spent at them might be to use fuzzy markers. In Figure 4.15, we have adapted a technique pioneered by the *Literary Atlas of Europe* to try and capture something more of the nature of rambling that Waugh describes.[90] In a sense, visualizations like these turn the GIS against itself, both indicating its limitations and highlighting how necessary it is to treat such maps like texts in themselves, to be interpreted in light of the more personal accounts offered by the written works on which they are based.

Maps like these can, however, help us to develop more nuanced understandings of these terms as spatial, experiential, and aesthetic categories. Waugh begins as a rambler who sees into the life of things—but as a wanderer he enters into them. In fact, he can *only* become a wanderer when the paths around Swarthmoor Hall have become familiar to him, for wandering is properly predicated on the careful retracing of earlier steps.[91] Waugh is responsible for the dramatic increase in the uses of the term in the 1860s (see Figure 4.16). He uses "wander" or one of its derivatives on sixty-six occasions across his two publications; that is 90 percent of the total number of uses for these terms in the corpus for that decade, and 15 percent of their occurrences in the entire corpus. "Wander" is the only term for peripatetic motion that is used consistently throughout the corpus; the only decade in which it does not feature after 1750 is the 1760s. Over the course of these years, however, its meaning shifted in response to its literary uses.

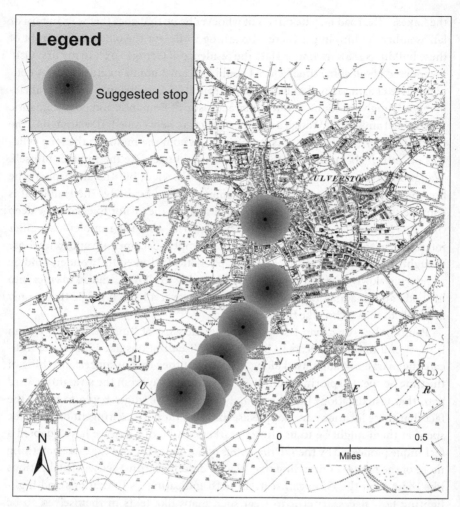

Figure 4.15. Edwin Waugh's suggested journey to Swarthmoor Hall using fuzzy symbols. Background map as for Figure 4.14.

The earliest reference to a wanderer—and, in fact, to any kind of peripatetic movement—in our corpus is not to a person, but to a part of the landscape itself. In *Poly-Olbion*, Michael Drayton describes how the "two mightie Meres," Thurstan and "the famouser Winander," "wander" through their valleys. The lakes, he writes, are "out-stretched," and their meandering shape affirms their lazy movement.[92] A similar paradox characterized nineteenth-century wanderers' accounts; like these lakes, the nineteenth-century wanderer moved with a form of productive lethargy. In the parodic poem *The Tour of Doctor Syntax in Search of the Pictur-esque*, William Combe playfully indicated a connection between wandering feet and a wandering mind: the treatment the doctor suggests for wandering is a "broad blister" applied to the back.[93]

After the Romantics, wandering became a form of movement that was oxymoronic at its heart: it was a contained form of freedom. As M. H. Abrams famously summarized, Romantic wandering is a journey "in search of an unknown or inexpressible something which gradually leads the wanderer back toward his point of origin."[94] That point might be either a geographical location or, more properly, a site in the wanderer's personal development. The Romantic and post-Romantic wanderer pays attention to details near to hand—people and objects—in order to reveal something about the point of their imaginative journey. If excursionists knew to what they were making their pilgrimage, for the wanderer it was more complex; the destination, such as it was, revealed itself over the course of an apparently aimless journey.

This kind of wandering was inherited from one particular text: William Wordsworth's *Excursion* (1814). For Houghton Walker, this poem is a key text in the development of a complex distinction between walking and wandering that does not pass moral judgement on either activity.[95] It was the appearance of vagrancy that gave pre-Romantic wanderers a bad reputation, but Wallace credits Wordsworth with changing the wanderer's status from the "bad old sense of aimless, socially disruptive walking" to someone imaginatively invested in the landscape.[96] She means principally along roadways but, in fact, the Lake District wanderer had discovered much earlier the potential in wandering for developing a sense of embodied connectivity to the landscape. In David Simpson's words, the Wordsworthian wanderer is always "*between* places, and often with no implied destiny at all."[97] It is that very liminality which enables the Wanderer to discover and communicate meaning; the Wanderer himself becomes the link between places and peoples. Wordsworth's Wanderer exemplifies the ideal peripatetic Lakeland traveler because he moves in unplanned ways within the confinement of the region's limits. He roamed around the landscape with an aim of confirming a place's cultural identity; this figure, according to Wallace, "returns continually along paths already walked, effecting connection and stabilization as he goes."[98] In *The Excursion*, the Wanderer has learned how to become one with the landscape. The speaker recalls the Wanderer as a boy:

> So the foundations of his mind were laid.
> In such communion, not from terror free,
> While yet a child, and long before his time,
> Had he perceived the presence and the power
> Of greatness; and deep feelings had impressed
> So vividly great objects that they lay
> Upon his mind like substances, whose presence
> Perplexed the bodily sense.[99]

This child is penetrated with the sense of divine presence that we have seen West describe; he deeply feels the "great objects" of the natural world, and in fact his mind seems to absorb them in an almost chemical fashion. Although this wanderer pursues the withdrawal from community life associated with the wandering

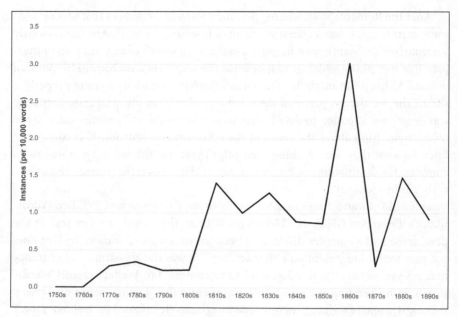

Figure 4.16. Time series graph of instances of "wander" and its lexeme.

vagabond, he does so to better understand the imaginative and spiritual connection between himself and the world in which he lives. He performs, in Wallace's words, "a deliberate, directed labor undertaken to make self and home."[100]
In so doing, he searches out his own point of origin as part of a natural ecology
that permits him to access a supernatural understanding of the celestial order.

The publication of *The Excursion* was the turning point for the Lake District
wanderer.[101] In the years following its publication in 1814, the popularity of "wandering" to describe a certain kind of self-consciously embodied, slow movement
that generated a sense of intimacy with the surrounding landscape increased dramatically (see Figure 4.16). As early as 1829, Edward Baines thinks of Wordsworth
"draw[ing] his sketch" of "his friend, the Wanderer" as he passes up Little Langdale toward Blea Tarn.[102] Later, Ellis Yarnall attributes Wordsworth's poetic talent
to his perennial wanderings over his native hills: "Surely to any man such sights
as these must give elevation of mind," he exclaims: "how much more to a poet!"
For Yarnall, Wordsworth's wanderings are essential to his trade: it was Wordsworth's "work," so Yarnall thought, to "interpret [Nature] to men."[103] Wordsworth's
wanderings afford him an intimate knowledge of the Lake District's pathways,
and, crucially, of the unmapped places between them. Writers like Baines and Yarnall attributed Wordsworth's unique ability to see into—and even beyond—the life
of things to this detailed acquaintance with the Lake District landscape.

Harriet Martineau similarly discovered in pedestrianism a means of engaging
in the Lakeland landscape in ways that helped her to re-evaluate her life, work, and
status as part of the Lake District community. On moving to Ambleside, walking
became one of the means by which she demonstrated the ability of women to, in

Alexis Easley's words, "assume positions of agency and independence through their engagement with the natural world."[104] For Martineau, walking became the central activity around which her days were structured.[105] She described the benefits of this lifestyle to Ralph Waldo Emerson as early as 1845, just before she acquired the land for her cottage, *The Knott*:

> It is with as much wonder as pleasure that I write to you. Here I am looking out on blue Windermere, on the mountains all sun and shadow,—feeling myself full of health through my whole frame,—strong, peaceful, *well* in mind and body. . . . For the first time in my life I am free to live as I please;—and I please to live here. My life is now (in this season) one of wild roving, after my years of helpless sickness. I ride like a Borderer,—walk like a pedlar,—climb like a mountaineer,—sometimes on excursions with kind and merry neighbours,—sometimes all alone for a day on the mountains. I cannot leave this region.[106]

Martineau's language is, as Kerri Andrews has recognized, that of the "explorer"[107]; like Waugh, Martineau discovers in wandering a sense of wonder at the natural world, and at her place within it. The health she derives from her days roaming around the mountains and lakes fills what appears here to have been a body previously empty. Walking makes her "full of health"; in an almost literal way, it seems to complete her so that she comes to feel that the Lake District is indispensable not only to her well-being but to her identity as well. Easley suggests that "the social and geographical space of the Lake District is interpreted by Martineau as a female-dominated environment ruled by Mother Nature herself, where women are able to achieve freedom from the social constraints faced by those in more conventional environments."[108] Certainly, Martineau rebels against feminine walking practices, embracing instead the practiced pedestrianism of the peddler and mountaineer. In her guidebooks, Martineau is more restrained; she describes walking, wandering, and rambling throughout the Lake District but, as Figure 4.17 shows, her focus was on the central Lakes. She did, however, encourage her readers to venture into those areas—particularly in the western part of the region—which were, as we have already described, less frequented by tourists. Martineau distinguishes here between her "day[s] on the mountains" and the smaller "excursions" practiced by her neighbors. Both types of activity have their place in Martineau's life, which is built around a mixture of solitary freedom and community-mindedness. The routes she advocates in her publications were distinct from her "wild rovings." These solitary walks were for her alone, and helped to secure her status as an inhabitant of the Lake District; as we saw in chapter 2, Martineau was a valued part of the local community.[109]

For Martineau, like other writers discussed in this chapter, walking itself acted as a form of deep mapping that inscribed subjective embodied experiences onto specific locations. Situating these personal records within our corpus reveals the development of distinct genres of walking that each had particular spatial and creative characteristics. As we have shown, different kinds of peripatetic activity resulted in variant levels of connection between the traveler and the landscape, and

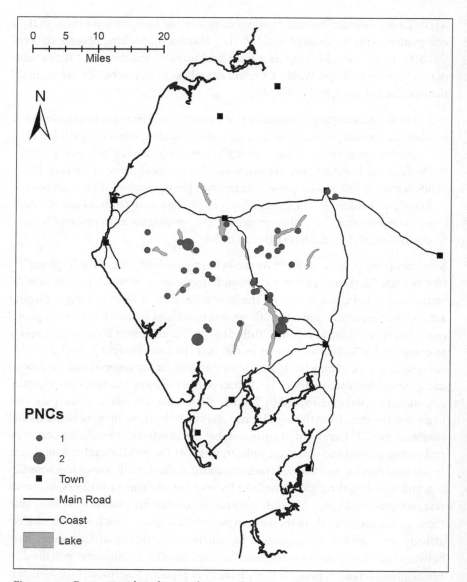

Figure 4.17. Proportional circle map showing the PNCs related to walking, rambling, and wandering from Harriet Martineau's two guidebooks (1855 and 1861).

travelers employed specific terms to describe their journeys that were well understood within the wider context of Lake District travel writing throughout this period. We have shown that walking in the Lake District was an imaginatively complex activity that had its own set of nuanced terms predicated on linguistic and geographical understandings. Visitors used walking as one tactic in their quest to imbibe the Lake District's atmosphere, but they did not travel away from the beaten paths only to look at the scenery. Their search for a truly embodied experience extended beyond their feet, and engaged all of the body's senses.

CHAPTER 5

Seeing Sound

MAPPING THE LAKE DISTRICT'S SOUNDSCAPE

In December 1844, William Wordsworth wrote a pair of now infamous letters to the editor of the *Morning Post*, in which he decried the proposal to extend the railway to Windermere. One of Wordsworth's central arguments was that the railway—and the countless numbers of visitors it would bring—would disrupt a much-loved characteristic of the Lake District: its quietness. "The wide-spread waters of these regions," he declared, "are in their nature peaceful; so are the steep mountains and the rocky glens; nor can they be profitably enjoyed but by a mind disposed to peace."[1] A person who could enjoy quiet and solitude "profitably" by discovering meanings in them was the only kind of person Wordsworth considered qualified to appreciate his native region. He concluded with a damning suggestion of where minds disposed to noise could go: "Go to a pantomime, a farce, or a puppet-show, if you want noisy pleasure."[2]

These were personal judgments; as Peter Coates puts it, "Just as beauty is in the eye of the beholder, noise frequently resides in the ear of the listener."[3] One era's noise might become another's sound—or even another's silence. Acoustic experiences were as subject to contemporary fashion as visual ones, and the late eighteenth century catalyzed the emergence of hearing as what Sophia Rosenfeld calls "a cultural effect as much as a physiological one."[4] Wordsworth's considerations of the relationship between noise, sound, and silence in the Lake District advanced a debate on the role of sound in the artistic imagination, and in the environment, that was at the foreground of aesthetic thinking in the eighteenth and nineteenth centuries.[5]

The relationship between landscape and soundscape in the Lake District forms the main theme of this chapter. Our central claim is that the soundscape as represented in our corpus developed a connection between the region's natural features and its human visitors. The Lake District's valleys and mountains form a natural amphitheater that witnessed what Martin Kaltenecker has called "the materialization of a listening discourse," whereby the venue for a sonic experience indicates how the listener should respond to the sounds heard there.[6] In the Lake District, this "materialization" resulted in a form of acoustic sublimity where sound was experienced as something tangible through its interactions with the region's geological forms and each listener's body. That experience might be rematerialized through its written communication. "Words work in the sounding," Susan Wolfson writes,[7] and we will see that sounds also work in the words; literary form could offer a vehicle through which to communicate and preserve the acoustic sublime.

Deep mapping has a significant role to play in demonstrating what these historical soundscapes comprised, and why they matter for today's environmental thinking. Indeed, projects in landscape planning and archaeology have started to indicate the importance of geospatial technologies such as GIS in incorporating sound studies in our thinking about future environments.[8] However, the importance that particular places have for human experiences of sound has remained underacknowledged. Stephanie Kuduk Weiner would class the acoustic sublime as an "aural aesthetic that raises a series of questions—about sensation and knowledge, reality and representation, words and things—analogous to those raised by the discourse of vision."[9] In this case, the unique acoustic effects created by the way sounds interact with the Lake District's distinctive terrain encouraged listeners to place themselves in imaginative and embodied conversation with the source of the sound and the landscape, which effected a deeper sense of belonging within the region's ecology. Matthew Rowney writes that "sound both determines and is determined by the spaces in which it occurs,"[10] and we demonstrate here that Romantic-era visitors to the Lake District took advantage of the topography to emphasize certain acoustic experiences that, in turn, influenced their imaginative and written responses to the landscape. As Emily Thompson summarizes, the soundscape is "simultaneously a physical environment and a way of perceiving that environment."[11]

We are interested here in exploring how sound acted as what Henri Lefebvre called a "spatial code" that was used by visitors to the Lake District to read and interpret the space that surrounded them.[12] In so doing, we engage with the recent, rapid growth of interest in critical sound studies that has occurred in both scientific and humanist study. Indeed, Mark Smith has suggested that "historians are listening to the past with an intensity, frequency, keenness, and acuity unprecedented in scope and magnitude."[13] This increased interest followed R. Murray Schafer's introduction of the term "soundscape" in the late 1960s and early 1970s. In his definition, the term might signify the sounds heard or the environment itself, and he identified three main components. Keynote sounds are the "fundamental tone[s]" of a soundscape; they are created by features in the local environment, such as water, wind, or birds. Schafer suggested that these sounds are often taken for granted, but he acknowledged that keynote sounds are the "anchor[s]" of a soundscape, around which all other sounds are arranged. The second type of sound, signals, are the "foreground sounds" that we listen to consciously, including alarms and sirens. Finally, soundmarks are any sounds that are specific to a community; they are the acoustic equivalent of landmarks. As such, Schafer argued that soundmarks especially deserve "to be protected" because they make the "acoustic life of the community unique."[14] A listener who has developed "exceptional powers of hearing," becomes what Schafer termed a "clairaudience,"[15] and it is precisely such an audience that Wordsworth desired for the Lake District's soundscape.

"Acoustic ecology" is another term that emerged from Schafer's World Soundscape Project. This concept concentrates on subjective responses to objective sounds, rather than simply the sounds themselves.[16] Timothy Morton argues that acoustic ecology is a Romantic form of understanding; it yearns, he writes, "for an organic world of face-to-face contact in which the sound of things corresponds to the way they appear to the senses and to a certain concept of the natural."[17] This kind of acoustic ecology relies on phenomenological responses to confirm cultural understandings of the natural world. It is affected by what Peter Szendy calls "regimes of listening," or the different ways that people are conditioned to respond to the sounds they hear.[18] It privileges interactions between the human and the natural that are inevitably understood through specific sociocultural values, and as a result its conclusions on the whole soundscape are limited.

Pijanowski and his coauthors have proposed a compromise between these alternative terms by advocating the use of "soundscape ecology" instead. For them, soundscape ecology emphasizes "the ecological characteristics of sounds and their spatial-temporal patterns as they emerge from landscapes."[19] Rather than focusing on individual components of the soundscape, soundscape ecology prioritizes interactions between sonic elements. Like Schafer, Pijanowski's team also develop a three-way classification for types of sounds: the biophony, which are sounds created by living organisms such as birds; the geophony, which includes sounds from nonbiological natural elements, such as wind and rain; and the anthrophony, which are sounds caused by humans.[20] To these, we add a fourth: the "topophony," the way in which sounds interact with the environment to generate distinctive acoustic events.[21] The topophony was particularly notable in the Lake District; the region's mountains and valleys affected sound in such a way as to produce distinctive acoustic experiences. As described later in the chapter, during the Romantic period in particular, visitors to the Lake District utilized its unusual topophonies to produce certain acoustic and imaginative effects.

For the years prior to the widespread use of recording equipment, written sources are the most reliable way of accessing a historical soundscape by preserving, however imperfectly, sounds that risk being forgotten or lost as a result of social, cultural, and technological change.[22] Travel writing provides a particularly useful record of lost soundscapes, since what was a keynote for someone familiar with a region was often a soundmark for a visitor.[23] As Wordsworth argued in his letters, a distinctive quality of the Lake District's soundscape seemed to be its quietness, but more discerning travelers distinguished themselves by recognizing the region's acoustic complexity. Travelers variously engaged with close evaluations of the soundscape's details and with distant appreciations of its overall effect. We argue that deep mapping allows us to begin to understand the role played by geography and topography in the formation of a specific historical-cultural soundscape.

THE POWER OF SOUND, NOISE, AND SILENCE

Many scholars, including Lucien Febvre, Alain Corbin, Bruce Smith, and Sophia Rosenfeld, have commented on how difficult it now is to comprehend the importance and diversity of historical soundscapes.[24] Compared to modern soundscapes, historical observers were exposed much less often to the loud anthrophonic noises that conceal multitudinous quieter sounds. Noise control had been a concern, in urban environments in particular, throughout the eighteenth century. Sound and hearing remained popular topics well into the nineteenth. John Andrew Fisher has demonstrated that John Tyndall's work on the physiology of hearing in his important book *Sound* (1867) was used in popular advertising campaigns,[25] while John M. Picker has traced the influence of Hermann von Helmholtz's research on sound and hearing in Dickens's novels.[26] Henri Lefebvre inherits Romantic definitions when he identifies three main rhythmic categories: noise, which is "chaotic"; sound, wherein harmonies can be discerned; and "silence."[27] In the late eighteenth century and the Romantic period these distinctions became the subject of a particularly active debate, a fact that goes some way toward explaining the rapid rise in interest in acoustics that, we argue, occurred in the Romantic Lake District.

When Wordsworth wrote his letter to the *Morning Post*, the peace he was defending did not necessarily mean silence; it meant the right kinds of sound. For him, the Lake District had a unique aural identity, not least because of what we are calling its topophony. In other words, the Lake District's physical geography interacted with other elements of the soundscape to form a distinctive acoustic ecology. Wordsworth's considerations of the relationship between noise, sound, and silence within his native landscape advanced a debate on the role of sound in the artistic imagination and in the environment that was at the foreground of aesthetic thinking in the eighteenth and nineteenth centuries. Travelers to the Lake District, encouraged by writers in the Wordsworthian mold, became interested in the interplay between noise, sound, and silence in the formation of characteristic spatial identities.

Wordsworth's letter represented a hierarchy of noise, sound, and silence that was well understood by his contemporaries. We can see from Figure 5.1 that, from the late eighteenth century onward, these three terms were used consistently in the texts that make up our corpus. It is evident that it was not just Wordsworth who celebrated the Lakeland "peace"; writers talk about listening to silence as much as four times as often (in the case of Edwin Waugh in the 1860s) as to sound. Despite this, sound was most frequently associated with named locations in the corpus (Figures 5.2 and 5.3). "Noise," or its lexeme "noisy," has slightly less than half of the PNCs as does "sound" or its lexemes ("sounds" or "sounding"); the noise group co-occurs with a place name in twenty-seven cases, and the sound group in fifty-nine. "Silence" or "silent" co-occurs with place names on thirty-one occasions. It is notable that, as Figure 5.2 indicates, "sound" becomes significantly more related to place in the Romantic era, a point to which we will return. Noise, like sound, enjoys a closer connection to place from the Romantic era, but the

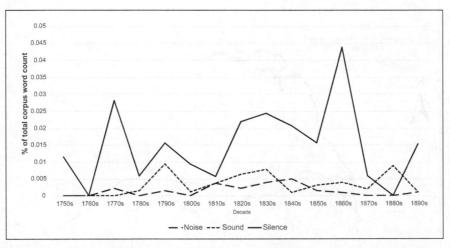

Figure 5.1. Frequency of "noise," "sound," "silence," and their lexemes as a proportion of the total corpus word count.

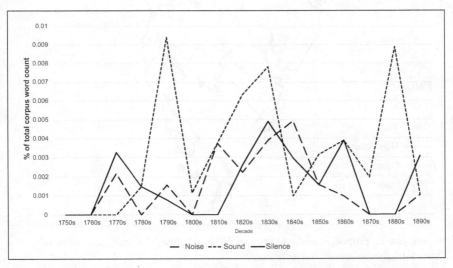

Figure 5.2. Frequency of PNCs of "noise," "sound," "silence," and their lexemes as a proportion of the total corpus word count.

locations with which it co-occurs are more condensed. As shown in Figure 5.4, in the Romantic and Victorian texts, "noise" is—with only two exceptions—concentrated from the Kirkstone Pass, over Langdale and through the Duddon Valley. This geography was thanks to two phenomena: the sound of the River Duddon, which appears to have seemed less harmonious than other Lakeland watercourses; and Wordsworth's record of the echoes that rebounded from the mountains when his sister-in-law, Joanna, laughed—an experiment revisited by literary tourists such as Samuel Leigh.[28]

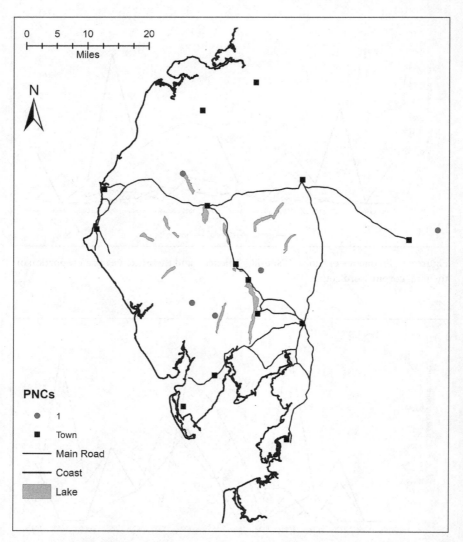

Figure 5.3a–c. Proportional circle maps of PNCs of "noise," "sound," and "silence." Above, (a) shows "noise" and its lexeme.

These patterns corroborate Murray Cohen's intuition that the relationship between sound and place was of particular interest to poets and philosophers in the Romantic period.[29] At the heart of that debate were deliberations as to what could be classed as sound and what was just noise. Writers such as Charles Burney, James Beattie, and William Duff agreed that the combination of certain sounds formed inherent harmonies, and so might produce pleasurable emotional responses in the listener.[30] Noises, on the other hand, were disagreeable; according to Beattie, they "hurt the ear by their shrillness" or required "painful attention on account of their exility." The converse was true of pleasant sounds: "Sweetness of tone, and beauty of shape and colour, produce a placid acquiescence of mind, accompanied

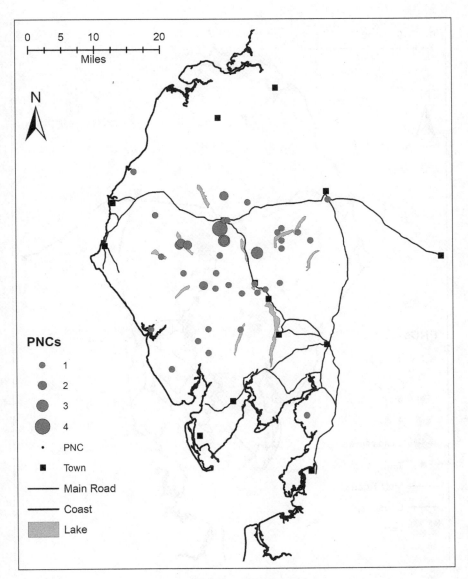

Figure 5.3b. "Sound" and its lexeme.

with some degree of joy, which plays in a gentle smile upon the countenance of the hearer and beholder. Equable sounds, like smooth and level surfaces, are in general more pleasing than such as are rough, uneven, or interrupted."[31] Beattie's distinction between "disagreeable" and "equable" sounds recalls Edmund Burke's definition of the sublime and the beautiful. For Burke, a "smooth" landscape was beautiful, but the rough surfaces of, for example, a mountain rendered such settings awe-inspiring or terrifying. Just as, for Beattie, excessively quiet sounds could be as disagreeable as shrill ones, so for Burke could the sublime be discovered in "extremes of littleness" as well as grandeur.[32] For both Burke and Beattie,

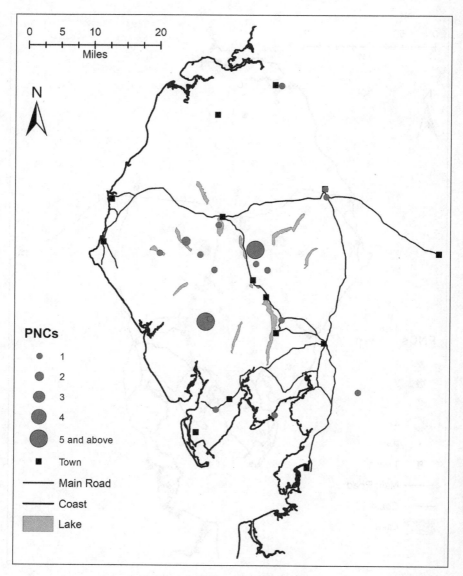

Figure 5.3c. "Silence" and its lexeme.

smoothness equated to pleasure, while the discordancy of uneven or "interrupted" elements rendered an experience displeasing. As we will see shortly, the Lake District's topophonic ability to render a rough sound smooth was one of its most notable characteristics.

William Duff, meanwhile, asserted that there were many ways "of affecting the human heart by the power of sounds."[33] Significantly, Duff's claim about sound here is echoed by Wordsworth's about poetry in his "Preface" to the Lyrical Ballads; that is, that poetry communicates "passions" to a reader, which should, if the "Reader's mind be sound and vigorous," also impart an "overbalance of pleasure."

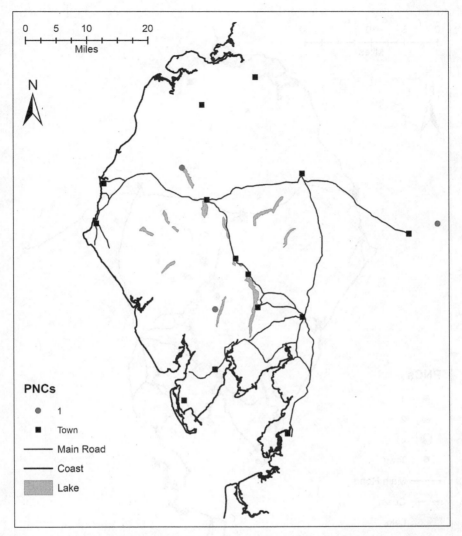

Figure 5.4a–c. Proportional circle maps of PNCs of "noise" and its lexeme in various periods. Above, (a) shows the eighteenth century.

These emotions are communicated by the sound of poetry; the "music of harmo-nious metrical language" contributes to the "powerful descriptions" that should, Wordsworth thinks, be poetry's aim.[34] Wordsworth recalled work like Duff's, too, when he recollected the Lake District soundscape's effect on his childhood devel-opment. In the *Prelude*, he remembered how he had "felt whate'er there is of power in sound | To breathe an elevated mood."[35] The sounds of the Lake District, whether in "storm and tempest, or in starlight nights | Beneath the quiet Heavens,"[36] infused him with a mood that might be both pleasurable and extraordinarily receptive to creative opportunities; when the poet imbibes the "power in sound" it is translated to a power in sight (or even insight).

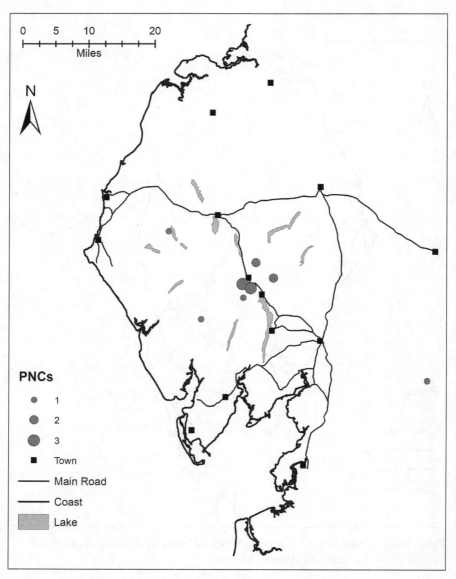

Figure 5.4b. The Romantic period.

Wordsworthian Listening

Distinctions between sound, noise, and silence were not stable in large part because the differences between them depended on the listener. A careful listener might establish harmony in an apparent cacophony. Lefebvre, for instance, writes that "the attentive ear" might bring the chaotic noises of multiple lives "back together by perceiving interaction."[37] Lefebvre suggests that the interaction between a noise and the subject who listens results in sound; in other words, for Lefebvre sound is not a result of the noise itself, but rather a phenomenological product that arises from close listening.

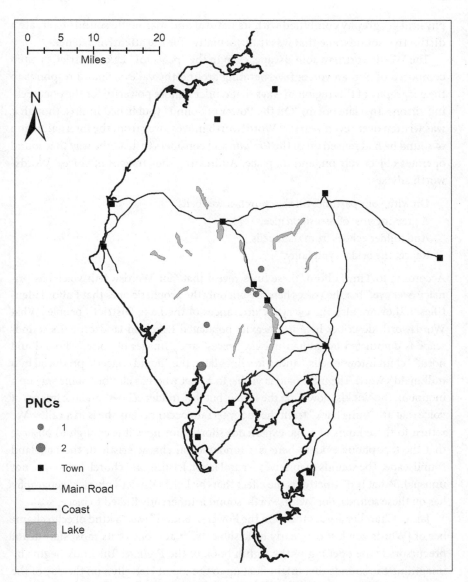

Figure 5.4c. The Victorian period.

Wordsworth's understanding of noise and sound anticipated Lefebvre's in its emphasis on attentive listening. One of Wordsworth's early editors, A. J. George, wrote that Wordsworth "hears no noises in Nature; he hears voices."[38] In fact, Wordsworth presents us with conversations: sounds that overlap in nature are brought into communion through the listener's attention. In his Lake District writing, sound is a result of the listener's personal response to the region's topophony; that is, the mountains and valleys of Wordsworth's native region were crucial for his understanding of noise, sound, and silence. The Lake District's physical geography combined with its natural and manmade sounds to create a distinctive soundscape that was transformative for the attentive listener.

The Wordsworthian soundscape, even in the "peaceful" Lake District, is often composed of human voices reverberating around the valleys. Sound responds to the geography of this region in ways that render it more powerful for the poet seeking visions. In a late poem, "On the Power of Sound" (published in 1835, though it was written over seven years),[39] Wordsworth moves away from the internalization of sound he had mused on in the *Prelude* and considers instead the way that sound operates objectively on, and in, place. Addressing the "Images of voice," Wordsworth advises:

> On with your pastime! till the church-tower bells
> A greeting give of *measured* glee;
> And milder echoes from their cells
> Repeat the bridal symphony.[40]

According to Tim Fulford, these lines reveal that "for Wordsworth voice has primacy over eye," but the voices here are not only the prophetic ones that Fulford identifies.[41] They are also the everyday utterances of the Lake District's people. What Wordsworth describes here is a heavily populated Lakeland landscape. Its soundscape is dominated by human noises: "voices" and "Images of voice," "hound and horn," "church-tower bells," and, a few lines later, the "liquid concert" produced by a milkmaid's work. The milkmaid is visible to a poet who has climbed some way up a mountain (he "look[s] down" on the scene), but the "milder echoes" and the images of voice that are "flung back" from the rocky terrain occur because he is in a valley. We return to these kinds of sonic experience shortly; for now, it is enough to observe that the topophony evident here is a fundamental characteristic of the Lakeland soundscape. The sounds themselves—rural labor, leisure, and church bells—are not unusual. What is distinctive is the effect that the Lake District's physical geography has on these sounds. For Wordsworth, sound is inherently linked to place.

James Chandler argues that "On the Power of Sound" was "a kind of echo chamber of [Wordsworth's] own early lyric subjects,"[42] and one of its most significant precursors is the opening of the eighth book of the *Prelude*. The book begins by imagining the sounds that might float up to the top of Helvellyn on the day of the Grasmere summer fair: noises of families with children; of the auctioneer "chaffering" as he sells livestock; of cattle lowing; flocks of sheep "bleating"; musicians playing; hawkers selling their wares; showmen demonstrating their talents.[43] The speed with which these sounds are introduced, and the short clauses that contain them, create a poetic cacophony that recalls the chaotic aurality of a Lakeland village on a festive day. Helvellyn stands above this acoustic chaos "in the silence of his rest."[44] Wordsworth again finds that mountains do strange things to sound:

> What sounds are those, Helvellyn, which are heard
> Up to thy summit? Through the depth of air
> Ascending, as if distance had the power
> To make the sounds more audible.[45]

Sound appears simultaneously to emphasize the mountain's height and the valley's depth; the combination of Helvellyn's high summit and the peculiar "depth" of the air—which appears to be a quality of the air itself as well as being reflective of the terrain—magnifies the sounds. This phenomenon affords the poet the chance to listen in on the goings-on of the fair even as he surveys it from a distance. In other words, the way that the mountains amplify the sounds in the valley allow the poet to offer two perspectives: his distant reading of what he can see is elucidated by the close aural experience provided by the Lake District uplands' distinctive auditory effects.

Wolfson argues that "the iconic Wordsworthian poet is a famously silent type,"[46] and, as Wordsworth discovered from the peak of Helvellyn, mountains were peculiarly effective defenders of silence. Figure 5.3c demonstrates that writers in our corpus usually labeled places as "silent" if they were away from towns. For some, this rural quietude could seem almost eerie. Charles Cooke, for instance, found Buttermere to be all "barrenness, solitude, and silence, only interrupted by the murmurs of a rill, running unseen in the narrow bottom of a deep dell."[47] For him, what is unheard is matched by what is unseen to form an unnerving loneliness. The only sound he does acknowledge, the stream's "murmur," is a form of subvocalization that does not quite attain the significance of a proper sound.

Silence could be either a good or a bad quality, depending on the listener's perspective.[48] Coates observes that quietness could be a sign of commercial backwardness, attractive only to a certain set of "disaffected literary gents."[49] As urban centers became increasingly noisy, however, silence became a precious, sought-after commodity.[50] Henri Bosco claims that silence suggests "a sense of unlimited space": "in the silence, we are seized with the sensation of something vast and deep and boundless."[51] By this reading, silence strips a landscape of its topophonic identity; it flattens out the nonvisual sense of a place's contours. Yet, as John Cage claims, there is no such thing as true silence; rather, what is perceived as silence is in fact an environment where the keynote sounds are amplified.[52] Sensitive travelers to the Lake District made the same discovery; thus, in Cooke's account of Buttermere, "silence" actually comprises a range of sounds that lie outside of urbanized cultural recognition. Coates summarizes the paradox inherent to the notion of a silent place when he writes that "a condition of silence does not imply the absence of sound";[53] as Fisher concludes, "something is always making sounds."[54]

When Wordsworth discovered the "power in sound" it was thanks to the acknowledgment of sound in silence. Like Wolfson, J. H. Prynne considers silence to be integral to Wordsworth's imagination: for Prynne, the gap between the sounds the poet hears and the "inward silence of his thought-world" was bridged by an "interval space" that formed "a hybrid between sound and silence." That hybrid found necessary expression in Wordsworth's poetry; as Prynne continues, unless Wordsworth expressed his "interior silence" in text, the topographies of his inner landscape would have been forever lost.[55] But the inverse was also true; silence might become sound in that interval space. Wordsworth discovered that the Lake District's very rocks were not truly silent:

> I would stand,
> Beneath some rock, listening to sounds that are
> The ghostly language of the ancient earth,
> Or make their dim abode in distant winds.
> Thence did I drink the visionary power.[56]

What seems like silence to the inattentive ear is, in fact, the "ghostly language of the ancient earth" that rumbles on outside the limits of most human hearing. In Mary Jacobus's words, this is a "half-heard" language from the "ancient past."[57] The poet hears these sounds, and his heightened powers of listening are translated into greater powers of seeing; by listening to that "ghostly language," this poet imbibes "visionary power."

A later, anonymous traveler advanced a similar conclusion. Walking in "deep solitude," this rambler remains in "awe-struck silence." After a time, though, he realizes that the region teems with sound: "Strangely impressed with the deep solitude, in awe-struck silence, I held on my way for an hour or so, now and then startled by the bleating of a lamb, the lowing of a cow afar off, and the flapping of the wings of a large bird, probably a heron, taking its heavy flight at my untimely approach."[58] His "deep solitude" here is reinforced by the silence that seems to surround him, but unlike Cooke, this rambler discovers a reflective, rather than "barren," state. Yet, as he moves through the landscape, he begins to discover that he is not alone after all—and nor is this part of the world silent. He begins to become aware of the animals' noises; in fact, he begins to develop such a nuanced approach to listening that he thinks he is able to distinguish the noise of ungainly flapping wings as a heron's take-off. In other words, this rambler discovers what Wordsworth had known: that listening carefully to the sounds and silences in the landscape creates and sustains a connection between person and place.

Most of these writers, including Wordsworth, overlooked other sources of sound. The mining industry that, as we have seen, proliferated in the Western Lakes particularly, is almost entirely ignored; so, too, are the quarries and other sites of industrial development that were found throughout the region. Wordsworth, like the majority of travelers to Lakeland throughout our period, constructed a certain type of cultural soundscape that affirmed the Lake District's status as a region of peace and tranquility that was increasingly unusual in industrializing and urbanizing Britain. It is another instance of what Marjorie Levinson, in reference to "Tintern Abbey," has called Wordsworth's "fragile" pastoral prospect, one that is "artfully assembled by acts of exclusion."[59] For Rowney, meanwhile, this perception of the silencing of the natural soundscape is a defining characteristic of the Anthropocene, which, he writes, "can at least be partially defined as the successful transduction of non-human sound into background music."[60] One nonhuman sound that was central to this cultural soundscape was the sound of water. We want to turn now to the first of our two case study sounds: the waterfall. Waterfalls were a peculiar acoustic experience because they seemed to slip between being a noise

TABLE 5.1

WATER-RELATED COLLOCATES OF "NOISE" AND "SOUND"

	T-score with "noise"	T-score with "sound"
Water	3.89	4.12
Waters	2.63	2.43
Lake	2.12	2.22
Falls	2.22	2.20
Sea	N/A	2.19

and a sound. It took an unusually attentive level of listening to uncover the music hidden behind a waterfall's deceptive monotonality.

How the Water Comes Down: Listening to Waterfalls

It will surprise no one familiar with the Lake District that water is a particularly pervasive keynote sound here; the various becks, rills, rivers, waterfalls, lakes, plentiful rain, and the sea that encloses it on one side provide a constant refrain that—especially before the noises of industrialization became "inescapable"[61]—could be heard almost anywhere in the region. Water is mentioned frequently in the Lake District corpus as being the loudest sound in the area, but it seems to have been an aural experience that was difficult to define. The most significant collocates with both "sound" and "noise" are dominated by "water" and related terms, including "waters," "waterfalls," "fall(s)," and "lake" (Table 5.1). Significantly, though, "sea" only co-occurs with "sound," indicating that it was one of those instances where its auditory character was possessed of inherent harmonies, while noise was more of an inland trait (see Figure 5.3).

At times, the sound of water seemed to disrupt the peace that, as we have seen, was so important to the Wordsworthian Lake District: the anonymous traveler we met earlier wrote in 1861 that the River Duddon wended its way "noisily . . . through the otherwise quiet and peaceful dale."[62] On other occasions, the same traveler discovered a soothing harmony in the "soft musical notes" of the becks; a "small beck" in Newlands, for instance, seemed to him to be "singing its evening lullaby."[63] The water's location, and the way it interacted with that place's topography, had important influences over the way its sound was perceived.

For visitors to the region, the waterfalls were a particularly notable element of the Lakeland geophony; Figure 5.5 indicates that the most mentions of water in the region occur at the sites of the main lakes and waterfalls, including the famous falls at Lodore (just south of Keswick and Derwentwater) and Rydal (between Grasmere and Ambleside). There are 338 mentions of waterfalls in the corpus; of these,

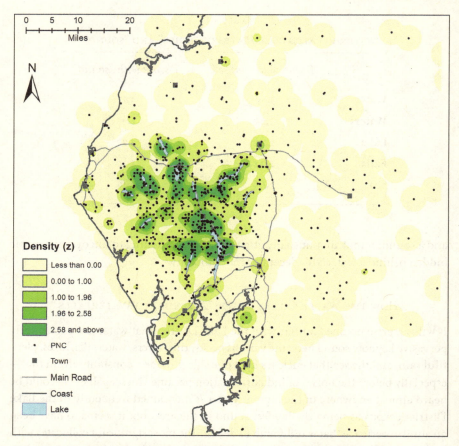

Figure 5.5. Density-smoothed maps of PNCs for a variety of water-related terms, including "water," "waters," "waterfall," "waterfalls," "lake," "sea," "mere," "tarn," "stream," "beck," and "rain."

253 occur within ten words of a place name (see Figure 5.6). In 70 percent of cases, as we can see from Figure 5.7, the place names that co-occur with "waterfall(s)" also co-occur with "sound." Waterfalls were, then, often memorable as much for the sound they made as for their sublime appearance. But waterfalls were especially complicated acoustic experiences. They presented sites at which distinctions between noise and musical sound might be challenged.

The water's sound quality was affected not only by its location but also by the local weather. In his *Guide*, Wordsworth recorded the weather's effect on the musicality of the local soundscape: "The rain here comes down heartily, and is frequently succeeded by clear, bright weather, when every brook is vocal, and every torrent sonorous."[64] The brooks seemed to take on a human quality; in Wordsworth's account, they seem to call to each other across the valleys. The acoustic qualities of the torrents (including waterfalls), on the other hand, were more complicated. "Sonorous" underwent a subtle shift in definition in the early nineteenth century. Initially, it meant a noise that was shrill or roaring; in either case, a sono-

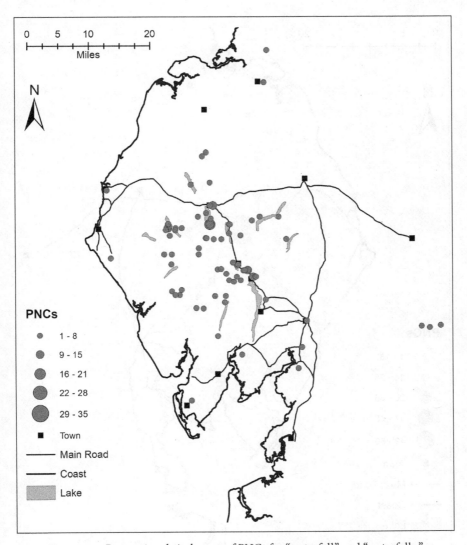

Figure 5.6. Proportional circle map of PNCs for "waterfall" and "waterfalls."

rous noise was something deep but monotonous.[65] By 1861, however, when the great writer of soundscapes, Henry David Thoreau, described his "Concord life" as "sonorous" he meant that it was acoustically diverse. The "crickets, and the lowing of kine, and the crowing of cocks" to which he listened emphasized space over time, since these sounds all made Thoreau feel as though he "might have been born any year for all the phenomena [he knew]" (Letter to Lucy Jackson Brown, September 8, 1841).[66] For Wordsworth, the torrent's "sonorous" quality seems to indicate a pleasing, constant background to the brook's more diverse voices; it was the Lakeland equivalent of white noise. Wordsworth's responses to waterfalls provided rare occasions when his ear could be critiqued for insensitivity by others in the Lake School.

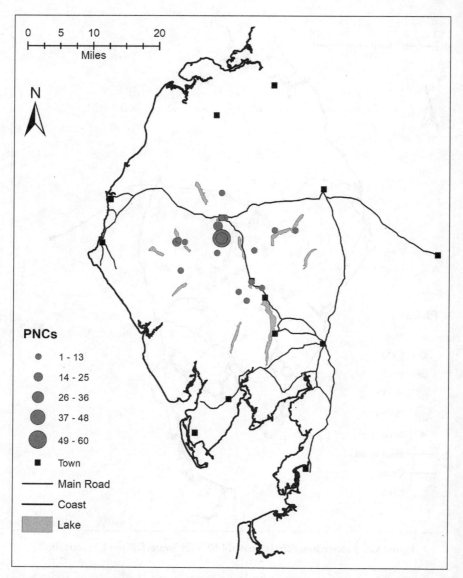

Figure 5.7. Proportional circle map of PNCs that include "waterfall(s)" with "sound" and its lexeme.

We saw earlier that eighteenth-century thinkers discussed acoustic phenomena in ways that recalled Burke's definitions of the sublime and beautiful: beautiful sounds were smooth, but unpleasant ones had a rough quality. Waterfalls presented difficulties with these classifications. Context was key for the interpretation of these sounds; as Fisher observes, a waterfall's roar can sound like that of an engine, but whereas for post-Kantian responses the natural sound seemed "majestically powerful," the industrial one was unpleasant.[67] Significantly, there are no overlaps between "waterfall(s)" and "noise" in our corpus. Waterfalls seem to have appeared to our writers to be possessed of inherent harmonic qualities; as

Figure 5.7 indicates, mentions of "waterfall(s)" and "sound" co-occurred together frequently.

To an eighteenth- or early nineteenth-century ear unaccustomed to loud noises, a powerful waterfall could be enough to disorient the senses. Samuel Taylor Coleridge noticed that the noise from waterfalls had marked the landscape etymologically as well as acoustically: "The word Scale & Scales is common in this Country—& is said . . . to be derived from the Saxon Sceala; the wattling of Sheep—but judging from the places themselves, Scale Force & this Scale Gill Force—I think it as probable that it is derived from Scalle—which signifies a deafening Noise."[68] Coleridge suggests an alternative onomastic history for the Lakeland word "scale" to that "said . . . to be derived from the Saxon." His own experience of exploring the areas around waterfalls—specifically, here, Scale Force near Buttermere—indicates to him that the word's development has more to do with responses to the soundscape than with the landscape's agricultural history. In a similar way to Wordsworth's identification of the torrent's sound as "sonorous," the noise of the scale is hyperbolically monotonous for Coleridge; it is "deafening," thereby removing the individual's ability to recognize separate components in the waterfall's sonic identity.

Coleridge's definition of "scale" implies a certain carelessness in his approach to waterfalls; like Wordsworth, Coleridge finds monotonality where, in fact, waterfalls generate a series of interconnected sounds. By contrast, Robert Southey knew that the listener who spent time at a waterfall paying attention to its acoustic qualities could recognize these complexities. Southey's most reprinted poem, "The Cataract of Lodore," is what Fulford calls "a humorous exercise on not-being-Wordsworth."[69] It offers a reading of the waterfall at Lodore that was distinct from Wordsworth's dismissal of it as a simple "roar." The poem plays with what Richard Terry terms "sound enactment," or the way that poets "exploit rhythm and phonology in such a way that these effects seem to corroborate, mimic, or enact the content of the lines in which they occur."[70] It is written in what one later writer called "dithyrambics, playful and irregular as [Lodore's] waters";[71] the words imitate in lively ways the sounds of the water as it comes over the rocks. Susan Wolfson calls it his *jeu d'esprit*, "a poem shaped, phonically and metrically, into a cascade of sounds that not only coincide with lexical sense but drive it as a primary expressive force."[72]

Southey originally wrote "The Cataract of Lodore" for his children.[73] It evinces the use of a picturesque location as what Fulford calls a "starting point . . . for a hands-on, active movement through the place."[74] "The Cataract of Lodore" investigates the transformation by attentive listening of a waterfall's "deafening noise" into musical—and metrical—sound. Southey's poem turns poetic cliché on its head; as John Hollander and Claire Téchené both remark, since the early eighteenth-century water had become an overused image of the pastoral, and one which writers such as Alexander Pope gleefully mocked.[75] Southey goes beyond this type of pastoral. Instead his onomatopoeic lines indicate that the traveler who paid attention to the relationship between a waterfall's geophonic identity and its local topophony could uncover an elaborate natural melody.

Southey's poem asks: "How do the waters come down at Lodore?" The question is answered by an exploration of the waterfall's physical journey, and demonstrates how that is inherent in its acoustic effects. As the poem concludes, the cataract's "motions" are blended intrinsically with its "sounds."[76] Lodore Falls have a distinctive sound, thanks to their drop of over a hundred feet from Watendlath Tarn near Grange. The way that the falls meander around and through the rocks on the cliff face gives this location a distinctive acoustic quality. "The Cataract at Lodore" offers a conceptual map of the waterfall; in fact, by claiming the name of the waterfall for the poem as well, the poem offers a textual portrait of the cataract. It demonstrates what Fulford has called the "re-materialization" of Romantic lyrics. "The Cataract of Lodore," perhaps more evidently than any other Romantic poem, reinscribes itself "onto the landscape to which it points." The effect, as Fulford concludes of Romantic poetry in general, is to bring "a material place, both mundane and sacred—in effect, uncanny—into being."[77]

When it was published in Joanna Baillie's anthology *Poems, Chiefly Manuscript, and from Living Authors* in 1823, Baillie wrote to Southey to say how the poem had "pleased and amused her." She predicted that "the younger part of my readers [will be] running about with portions of it in their mouths and shaking their heads to the measure, for these six months to come."[78] Baillie imagines these young readers becoming uncannily infected with Lake District rhythms; through Southey's verse, the waterfall produces an effect that might be said to be a form of natural supernaturalism, even on those who only hear its rhythms secondhand.

The poem's shape maps onto that of the cataract and it thereby emphasizes the importance of looking at as well as listening to the waterfall (Figure 5.8).[79] The movement of the water is decipherable through the poem; each line stands in for the rocks that make up the drop. The poem begins slowly, with the waters in Watendlath Tarn: "its own little lake." We pause here, halted by the full stop, waiting just like the water in the tarn taking a breath before the plunge down the cliff-face.

> And foaming and roaming,
> And dinning and spinning,
> And dropping and hopping,
> And working and jerking,
> And guggling and struggling,
> And heaving and cleaving,
> And moaning and groaning;
>
> And glittering and frittering,
> And gathering and feathering,
> And whitening and brightening,
> And quivering and shivering,
> And hurrying and skurrying,
> And thundering and floundering;
>
> Dividing and gliding and sliding,
> And falling and brawling and sprawling,
> And driving and riving and striving[.][80]

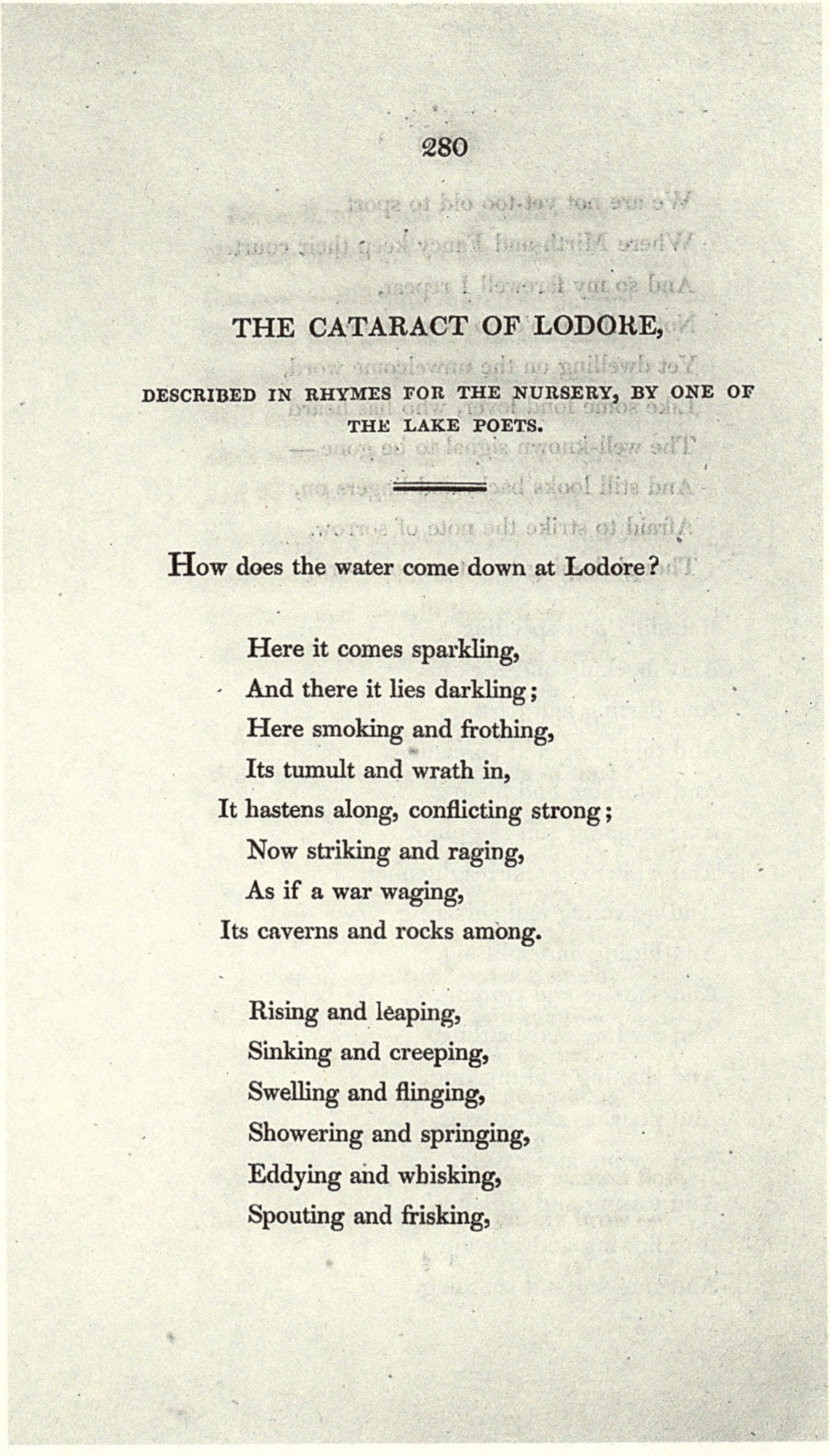

THE CATARACT OF LODORE,

DESCRIBED IN RHYMES FOR THE NURSERY, BY ONE OF THE LAKE POETS.

How does the water come down at Lodore?

Here it comes sparkling,
And there it lies darkling;
Here smoking and frothing,
Its tumult and wrath in,
It hastens along, conflicting strong;
Now striking and raging,
As if a war waging,
Its caverns and rocks among.

Rising and leaping,
Sinking and creeping,
Swelling and flinging,
Showering and springing,
Eddying and whisking,
Spouting and frisking,

Figure 5.8. Robert Southey, "The Cataract of Lodore," in *Collection of Poems, Chiefly Manuscript, and from Living Authors*, ed. Joanna Baillie (1823), 280–283. Images from archive.org.

281

Turning and twisting
    Around and around,
Collecting, disjecting
    With endless rebound;
Smiting and fighting,
A sight to delight in,
Confounding, astounding,
Dizzying and deafening the ear with its sound.

Receding and speeding,
And shocking and rocking,
And darting and parting,
And threading and spreading,
And whizzing and hissing,
And dripping and skipping,
And whitening and brightening,
And quivering and shivering,
And hitting and splitting,
And shining and twining,
And rattling and battling,
And shaking and quaking,
And pouring and roaring,
And waving and raving,
And tossing and crossing,
And flowing and growing,
And running and stunning,

Figure 5.8. *(continued)*

And hurrying and skurrying,
And glittering and frittering,
And gathering and feathering,
And dinning and spinning,
And foaming and roaming,
And dropping and hopping,
And working and jerking,
And guggling and struggling,
And heaving and cleaving,
And thundering and floundering,
And falling and brawling and sprawling,
And driving and riving and striving,
And sprinkling and twinkling and wrinkling,
And sounding and bounding and rounding,
And bubbling and troubling and doubling,
Dividing and gliding and sliding,
And grumbling and rumbling and tumbling,
And clattering and battering and shattering,
And gleaming and streaming and steaming and beaming,
And rushing and flushing and brushing and gushing,
And flapping and rapping and clapping and slapping,
And curling and whirling and purling and twirling,
Retreating and beating and meeting and sheeting,
Delaying and straying and playing and spraying,
Advancing and prancing and glancing and dancing,
Recoiling, turmoiling and toiling and boiling,

Figure 5.8. *(continued)*

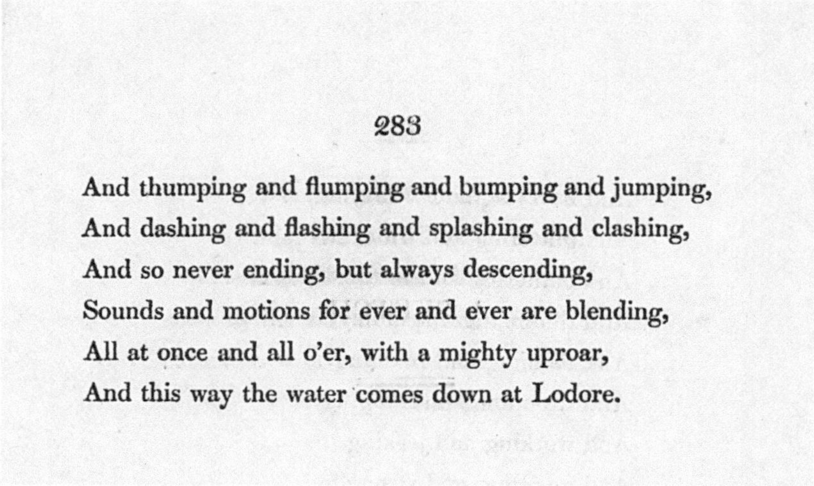

283

And thumping and flumping and bumping and jumping,
And dashing and flashing and splashing and clashing,
And so never ending, but always descending,
Sounds and motions for ever and ever are blending,
All at once and all o'er, with a mighty uproar,
And this way the water comes down at Lodore.

Figure 5.8. *(continued)*

The poem quickens as it follows the water over the edge; it becomes a profusion of active verbs ("Rising and leaping, | Sinking and creeping, | Swelling and sweeping, | Showering and springing")[81] that imitate the water's rapid descent. The poem provides a highly specific—if not exactly accurate—map of the waterfall that imagines details down to the way that individual rocks might disrupt the flow of the water.

The short vowel sounds that replicate the water's quick falls—"dinning and spinning," "dropping and hopping"—lengthen as the words mimic the way that the water slows momentarily as it reaches one of the small pools that gather along the waterfall's descent. The poem, like the cataract, demands slower reading at these junctures: where the water lies "moaning and groaning" or "thundering and floundering," the poem also requires a pause. The semicolons confirm a change of pace, before the stanza breaks imitate the next short drop. As the poem follows the waterfall to the bottom, it mimics the change in the water's movement. Syllables become consistently long, and the sound of the consonants is heavier in mimicry of the water's more lumbering flow in the lower stages of the fall: "And sprinkling and twinkling and wrinkling, | And sounding and bounding and rounding, | And bubbling and troubling and doubling." Finally, the poem, like the cataract, splashes into the stream at the bottom.

The poem's final lines are gently ironic: "All at once and all o'er, with a mighty uproar; | And this way the water comes down at Lodore."[82] In fact, as this lively poem has revealed, the water does not fall "all at once"; it comes down in increments that produce an acoustic experience that, if listened to properly, comprises astonishing diversity. The poem reveals the breadth of sounds that actually compose this waterfall's roar. What Southey's poem uncovers is the transformation of a keynote sound into a dense series of soundmarks.

Following Southey, a number of later writers paused at the waterfall to consider the effect of his poem on location. The author of an anonymous guide published by John Garnett provided an extract from the poem to act as a substitute for the waterfall: "As the reader is supposed to be on the spot we cannot resist giving a few lines."[83] The anonymous author of *Nelson's Handbooks for Tourists: The English Lakes* noted, though, that the poem was accurate only "after heavy rains," since "during dry weather its vagaries are by no means so outrageous."[84] Derwent Coleridge—Samuel Taylor Coleridge's second son, who was largely brought up by Southey at Greta Hall—expanded on Southey's project by tracing the change in how the waterfall was heard as the listener's physical relationship to Lodore altered on the walk up to it:

> You hear the roar for several miles—losing it from time to time as we come near the lesser cataracts—reminding one of a great man's fame, seemingly overpowered by the prattling of some ephemeral reputation, but in reality keeping on in deeper note and swelling out again finely in the distance. Think of me, standing alone, beneath and among those great rocks, with the great waterfall before me. I got up close to it, grappled with it—it has many arms!—Lay at its feet, looked up at it—heard it declaim a grand epic *ore profundissimo*,—great primæval monster—bard of the mountains that it is—sitting in its winter house, bard of its laurels.[85]

Derwent finds both music and poetry in this waterfall. What he discovers here is not the "roar | that stuns the tremulous cliffs at high Lodore" that Wordsworth recorded. Instead, Derwent, like Southey, recognizes that Lodore's "many arms" each produce an astonishing variety of sounds as the millions of droplets of water hit the rocks on their way down the steep mountainside.

Southey's poem argues for a close reading of a deceptively homogeneous noise; it demands that its readers—and, subsequently, visitors to the Lake District—become more attentive to the small sounds that make up a soundscape. A trade had already developed in encouraging the kind of careful listening for which both Southey and Wordsworth—in different ways—advocated. By creating a very loud noise, Lakeland visitors discovered that they could conversely emphasize the region's peacefulness—and its inhabitants discovered that there was money to be made from this jarring practice. By the time of Southey's poem, another booming trade had been established at Lodore, one that—in a similar way to Southey's poem—sought to draw a listener's attention to the sounds that made up the iconic Lake District silence.

The "Most Expensive Luxuries": Cannon-Fire and English Echoes

To the seventeenth-, eighteenth-, or nineteenth-century ear, quietness ruled the countryside. It meant that subtle sounds were able to be heard, but it also meant that they were often taken for granted. Silence seemed to indicate a wilderness or, at least, what Fisher calls "untrammeled nature."[86] Rosenfeld claims that there was a change in listening culture between the late eighteenth and mid-nineteenth centuries, whereby city-dwellers "began to pay less attention to the sounds of nature," particularly since "new, typically endogenous or manmade noises . . . began to fill the sonic void."[87] But that "void" was not silent; the soundscapes—both natural and manmade—continued to display complex arrangements, even if they were not always attended to. Sometimes, visitors' sensitivities to the Lakeland soundscape needed a little encouragement. One way that this could be achieved, in the late eighteenth and early nineteenth centuries especially, was through the impressive echoes that could be produced as a result of the Lake District's topography.

The echo is a record—or a "memory," as Sean Street terms it[88]—of sound's interactions with the environment. An echo is formed by soundwaves' reflections from a surface. If an echo is to form, it requires a degree of containment, but its repetitions make it a vehicle for a physical and imaginative sense of vastness. The echo exaggerates what George Revill identifies as the core properties of heard sounds by giving "embodied sensation to properties of depth, distance and proximity."[89] Echoes emphasize an ecological relationship between sound and listener that is contingent on space. As Hollander explains, "in modern discourse, the word echo is used figuratively to indicate a musical or linguistic repetition, usually of a short utterance or the terminal portion of a longer one, with the additional qualification that the repeated sound is not only contingent upon the first, but in some way a qualified version of it."[90] These qualifications are both physical, since each echo returns a weaker version of the original sound—a kind of "speaking silence," Christina Rossetti called it[91]—and figurative; each repetition of an image or idea alters the original in some way that develops or complicates its meaning. An echo also changes the way sound is perceived in space, transforming it from a monodirectional entity into a multidirectional experience.

To our historical Lakeland travelers, echoes seemed to reveal aspects of the landscape that remained hidden to the eye, and this form of second sight was facilitated by the acoustic capacities of the Lake District's topography. The rocks that make up much of the Lake District reflect soundwaves in such a way that a loud noise could result in particularly impressive echoes that were not possible elsewhere. Figure 5.9 displays place names where "echo" or its lexeme occur in the same sentence rather than within ten words. (We chose this bandwidth in this instance because the echoes were frequently described using long lists of place names, so using a set span of words led to many place names being wrongly omitted.) We can see from Figures 5.9 and 5.10 that echoes co-occur most frequently with place names located in one of two main geological groups: the igneous Borrowdale Volcanic Group in the center of the region is formed largely of lava with some other significant intrusions; the Skiddaw Group to the north is sedimentary rock mostly formed of slate. Slate, as we will see momentarily, seems to have been the most effective surface from which to reflect sound.

These unusually effective echoes encouraged listeners to focus on sound's powerful imaginative and emotional effects. In "On the Power of Sound," Wordsworth attributes the Lake District's distinctive topophony to its geology, and suggests that this scientific phenomenon might have profound implications for personal responses to the landscape:

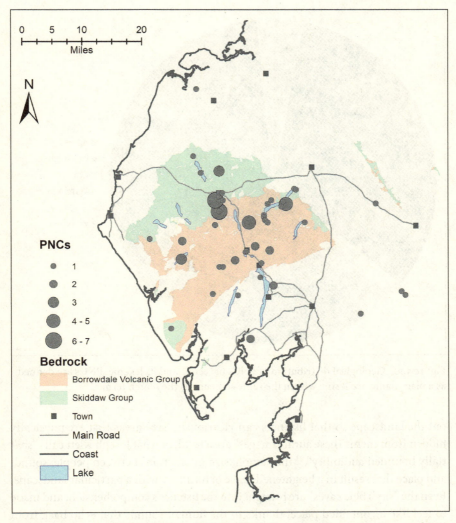

Figure 5.9. Proportional circle map of PNCs of "echo" and its lexeme, superimposed on two major Lakeland geological regions. PNCs are defined as a place name occurring within the same sentence as the search term.

> Ye Voices, and ye Shadows,
> And Images of voice—to hound and horn
> From rocky steep and rock-bestudded meadows
> Flung back, and, in the sky's blue caves, reborn.[92]

The echoes here have the potential to radically alter perceptions of both sound and place. Wordsworth envisages echoes as objectified forms of sound; they become "Images" that make the sounds of "hound and horn" tangible. More than that, though, these "Images of voice" allow the listener to imagine vividly the mountains and meadows that lie out of their line of sight. In other words, sound opens

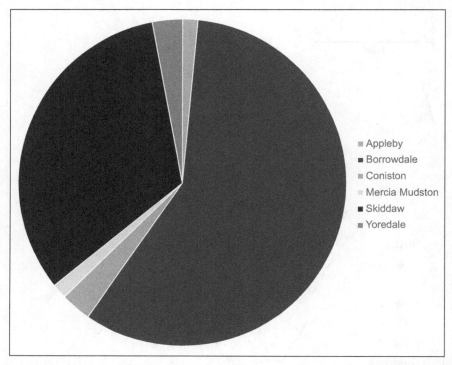

Figure 5.10. Geological distribution of PNCs of "echo" and its lexeme. PNCs are defined as a place name occurring within the same sentence as the search term.

out the landscape so that listeners can vicariously "see" areas that are physically hidden from them. These aural "Images" are a result of what Joseph Klett calls "spatially bounded audibility";[93] they emphasize interactions between people, sound, and place that result in a heightened sense of intimacy with a particular landscape. Even the "sky's blue caves" are brought into the listener's comprehension, and made to feel like a contained place, thanks to the human sounds that echo back from them. At the very least, the creation of hyperbolically loud noises in an otherwise unusually quiet environment emphasized the way that sound responds to place, and how, in turn, a listener's connection to the landscape is altered.

This interest in echoes led to one of the Lake District's stranger tourist attractions: the deliberate creation of loud noises so that the listener could hear the echoes. A variety of objects were used to generate these noises. Charles Cooke advocated the use of a clarinet and a few French horns to create an orchestral echo that would offer "a continuation of musical echoes, which reverberating round the lake, are exquisitely melodious in their several gradations, and form a thousand symphonies, playing together from every part."[94] Others were happy to use their own voices; Coleridge particularly enjoyed the sensation that the mountains were shouting back to him the names of the loved ones he called out.[95] For some, voices were not an effective instrument; Edward Baines records that women's voices particularly were neither deep nor loud enough to generate satisfactory echoes.[96] How-

TABLE 5.2

DIFFERENT SOUND INTENSITIES

Source	Intensity (decibels)
Rocket launching pad	180
Gunshot blast; jet plane	140
Threshold of pain; thunder; pneumatic hammer at 3 feet; amplified rock music in large arena	120
Chainsaw	100
Motorcycle at full throttle at three feet	95
Lawn mower	90
Average city traffic; Alarm clock at two feet	80
Human shout at three feet	75
Large dog barking at fifty feet; hairdryer	70
Conversation at three feet	60

Source: Simplified from Bruce R. Smith, *The Acoustic World of Early Modern England: Attending to the O-Factor*, 50.

ever, there was one object that emerged as being the clear favorite for creating impressive echoes: the cannon.

Wordsworth's claim in 1820 that "here no cannon thunders to the gale"[97] was right only for the Duddon Valley. In fact cannon-fire was a regular occurrence in the Lake District. These cannon, though, were not sounded as part of the military effort. At an early stage in the Lake District's emergence as a popular tourist destination, local boatmen and innkeepers began to charge their patrons for the firing of cannon across the prominent lakes. Cannon-fire was one of the loudest known sounds until the late nineteenth century (Table 5.2); according to Leigh Schmidt, sounds like it induced a *"sort of vertigo"* in listeners, and drove minds to distraction.[98] Corbin claims that before the "continuous noise of the internal combustion engine, electric motor, or amplifier," "people liked . . . being sporadically deafened" by noises such as cannon being fired.[99]

Cannon-fire provided regular acoustic attractions in the Lake District for several decades. Cannon were fired in the valleys to draw attention to the complicated forms of silence that followed a loud, and out of place, noise. There was, perhaps, still a remnant of the seventeenth-century belief that a powerful natural sound articulated terrifying divine intentions.[100] This belief altered in light of eighteenth-century developments in the understanding of the sublime, however, so that, in Isabelle Bour's words, "awesome noises could elevate the mind and extend the scope of man's understanding of nature."[101] In the Lake District, that extension seemed

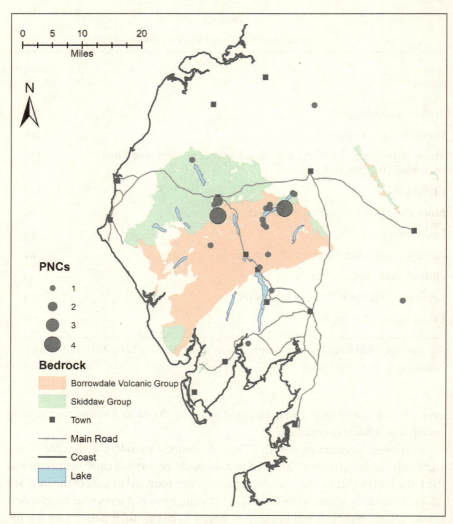

Figure 5.11. Geological distribution of PNCs of "cannon." PNCs are defined as a place name occurring within the same sentence as the search term.

almost literal. Cannon-fire, and, more importantly, the echoes it created, brought the soundscape's aesthetic qualities to the fore, and was used to develop a form of acoustic sublime that extended the traveler's knowledge of and feeling of connection with the Lakeland landscape.

These cannon could be found at various points around the Lake District, but they were mostly located around the main lakes, particularly those located within the geological Skiddaw Group—notably Ullswater and Derwentwater—but also including Windermere (Figure 5.11). Again, we have used the place names that co-occur in the same sentence as "cannon," since cannon tended to be associated with many places at once; the expansive echoes they created generated networks of place names. If we break these data down by period, a pattern emerges that is similar to

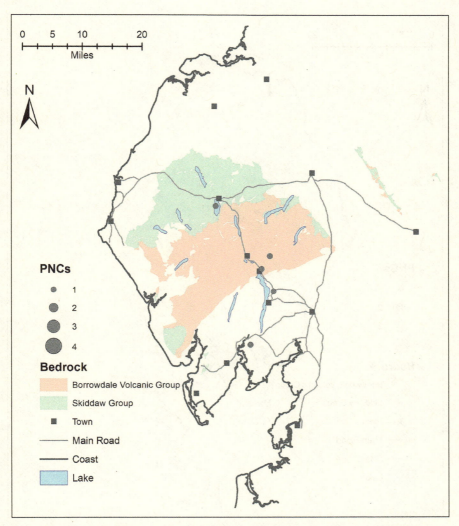

Figure 5.12a–c. Geological distribution of PNCs of "cannon" in various periods. Above, (a) the eighteenth century.

what we saw earlier with the sound and noise data: cannon were most popular during the Romantic period, and the concentration of the activity in these years confirms that sound was a particular concern for authors in the late eighteenth and early nineteenth centuries (Figure 5.12). Interestingly, all of the cannon sites mentioned in the eighteenth century had disappeared by the Romantic period, and only one Romantic-era cannon survived into the Victorian age. The popularity of cannon-fire in these years affirms that sound—and the echo especially—contributed to a form of place-making that was specifically Romantic.

The Lake District was certainly not the only location to put on an acoustic display for its visitors. Perhaps the most well-known listening experience on the Grand Tour was to be found in Venice; there, gondoliers would sing with each other

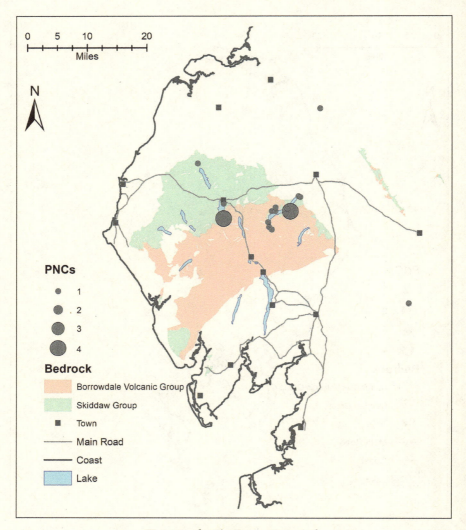

Figure 5.12b. The Romantic period.

loud enough to make their voices harmonize across the canals. Goethe's account of this spectacle emphasizes the acoustic aims of these singers: "The singer sits on the shore of an island, on the bank of a canal or in a gondola, and sings at the top of his voice—the people here appreciate volume more than anything else. His aim is to make his voice carry as far as possible over the still mirror of water."[102] This display was so striking because it emphasized harmonies; the listener, ideally, should be situated precisely half-way between two singers in order to fully appreciate the moving effect of the way the voices blended. It seemed that volume was preferable to tune, since the louder the singing, the more the sound of it merged with that of other voices. These voices were amplified by that "still mirror of water," to create a unique sonic effect that brought the gondoliers lucrative additional employment; by the time Goethe traveled to Venice in the 1780s, this display had

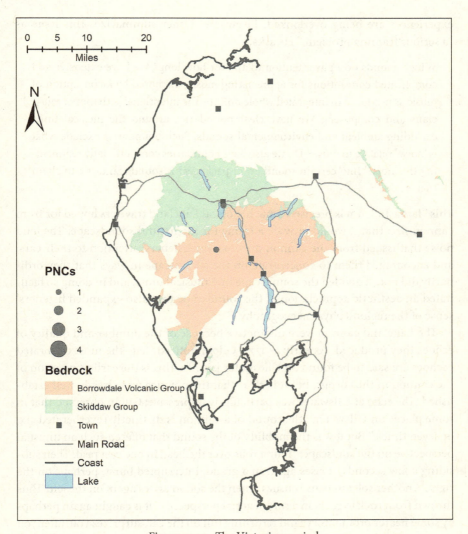

Figure 5.12c. The Victorian period.

to be ordered—and paid for—in advance.[103] To hear the gondoliers singing was to partake in an acoustic experience that linked the traveler imaginatively with Goethe and other ear witnesses.[104]

The Lake District cannon strived for a similar effect; they aimed to demonstrate a harmonic, sonic relationship between people and place. According to Fisher, the problem with natural sounds is that they are "not like music, not intentionally produced to be appreciated as expressive or aesthetic objects. Nor are they regimented into units as in music to be appreciated in spatial and temporal separation from other sounds occurring simultaneously. They surround us, occurring at many levels and distances from us, with no beginning or end."[105] This apparent endlessness of natural sounds means they can be taken for granted as part of a rural or wilderness setting without a listener being aware that a complex array of acoustic experiences are being overlooked. Elsewhere, Fisher summarizes this issue as "a serious framing problem." He asks,

> Which sounds do I pay attention to and for how long? We have extensive and complicated conventions for appreciating music, anchored by a conception of music as produced in integrated whole units by the intentional activities of musicians and composers. We have clear boundaries around the musical units excluding ambient and environmental sounds. Such boundaries exclude what is 'noise' relative to music. Do we also have boundaries conventionally regimenting the 'noise' into certain sound event packages? It sounds fantastic to claim that we do.[106]

This "fantastic" aim is precisely what historical Lakeland travelers hoped for from cannon-fire: that it would provide a frame for the natural soundscape. The loud noise that issued from the cannon drew nearby listeners' attention to their ears, and encouraged them to concentrate on the soundscape in ways that they ordinarily did not. It divided the soundscape into musical units, and in doing so facilitated an aesthetic appreciation of the soundscape that also expanded listeners' sense of the region's physical geography.

The Lakeland cannon were distinctive because of the number and quality of echoes they produced. As early as 1772, Gilpin noticed that "the most celebrated ecchoes are said to be found on Ulleswater [sic]."[107] This is the earliest mention of the cannon in the corpus, but it is clear that the practice was already well established. The echo at Ullswater was particularly impressive; Gilpin observed that in some places on Ullswater, "the sound of a cannon is distinctly reverberated six, or seven times." But it was the mobility of the sound that offered such an unusual perspective on the landscape: "It first rolls over the head in one vast peal. Then subsiding a few seconds, it rises again in a grand, interrupted burst, perhaps on the right. Another solemn pause ensues. Then the sound arises again on the left. Thus thrown from rock to rock, in a sort of aerial perspective, it is caught again perhaps by some nearer promontory; and returning full on the ear, surprizes you, after you thought all had been over, with as great a peal as at first."[108] Gilpin's sentences here attempt to mimic the effect of the echo; they roll over multiple commas as the echo builds, and then become staccato as he records the "solemn pauses" between those disorienting sounds. This sonic experience appears to raise the listener above the earth to offer them an "aerial perspective" that anticipates Wordsworth's cloud station and enables them to perform a kind of deep mapping of the landscape;[109] the echoes seem to reveal distant prospects as well as those "nearer promontor[ies]." Gilpin actually preferred the echo produced by French horns as being more musical, but he thought that there was something exceptionally powerful in the cannon's ability to highlight the Lake District's unusual topophonies.

A little later, William Hutchinson discovered something similar. He recalled embarking on a barge that was provided with "six brass cannon mounted on swivels." Hutchinson reports, in quasi-scientific fashion, the interaction of the sound waves with the surfaces of the surrounding mountains: "On discharging one of these pieces, the report was echoed from the opposite rocks, where by reverberation it seemed to roll from cliff to cliff, and return through every cave and valley, till the decreasing tumult gradually died away upon the ear."[110] The echoes demonstrate the interaction between the sound waves and the Lake District's material nature, and this phenomenon draws Hutchinson's attention to his own interactions with the soundscape. His astonishment at the effect this loud sound has on the region's quietness is palpable when he writes the following:

> The instant it had ceased, the sound of every distant water-fall was heard, but for an instant only, for the momentary stillness was interrupted by the returning echo on the hills behind; where the report was repeated like a peal of thunder bursting over our heads, continuing for several seconds, flying from haunt to haunt, till once more the sound gradually declined;—again the voice of the water-falls possessed the interval—till, to the right, the more distant thunder arose upon some other mountain, and seemed to take its way up every winding dell and creek, sometimes behind, on this side, or on that, in wondrous speed running its dreadful course; when the echo reached the mountains, within the line and channel of the breeze, it was heard at once on the right and left, at the extremities of the lake.—In this manner was the report of every discharge re-echoed seven times distinctly.[111]

The "momentary stillness" that follows the cannon-fire, as well as the "intervals" that succeed each echo, draws attention to what Fisher terms the "network of sounds that surround us."[112] At the center of that network is the listener, who suddenly finds that he is possessed of almost supernatural powers of hearing; he is able to hear "every distant water-fall" with an acuity that, before the cannon-fire, had not been possible. Klett explains this phenomenon: he writes that it is "not the presence of sound energy, but the dynamic variation of that energy that draws our attention to sound objects, as we register changes in air pressure."[113] The instant of quiet after an excessively loud sound draws the listener's attention to the minutiae of the soundscape, granting them an important, if fleeting, insight into the wild spaces of this region.

Southey provides a satirical account of these experiences when he describes a visit to the popular cannon at Lodore in his mock-tourist guide *Letters from Don Manuel Espriella* (1807). This account makes clear Southey's dismay that Lodore, in Fulford's words, "may have resounded with the waterfall that cascaded down the fellside, but it also echoed to the commodification of a place for a new market of sightseers."[114] The fictional protagonist visits the cannon, and, although he is impressed by the echo, he is appalled by how expensive this experience is:

> At a little public-house near, where the key of the entrance is kept, they have a cannon to display the echo; it was discharged for us, and we heard the sound rolling round from hill to hill, but for this we paid four shillings which are very nearly a peso duro, so that English echoes appear to be the most expensive luxuries in which a traveler can indulge. It is true there was an inferior one which

would have cost only two shillings and sixpence; but when one buys an echo, who would be content, for the sake of saving eighteen pence, to put up with the second best, instead of ordering at once the super-extra-double superfine?[115]

For Southey, the cannon's echo has become little more than a ridiculous tourist fashion; as Carol Bolton notes in her introduction to *Letters from England*, "The decision to get more 'bang for their buck' deliciously complements Espriella's London commentary on the ridiculousness of purchasing expensive luxuries."[116] The sound the cannon makes seems visible: the cannon *displays* the echo. Espriella writes as if it becomes a tangible artifact, a souvenir that affords an impressive acoustic experience. Of course, the irony is that the echo is the most ephemeral "display" imaginable; it is not even the sound itself, but the "memory" of one.[117] Moreover, it allows the listener to feel connections with parts of the landscape that they have not visited; the sound rolls "round from hill to hill," before returning to the listener's ear, so that the listener can claim to have experienced something of the region around the cannon site. The more expensive echo brings a wider range to the listener; this package offered a bigger noise, and so a more impressive "display." At the same time, the cannon-fire disrupts the natural soundscape, offering a demonstration of human power even over the Lake District's remaining wild places. Southey mocks Espriella's touristic response to the cannon, but for more sound-sensitive travelers the practice seemed to deepen their connection with the landscape.

The acoustic insights afforded by the cannon generated a new form of sublime experience. After a visit to the echo at Ullswater near Patterdale, Edward Baines paused to consider this precise effect: "There is something deeply impressive in the reverberation of such a burst of sound through a mighty theatre of mountains. It enlarges the conception of the mind with regard to the vastness of the surrounding objects: the ear supplies the deficiencies of the eye, and informs us of the loftier and more distant ranges which are shut out from our view."[118] For Baines, the echo displays the power of the landscape through the soundscape, and it allows the listener to access a sublime that is vaster than sight alone can allow. The mind seems to expand to match the reach of the echoes, so that the mind in listening seems better able than the mind looking to match the impressiveness of the surrounding scenery. That is the power of the echo: it not only brings together the noises of one area into a distinctive soundscape, but it unites multiple soundscapes under one soundmark. Like the landmark, this soundmark affects perceptions of the scenery for miles around. This is not an acoustic ecology, at least by Timothy Morton's definition, because this sound-making does not seek "face-to-face contact";[119] instead, it privileges interactions between the sound, the landscape, and the human listener. In fact, it is rhythm analysis at its best. It offers a physical demonstration of the interaction between the human and the natural: the cannon is fired, and the mountains fire the sound back. The echo transforms the noise of the cannon into a sound through which the listener might begin to comprehend the hidden features of the landscape and, more than that, to understand their place within it.

We have shown in this chapter that deep mapping the Lakeland soundscape reveals unacknowledged spatial networks and, more significantly, acknowledges previously obscured aspects of established aesthetic and phenomenological practices that had profound implications for the way historical travelers negotiated this landscape and places beyond it. We have demonstrated, too, that certain types of sound in specific locations were cherished for their aesthetic properties and capacities to encourage particular imaginative responses that became central to Lake District literature in the Romantic period especially. Sounds—both natural and manufactured—were a crucial means by which tourists and travelers sought to understand and engage with this region from new perspectives. That was particularly true of the unvisited places that echoes seemed to bring into the traveler's comprehension. There was no replacement for actually going into these wild places, though—but they required a different kind of reading altogether.

CHAPTER 6

Digital Cartographies and Personal Geographies

(RE-)MAPPING SCAFELL

Late eighteenth- and early nineteenth-century travelers were ill prepared for Scafell. Scafell—the massif containing both of England's tallest peaks—remains one of the most challenging climbs in the Lake District. It also boasts the region's most extensive, and sublime, views. Intrepid mountaineers found that Scafell and Scafell Pike concentrated thoughts about the relationship between cartographic interpretation and personal experiences of the Lake District's geography. Climbing Scafell encouraged experiments with representations of spatial experiences, via both maps and written texts. As we will see in this chapter, writers, artists, and mapmakers throughout our period discovered at Scafell an imaginatively lucrative site at which to explore the relationship between the experience of being in a challenging landscape and how it was represented on a flat page. These historical creative experiments have led us, in turn, toward some more playful ways of using GIS to do a close reading of literary works.

It has become something of a critical truism that developments in cartography, alongside the concurrent establishment of the picturesque, had pervasive effects on the Romantic spatial imagination; Julia S. Carlson, Dewey W. Hall, Rachel Hewitt, and Michael Wiley have all done important work that demonstrates the extent to which evolutions in mapmaking influenced the rhythms, forms, and themes of the period's literature.[1] The same claim might, we think, be made for our own age. Digital mapping technologies have transformed how users engage with the world around them. The transition away from the horizontal perspective that characterizes paper maps toward the vertical plane that, increasingly, make digital cartographies distinctive has had as profound an effect on modern spatial experiences as late eighteenth-century developments in mapping techniques and technologies had on the Romantic imagination. Virtual globes, notably Google Earth, are increasingly interested in representations of space that privilege egocentric or embodied human experiences over objective data.[2] One way they do this is by encouraging the user to interact with the world as a vertical space; Google Street

View, for instance, allows the user to place themselves in a land- or cityscape and gain a sense of how their body will stand in relation to these spaces. In doing so, these kinds of maps encourage a greater focus on the relationship between the individual body, mapped space, and a lived experience that combines the two.[3] This shift opens up opportunities for research into historical experiences of space, and necessitates new ways of thinking about how we engage with the world around us.

As early as 2008, the historian Heidi Scott issued a call for "stronger theorizations of verticality" to counteract the "implicit horizontalism" she found in cartographic studies.[4] Scott joined postcolonial scholars in finding such "horizontalism" to be inherently imperialist; the "God's-eye" view of a landscape transforms the terrain into something to be conquered and controlled.[5] However, Jess Edwards's claim that "every cartographic text" conceals "histories of encounters: some violent and exploitative, some more co-operative and transactional" is as applicable to modern digital cartographies that privilege verticality as it is to analog maps that operate on horizontal planes.[6] Peter Adey, Mark Whitehead, and Alison J. Williams have demonstrated that modern maps' engagements with verticality reflect the ways in which that perspective has become a ubiquitous instrument of geopolitical power in the twenty-first century, via technologies such as surveillance cameras and military drones.[7] Nevertheless, these authors, along with Stephen Graham and Lucy Hewitt,[8] agree that more work is needed on the social, cultural, and imaginative implications of engaging with the world as a vertical space.

For Eyal Weizman, focusing on the horizontal at the expense of the vertical has serious intellectual implications too; he argues that spatial research is a "flat discourse" that all too often "look[s] across rather than . . . cut[s] through the landscape," so that academic research on landscapes risks replicating the same problems as the maps and texts on which it is based.[9] The digital humanities might be uniquely positioned to address this problem; after all, as Kevin Lewis O'Neill and Benjamin Fogarty-Valenzuela note, digital methods like bar charts and spreadsheets are essentially vertical forms.[10] But digital humanists are also uniquely placed to address a question that Stuart Eve has identified as being at the heart of contemporary humanities research: that is, the need "to marry the advantages of computer-based analysis (simulation, prediction, etc.) with embodiment (being able to travel through and experience the landscape from a situated perspective)."[11]

Combining digital mapping technologies with analyses of texts that explicitly meditate upon what it feels like to live in or move through an unusually vertical landscape can help us to contemplate in unprecedented ways both why the vertical matters for experiences of space, and how historical texts can give us new perspectives on the ways we use modern cartographies. Our central premise in this chapter is that modern digital maps face many of the same issues that beset eighteenth- and nineteenth-century map-makers—but that these apparent limitations open up new possibilities for creative close readings of textual geographies. Using new forms of cartographies which emphasize verticality can, we suggest, extend the reconsiderations of what David Cooper and Gary Priestnall term the "complex imaginative geographies" communicated by analog maps and provide new opportunities "to reflect upon the relationship between textual and mapped space."[12]

We are especially interested, here, in how viewshed analyses can generate new ways of reading texts written on and about Scafell. Viewsheds allow us to model what might be seen from a certain location in different conditions, or even what different people might witness under the same conditions.[13] Yet, as Stuart Eve has lamented, viewshed analyses, like other kinds of sensory "sheds," imply that historical people and places existed "within a mathematically calculated sensory bubble."[14] Mark Gillings concurs, arguing that the viewshed simply "marks the starting point for an investigation of experiential affordance."[15] While we fully agree that these kinds of shed can offer only starting points rather than complete analysis, we do not see that as a limitation. Instead, we suggest here that viewsheds offer means by which we can begin to investigate spatial nuances that may not be evident from an unguided reading of the text alone. In this sense, we use GIS to create visualizations through which we might read our primary sources, while at the same time using our texts to inform interpretations of the digital maps we employ. Using this approach moves away from an understanding of GIS and other forms of cartographic visualization as objective, data-driven forms and posits them instead as texts to be interpreted in light of subjective phenomenologies. Alongside photographs of the place and texts describing the place, these viewsheds develop a more tangible sense of the place for readers and researchers who are not necessarily able to visit the spot themselves.

Up to now, we have taken a distant view of the entire Lake District region. In this chapter, our focus is much narrower. Our aim is, in part, to demonstrate how GIS and other geospatial technologies might be used to do a close reading of individual places and texts. We demonstrate here that combining written accounts with geographical data can generate a more nuanced understanding of both Scafell's cultural geography and the texts that describe it. In doing so, we hope to show another way in which reading texts and maps side by side can uncover new perspectives on historical experiences of space.

MAPPING SCAFELL

The cartographic and phenomenological issues with which virtual globes and the like attempt to engage are not new. In fact, they are remarkably similar to those faced by eighteenth- and early nineteenth-century mapmakers: as Robert Macfarlane summarizes, "conventional plane-view maps are poor at registering and representing land that exists on a vertical plane."[16] In the late eighteenth century, this problem was exaggerated for visitors to the Lake District when they arrived in the remote valley of Wasdale, the location of both England's deepest lake, Wastwater, and its highest mountains. Scafell seemed, to these early visitors, to block off the exit roads. Thomas Wilkinson—a Quaker mountain lover based in Penrith who is remembered now principally as an abolitionist and for inspiring William Wordsworth's poem *The Solitary Reaper*—summarized the feelings of several early nineteenth-century travelers when he mused that Scafell was a relic of the "primeval solitude" that had enveloped the earth after the Creation: "It still remains," he wrote, "a labor for the shepherd, or a pilgrimage for taste, to ascend its lofty summit."[17]

The Scafell massif was confirmed as containing England's two highest peaks by Joseph Banks's Trigonometrical Survey in 1790, which recorded Scafell at 3,092 feet and Scafell Pike at 3,165 feet.[18] Hewitt has expressed justified admiration for the accuracy of the technologies and techniques employed by these early surveys,[19] and the Scafells are a case in point: Banks's survey was out by less than 100 feet according to modern measurements taken using satellite technology, which measure Scafell and Scafell Pike at 3,162 feet and 3,209 feet, respectively.[20] Scafell's height distinguished it from other English peaks; Thomas Wilkinson went so far as to declare Scafell "the Goliath of our northern mountains, or the first of the British Alps,"[21] an Anglocentric view that pointedly overlooks the forty-five Scottish and Welsh mountains that are taller than it.[22] Nevertheless, Scafell's height—exaggerated by the sheerness of its sides—continued to fascinate visitors throughout the nineteenth century. Successive guidebooks offered increasing amounts of detail for the walker hardy, brave, or stubborn enough to attempt the climb.

Scafell is actually, as *Black's Shilling Guide to the Lake District* put it, an "aggregation of mountains" comprising four primary summits, and it is perhaps unsurprising that these were the focal points for writers intent on describing or climbing Scafell.[23] Figure 6.1, a density-smoothed map of all the PNCs for this part of the region in our corpus (236 in total), indicates the extent to which writing about this part of the region concentrated on Scafell's peaks: Scafell, Scafell Pike, Great Gable, and Lingmell. *Black's* (1853 and 1900) records that Scafell Pike was the main goal for most visitors to the massif in the Victorian period, although it warns visitors to check their maps carefully: it was common for hapless walkers, confused "by the similarity of names," to climb Scafell thinking they had achieved Scafell Pike. It notes, though, that the Trig Point on Scafell Pike—initially erected in 1826[24]—should help to minimize such mistakes (Figure 6.2).[25] *Black's* advises that the two summits are a little more than a mile apart, but are separated by the "fearful chasm" of Mickledore Gap.[26]

Black's has less to say of the other two summits, although it does acknowledge that each of these smaller peaks played an important role in Scafell's character overall. Lingmell was derided by the 1853 edition of *Black's* as being of "considerably inferior elevation" to the other summits.[27] M.J.B. Baddeley, the author of the 1900 edition, is more generous; this later version described Lingmell as "a sort of buttress for the support of the loftier heights."[28] The implication in the 1900 edition is that, without Lingmell, the improbably perpendicular rocks that form Scafell and Scafell Pike might collapse. Great Gable, meanwhile, forms "the advanced guard on the north east."[29] In this account, Scafell was transformed into an opposition force to be conquered by intrepid mountaineers. This alteration reflects the significant changes to Scafell's cultural status in response to a century in which

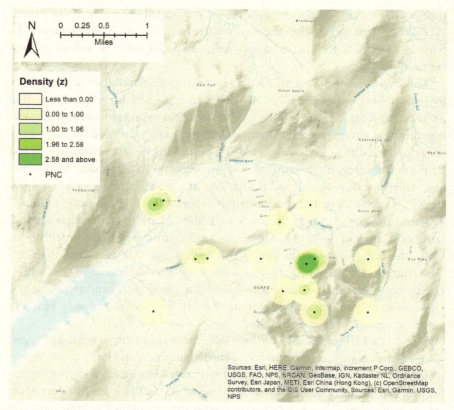

Figure 6.1. Density-smoothed map of all PNCs around Scafell.

mountaineering activities had become increasingly popular, and the people who undertook them increasingly diverse.[30] Scafell's status as England's highest mountain was crucial for this rise in its cultural capital; its statistics offered a way of comprehending the mountain so that its previously unfathomable heights and depths were brought into human order.

Mapping the mountain was an important way through which attempts at this kind of control were exerted. The Trig Point on Scafell Pike (Figure 6.2)—the "highest point of honour" for the climber, as Dorothy Wordsworth called it[31]— remained a tantalizing reminder that, even when it seemed impossibly steep and hostile, the mountain was both climbable and mappable. Trig Points act as memorials to the Enlightenment mapmaker's aim, in Hewitt's words, to "create a universal bird's-eye image of a landscape drawn from the perspective of an imaginary eye suspended many miles above the landscape, a scene unified through geometric sightlines linking elevated triangulation stations."[32] William Wordsworth put this perspective to imaginative use when he asked the reader of his *Guide* to imagine themselves floating on a cloud hanging midway between Great Gable and Scafell. From this cloud station, the reader could imagine the ideal cartographer's-eye view of the Lakeland valleys "diverging from the point,

Figure 6.2. The Trig point on Scafell Pike. Skiddaw and Blencathra can be seen on the horizon in the background, with Derwentwater also visible. Image Credit: Scafell Pike Trig Point. © Gareth James. Licensed for reuse under Creative Commons (CC BY-SA 2.0).

on which we are supposed to stand, like spokes from the nave of a wheel."[33] The Ordnance Survey (OS) sheet for Scafell (1865) was a triumph of this kind of map-making; the confident contour lines outline Scafell's topography in some detail, and seem to contain its massiveness in a manageable frame (Figure 6.3). Like the Trig Point, the OS was evidence that Scafell was not only walkable, but that it could be deconstructed and understood in manageable portions. By the late nineteenth century, this map—along with the increasing numbers of accounts of ascents of the mountain—had secured Scafell's place as one of the key sights, and most ambitious walks, for visitors to the region.

The OS for Scafell was particularly notable because it signified a step change in representations of—and subsequent understandings about—the massif. The OS's success more generally was attributable in large part to its development of contour lines, an innovation that finally standardized cartographic representations of height.[34] In the late eighteenth century, cartographers experimented with shading and hachuring to outline mountains. While these "visual grammar[s]" were revolutionary in representing the idea of height,[35] these techniques were not sufficient to represent the uplands in any detail. That had not mattered in a period when a mountain was simply an uninteresting barrier, and notions that it might be necessary to understand the specific shapes and terrains of these forms were slow to develop. Works like Thomas Burnet's *Sacred Theory*—one of the most widely read

Figure 6.3. Scafell, from Ordnance Survey First Series, Sheet 98 (1865). Data provided through www.VisionofBritain.org.uk, with historical material which is copyright of the Great Britain Historical GIS Project and the University of Portsmouth. Image licensed under Creative Commons (CC BY-SA 4.0).

books of the eighteenth century—had done much to transform mountains in the popular imagination from frightening, barren wildernesses to exhilarating meta-phors for adventure, freedom, and divinity.[36] In the Lake District, guidebooks like West's had advanced opinions that the mountains were, in their own ways, as entic-ing as the lakes. By the time Wilkinson set out to discover "the sublime in Nature," he could expect a reader sympathetic to his feeling that mountains were "amongst the finest specimens of the sublime" and "the most stupendous specimens of Almighty Power that we see around us."[37] As such, they were a worthwhile fasci-nation for lovers of the natural world and national heritage: "*Mountains* are my flower-garden, or my museum," Wilkinson wrote, "and they exhibit the oldest and most magnificent specimens of pristine grandeur."[38]

Yet the maps of Scafell from the crucial century in the Lake District's emergence as a tourist destination (1750–1850) reveal how long it took for mountains gener-ally, and Scafell in particular, to be appreciated as a significant aspect of the region's cultural ecology. In early maps of the western Lakes, Scafell often appeared as a blank space, and maps that did offer topographical representations were frequently experimental. C. Smith and William Hutchinson (Figures 6.4 and 6.5) both depict mountains using the precursor to contour lines: shading. Hutchinson's map sug-gests something of the massif's broad base, but it, and the disproportionately wide Screes beside it, feature as mostly white space. Indeed, the Screes appear as a dis-tinct adjacent feature, rather than as part of the mountainside. The shading does

Figure 6.4. Scafell, detail from C. Smith, *New Map of Great Britain and Ireland* (1806). Source: The British Library, www.bl.uk and visionofbritain.org.uk. Image licensed under Creative Commons (CC BY-SA 4.0).

little to indicate that Scafell is higher than any of the surrounding mountains. Smith's map has the opposite problem; whilst its more dense shading does suggest height, Scafell appears very small, and to be located some distance from Wastwater. These maps both demonstrate the pitfalls of mapmaking in regions that were not, yet, very well known.

What these maps strive, and ultimately fail, to represent is the lived experience of moving through the complex topographies of the Lake District. Several early Lakeland maps experimented with different perspectives to try to encapsulate more clearly the relationship between human and mountain. Hutchinson offered an alternative map of the mountains, which attempted to show their heights in ways to which his reader could relate. By drawing them in profile (Figure 6.6), Hutchinson depicted something of the experience of moving through a landscape dominated by verticalities. He indicates the vast size of the mountains by comparing them to miniature depictions of trees and settlements. Although Saddleback and Skiddaw are both included, Helvellyn is missing—and so, too, is Scafell. In fact, the part of the map which Scafell should occupy appears as a blank space labeled, simply, "Desolate and Mountainous."

Hutchinson was not alone in dismissing some of the Lake District's more dramatic upland scenery as unworthy of mapping; in 1751, George Smith had similarly

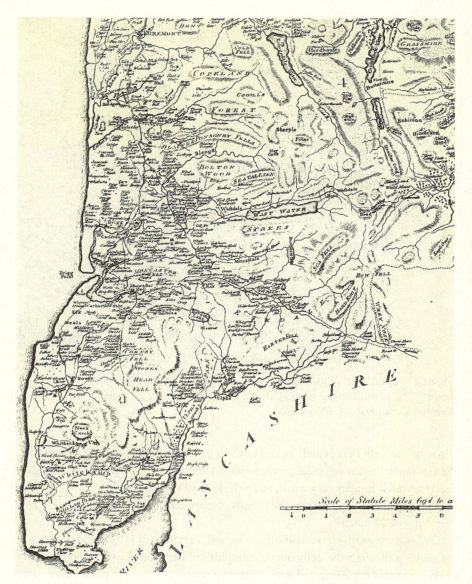

Figure 6.5. Western Lakes, from William Hutchinson, *The History of the County of Cumberland* (Carlisle: F. Jollie, 1794). Source: archive.org (https://archive.org/details/historyofcountyoo1hutc).

described a section of the Western Fells he was uninterested in mapping as "All rocky and pik'd Mountains" (Figure 6.7). Scafell does not feature on his map either, although Styhead Pass—the main route between Wasdale and Ravenglass that cuts between Great Gable and Great End—is noted for its importance to trade routes from the slate and lead mines near Keswick. Not until Jonathan Otley's superb map of the Lake District (Figure 6.8), published in 1818, was there a credible representation of Scafell on paper. The difference was that Otley, "an ingenious

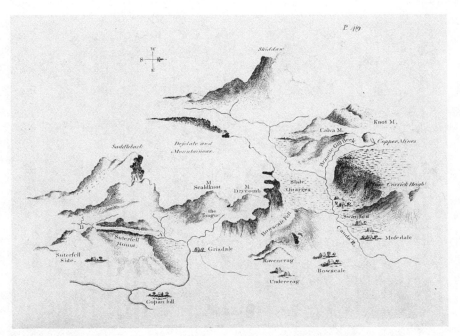

Figure 6.6. Profile map from William Hutchinson, *The History of the County of Cumberland* (Carlisle: F. Jollie, 1794). Source: archive.org (https://archive.org/details/historyofcountyo01hutc).

mechanic of Keswick" as an advertisement for the map in *Blackwood's Edinburgh Magazine* described him, had an "intimate acquaintance" with the mountain;[39] he had repeatedly climbed Scafell and the Pike as part of his mapmaking project. Indeed, an excursion of Otley's up the Pike in 1816 is the earliest recorded recreational ascent of the mountain.

Otley's achievement is even more remarkable because Scafell seemed to both contemporary and later cartographers to actively elude mapping. When Eliza Lynn Linton climbed the mountain in 1864, she noticed that the distance to the massif seemed to be continually shifting: "Great End had slipped away," she wrote, "leaving us to climb an empty sleeve, in which he was only laughing at us."[40] The personified mountain has tricked the travelers into thinking they were upon him, but in fact "there he was as far off as ever, with Scawfell Pike in the distance."[41] As they continued toward Scafell, Lynn Linton recorded how the mountain seemed to change: "Scawfell rose up, and looked bigger and more formidable than ever. As we proceeded he grew, and our work seemed only beginning: all the climbing we have had mere child's play to what was to come. This was his next aspect, still bigger, yet seeming no nearer for his enlargement; and again he became bigger and bigger yet again, till we rose above everything else, and saw only himself before us, more gigantic than ever."[42] How, Lynn Linton's text asks, can a mountain be mapped if its very geographies seem to be constantly shifting? Lynn Linton's answer was to include more personal, quasi-cartographic representations of the experience of ascending

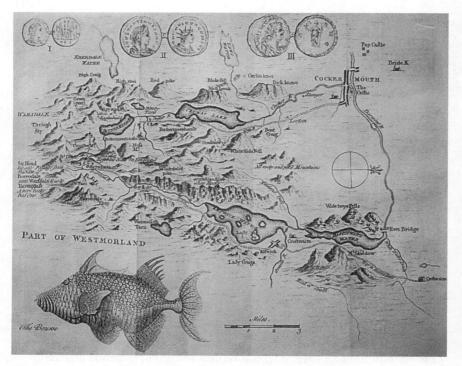

Figure 6.7. George Smith, engraving of "Map of the Black Lead Mines &c. in Cumberland" (London: *The Gentleman's Magazine*, 1 June 1751). By permission of The Wordsworth Trust, Grasmere.

the mountain that anticipate Alfred Wainwright's multimedia representations of the Lakeland peaks. Accompanying Lynn Linton's description are a series of engravings by her husband and traveling companion, William Linton (Figure 6.9). These engravings are deliberately rudimentary, and what Ann C. Colley has written of Ruskin's pedestrian sketches might be equally applied to Linton's; that is, they are attempts to "replicate the various foci of the eye's attention as it guides the body's ascent" in ways that "reflect the anxiety that emanates from there being no stable point of reference, and hurriedly catch a view . . . just before it disappears."[43] Like Lynn Linton's text, they chart Scafell's changing appearance and attempt to capture something slippery, even multiscalar, about experiences of the mountain.

Lynn Linton's account makes clear the very real danger that the mountains might shift, or suddenly be found to have "slipped away" entirely.[44] Even when they finally made it to Scafell, its geography threatened to alter beneath their feet: they climbed "up the corner, through the steep loose screes; digging places for our feet, and afraid at every step of disturbing the stones and bringing down a torrent of slates and boulders upon us."[45] The instability of the mountainside suggests to Lynn Linton a threatening contingency: the mountain may or may not permit them to climb; they may or may not fall down or be knocked off by falling rock; and no map is sufficient to capture a landscape that performs this kind of mobility. Lynn

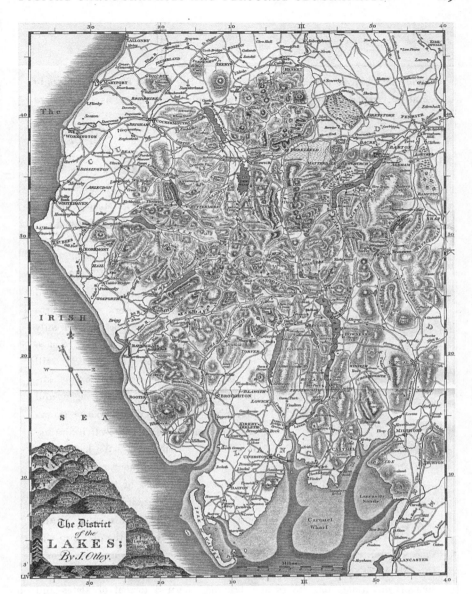

Figure 6.8. Jonathan Otley, *A New Map of the District of the Lakes* (Keswick: Jonathan Otley, 1818). Source: Martin Norgate and Jean Norgate, *Guides to the Lakes* (http://www .lakesguides.co.uk/html/maps/typo401.htm). Reproduced by permission of Jean Norgate.

Linton's fears focus on the mountain's threatening verticality, which might injure the walker in a variety of ways. What appear in Linton's sketches, or on the map that accompanied the guide book, to be solid physical formations are revealed when under the climber's foot to be unstable features that cannot be contained by the cartographer's gaze or pen; they might, Lynn Linton implies, decide to leave at any moment. Even on the ground, Scafell seems to resist cartographic endeavors.

found that while we were toiling on, Great End had slipped away, leaving us to climb an empty sleeve, in which he was only laughing at us; and there he was as far off as ever, with Scawfell Pike in the distance—yet in the distance. To the left again—another steep climb; and to  the right, below us, a pit, bottomless for aught that we could see; but a little farther on, a green platform rose in the midst, with Sty Head Tarn shining like a star upon it, and the great black mountains steeply walling it round. Yet all below us; great as they were, we looked over their tops.

Then a quarter of a mile of scrambling over a sea of rocks—rough as any sea-shore scrambling; only there was no sea-weed to make them slippery, nor growth of any kind till they were crossed; and then  Scawfell rose up, and looked bigger and more formidable than ever. As we proceeded he grew, and our work seemed only beginning: all the climbing we have had mere child's play to what was to  come. This was his next aspect, still bigger, yet seeming no nearer for his enlargement; and again he became bigger and bigger yet again, till we rose above everything else, and saw only himself before us,  more gigantic than ever. We had to get down this steep embankment, over the shale and rocks, to the foot of the Pike itself; but before we went forward we looked down over the tops of the other mountains and saw a lake of gold lying in the grey formless mist beyond them—the lonely lake of Ennerdale. Then up the corner, through the steep loose screes; digging places for our feet, and afraid at every step of disturbing the stones and bringing down a torrent of slates and boulders upon us (it was like going up the corner of a crumbling house

Figure 6.9. Eliza Lynn Linton, *The Lake Country* (Smith, Elder & Co., 1864), 210. Source: Google Books (https://books.google.co.uk/books?id=HYTUB1CF83kC&printsec).

Figure 6.10. Philip James de Louterbourg (1740–1812), *Skiddaw, Cumberland, a Summer Evening with a Stage Coach* (date unknown, but ca.1785). Oil on canvas, 41 × 59.7 cm. Government Art Collection. © Image: Crown Copyright, UK Government Art Collection.

These challenges evidently did not deter everyone. William Wilberforce was one of the earliest travelers into Wasdale; certainly, he is the first to mention the valley in our corpus. Wilberforce visited Wasdale on September 20, 1779, and records that the locals needed no survey to tell them which of the Lakeland mountains was highest; he wrote of Scafell that it was "said by the People thereabouts" to be "higher than Skiddaw."[46] There were other differences, too, not least in artistic representations of the two mountains. Skiddaw, being close to Keswick, was at the heart of the tourist's Lakeland. Ponies, horses, and even carriages could get most of the way up the well-known route; Ann Radcliffe rode up in 1794, though she noted that "the ascents were such, that the horses panted in the slowest walk, and it was necessary to let them rest every six or seven minutes."[47] Philip de Louterbourg's painting of Skiddaw (ca.1785) contributed to the exaggeration of Skiddaw's picturesqueness: the rocks are rounded and softened by the early evening light, and the close perspective on the mountaintop minimizes the viewer's awareness of Skiddaw's height (Figure 6.10). The stagecoach implies that the mountain is easily accessible even for those unwilling or unable to walk up it. Scafell's steep sides, on the other hand, exaggerated the massif's proportions. Frederick Clive Newcombe's painting *The Gates of Borrowdale* (1874) reflected literary as well as artistic trends in depicting Scafell as being archetypally sublime:[48] it appears awe-inspiringly dangerous, and seems to block access into the southwestern Lake District.

Yet Scafell was by no means forbidding to everyone. Indeed, Newcombe's painting indicates as much: on the road to the right of the painting, we see a shepherd guiding his sheep into the fells. Newcombe recognized that, threatening as Scafell seemed to many of the Lake District's visitors, it was an integral part of the Western Lakes' agricultural economy. Shepherds had grazed their sheep on Scafell for hundreds of years. Indeed, the massif's name indicates as much; it originates from the Old Norse elements *skali* (shieling, summer pasture) and *fiall* (hill).[49] Additionally, according to James Plumptre, the ochre used to raddle the sheep was taken from the Screes on Scafell's side.[50] Scafell's sparse population and remoteness from the rest of the Lakes—let alone the rest of the country—established it as a sublime relic of a lost rustic golden age.

For Wilkinson, Scafell offered an "idea of the world before it was peopled."[51] As a result, it seemed to early travelers to preserve something that was almost pre-Lapsarian. When Plumptre visited the valley on his pedestrian tour in 1799—and subsequently published one of the earliest substantial accounts of life in Wasdale—he implored his readers to "put off and forget the dissipated world" before they reached these lesser-known valleys:

> Their difficulty of access has, as yet, secured them from the visits of the great with splendid equipages, and swearer and blasphemer, the gamester and the prodigal with their trains of Envys, Hatreds & Malignancies, are, I hope, as yet strangers to them: the lover of the Works of nature, as a humble pedestrian, will, I hope, alone traverse these delightful regions; should *Sin* overleap the barriers of this little paradise, and teach them vices,—the names of which they would be strangers to but for their prayers to the Almighty to defend them from them,—tremendous will be his account at the last solemn audit: to his own burden of guilt will be added that of every one, whom his wilful or unguarded profligacy has corrupted.[52]

Plumptre does not go quite as far as Wilkinson, for whom the very sheep seemed peculiarly "innocent,"[53] but he does suggest that Wasdale's seclusion has protected it from the greater number of modern vices. The traveler who introduces sin here—even, Plumptre declares in a proto-Ruskinian mode, quicker forms of transport—should be held to account for any destruction of the simple human and physical nature enclosed by the mountains that form the "barriers" around "this little paradise."

Dorothy Wordsworth also thought that the rusticity of Wasdale's inhabitants was protected by—and even echoed in—the valley's geography. Writing to Lady Beaumont after a visit to the area in 1804, Wordsworth declared it to be "exceedingly wild but in entire simplicity." If she had even a "small share" of Sir George Beaumont's artistic talents, she continued, she might capture it "with half a dozen strokes of the pencil."[54] Indeed, Beaumont had made several studies of the kinds of mountain scenery Wordsworth discovered in Wasdale. In his study *Mountainous Landscape with a Lake* (Figure 6.11), for instance, the rocky terrain is foreboding but the sunlight that shines on the mountains indicates a more benign reading of these sublime forms. Plumptre, Wordsworth, and Beaumont were all part of the vanguard that offered reassessments of Scafell in the late eighteenth and early

Figure 6.11. George Beaumont (1753–1827), *Mountainous Landscape with a Lake*. Oil on millboard, 28 × 44.3 cm. New Walk Museum & Art Gallery, Leicester Arts and Museums Service. With permission, Leicester Arts and Museum Service.

nineteenth centuries. Their example would later be taken up, as Jonathan West-away summarizes, by the "liberal middle-classes of the late nineteenth century" who "valued the un-regulated space and the opportunities for maximizing indi-vidual freedoms" in the Lake District's more remote uplands.[55] They anticipated the cultural transformation of Scafell that saw it change from an inaccessible wil-derness to a challenging and exciting hub for adventurous mountaineers.

Climbing Scafell

When Thomas Wilkinson climbed Scafell sometime before 1807—the precise date is uncertain, and his account remained unpublished until 1824—he mused that it had perhaps taken "two millenniums" for any human to walk the same route. Other than the region's shepherds, whose herds of "innocent" sheep he admired as he ascended, he may well have been right: sheep trails were the only well-trodden paths anywhere on the Scafell massif until significantly later in the century. Wilkin-son's exhilaration at seeing the summit of Scafell—it "elevated [his] spirits," he wrote—was still unusual in the early 1800s; more normal was the response of his companion who felt "depressed" by the sight of the mountains looming above them (Wilkinson was not sympathetic to his friend's response, writing "I am not sure that he was quite well").[56] By the early 1820s, though, both Scafell and Scafell Pike had been repeatedly climbed: Samuel Taylor Coleridge, famously, ascended Scafell in August 1802; Jonathan Otley reportedly climbed it in June 1815, and then ascended the Pike with William Green in September 1816;[57] and Dorothy Words-worth's account, revised for her brother's *Guide* (1822), became one of the best-known and most frequently quoted records of climbing the Pike. These exploits ensured that the Scafell massif entered into the list of sights necessary for the more adventurous Lakeland visitor.

This shift was facilitated by a change in the occupations of Wasdale's residents in response to the Lake District's growing tourist numbers and the concurrent popularization of mountaineering activities. The Scafell region offers a distinctive challenge to O'Neill and Fogarty-Valenzuela's claim that "verticality stratifies society one layer atop another."[58] In the city, that might be true, and it is perhaps no coincidence that high-rise living became common in London at the precise moment that rock climbing was becoming a popular sport in the Lake District.[59] But in the mountains, verticality was a social leveler.[60] Thanks to the locals' highly developed knowledge of the dangerous yet alluring mountainside, during the nineteenth century Wasdale developed what we might think of as a knowledge economy; only those who could navigate the mountain safely were welcome, regardless of social class. The shepherds' working knowledge of Scafell led to the development of a parallel industry that opened up the mountain to more adventurous travelers. The regularity of reports of death or injury on Scafell was sufficient to maintain the mountain's reputation as a feat beyond the endurance of the casual tourist. This caution was necessary because, as Samuel Leigh explained, Scafell is "far more difficult of access than Helvellyn or Skiddaw."[61] The result was that the guiding industry flourished rapidly as Wasdale and Scafell's visitor numbers increased. Those who attempted the mountain without a guide were foolhardy at best.

Samuel Taylor Coleridge thought that the sublime simultaneity of excitement and danger was one of Scafell's attractions. He left his home, Greta Hall in Keswick, at half past twelve on August 2, 1802, equipped with a "net Knapsack" containing what he considered to be the essentials for a walking tour of the Lakes: "a Shirt, cravat, 2 pair of Stockings, a little paper & half a dozen Pens, a German Book (Voss's Poems) & a little Tea & Sugar, with my Night Cap, packed up in my natty green oil-skin."[62] Coleridge also removed the kitchen broom from its normal spot and proceeded to de-broom it to use as a walking stick; he "left the Besom scattered on the Kitchen Floor." It is fair to say that he was significantly more pleased about this innovation than was his wife, who he left to clean it up. Coleridge traveled extraordinarily lightly; if we compare his belongings with the "essentials" carried by the volunteer rifleman we met earlier undertaking his own pedestrian tour in the 1860s, we get a sense of how hyperbolically lightly Coleridge packed. The rifleman notes that he had packed carefully, and with a cautious economy so as not to overload himself as he walked the difficult mountain routes. The rifleman took with him two shirts, one night shirt, one pair of shoes, a pair of slippers (for the better lowland paths), six shirt collars, a traveling map, a pocket compass, toilet articles, scissors, needles and thread for the inevitable repairs to his clothing, a penknife, some cord, a pencil and "a small note-book to dot mental impressions upon," along with "a good guide book."[63] Coleridge also packed writing materials—but that he needed six pens, as opposed to the rifleman's single pencil, is revealing about the aims for their respective journeys.

The "circumcursion," as Coleridge called it, was about connecting with a landscape in ways that were both literary and embodied.[64] As Richard Holmes puts it, "Coleridge was in effect inventing a new kind of Romantic tourism, abandoning the coach and the high-road for the hill, the flask and the knapsack."[65] To this end, rather than pack a guidebook, Coleridge took with him a copy of the recently published *Lyrical Poems* by Johann Heinrich Voss (1802), a collection that imagined the speaker's wanderings around his rural north German home. Goethe, reviewing the volume in the same year, described a "level northern landscape" where the poet was found "rejoicing in his existence, in a latitude in which the antients hardly expected to find a living thing."[66] In fact, what Goethe discovers in Voss's poetry of northern Germany is remarkably similar to what Raimonda Modiano finds in Coleridge's account of northern England; that is, a wholeness of vision produced by uniting disparate geographical and imaginative parts.[67]

Coleridge had undertaken walking tours of the Lake District before; in 1799, he had accompanied William Wordsworth on the tour that would result in the Wordsworths moving to Dove Cottage. That tour had focused largely on the corridor between Penrith, Keswick, and Ambleside that, later, became the heart of Wordsworthshire.[68] What Coleridge sought on his circumcursion was, in part, to define an alternative area in the Lakes as Coleridgean, rather than Wordsworthian. Perhaps the best indication of Coleridge's daring—and foolhardiness—was his decision not to employ a guide. Instead, he planned a solitary route that would see him walking 76 miles in a week. In the event, he was gone for nine days and walked 240 miles on a route that took him through the heart of that "desolate and mountainous" region that Hutchinson had identified. As Cooper, Gregory, and Bushell showed on the "Mapping the Lakes" project, Scafell was the "imaginative core" of the journey;[69] Coleridge mentions Scafell more than any other location on his tour (Figure 6.12). They note, too, that "verticality . . . is central to Coleridge's spatialization of the Lake District landscape."[70] The sketches Coleridge took down in his notebook as he walked, as well as the cartographic grammars in his written text, offer experiments in representing phenomenologies of verticality that were central to Coleridge's imaginative and physical experiences. As we now want to explore, playing with how to translate Coleridge's account into a GIS environment can also offer new approaches to analyzing textual geographies in this and other accounts, which seek to communicate something of the embodied feeling of being in the mountains.

Coleridge did not take a proper map with him on his circumcursion. Instead, he copied into his notebook a sketch of a map of the Western section of the Lake District that, according to Kathleen Coburn, was based on Hutchinson's map from his *The History of the County of Cumberland* (1794) (Figure 6.13).[71] There are notable similarities between Coleridge's sketch and Hutchinson's original: the strangely flat coastline, for instance, and the related linearity of the interior landscape, with the inevitable compression that entails, is evident in both Hutchinson's map and Coleridge's copy. Before he set out, Coleridge marked on his sketch the places he initially intended to visit, following in Hutchinson's footsteps, including St. Bees,

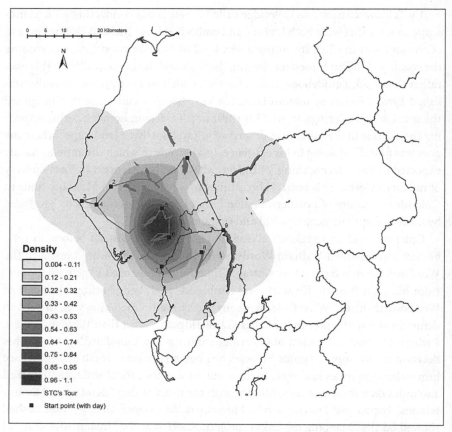

Figure 6.12. Density-smoothed map of locations mentioned in Coleridge's account of his circumcursion. Modified from Cooper and Gregory (2010), 100.

Ravenglass, and Devock. But this sketched map cannot have been of much use in a practical sense; its central focus is the main road leading from St. Bees to the Duddon Bridge near Broughton-in-Furness, and thence to Kendal. Coleridge actually intended on spending very little time on the road: he planned to use it just once, for a brief period "on the South of Melthwaite Side," to the south of Wastwater.[72]

In fact, the region Coleridge was most interested in on his tour appears on his sketch, as on Hutchinson's profile map, as a blank space: the mountains and dales of the western Lakes from Buttermere, down through Wasdale and Eskdale, to Coniston. Coleridge's sketch map anticipates a phenomenological landscape, one that cannot be mapped until the cartographer has experienced it.[73] The blanks, in short, are regions to be explored, and Coleridge is reluctant to reduce them to marks on the page until he has seen them for himself. Coleridge's sketches are evidence of what Harold Baker calls the "sense of liberation" from literary convention;[74] Coleridge finds that words fail in describing his spatial experiences, but his quasi-cartographical sketches communicate a landscape that is phenomenological rather than geographical. In other words, the sketches offer visual clues as to how Coleridge

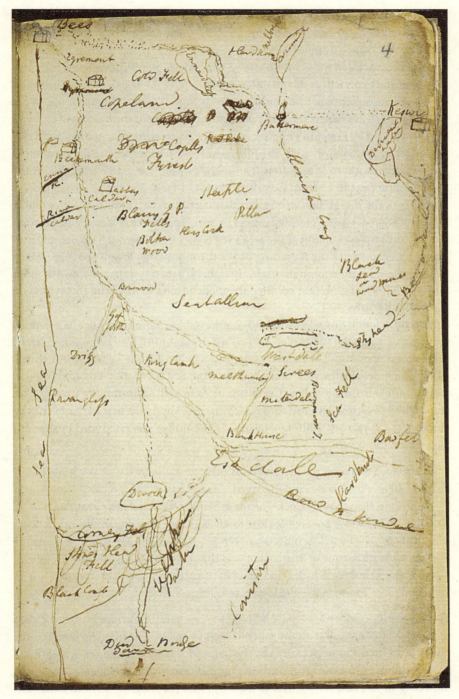

Figure 6.13. Samuel Taylor Coleridge, sketch map adapted from William Hutchinson's *The History of the County of Cumberland* (1794) (Figure 6.5). From *The Notebooks of Samuel Taylor Coleridge*, I.1206. © The British Library Board (47497, f.4r). Reproduced with permission of the British Library Board, 12/4/21.

sees the mountains in relation to himself. As with so many of Coleridge's land-scape descriptions, to understand what he means requires looking from a particular location, and from a unique body.

The sketches fill in the blank spaces on Coleridge's map with personal interpre-tations of the experiences of verticality in these fells. At Wastwater, for instance, he paused to sketch what he could see from Scafell's base (Figure 6.14). What Coleridge portrays here is the sense of enclosure he feels at the bottom of this val-ley, surrounded by England's highest peaks. The mountains—including "Sca' Fell," Great Gable, Yewbarrow, and "The Pike"—surround the lake, and the position of the text in relation to Wastwater demonstrates what the relative heights of the mountains appear to be from Coleridge's point of view. The sketch evidently gets the order of the mountains wrong, but that hardly matters; this is a cartographic representation of what Coleridge thinks he sees. The sketch is also a visualization that explores his conception of the area's verticality by rendering it excessively hor-izontal; it exaggerates the flattening out of the mountains to suit the map. When Coleridge got up the mountain itself, though, he began to experiment with other forms of representation that revealed the inadequacies of mapping this region on a horizontal plane.

Coleridge found himself less able to compress these mountains once he ascended up into them; in fact, they seemed to crowd around him. Coleridge summarized the opinion of many a Lakeland traveler when he wrote that "of all earthly things which I have beheld, the view of Sca'fell and from Sca'fell (both views from it's [sic] own summit) is the most heart-exciting."[75] At Scafell's summit, he used a "nice stone table" to write a letter to Sara Hutchinson—"surely the first Letter ever writ-ten from the Top of Sca' Fell!" he exclaimed.[76] Coleridge was astounded by the view from the summit:

> O my God! what enormous Mountains these are close by me, & yet below the
> Hill I stand on / Great Gavel, Kirk Fell, Green Crag, & behind the Pillar, then
> the Steeple, then the Hay Cock—on the other side & behind me, Great End, Esk
> Carse [Esk Hawse], Bow-fell & close to my back two huge Pyramids, nearly as
> high as Sca' Fell itself, & indeed parts of Sca' Fell known far & near by these
> names, the hither one of Broad Crag, and the next to it but divided from it by a
> low Ridge Doe Crag, which is indeed of itself a great Mountain of stones from a
> pound to 20 Ton weight embedded in woolly Moss.[77]

There is a conflicted sense of space here: on the one hand, Coleridge is overwhelmed by how far he can see, but on the other he feels closed in. The frequent, and erratic, punctuation marks—especially the dashes and slashes—make for a breathless account. It mimics in text the kinds of physical response Coleridge was having to the vertiginous prospect, as well as the ways that these peaks seem to close him in—and not in the comforting way experienced by Wordsworth in "Home at Gras-mere." These mountains, looming "close to [his] back" and surrounding him on all sides, seem to trap him in a way that is almost threatening. This nightmarish sense of entrapment is heightened if we read this account alongside a ground-level

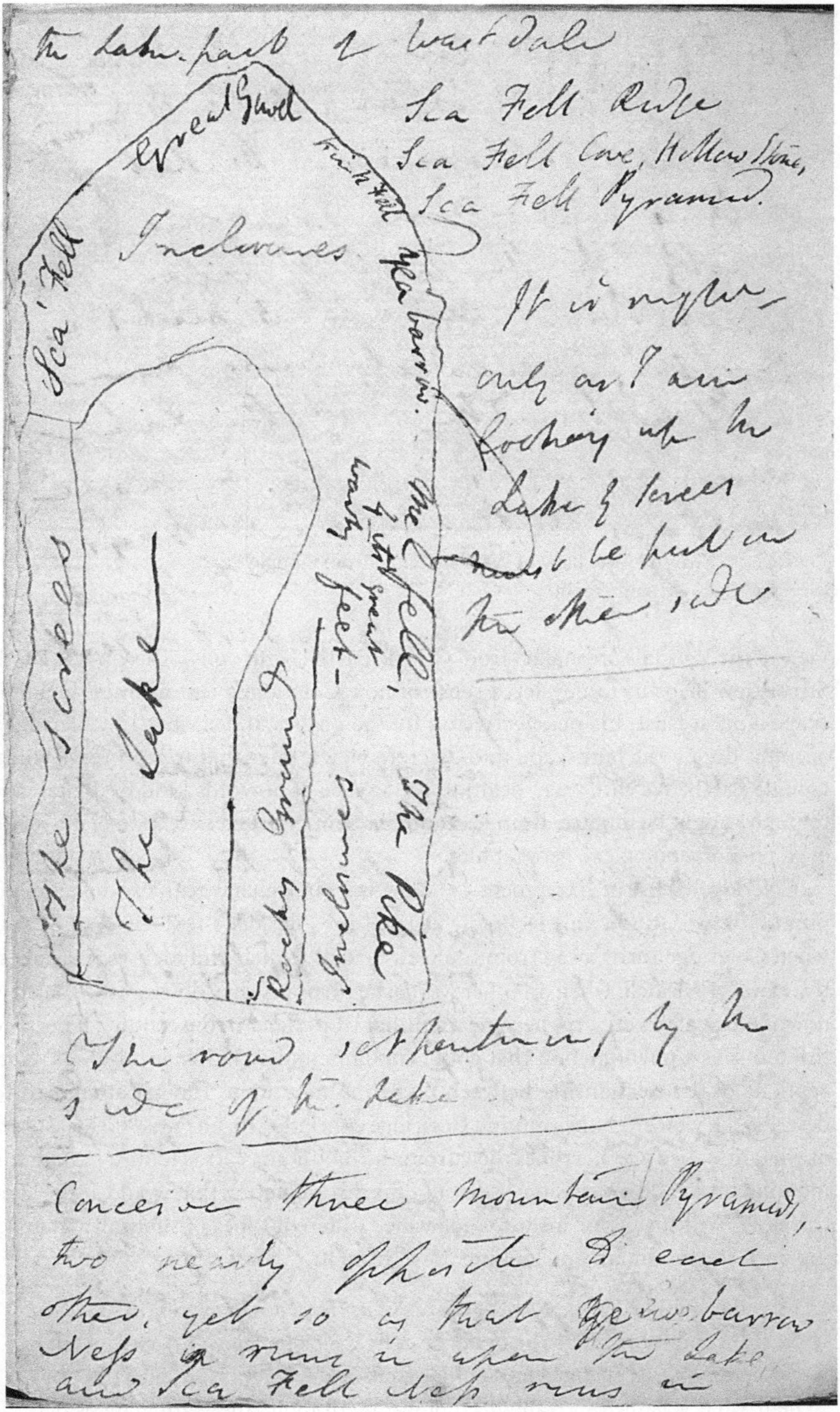

Figure 6.14. Samuel Taylor Coleridge, sketch map of Wastwater. From *The Notebooks of Samuel Taylor Coleridge*, I.1213. British Library. © The British Library Board (47497, f.11v). Reproduced with permission of the British Library Board, 12/4/21.

Figure 6.15. Ground level view of Wasdale taken from Google Earth.
(See: www.google.com/earth.)

view of the Wasdale area taken from Google Earth (Figure 6.15). The Google Earth StreetView helps us to develop a sense of how Coleridge's text mimics the landscape—or, at least, his perspective on it. The dashes and slashes in Coleridge's account divide the landscape into discrete views, ones that we can replicate in Google Earth. We can, then, begin to get a sense of how this kind of digital cartography might facilitate new understandings about the text's creation of personal, even phenomenological, geographies.

Coleridge's sense of entrapment—and the ways in which we can use digital mapping to draw out how this feeling is enacted in Coleridge's text—is even clearer when Coleridge turns away from the view "from" Scafell and focuses instead on the view "of" Scafell: when, in other words, he turns his gaze downward. The view down into Scafell's crevices became a familiar trope; later in the century, it became infamous as a phenomenon that could fundamentally challenge climbers' conceptions of the relationship between body and mountain. Having attempted to describe the view from the summit, Coleridge concluded that he was "no measurer" of what he called the "terrible" view from the mountain.[78] This failure to map the mountain is a mild expression of the sublime disorientation that would afflict later travelers. Wilkinson, for instance, identified different types of sublimity in looking up at the mountain and looking down from it:

> I should have liked to explore the terrors of its tremendous precipices: but these fearful exhibitions would be better seen by me from below; my terrors are in precipices and perpendiculars. Looking from below, we only lose of terrific grandeur what is gained in tranquil, sublime admiration. There are many fearful and majestic forms amid these mountains yet unexplored by me: perhaps I may some time ascend to favourable points, and I treat myself with a sight of their solitary magnificence.[79]

Wilkinson recognizes two forms of the sublime. The view from the base of the mountain had offered sublimity combined with tranquility, but the view from the summit was different. Looking down, the climber can only focus on those "tremendous precipices," which seem to isolate the mountain—and the traveler—from the rest of the landscape. This was not simply a Burkean sublime that thrived on the threat of danger: the risk, standing on the edge of one of Scafell's gullies, was very real.[80]

More than that, though, looking down at the mountain challenged the dichotomy between earth and sky in ways that could have serious consequences for the climber's sense of space. From the summit of Scafell, the very foundations of natural vertical orders seemed to be disrupted. This feeling could disorient even the experienced climber, and one of the sources of sublimity from Scafell's summit was the fact that this vantage point challenged the mountaineer's fundamental understanding of their relationship to the earth. C. N. Williamson, in what Westaway recognizes as "the first climbing guide to the region,"[81] offered an incisive account of this sensation in a piece titled "The Climbs of the English Lake District" for the magazine *All the Year Round* (edited by Charles Dickens Jr.) in 1884: "A sudden seizure akin to sea-sickness may assail the cragsman who has not his nerves under thorough control. All who have been on the top of Scafell, near Mickledore, must have looked down with wonder and admiration into Deep Ghyll, that vast, almost vertical funnel, which descends from the top of the mountain to the Lord's Rake."[82] Tim Ingold might see this as a moment of sudden realization that Williamson lives "in" the earth, not on it. Ingold argues that "to feel the air and walk on the ground is not to make external, tactile contact with our surroundings but to mingle with them."[83] Williamson discovers precisely such a "mingl[ing]" of himself with sky and earth on the summit of Scafell, but the effect is disorienting. In fact, what Williamson describes here is vertigo. From the summit, the body seemed to attempt to flatten out the landscape; vertigo became a symptom of the body's ingrained inclination to impose human cartographic order on the mountain. Vertigo challenges distinctions between the surface and the sky; the sky seemed to be above the climber and below them, in the mountain's gullies and precipices. In an age before aerial travel particularly, this was a sensation for which there was little precedent. For Williamson, the feeling seemed to destabilize the very ground; he describes a "seizure akin to sea-sickness" that indicates the way that the sudden drop into Deep Ghyll challenged his confidence in the earth's stability. Like Eliza Lynn Linton twenty years previously, Williamson discovered that any form of cartographic engagement with Scafell—whether that meant mapping it or climbing it—depended on the connection between the individual's body and the mountain.

Coleridge's account describes a similar realization. Yet Coleridge did attempt to "measure" the mountains using the only frame of reference he had at his disposal: his own body. Coleridge decided to take the most direct route down from the summit, down the cliff face known as Broad Stand and Fat Man's Gully. As Bainbridge has shown about William Wordsworth's response to Black Comb, Coleridge found that attempts to "impose a cartographic understanding on the mountain [met] with failure."[84] Recalling the experience in his letter to Sara Hutchinson, Coleridge described his attempts to measure his descent:

> the first place I came to, that was not direct Rock, I slipped down, & went on for a while with tolerable ease—but now I came (it was midway down) to a smooth perpendicular Rock about 7 feet high—this was nothing—I put my Hands on the Ledge, & dropped down / in another few yards came just such another / I *dropped* that too / and yet another, seemed not higher . . . the next 3 drops were not half a Foot, at least not a foot more than my own height / but every Drop increased the Palsy of my Limbs—I shook all over, Heaven knows without the least influence of Fear / and now I had only two more to drop down / to return was impossible.[85]

Alan Vardy notes that we get a sense in this letter of Coleridge's "giddiness"; this bodily fragility creates an alternative form of sublime that is at odds with how we usually understand that aesthetic.[86] But the sense of vertigo Coleridge implies here does something important for his conception of the relationship between himself and the landscape. This climb developed in Coleridge what Westaway calls "a highly embodied understanding of topography," and this personal version of the mountain's form is evident in the text.[87] As in his description of the view from the top of Scafell, these punctuation marks become an alternative "visual grammar" for the rocks.[88] The dashes and slashes here mimic his physical movements: each of these grammatical marks stands in for the narrow ledge onto which Coleridge lowers himself. The climb forces Coleridge to stretch his muscles and push his limbs to their utmost. He finds himself unable to measure the mountain, but in that failure he realizes that the mountain seems to have measured *him*—and found him wanting.

Once he had reached the bottom of Broad Stand, Coleridge continued on his journey overwhelmed by a sense of relief that he had completed a dangerous climb safely. Reaching the glacial depression at Hollow Stones, Coleridge welcomed the sense of enclosure that offered a sharp distinction from the overexposure he had felt on Broad Stand. In his notebook, he recorded the sense of being contained by the mountain:

> Just by the hollow stones are two enormous Columns / I am no measurer—they were vaster than any that I have ever seen, & were each a stone Mountain / they could not be less than 250 yards high / for they reached halfway, or more, down into the vale / The whole Head of Scafell, & its Bowfell & Eskdale Head & Side bare Stone, in many places more than perpendicular / Came to a waterfall, down a slope of Rock just 80 yards steep / not far from perpendicular / below this is a succession of Falls, some more sloping than others, to the number of 8—nearly at the bottom of the Hill, you may stand so as to command 5 of them <with Δ looking in over above.[89]

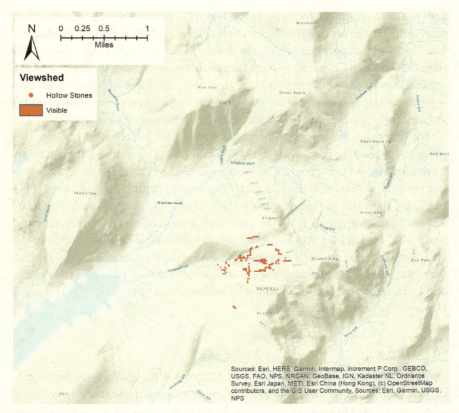

Figure 6.16. Viewshed analysis from Hollow Stones, a glacial depression on the side of Scafell. Only pixels shaded orange are visible from this location.

Coleridge tries to map his sense of enclosure; when words fail him, he attempts to draw what he can see. Moreover, Coleridge's punctuation marks once again offer a form of phenomenological cartography that maps out a personal perspective of the mountain.

A viewshed analysis from Hollow Stones offers a guide to reading the text's mimicry of the landscape's physical geography. A viewshed is created by using the values on a raster surface (see chapter 1) to create a three-dimensional model of the area's terrain, known as a digital terrain model (DTM). A viewshed analysis, using a DTM of the Lakes region, allows us to calculate where a person standing at Hollow Stones should be able to see. These calculations take the curvature of the earth into account, but they represent an optimum visibility that is uncontaminated by air pollution or unobstructed by inclement weather—though that hardly matters in this case. As Figure 6.16 indicates, the view from Hollow Stones is restricted to the very narrow enclosure that this glacial depression creates. Using this viewshed as an analytical guide for the text as well as the terrain reveals how Coleridge tried to capture something of the physical landscape in his written descriptions of it. Coleridge's slashes enclose the clauses in a way that reflects his sense of imprisonment by those immeasurable columns. Like the mountain's slopes, the slashes are hyperbolically vertical; they are "more than perpendicular" and "not far from perpendicular." The slashes stand in place of the columns and cliffs that seem, to Coleridge, to form the mountainside. In short, these grammatical marks map that sense of verticality onto the page more effectively than contemporary maps seemed able to. The viewshed map, meanwhile, emphasizes the degree to which Coleridge's grammar mimics the mountain's topography.

For Coleridge, as for many others after him, Scafell offered an extraordinarily powerful adrenaline rush wherein the physical effects of climbing the mountain were transformed into imaginative—even spiritual—effects. This was because of one obvious, yet easily overlooked, fact: that, in an age unfamiliar with aerial photography, high-rise buildings, or air travel (although the hot air balloon had already begun to remedy this), the view from a mountain as high as Scafell or— better yet—Scafell Pike was extraordinary. Whether looking down into the massif's fearful chasms, or out across the expansive prospect that a clear day afforded, there was something sublimely invigorating about the views from Scafell's peaks, and Coleridge was by no means the only author to attempt to re-create that experience in the forms of his writing.

The View from the Top

Simon Bainbridge rightly notes that it is difficult for the modern reader to comprehend what "the sensations of altitude" must have been like when recreational climbing was still in its infancy.[90] On a clear day, it is possible to see from Scafell to Snowdonia in one direction and the Cairngorms in the other, and from the Yorkshire Dales across to the Isle of Man over the Irish Sea. However, this kind of perfect visibility certainly is not experienced by many of Scafell's climbers. Charles Mackay's complaint that the limited view on one of Scafell's frequent cloudy or rainy days did not "warrant the ascent of Scawfell" must have been echoed many times.[91] But for some, who ascended on the kind of clear day needed to see across these vast distances, the view could seem literally breathtaking.

Thomas Wilkinson captures how exhilarating beholding a view from this altitude for the first time really was; as he ascended, he recorded his excitement as "the sea began to appear in the south-west," and the "stately assemblage of mountains" which, he writes in similar terms to Coleridge, seemed to "[crowd] the western hemisphere." From the summit, he looked "down on Langdale Pikes, the Man Mountain of Coniston, and others of [his] old acquaintances."[92] He slipped into a present tense that communicates the immediacy of his experience, and transports the reader to the summit with him: "I am alone on the mountains, and there is nothing but majesty and innocence around me."[93] Yet this scene also appeared peculiarly domestic to Wilkinson: "How delightful to look round and meditate on these serene regions—the loftiest mountains our next neighbours, and the valleys their gardens and domains!"[94] Wilkinson imagines the Lakeland mountains as a suburban community. More than that, he positions himself as part of it: the "our" to which he refers is himself and Scafell. Both man and mountain become, for a moment at least, masters and protectors of all they survey. Ron Broglio aligns this kind of colonial desire for possession with the picturesque; he claims that "both surveyor and tourist map the land with a sense of possessing it."[95] On a clear day, Scafell was the best place to attempt this form of possession; from its summit the traveler could command the most extensive view in the country.

Dorothy Wordsworth discovered a similar mix of sublimity and serenity when she climbed Scafell Pike on October 7, 1818—though notably without that desire for conquest. She undertook this pioneering ascent—one of the earliest accounts of the feat, and the earliest surviving account by a woman—with her friend Mary Barker. Barker was "an unmarried Lady" who lived at a house she had built in Rosthwaite, dubbed "Barker's Folly" by Robert Southey on account of it being erected foolishly close to the river.[96] Wordsworth reported that Barker had been "bewitched with the charms of the rocks, & streams, & Mountains, belonging to that secluded spot," and had "there built herself a house." Barker occupied herself with painting, music, reading, and in becoming an "active Climber of the hills."[97]

Wordsworth recorded the ascent of Scafell in a letter written to William Johnson, Grasmere's former curate (the fair copy is now at the Wordsworth Trust, and it is from this source that we quote here). Her letter was composed as a retrospective reflection on the adventure of climbing several of England's highest peaks on the same day. Fortunately, since only part of the original letter survives, the account was considered by Dorothy's friends and family to be of sufficient literary merit to be transcribed into a fair copy, and revised for inclusion, without attribution, in William Wordsworth's *Guide to the District of the Lakes* from the second edition in 1822 onward. This meant that many of the people who followed in the *Guide*'s footsteps believed that it was William who they were emulating, not Dorothy (in fact, William has left no record of ever climbing Scafell or the Pike). And it was hugely influential on Scafell Pike's introduction into the walker's canon; over thirty years later, Harriet Martineau still believed that, for a description of the view, the stranger could do no better than "to copy portions of that 'Letter to a friend' which Mr. Wordsworth published many years ago, and which is the best account we have of the greatest mountain excursion in England."[98] Her vagueness as to who wrote the account—"Mr. Wordsworth" here is merely the publisher—indicates that Martineau may, perhaps, have known who the author was; she was intimate with the Wordsworth household after she moved to Ambleside in the 1840s.

Wordsworth's letter remarks on phenomena seen for the first time using, as Mary Ellen Bellanca has written of Wordsworth's account of the Scottish tour, "a nature diary convention marking acquisition of new knowledge with wonder or surprise."[99] It is a document that reveals an extraordinary sensitivity not only to both close and distant aspects of the landscape but to the contingencies imposed on summit views by personal perspective. Wordsworth and Barker had not intended to climb Scafell Pike; their original plan was to go only as far as Esk Hause, from which Barker promised a "magnificent prospect."[100] They traveled by cart from Rosthwaite to Seathwaite, where they acquired a guide, and set off up the

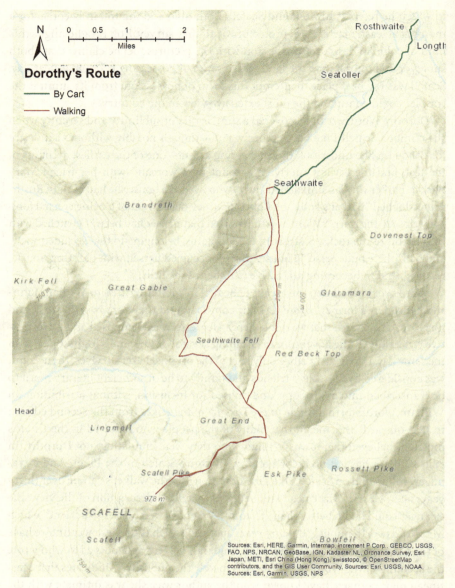

Figure 6.17. Dorothy Wordsworth's route up Scafell Pike, October 7, 1818, combining data from her letter with the Lake District National Park's Digital Public Rights of Way dataset (2018).

fell feeling refreshed by the autumn air and "the sweet warmth of the unclouded sun." An approximation of their route is represented in Figure 6.17, using open-access data about public footpaths from the Lake District National Park Authority (2018); the route up Esk Hause and Scafell has barely altered since Wordsworth and Barker undertook their climb, thanks in large part to readers reinscribing the route in their footsteps. When they reached the summit of Esk Hause, Wordsworth was not dis-

Figure 6.18. John Constable (1776–1837), "Eskhause, Scawfell" (1806). Watercolor on paper, 12.9 × 27.4 cm. © Leeds Museums and Galleries / Bridgeman Images. Used with permission.

appointed with the view. Feeling grateful for "that vigour of body, which enabled [her] to climb the high mountain, as in the days of [her] youth," Wordsworth recorded her exhilaration as she looked out across the region: "Three views, each distinct in its kind, we saw at once—the Vale of Borrowdale, of Keswick, of Bassenthwaite Skiddaw, Saddleback, Helvellyn, numerous other Mountains, and; still beyond; the Solway Firth, and the Mountains of Scotland. Nearer to us on the other side, and below us were the Langdale Pikes—their own vale below *them*, Windermere and, far beyond Windermere, after a long long distance we saw Ingleborough in Yorkshire."[101] As we saw with Coleridge's account—which Wordsworth had certainly read, and which she recalled on the spot by writing a (now lost) letter to Sara Hutchinson from the summit of the Pike—Wordsworth's sentences mimic the visual leaps from mountain to valley; the frequent commas each register movement onto a new feature.

That attempt to re-create the landscape's topography in her own textual geographies is emphasized when Wordsworth describes what she saw as she turned to look out across Wasdale. Her viewpoint emphasized a contrast between Eskdale's green fertility and Wasdale's dark sublimity:

> But how shall I speak of the peculiar deliciousness of the third prospect! At this time that was the most favoured by sunshine & shade. The green Vale of Esk deep & green, with its glittering serpent stream was below us; and on we looked to the Mountains near the sea—Black Coombe and others and still beyond to the sea itself in dazzling brightness. Turning round we saw the Mountains of Wasdale in tumult; and Great Gavel, though the middle of the Mountain, was to us as its base, looked very grand."[102]

This description is evidence of what Maria Jane Jewsbury called Wordsworth's "embodied spell";[103] she captures here a moment of personal, embodied landscaping. This is the same view that John Constable recorded in his painting "Eskhause, Scawfell" (1806) (Figure 6.18). Constable captures the mountains in precisely such a "tumult" as Wordsworth records; indeed, as Suzanne Stewart has shown, this was not the only occasion when Wordsworth's and Constable's interpretations of landscape would overlap (unwittingly, since the two never met).[104] The "tumult" that Constable depicts is reflected in Wordsworth's grammar; the long sentence, broken up by commas and dashes, mimics the quick, glancing motion of the eye as it trips over the mountains that crowd in around her. Stewart notices the almost painterly attention Wordsworth pays to the qualities of light in her writing,[105] and in this letter Wordsworth observes the difference that the passing of time makes to the view; as the sun moves across the sky, the interplays of light and shade alter and have the potential to change the prospect radically. It was further evidence of the massif's exhilarating contingency.

Helen Boden has commented of Wordsworth's alpine climbs that seeing the mountains seems to have physically invigorated her, and the same thing happened on the Scafell excursion.[106] Notwithstanding the miles they had already walked that day, gazing out to Great Gavel she and Barker agreed to attempt an ascent of Scafell. They had climbed so high in any case that, Wordsworth thought, they already seemed to be "three parts up that Mountain." Although the distance turned out to be "greater than it had appeared," Wordsworth wrote that still their "courage did not fail."[107] On reaching the base, however, the climbers discovered that the mountain at this point is too steep to attempt. They changed course slightly, and began to ascend Scafell Pike instead.

By the time Wordsworth wrote the letter some days later, she had discovered that "the Measurers of Mountains" (by which she meant Joseph Banks and his surveyors) estimated the Pike to be the higher summit, but that was not Wordsworth and Barker's motivation for making the climb. It was to gain a new perspective on that magnificent prospect: "The Vales before described lay in view; and, side by side with Eskdale, we now saw the sister Vale of Donnerdale terminated by the Duddon Sands: But the majesty of the Mountains below us, & close to us is not to be conceived. We now beheld the whole Mass of Great Gavel [sic] from its base, the Den of Wasdale at our feet, the Gulph immeasureable—Grassmire [sic], & the other mountains of Crummock, Ennerdale & its mountains; and the Sea beyond."[108] Bainbridge observes that Wordsworth here "identifies a visual sensation available to only the very few who reach that remote spot."[109] From the top of Scafell Pike, Wordsworth recaptures that sense of fragmented unity she had expressed from Esk Hawse: her new, higher viewpoint allows her to see with even more clarity the connections between the disparate elements of the landscape. And, just as we witnessed with Coleridge and the viewshed from Hollow Stones, those connections between parts of the landscape, and between landscape and text, become clearer when we read Dorothy's letter alongside the viewshed analysis from Scafell Pike (Figure 6.19). The viewshed makes clear that the view is not experienced as one continuous landscape, and Wordsworth's grammar replicates that sense of fragmentation. A colon indicates the termination of Donnerdale by the Duddon Sands, but

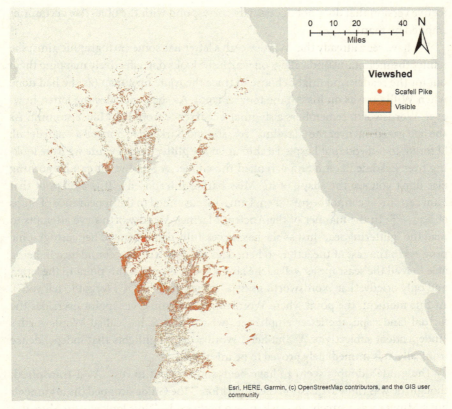

Figure 6.19. Viewshed analysis from Scafell Pike. Orange pixels are land areas that are visible from Scafell Pike. Note that the sea is not included in the analysis.

it allows, too, for a connection between the estuary and the "Mountains below us." From this vantage point, the Wasdale mountains seem to belong in a group of their own; the full stop separates the Scafells from the Crummock mountains. The dash, meanwhile, mimics the "Gulph immeasurable" that seems to separate the Pike from Wasdale. Wordsworth's grammar re-maps the mountain, and the view from it, in line with her personal experience of the geography.

Yet the certainties Wordsworth implies in her letter are quickly undercut when she sees in practice the very different interpretations two walkers could reach about the same view. Her account manipulates the objective, mappable elements she identifies as part of a textual construction of a phenomenological account. Her grammar reconstructs the picturesque frame created on the spot by her concentrated gaze, with the result that, as Denys Van Renen writes of the Scottish tour, Wordsworth is led toward "the potential for radical revelation (unconcealedness) of her surroundings."[110] Wordsworth's "radical revelation" from Scafell Pike is twofold. First, it recognizes her role in a picturesque ecology that, from this vantage point, evidently operates on a massive scale—but which is underpinned by small details. Second, it acknowledges that each account of the mountain relates a subjective version that does not necessarily correspond with the objective certainties implied by maps.

We have seen already that Wordsworth's letter has some cartographic aims; she names the mountains and valleys on which she looks out; effectively mapping them out for the reader who might choose to trace the route on a map (as she had done when William was on his Alpine tour in 1790). As she concludes the letter, however, Wordsworth remembers a singular occurrence from Esk Hause summit. As she had gazed out over the "dazzling" sea, she and Barker had noticed a small detail: "I forgot to tell you that I espied a ship upon the glittering sea while we were look-ing over Eskdale, 'Is it a Ship?' replied the Guide. 'A Ship! yes it can be nothing else don't you see the shape of it?' Miss Barker interposed—'It is a Ship, of that I am certain—I cannot be mistaken, I am so accustomed to the appearance of Ships at Sea—'"[111] In the manner of the Ancient Mariner, Wordsworth's eye attempts to read the "glittering sea." Just as she has successfully demonstrated her cartographic prowess in the rest of the letter, so here does she proclaim her confidence in being able to read the seascape as well as the landscape. It is only at this point in the letter, and only briefly, that Wordsworth uses "I" rather than "we" ("*I* forgot to tell you"). At this moment, the point where Wordsworth's personal viewpoint overrides the factual landscape, the letter emphasizes what Bellanca has called Wordsworth's "independent subjectivity."[112] But here, Wordsworth highlights that independence ironically; it is immediately proved to be misguided.

The guide's doubts seem to have been soundly put to rest. As it transpired, though, he was right to question the apparition: "The Guide dropped the argument; but a Minute was scarcely gone when he quietly said—'Now look at your Ship, it is now a horse'—So indeed it was, with a gallant neck and head—We laughed heart-ily, and I hope when I am again inclined to positiveness I may remember the Ship and the horse upon the glittering Sea; and the calm confidence, yet submission of our wise man of the mountains; who certainly had more knowledge of *Clouds* than we, whatever might be our knowledge of Ships."[113] The Guide's detailed knowledge of the local weather enables him to closely read details at a distance. It is a knowl-edge that neither Wordsworth nor Barker possesses. The passage mocks the car-tographic certainties on display in the rest of the letter. The ship-cloud challenges Wordsworth's faith in positivism—and rightly so, for this experience indicates the extent to which objective geographical knowledge relies on the viewer's per-ceptions. Wordsworth learns to mistrust her faith in certainties. Instead, she highlights a "new form" of reading the landscape that allows for—even thrives on—a contingency that produces a textual cartography that is also a form of phe-nomenological geography. As we have indicated throughout this book, and as the accounts on which we have focused in this chapter have especially intimated, similar reservations should inform our readings of digital maps.

This need for caution is even clearer when Wordsworth turns her gaze down-ward. Unlike Coleridge or Williamson, Wordsworth is not interested in the sub-lime depths of the mountain's fissures; instead, she is captivated by the beauties uncovered in a careful reading of the mountaintop. Digital maps share with the analog versions with which Wordsworth was familiar the problem that they are designed to represent a distant view of the terrain that enables navigation at the expense of a detailed account of the nuances of a place's character. That, of course, is where a deep map comes in, and, once Wordsworth has sufficiently described the distant prospect, she switches focus toward a deeper account of the spot on which she stands. In doing so, Wordsworth achieves in this letter what Rachel Feder has suggested she does in her other writing: she "produces a discursive field" that "activate[s] poetic experiments and invent[s] new forms of reading."[114]

Wordsworth's letter about the Scafell Pike walk effects a multiscalar viewshed: in one moment, she offers a reading of the landscape that literally and figuratively explores distance by both describing a landscape that stretches out for miles from the summits on which she stands, and offers a distant reading of it that highlights connections between its various elements. In the next, when she looks down, Wordsworth realizes that the summit itself deserves more sustained attention. Beauty, she realizes, could be found clinging to the rocks if one looked closely enough:

> I ought to have described the last part of our ascent to Scaw Fell pike. There, not a blade of grass was to be seen—hardly a cushion of moss, & that was parched & brown; and only growing rarely between the huge blocks & stones which cover the summit & lie in heaps all round to a great distance, like Skeletons or bones of the earth not wanted at the creation, & here left to be covered with never-dying lichens, which the Clouds and dews nourish; and adorn with colors of the most vivid and exquisite beauty, and endless in variety.[115]

Black's Shilling Guide—unaware of this account's prepublication history—considers this passage to be evidence of William Wordsworth's "usual poetic feeling."[116] What it actually communicates is Dorothy Wordsworth's "climber's eye view,"[117] which she employs to focus on the summit's own beauties rather than only on the view from it. The mountain seems to be a site at which a forgotten part of the creation myth might be discovered; for Wordsworth, this might be a Gothic cemetery, or maybe a celestial dumping ground. But when she looks closely, Wordsworth discovers "never-dying lichens" being nourished by their sheer proximity to the clouds. This was a point that later writers borrowed; Jonathan Otley, for instance, also noticed that "here the *lichen geographicus* appears in peculiar beauty."[118] It was an appropriate observation for these map-minded authors; this particular species is commonly known as the "map lichen." Even nature seemed to be conspiring in attempts to map the mountain.

Allusions like Otley's indicate the success Wordsworth had in promoting an alternative way of reading the mountain that valued detail as well as distance. While this narrative did not exert the same kind of imaginative grip as the view from the summit, it nevertheless had some important consequences for later engagements with Scafell and the Pike. Their close readings of the mountain depended on a different kind of attention to verticality that acknowledged its power on small scales as well as grand ones. Wordsworth's and Otley's references to the beauty of the lichens anticipates a mode of reading the mountain that would be crucial for one later group of visitors to it: rock-climbers. By 1884—comfortably less than a century after Thomas Wilkinson's assumption that no one had climbed Scafell in millennia—C. N. Williamson could confidently declare that there were too many routes up Scafell to describe in a few column inches: "the cragsman," and, as Wordsworth had shown, "cragswoman," "could well spend a fortnight in clambering about the mountain, and even then its climbs would not be exhausted."[119] This was a dramatic change from Scafell's reputation as a barren wasteland. Now, the rock faces that seemed bare from a distance were found to be intersected with cracks, crevices, and holds, overlaid with rare lichens and mosses, which transformed the mountainside into a text that required careful haptic reading. Once the climber started looking upward or downward, rather than outward, their relationship to the mountain changed.

In this chapter, we have shown how digital maps can be read alongside written texts to develop geographical and topographical close readings of a written work. More than that, we have revealed that digital cartographies continue to negotiate the same issues as have beset cartographers for centuries. They continue to experiment with ways of representing verticality and of capturing subjective experiences of specific locations. Reading visualizations created in GIS or virtual globes alongside, and in light of, written texts offers a new dimension through which to understand these cartographies. Like historical maps, these new forms of geovisualization can be reinterpreted in more meaningful ways by applying experiences described in historical accounts. At the same time, reading the texts in light of those maps unveils new ways of understanding written creations of phenomenological geographies. It becomes clear that the text's grammars offer re-mappings of the physical landscape in ways that re-create the author's experience of them. In these ways, digital maps have the potential to become powerful tools for close reading of written works.

Conclusion

THE FUTURE OF DEEP MAPPING

We began this book by arguing that digital humanities research moves through three phases. First, the datasets and computational techniques are developed. Second is the exploratory research, which tends to be driven by the desire to test what can be done using the data set, the technique, or both. The problem with this phase, though, is that it puts the digital first, and the humanities second. In the third phase, this prioritization needs to be switched around, so that the humanities are brought to the fore, and the digital becomes the means to an end. This third phase is inspired by humanities research questions that seek to make a contribution to humanistic knowledge, including for researchers who may have little or no interest in the digital approaches used.

That is what we aimed to achieve here. Chapter 2 uses eighteenth- and nineteenth-century theories of the picturesque as a lens through which to critique the digital methodologies we employ. Chapters 3, 4, and 5 demonstrate the Lake District's various and multifarious cultural geographies by revealing how different parts of the region were associated with different kinds of people, activity, and practice. For instance, in chapter 4 we reveal that terms for walking, which previous scholarship has understood as synonymous (e.g., "ramble" and "wander") actually connoted distinct geographical responses to the landscape that were inherently linked to contemporary readings of Lake District literature. Finally, chapter 6 reverses this interest in scale to focus in on one particular location—Scafell—rather than a theme, and uses the analytical tools available in a geographical information system to explore how this vertiginous peak was represented and experienced by the writers in our corpus. Together, these chapters illustrate that the Lake District's literary landscape is much richer—and has far wider reaching consequences for literary, cultural, and environmental histories—than studies that focus only on its canonical literature suggest. Methodologically, what draws these chapters together is that in each case, although the approaches and themes vary, we employed digital approaches to explore humanities research questions. In every case, our aim has been to keep the humanities are in the foreground, while the digital approach provides the supporting architecture. It is research enabled by the digital but driven by the humanities.

We will not have convinced everyone who is skeptical about digital approaches to literature that this kind of methodology has much to offer literary study: Why not start by simply reading the books, rather than beginning with computer-aided distant reading? But there are practical advantages. Adapting a corpus linguistics methodology, and embedding it in a practice that continues to prioritize close reading, has allowed us to consider an otherwise unfeasible scope of material. There often seems to be a contradiction between the rule-based digital approaches favored by computer-based research, and the nuance and interpretation required by the humanities. Yet the computer's distant approach need not be a limitation; rather, it can be used as an opportunity to understand the broad patterns in a dataset, as well as the intricacies and variables that create them. By close reading these patterns, alongside the individual texts, we have tried to demonstrate an enhanced version of the reading "ecosystem" for which Hammond, Brooke, and Hirst advocate.[1] In our deep mapping practice, distant and close reading work synergistically: distant techniques reveal trends (or silences), and guide us toward which texts are involved in that data anomaly; close readings of those individual texts, in turn, reveal new elements to the pattern that can be further explored through distant readings—and so on. In this way, the reading ecosystem works through an iterative cycle that privileges interconnection between media and methods, and interaction across methods and researchers. This ecosystem comes to house a community of texts, approaches, and interdisciplinary scholars that would not ordinarily be possible in literary studies without a digital element.

By adapting this ecosystem to include mapping technologies—particularly GIS—alongside these reading methodologies, our deep mapping practice prioritizes these facets of interactivity and community. In doing so, it addresses one of the most persistent problems in GIS-based research: that quantitative results[2] and positivist analysis[3] are not, by themselves, sufficient to account for the complexities of lived geographies. But neither can written accounts alone fully absorb the broader—and more broadly quantifiable—contexts that also shape our experiences of the world around us. Together, the texts can indicate new understandings of other kinds of data, and quantitative results can suggest new modes of interpreting written representation. The GIS allows us to overlay this information in a practical way—but it is only when we embed GIS research as part of the reading ecosystem—by treating its maps as texts—that its potential for humanities research becomes clear. As this ecosystem of distant reading, close reading, and GIS develops, and as practitioners more thoroughly explore the potential of GIS and other digital maps for artistic practices,[4] we hope we will see this method being employed in creative, as well as critical, ways.

Arriving at this point, where these forms of humanities-driven digital analyses can be conducted, is a lengthy and time-consuming process. More than that, it relies on forms of collaborative and interdisciplinary research—and scales of external funding—that are not yet the norm in the humanities. Reaching the point where we could produce this book has involved a multiyear and multiphase collaboration with more than a dozen researchers from natural language processing, corpus linguistics, archaeology, and history as well as geography and literary studies. The research that led to this book started around a decade ago with the Mapping the Lakes project, which investigated if we could use GIS to explore two short texts of Lake District writing.[5] Following this project, the research broadened and began exploring ways that larger volumes of text could be converted into a format suitable for use within GIS, and investigating the use of corpus linguistics as a tool that could be used in combination with GIS.[6] Only once these ideas had started to develop did the concept of Geographical Text Analysis (GTA) begin to crystallize as a way of implementing a deep mapping approach.[7] Finally, we moved toward the more humanities-centric ideas on which we have expanded in this book.[8] This process has required extraordinary levels of intellectual and practical generosity from the multidisciplinary scholars who have contributed to these research teams. No less, it has required generous leadership that recognizes, encourages, and acknowledges the contributions of students and junior staff members in driving both the research questions and the methodologies forward.

The ultimate end-point of this research, if indeed this is where we are, was not clear at the outset. But even when the aims were more focused on technical approaches, we have always been clear that our ultimate goal was to use the digital to do humanities research. Underlying our methodology is the belief that the digital humanities cannot exist in isolation from the humanities mainstream. This is not to say that the significant amounts of work that go toward developing digital datasets and methodologies, and employing data-driven approaches, cannot exist in a relatively self-contained subfield called digital humanities. And developments in technology—including GIS, spatial analysis, and corpus linguistics—rarely originate in the humanities; indeed, the humanities traditionally have been relatively late adopters. Nevertheless, if research from this area is not made more widely relevant, the danger is that the field becomes isolated and irrelevant to most humanists. The challenge is to adopt the technology available in an appropriate and self-critical way, and then to adapt it in ways that make it more suitable for humanities sources and paradigms.

With or without funding, there are many other significant practical challenges facing researchers in this field. Many—if not most—humanities scholars are not fluent in any programming language. This is not necessarily a problem if we see a central pillar of digital humanities research as being collaborative, whereby the computer scientist provides the code. But this approach risks reducing the digital humanities to a problem/solution model, which undercuts the kinds of nuance that characterize humanities research. More than that, it limits the extent to which humanities research questions can be imbricated in a project from the outset. But coding can be a tough skill to crack: it takes time, of course, but it is also often taught through courses designed for social or computer scientists who are more fluent in languages about data, which can be baffling for the researcher trained to speak and think in more narrative-driven forms. Coding courses specifically for humanists—such as Duncan Hay's "Python for the Spatial Humanities" (2018)[9]—emphasize how coding functions as a language that is deployed to write new forms of narrative. Expanding from that approach, as J. R. Carpenter's poetry collection *An Ocean of Static* (2018) begins to do, we might also think about ways in which recognizing the creative poetics of coding—the forms, structures, metaphors, and dictions essential to these languages—can offer new forms of literariness, as well as literacy. Humanities researchers who also know how to think and write in code are a valuable asset: not only can they produce their own script-lines or programs, but they can bring their interpretative expertise to bear on the interpretation of coding. At a moment when coding languages are being used to write increasingly complex literatures, including algorithms so complicated and multi-layered that their own programmers struggle to explain them,[10] that underpin the ever more pervasive elements of our digital lives, it is perhaps more important than ever to develop researchers who are trained both in coding and in interpretative analysis.

This challenge is enhanced by the traditional perception that the humanities and computer sciences are almost diametric opposites. Where computing was used in the humanities it was often seen as being associated with applying positivist approaches to quantitative sources, meaning that both the approaches and the sources were seen as, at best, a minority interest and, at worst, an anathema to humanities scholarship.[11] Today, however, computers deal with a lot of textual data, whether libraries of digitized material (such as archive.org, the site from which many of our sources have been taken), born-digital archives, or social media material. Computers—and computer scientists—are exceptionally skilled at aggregating massive quantities of data, recognizing and evaluating the patterns in them, and developing visualizations and interactivity that represent those data in new ways. However, analyzing this kind of content is a major challenge for both computers and computer scientists. Yet this is precisely where humanists are trained to work. Computer scientists have long been aware that analyzing text requires a different skill set than that provided by the training they undergo for working principally with quantitative data. Interpretative issues such as ambiguity, vagueness, nuance, tone, and the expression (explicit or otherwise) of feeling require a human reader to unpack. Both fields, therefore, have much to offer, and both disciplines can—and, we think, should—assist, complement, and enhance the other without seeking to subdue or replace existing approaches in either subject.

Deep mapping is coming of age. We have shown in this book that a deep mapping practice can deliver new forms of analysis and new insights into scholarly challenges. However, much can still be done to evolve a deep mapping methodology. Technologically, there is great potential in the vision of a deep mapping product that uses space as the platform on which to bring together a wide variety of different types of sources and allows them to be integrated and visualized through location. One of the major challenges here is to move beyond the simple Euclidean two-dimensional maps that GIS outputs very easily, and that we have used extensively in this book, to more advanced forms of visualization and participation. Gaming engines have much to offer here,[12] as do wearable technologies.[13] As with other aspects of geospatial technologies, the challenge is twofold: first, to create effective visualizations, and, second, to use these to advance knowledge of the sources they portray.

As part of this ambition, deep mapping needs to develop ways of representing uncertain, textual, or imaginary space alongside place. Geographical Text Analysis (GTA) is based on geoparsed texts, where place names are extracted from the texts and topographic mapping with Euclidean distance is used as the basis for analyzing their literary geographies. But place names are only one form of geography, and there are many other ways of writing about spatial information. Representations of physical features ("the mountain," "along the road") are not included in GTA, nor are abstract representations of place, such as "the view" or "the scenery," or directions based on personal perspective ("to the left," "across from," "in front of"). The question of how to include these other, less certain kinds of geography as part of a deep map represents a new research challenge.[14]

Building on this, a further difficulty is how we "locate" places once we have identified them. In the maps and spatial analysis used by GTA, we are interested in real-world locations: the analysis is based on straight-line distances between two or more points. But does this really represent the geography as the writers themselves would have experienced it? The human perception of geography is very different from that found on the topographical map. Human perception—the kind of geographies with which our corpus writers deal—tends to simplify and straighten geographies: this approach often simply does not know much about where different places are in relation to each other. Representing these connections requires very different forms of representation than the topographic map. A range of options might be explored here. Topological mapping—made famous by the London Underground map—can show how writers connect places. More complex network or graph representations, often used to show networks of people but less commonly applied to place, might also be built into a deep map. Conceptual cartographies are another option, based largely around detailed manual markup of the texts under study.[15] One approach drawn from mathematics, qualitative spatial reasoning (QSR), involves representing places as regions and identifying the relationships between them. QSR understands space and place as inherently representational and offers some intriguing opportunities for experimenting with how to translate geographical representation from text to a new kind of human- and humanist-oriented map.[16]

All of these models have something in common: they each rely on some form of the deep mapping ecosystem that we have advocated throughout this book. Like our readings here, they require collaborative and generous interdisciplinary, multimedia and multiplatform approaches. A deep mapping practice encourages both digital and humanities researchers to cross, recross and, ultimately, blur the boundaries between space and place, map and text, digital and humanities.

Appendix

THE CORPUS OF LAKE DISTRICT WRITING

Anon. *Observations, Chiefly Lithological, Made in a Five Weeks' Tour*. London: T. Ostell, 1804.

———. *Gleanings of a Wanderer, in Various Parts of England, Scotland, & North Wales, Made during an Excursion in the Year 1804*. London: Richard Phillips, 1805.

———. *Keswick and Its Neighbourhood: A Hand-book for the Use of Visitors*. Windermere and London: J. Garnett, and Whittaker and Co., 1852.

———. *Black's Shilling Guide to the English Lakes*. Edinburgh: A. and C. Black, 1853.

———. *Nelson's Handbooks for Tourists: The English Lakes* [1857]. London: Thomas Nelson & Sons, 1859.

Baddeley, M.J.B. *Black's Shilling Guide to the English Lakes*. Edinburgh: A. and C. Black, 1900.

Baines, Edward. *A Companion to the Lakes of Cumberland, Westmoreland, and Lancashire: In a Descriptive Account of a Family Tour and Excursions on Horseback and on Foot*. London: Simpkin and Marshall, 1829.

Barber, Samuel. *Beneath Helvellyn's Shade: Notes and Sketches in the Valley of Wythburn*. London: E. Stock, 1892.

Bree, John. *Saint Herbert's Isle: A Legendary Poem: In Five Cantos*. London: Longman, 1832.

Brown, John. *Description of the Lake and Vale of Keswick*. Newcastle and Kendal: J. Ashburner, 1767.

Budworth, Joseph. *A Fortnight's Ramble to the Lakes in Westmorland, Lancashire, and Cumberland*. London: Hookham and Carpenter, 1792.

Burroughs, John. *In Wordsworth's Country*. Edinburgh: David Douglas, 1884.

Carter, Nathaniel Hazeltine. *Letters from Europe: Comprising the Journal of a Tour Through Ireland, England, France, Italy, and Switzerland*. New York: G. and C. Carvill, 1827.

Clarke, James. *A Survey of the Lakes of Cumberland, Westmorland, and Lancashire*. London: J. Clarke, 1787.

Cockin, William. *Ode to the Genius of the Lakes. A Poem*. London: Richardson and Urquhart, J. Robson, W. Pennington, 1780.

Coleridge, Samuel Taylor. *Letters of Samuel Taylor Coleridge: Volume II*, ed. Earl Leslie Griggs. Oxford: Clarendon Press, 1956.

———. *The Notebooks of Samuel Taylor Coleridge*, vol. 1, ed. Kathleen Coburn. London: Routledge and Kegan Paul, 1957.

Collingwood, W. G. *Coniston Tales*. Ulverston: William Holmes, 1889.

Combe, William. *The tour of Doctor Syntax in Search of the Picturesque*. London: R. Ackermann, 1812.

Cooke, Charles. *The Tourist's and Traveller's Companion to the Lakes of Cumberland, Westmoreland, and Lancashire*. London: Sherwood, Jones and Co., 1827.

Cumberland, Richard. *Odes*. London: J. Robson, 1776.

Dalton, John. *A Descriptive Poem, Addressed to Two Ladies, at their Return from Viewing the Mines near Whitehaven*. London: J. J. Rivington and R. and J. Dodsley, 1755.

Defoe, Daniel. *A Tour thro' the Whole Island of Great Britain*. London: G. Strahan, J. Mears, J. Stagg, 1727.

Denholm, James. *A Tour to the Principal Scotch and English Lakes*. Glasgow: A. Macgoun, 1804.

Dickinson, William. *Cumbriana: Or Fragments of Cumbrian Life*. London and Whitehaven: Whittaker and Co., and Callander and Dixon, 1875.

Drayton, Michael. *Poly-Olbion; or, A Chorographicall Description of All the Tracts, Rivers, Mountains, Forests, and Other Parts of This Renowned Isle of Great Britain*. London: A. Mathews, J. Marriott, J. Grismand and T. Dewe, 1622.

Fiennes, Celia. *Through England on a Side-Saddle in the Time of William and Mary*. 1698. London and New York: Field and Tuer, and Simpkin, Marshall and Co., 1888.

Freeman Clarke, James. *Eleven Weeks in Europe; and What May Be Seen in That Time*. Boston: Ticknor, Reed, and Fields, 1852.

Frith, Henry. *Wanderings in Wordsworthshire*. London, W. Poole, 1881.

Gell, William. *A Tour in the Lakes, 1797*. Newcastle: Frank Graham, 1968.

Gibson, Alexander Craig. *The Old Man; or Ravings and Ramblings round Conistone*. London and Kendal: J. Whittaker and Co., and J. Garnett, 1849.

Gilpin, William. *Observations, Relative Chiefly to Picturesque Beauty, Made in the Year 1772, on Several Parts of England; Particularly the Mountains, and Lakes of Cumberland, and Westmoreland*. London: R. Blamire, 1786.

Gray, Thomas. *Journal of a Visit to the Lake District in October 1769* [1775], ed. William Roberts. Liverpool: Liverpool University Press, 2001.

[Hammond, Lieutenant]. *A Relation of a Short Survey of 26 Counties*. 1634. London: F. E. Robinson and Co., 1904.

Hawthorne, Nathaniel. *English Notebooks* [1855]. Boston, New York and London: J. R. Osgood and Co., and Routledge, 1871.

Hoare, Richard Colt. *The Journeys of Sir Richard Colt Hoare through Wales and England [1793–1810]*. Gloucester: A. Sutton, 1983.

Housman, John. *A topographical description of Cumberland, Westmoreland, Lancashire, and a Part of the West Riding of Yorkshire*. Carlisle and London: F. Jollie, 1800.

Hutchinson, William. *An Excursion to the Lakes in Westmoreland and Cumberland*. London: J. Wilkie, 1776.

Hutton, Catherine. *Oakwood Hall, a Novel, Including a Description of the Lakes of Cumberland and Westmoreland, and a Part of South Wales*. London: Longman, 1819.

Keats, John. "Letter to Thomas Keats, 25–27 June 1818," in *The Letters of John Keats*, ed. Maurice Buxton Forman, 154–157. Oxford: Oxford University Press, 1947.

———. "Letter to George Keats, 27–28 June 1818, in *The Letters of John Keats*, ed. Maurice Buxton Forman, 157–164. Oxford: Oxford University Press, 1947.

Leigh, Samuel. *Leigh's Guide to the Lakes and Mountains of Cumberland*. London: Samuel Leigh, 1830.

Mackay, Charles. *The Scenery and Poetry of the English Lakes: A Summer Ramble*. London: Longman & Co., 1846.

Malleson, Frederick Amadeus. *Holiday Studies of Wordsworth by Rivers, Woods and Alps*. London: Cassell and Co., 1890.

Manners, John Henry. *Journal of a Tour to the Northern Parts of Great Britain*. *1796*. London: J. Triphook, 1813.

Martineau, Harriet. *A Complete Guide to the English Lakes*. Windermere and London: J. Garnett, and Whittaker and Co., 1855.

———. *The Lights of the English Lakes*. Boston: Ticknor & Fields, 1861.

Mawman, Joseph. *An Excursion to the Highlands of Scotland and the English Lakes*. London: J. Mawman, 1805.

Newte, Thomas. *A Tour in England and Scotland, in 1785*. London: G.G.J. and J. Robinson, 1788.

Otley, Jonathan. *A Concise Description of the English Lakes and Adjacent Mountains: With General Directions to Tourists, Notices of the Botany, Mineralogy, and Geology of the District, Observations on Meteorology, the Floating Island in Derwent Lake, and the Black-Lead Mine in Borrowdale*. Keswick and London: J. Otley and J. Richardson, 1823.

Pennant, Thomas. *A Tour in Scotland, 1769*. Chester: John Monk, 1771.

———. *A Tour in Scotland, and Voyage to the Hebrides, 1772*. Chester: John Monk, 1774.

Plumptre, James. *The Lakers: A Comic Opera in Three Acts*. London: W. Clarke, 1798.

Radcliffe, Ann. *A Journey Made in the Summer of 1791*. London: G. G. and J. Robinson, 1795.

Rix, Herbert. *Down the Duddon with Wordsworth* [1883–1893]. London: Bouverie, 1893.

Robinson, John. *A Guide to the Lakes, in Cumberland, Westmorland, and Lancashire*. London: Lackington and Co., 1819.

———. *Views of the Lakes in the North of England, from Original Paintings; with Historical and Descriptive Illustrations*. London, Penrith and Carlisle: Whittaker and Co., J. Brown, and J. Cockburn, 1833.

Ruskin, John. *Iteriad; or, Three Weeks among the Lakes* [1830–1832]. Newcastle: Frank Graham, 1969.

Shaw, Stebbing. *A Tour in 1787, from London to the Western Highlands of Scotland*. London: L. Davis, Robson and Clarke, W. Lowndes, H. Gardner, 1788.

Skrine, Henry. *Three Successive Tours in the North of England, and Great Part of Scotland: Interspersed with Descriptions of the Scenes They Presented, and Occasional Observations on the State of Society*. London: W. Bulmer and Co., 1795.

Smith, George. *A Journey up to Cross-Fell Mountain*. London: E. Cave, 1747.

———. *A Journey to Caudbec Fells*. London: E. Cave, 1747.

———. *A Survey of the Northwest Coast of England*. London: E. Cave, 1747.

Southey, Robert. *Letters from England, by Don Manuel Alvarez Espriella*. London: Longman, Hurst, Rees and Orme, 1807.

Spiker, Samuel Heinrich. *Travels through England, Wales & Scotland in the Year 1816*. London: Lackington and Co., 1816.

Sullivan, Richard Joseph. *Observations Made during a Tour through Parts of England, Scotland, and Wales, in a Series of Letters*. London: T. Becket, 1780.

Thorne, James. *Rambles by Rivers*. London: Charles Knight and Co., 1844.

Thornton, Thomas. *A Sporting Tour through the Northern Parts of England, and Great Part of the Highlands of Scotland*. London, Edinburgh and Glasgow: Vernor and Hood, Constable and Hunter, Brash and Reid, 1804.

Wakefield, Priscilla. *A Family Tour through the British Empire*. London: Darton and Harvey, 1804.

Walker, Adam. *Remarks Made in a Tour from London to the Lakes of Westmoreland and Cumberland, in the Summer of 1791*. London: G. Nicol and C. Dilly, 1792.

Waugh, Edwin. *Over Sands to the Lakes*. Manchester: A. Ireland and Co., 1860.

———. *Rambles in the Lake Country and Its Borders*. Manchester and London: John Heywood, and Simpkin, Marshall and Co., 1861.

Wesley, John. *An Extract of the Rev. Mr. John Wesley's Journal*. Bristol: William Pine, 1764.

West, Thomas. *A Guide to the Lakes: Dedicated to the Lovers of Landscape Studies, etc.* London and Kendal: Richardson and Urquhart, and W. Pennington, 1778.

Wilberforce, William. *Journey to the Lake District from Cambridge*. Hull: Oriel Press, 1983.

Wilkinson, Thomas. *Tours to the British Mountains, with the Descriptive Poems of Lowther*. Taylor and Hessey, 1824.

Williamson, C. N., "The Climbs of the English Lake District," Part 2, *All the Year Round*, 110–114. November 8, 1884.

Wordsworth, William. *The River Duddon: A Series of Sonnets*. London: Longman & Co., 1820.

———. *A Description of the Scenery of the Lakes in the North of England*. London: Longman & Co., 1822.

———. *Wordsworth's Guide through the District of the Lakes, Fifth Edition. 1835*, with notes by Ernest De Sélincourt. London: Henry Frowde, 1906.

Yarnall, Ellis. *Walks and Visits in Wordsworth Country* [1876]. New York and London: Macmillan and Co., 1899.

Young, Arthur. *Six Months' Tour through the North of England*. London, Salisbury and Edinburgh: W. Strahan, W. Nicoll, B. Collins, J. Balfour, 1770.

Acknowledgments

Our first thanks must go to Suzanne Guiod and Pamela Dailey at Bucknell University Press, and to the production team at Rutgers University Press, for helping us turn our manuscript into this book. *Deep Mapping the Literary Lake District* is one of the major outputs of the Leverhulme Trust–funded project Geospatial Innovation in the Digital Humanities: A Deep Map of the English Lake District (RPG–2015–230). We are very grateful to the Leverhulme Trust for supporting this work, and to the project's co-investigators—Sally Bushell, Paul Rayson and especially Christopher Donaldson—for their input, advice, and discussions throughout the process of writing the book. Alex Reinhold, the project's PhD student, developed the idea of deep mapping in new and exciting ways that were not evident when we started. James Butler produced the gold-standard corpus, with place names manually identified. We have taken the work from this book to many conferences and other meetings, and we are grateful to listeners and interrogators at these events for their insights and suggestions. Hopefully it will be as clear from reading this book as it was from writing it that the kind of generous interdisciplinary conversations we enjoyed with each of these exceptional scholars, alongside too many others to name here, is invaluable in the production of this form of scholarship.

Notes

CHAPTER 1 — DEEP MAPPING AND THE CORPUS OF LAKE DISTRICT WRITING

1. Oldroyd, *Earth, Water, Ice and Fire*, 6.
2. Housman, *A Topographical Description of Cumberland, Westmoreland, Lancashire*, iv.
3. Housman, iv.
4. Housman, iv.
5. Housman, iv.
6. Nicholson, "Algorithm and Analogy," 643–650.
7. Walton, "Setting the Scene," 47.
8. Williams, *Problems in Materialism and Culture*, 67.
9. Lake District National Park Partnership, *Nomination of the English Lake District for Inscription*.
10. Piper, *Enumerations*, xii.
11. Risen and Lichtblau, "How the U.S. Uses Technology to Mine More Data More Quickly."
12. Underwood, *Distant Horizons*, ix.
13. Bode, *A World of Fiction: Digital Collections and the Future of Literary History*, 13.
14. Hitchcock, "Confronting the Digital," 9–23.
15. Leetaru, "In Machines We Trust."
16. Piper, *Enumerations*, 6; Felluga and Rettenmaier, "Can Victorian Studies Reclaim the Means of Production?" 331–343.
17. Underwood, "Distant Reading and Recent Intellectual History."
18. Goldstone, "The Doxa of Reading," 636–642.
19. Clement, *Text Analysis, Data Mining, and Visualizations*.
20. Drucker, "Humanities Approaches to Graphical Display."
21. Weingart, *The Moral Role of DH in a Data-Driven World*.
22. Drucker, "Humanities Approaches to Graphical Display."
23. Piper, *Enumerations*, 3.
24. Weingart, *The Moral Role of DH*.
25. Weingart.
26. Tavel Clark and Wittenberg, eds., *Scale in Literature and Culture*.
27. Jockers, *Macroanalysis*.

28. Hammond, Brooke, and Hirst, "Modeling Modernist Dialogism," 50.

29. Eve, *Close Reading with Computers*.

30. Underwood, *Distant Horizons*, xviii–xix.

31. Goldstone, "The Doxa of Reading," 9.

32. Underwood, *Distant Horizons*, xvii–xviii.

33. Nicholson, "Algorithm and Analogy."

34. Taylor, Gregory, and Donaldson, "Combining Close and Distant Reading," 163–182.

35. Hitchcock, "Confronting the Digital."

36. Raymond and Moxham, eds., *News Networks in Early Modern Europe*; Piper, *Enumerations*, 10.

37. Allison, *Reductive Reading*; Piper, *Enumerations*; Underwood, *Distant Horizons*, xii.

38. Bode, *A World of Fiction*, 2.

39. Piper, *Enumerations*, 11.

40. Underwood, "Distant Reading."

41. Whitson, *Steampunk and Nineteenth-Century Digital Humanities*, 5.

42. Owens, "Defining Data for Humanists."

43. Clement, *Text Analysis*.

44. Piper, *Enumerations*, 5.

45. Svensson, "Humanities Computing as Digital Humanities," 178.

46. Wilkens, "Canons, Close Reading, and the Evolution of Method," 249.

47. Cooper and Gregory, "Mapping the English Lake District," 90.

48. Cooper, "The Poetics of Place and Space," 813.

49. Yoshikawa, *William Wordsworth and the Invention of Tourism*.

50. Baddeley, *Black's Shilling Guide to the English Lakes*.

51. Baddeley, np.

52. Holt, "Historical Landscape and the Moving Image," 182.

53. Scott, "The Cultural Economy of Landscape," 1567–1589.

54. Andrews, *The Search for the Picturesque*; Ritvo, *The Dawn of Green*; Walton and Wood, eds., *The Making of a Cultural Landscape*.

55. Fulford, *The Late Poetry of the Lake Poets*, 9.

56. Huggins, "Popular Culture and Sporting Life in the Rural Margins," 189–205.

57. Hess, *William Wordsworth and the Ecology of Authorship*; Yoshikawa, *William Wordsworth and the Invention of Tourism*; Carlson, *Romantic Marks and Measures*.

58. Kirschenbaum, "What Is Digital Humanities and What's It Doing in English Departments?" 195–204.

59. Rayson et al., "A Deeply Annotated Testbed for Geographical Text Analysis."

60. Inaki and Okita, "A Small-Corpus-Based Approach to Alice's Roles," 284.

61. McEnery and Hardie, *Corpus Linguistics*.

62. Hunston, *Corpora in Applied Linguistics*, 68–75.

63. Adolphs, *Introducing Electronic Text Analysis*; McEnery and Hardie, *Corpus Linguistics*; McEnery and Baker, *Corpus Linguistics and 17th-Century Prostitution*; Blaxill, "The Language of Imperialism," 416–448; Atkinson and Gregory, "Finding Child Welfare in Victorian Newspapers," 159–186.

64. Anthony, "AntConc," 7–13.

65. Rezaeian et al., "Geographical Epidemiology, Spatial Analysis and Geographical Information Systems," 98–102; Chainey and Ratcliffe, *GIS and Crime Mapping*.

66. Coppock and Rhind, "The History of GIS," 21–43.

67. Goodchild, "Geographical Information Science," 31–45.

68. Gregory and Geddes, *Toward Spatial Humanities*, 9.

69. Porter, "Introduction: The Importance of Place and Openness," 91–101.

70. Knowles, Westerveld, and Strom, "Inductive Visualization," 233.

71. Gregory and Ell, *Historical GIS*, 21–40.

72. Gregory and Ell, 41–62.

73. Gregory, Kemp, and Mostern, "Geographical Information and Historical Research," 7–23.

74. Mailing, *Coordinate Systems and Map Projections*; Snyder, *Flattening the Earth*.

75. Fotheringham, "Trends in Quantitative Methods I," 88–96; Fotheringham, Brunsdon, and Charlton, *Quantitative Geography*.

76. Kretzschmar, "GIS for Language and Literary Study."

77. Bushell, "The Slipperiness of Literary Maps," 149–160.

78. Heuser, Moretti, and Steiner, *The Emotions of London*; Reuschel and Piatti, "Ein Literarischer Atlas Europas," 254–272; Gregory et al., "Geospatial Innovation in the Digital Humanities"; Heuser, Moretti, and Steiner, *The Emotions of London*; Donaldson, Gregory, and Taylor, "Locating the Beautiful, Picturesque, Sublime and Majestic," 43–60.

79. Juvan, "From Spatial Turn to GIS-Mapping of Literary Cultures," 90.

80. Porter, Atkinson, and Gregory, "Geographical Text Analysis," 25–34; Murrieta-Flores et al., "Automatically Analysing Large Texts in a GIS Environment," 296–320; Gregory and Donaldson, "Geographical Text Analysis," 67–87; Donaldson, Gregory, and Taylor, "Locating the Beautiful," 46–48; Paterson and Gregory, *Representations of Poverty and Place*.

81. Hardie, "Modest XML for Corpora," 73–103.

82. Southall, Mostern, and Berman, "On Historical Gazetteers," 127–145; Berman, Mostern, and Southall, *Placing Names: Enriching and Integrating Gazetteers*.

83. Grover et al., "Use of the Edinburgh Geoparser," 3875–3889.

84. McDonough, Moncla, and van de Camp, "Named Entity Recognition Goes to Old Regime France," 2.

85. Butler et al., "Alts, Abbreviations, and AKAs," 66.

86. Rupp et al., "Dealing with Heterogeneous Big Data," 80–83; Gregory et al., "Geoparsing, GIS and Textual Analysis," 1–14.

87. Piper, *Enumerations*, 9–12.

88. Wilkens, "Canons, Close Reading, and the Evolution of Method," 256–257.

89. Wilkens, "The Geographic Imagination," 803–840.

90. Heuser, Moretti, and Steiner, *The Emotions of London*.

91. McEnery and Hardie, *Corpus Linguistics*, 122–165; Barnbrook, Mason, and Krishnamurthy, *Collocation: Applications and Implications*.

92. Donaldson, Gregory, and Taylor, "Locating the Beautiful," 46–47.

93. Fotheringham, Brunsdon, and Charlton, *Quantitative Geography*, 146–149.

94. Kulldorff, "A Spatial Scan Statistic," 1481–1496.

95. Openshaw et al., "A Mark 1 Geographic Analysis Machine," 335–358; Wakeford, Binks, and Wilkie, "Childhood Leukaemia and Nuclear Installations," 1–26; Cross, "Using a Geographic Information System to Explore the Spatial Incidence of Childhood Cancer in Northern England," 218–229.

96. Yoshikawa, *William Wordsworth and the Invention of Tourism*.

97. Rossetto, "Theorizing Maps with Literature," 516.

98. Taylor et al., "Mapping Digitally, Mapping Deep," 10–19.

99. Lynch, Glotfelty, and Armbruster, "Introduction," 7.

100. Taylor, "Editorial comment: GKS," 211–212.

101. Kwan Mei-Po, "Visualization: Re-envisioning GIS," 645–661; Kwan Mei-Po, "Is GIS for Women?" 271–279; Pavlovskaya and St. Martin, "Feminism and Geographic Information Systems," 583–606.

102. Knowles, Westerveld, and Strom, "Inductive Visualization," 234.

103. Knowles et al., 235.

104. Knowles et al., 235.

105. Wells, "La cartographie comme outil d'analyse littéraire," 170.

106. Bodenhamer, Corrigan, and Harris, "Introduction," 3.

107. Edwards, "How to Read an Early Modern Map," 2.

108. Hall, "I, Mercator," 19.

109. Donaldson, "Deep Mapping and Romanticism"; Bushell, *Reading and Mapping Fiction*, 20–26.

110. Bodenhamer, Corrigan, and Harris, "Introduction: Deep Maps and the Spatial Humanities," 1.

111. Harris, "Deep Geography—Deep Mapping," 28–53; Bodenhamer, "Making the Invisible Visible," 207–220.

CHAPTER 2 — PICTURESQUE TECHNOLOGIES
AND THE DIGITAL HUMANITIES

1. Anon, *The English Lakes*, 2.

2. Glickman, *The Picturesque and the Sublime*, 13; Holt, "Historical Landscape and the Moving Image," 185.

3. Byerly, "The Uses of Landscape," 52–68.

4. Williams, *The Country and the City*, 113.

5. Anon, *The English Lakes*, 2.

6. Ackerman, "The Photographic Picturesque," 73–94; Hewitt, *Map of a Nation*, 185; Rarey, "Camera Lucida Mexicana."

7. McGillivray, "The Picturesque World Stage," 128–129.

8. Broglio, *Technologies of the Picturesque*, 15–22.

9. Williams, *The Country and the City*, 193.

10. Porter, "Maps, Lists, Views," 168.

11. Broglio, *Technologies of the Picturesque*, 18–20.

12. Pfau, *Wordsworth's Profession*, 30; Glickman, *The Picturesque and the Sublime*, 12; Porter, "Maps, Lists, Views," 168.

13. *Samsung Galaxy S8 Commercial*.

14. Drucker, "Humanities Approaches to Graphical Display."

15. Drucker.

16. Owens, "Defining Data for Humanists"; Juvan, "From Spatial Turn to GIS-Mapping of Literary Cultures."

17. Schöch, "Big? Smart? Clean? Messy?"

18. Pressman and Swanstrom, "The Literary And/As the Digital Humanities."

19. Broglio, *Technologies of the Picturesque*, 46.

20. Southey, "The Collected Letters of Robert Southey, Part Three: 1804–1809," 1813, sec. 1348: Letter to John Aiken, July 1807 [original emphases].

21. Hipple, *The Beautiful, the Sublime and the Picturesque*, 186.

22. Ruskin, "The Seven Lamps of Architecture," 235.

23. Ruskin, "Modern Painters," 244.

24. Dixon Hunt, *The Figure in the Landscape*, 46–47.

25. Pfau, *Wordsworth's Profession*, 62; Townsend, "The Picturesque," 374; McGillivray, "The Picturesque World Stage," 128.

26. Carter, *The Road to Botany Bay*, 232.

27. Byerly, "The Uses of Landscape," 53.

28. Urry and Larson, *The Tourist Gaze 3.0*, 6.

29. Macpherson, "Walkers with Visual-Impairments," 251–258.

30. Auerbach, "The Picturesque and the Homogenisation of Empire," 47–48; Bohls, *Romantic Literature and Postcolonial Studies*, 30.

31. Pfau, *Wordsworth's Profession*, 69.

32. Fulford, *Landscape, Liberty and Authority*, 117.

33. Fulford, *The Late Poetry of the Lake Poets*, 31.

34. Fulford, *Landscape, Liberty and Authority*, 142.

35. Rutherford, "Claife Station and the Picturesque," 204.

36. Hill, "Keats, Antiquarianism, and the Picturesque," 122.

37. Wordsworth, *Wordsworth's Guide to the Lakes*, xx.

38. Dixon Hunt, *Gardens and the Picturesque*, 193.

39. Glickman, *The Picturesque and the Sublime*, 10.

40. Gilpin, *Observations, Relative Chiefly to Picturesque Beauty*, vii.

41. Gilpin, vii–viii.

42. Gilpin, ix.

43. Gilpin, 121.

44. Gilpin, 120.

45. Noggle, *The Temporality of Taste*, 77–78.

46. Gilpin, *Observations, Relative Chiefly to Picturesque Beauty*, xiii.

47. McGillivray, "The Picturesque World Stage," 132.

48. Barbier, *Samuel Rogers and William Gilpin*, 1.

49. Austin, "Aesthetic Embarrassment," 629.

50. Gilpin, 168–169.

51. Gilpin, 168–169.

52. Marr, *The Geology of the Lake District*.

53. Donaldson, Gregory, and Taylor, "Locating the Beautiful, Picturesque, Sublime and Majestic."

54. Glickman, *The Picturesque and the Sublime*, 10.

55. Hill, "Keats, Antiquarianism, and the Picturesque," 124.

56. Gilpin, *Observations*, 183.

57. Gilpin, 186.

58. Andrews, *The Search for the Picturesque: Landscape Aesthetics and Tourism in Britain, 1760–1800*, 122.

59. Austin, "Aesthetic Embarrassment," 646.

60. Rutherford, "Claife Station and the Picturesque in the Lakes," 207.

61. Plumptre, *The Lakers*, 21.

62. Robert Southey, *Letters from England, by Don Manuel Alvarez Espriella*, 261.

63. Carter, *Letters from Europe*, 215–216 [original emphasis].

64. Powell, ed., *Excursion to Wordsworthshire*, 190.

65. Austin, *Automatism and Creative Acts*, 76–77.

66. Austin, "Aesthetic Embarrassment," 645.

67. Linton, *The Girl of the Period*, 97.

68. Linton, *Lizzie Lorton of Greyrigg*, 74.

69. Linton, 147.

70. Hess, *William Wordsworth and the Ecology of Authorship*, 21.

71. Bohls, *Women Travel Writers*, 13; Labbe, *Romantic Visualities*; Barrell, *The Dark Side of the Landscape*, 70–76; Townsend, "The Picturesque," 370; Fairclough, *John Thelwall and the Politics of the Picturesque*, l; Gaunt, "Patrician Landscapes and the Picturesque," 173.

72. Anon, *Keswick and Its Neighbourhood*, 87.

73. Anon, 87.

74. Broglio, *Technologies of the Picturesque*, 59.

75. Walker, *Remarks Made in a Tour from London to the Lakes of Westmoreland and Cumberland*, 109.

76. Wainwright, *The Outlying Fells of Lakeland*.

77. Wainwright, 26.

78. Fulford, *Landscape, Liberty and Authority*, 125.

79. Hess, *William Wordsworth and the Ecology of Authorship*, 23.

80. Wordsworth, *Last Poems, 1821–1850*, 389–390.

81. Wordsworth, *Last Poems*, 389n.

82. Wordsworth, *Wordsworth's Guide to the Lakes*, 92.

83. Bate, *The Song of the Earth*, 148.

84. Cosgrove, "Seminar Discussion," 128.

85. Ellison, "The Suffocating Embrace of Landscape," 87.

86. Macarthur, *The Picturesque: Architecture, Disgust and Other Irregularities* (London: Routledge, 2007), 101.

87. Lindsay Smith, *Victorian Photography, Painting and Poetry: The Enigma of Visibility in Ruskin, Morris and the Pre-Raphaelites* (Cambridge: Cambridge University Press, 1995), 39; Dixon Hunt, *Gardens and the Picturesque*, 194.

88. Smith, *Victorian Photography*, 37.

89. Ruskin, "Modern Painters," vol. IV.14.

90. Ruskin, vol. V.21.

91. Ruskin, vol. V.20n.

92. Clement, *Text Analysis, Data Mining, and Visualizations*.

93. Porter, "Maps, Lists, Views," 173.

94. Gage, "The Distinctness of Turner," 448.

95. Gage, 449.

96. Fulford, *Landscape, Liberty and Authority*, 117.

97. Fulford, *The Late Poetry of the Lake Poets*, 30.

98. Underwood, *Distant Horizons*, xiv.

99. Broglio, *Technologies of the Picturesque*, 15.

100. Louv, *The Nature Principle*; Pergams and Zaradic, "Evidence for a Fundamental and Pervasive Shift," 2295–2300; Arts, Wal, and Adams, "Digital Technology and the Conservation of Nature," 661–673; Kesebir and Kesebir, "A Growing Disconnect from Nature," 258–269; Ives et al., "Reconnecting with Nature for Sustainability," 1389–1397.

101. Ruskin, *Sesame and Lilies*, "The Ethics of Dust," 212.

102. Pfau, *Wordsworth's Profession*, 67.

103. Hill, "Keats, Antiquarianism, and the Picturesque," 121.

104. Margaret Linley, "Lake District Online: Studies in Book Ecology and Digital Migration," *Victorian Studies* 58, no. 2 (2016): 264.

105. Linley, 263.

106. Hewitt, *Map of a Nation*, 185.

107. Gilpin, *Observations, Relative Chiefly to Picturesque Beauty*, 81.

108. Porter, "Maps, Lists, Views," 168.

109. Gilpin, *Observations*, xxiv [original emphasis].

110. Gilpin, xxv [original emphases].

111. Gilpin, xxiv.

112. Gilpin, xxv [original emphases].

113. Moretti, *Graphs, Maps, Trees*, 1.

114. Ascari, "The Dangers of Distant Reading," 1–19; Klein, "Distant Reading After Moretti."

115. Porter, "Maps, Lists, Views," 168.

116. Gilpin, *Observations on the River Wye*, 2.

117. Porter, "Maps, Lists, Views," 168.

118. Williams, *The Country and the City*, 64.

119. Williams, 86.

120. Pfau, *Wordsworth's Profession*, 21.

121. West, *A Guide to the Lakes: Dedicated to the Lovers of Landscape Studies, Etc.*, 197.

122. West, 200.

123. Porter, "Maps, Lists, Views," 178n.

124. Andrews, *Wanderers*, 139–140.

125. Martineau, *Harriet Martineau's Autobiography*, 513.

126. Martineau, *A Complete Guide to the English Lakes*, i–ii.

127. Martineau, ii.

128. Wells-Brown, *Three Years in Europe*, 199.

129. Wells-Brown, 198.

130. Liu, "Transcendental Data," 49–84.

CHAPTER 3 — TOURISTS, TRAVELERS, INHABITANTS

1. Gilpin, *Observations, Relative Chiefly to Picturesque Beauty*, 207–208.

2. Gilpin, 207.

3. Williams, *The Country and the City*, 185.

4. Mason, Westover, and Stimpson, "Introduction."

5. Bate, *Romantic Ecology*, 40.

6. Wilson, "Letters from the Lakes," 397.

7. Buzard, *The Beaten Track*.

8. Stewart, "'The Eye It Cannot Choose but See,'" 405–431.

9. White and Frew, "Tourism and National Identities," 2.

10. White and Frew, 3; St. Clair, *The Reading Nation*.

11. Groth, "Major Ideologies," 86; Anderson, *Imagined Communities*, 191; White and Frew, "Tourism and National Identities," 2.

12. Hanley and Walton, *Constructing Cultural Tourism*, 27.

13. Bui, Jolliffe, and Nguyen, "Heritage and Aspects of Nation," 151–175; Campelo and Aitken, "Travelling to the Past," 190–201; White and Frew, "Tourism and National Identities," 6.

14. Hanley and Walton, *Constructing Cultural Tourism*, 30.

15. Wyatt, *Wordsworth and the Geologists*; Heringman, *Romantic Rocks*; O'Connor, *The Earth on Show*.

16. Heringman, "Romantic Antiquarianism."

17. Denyer, "The Lake District Landscape," 3–30.

18. Kostelnick, "Wordsworth, Ruins, and the Aesthetics of Decay," 20; Wickman, "Travel Writing and the Picturesque," 63.

19. Wickman, "Travel Writing and the Picturesque," 61–63.

20. Ferri, "Time in Ruins," 204.

21. Hess, *William Wordsworth and the Ecology of Authorship*, 126–132.

22. Ottum, "Discriminating Vision," 168.

23. Fussell, *Abroad: British Literary Travelling*, 38.

24. "Tourist, n.," in *OED Online*.

25. Hanley and Walton, *Constructing Cultural Tourism*, 80.

26. MacCannell, *The Tourist*, 107.

27. Brendon, *Thomas Cook*, 188.

28. Hanley and Walton, *Constructing Cultural Tourism*, 143.

29. "Tourist, n."

30. Coleridge, *The Collected Works of Samuel Taylor Coleridge*, 1022.

31. Coleridge, 1023.

32. Livesey, *Writing the Stage Coach Nation*.

33. Donaldson, "'The Travelling Carriage in Old Times,'" 101–123.

34. Chard, "Introduction," 24; Urry and Larson, *The Tourist Gaze 3.0*.

35. Hanley and Walton, *Constructing Cultural Tourism*, 140.

36. Toner, "Landscape as Literary Criticism," 3.

37. Gray, *Journal of a Visit*, 87.

38. Martineau, *A Complete Guide to the English Lakes*.

39. Walker, *Remarks Made in a Tour from London*, 100.

40. Southey, "The Collected Letters of Robert Southey, Part Three: 1804–1809," sec. 1509.

41. Hembry, *The English Spa 1560–1815*.

42. Hanley and Walton, *Constructing Cultural Tourism*, 162.

43. Robinson, "A Guide to the Lakes," iv.

44. Martineau, *A Complete Guide to the English Lakes*, 177–178.

45. Anon, *The English Lakes*, 1.

46. Anon, *The English Lakes*, 1–2.

47. Urry and Larson, *The Tourist Gaze 3.0*, 7–8.

48. Urry, *The Tourist Gaze*.

49. Santesso, "The Birth of the Birthplace," 385.

50. Fussell, ed., *The Norton Book of Travel*, 651.

51. Bicknell, ed., *The Illustrated Wordsworth's Guide to the Lakes*, 21–22.

52. Baines, *A Companion to the Lakes of Cumberland, Westmoreland, and Lancashire*, v.

53. Wordsworth, *Wordsworth's Guide to the Lakes: The Fifth Edition (1835)*, 1.

54. Wordsworth, vi; Gill, *Wordsworth and the Victorians*, 56, 202.

55. Powell, *Excursion to Wordsworthshire*, 7–9.

56. Yoshikawa, *William Wordsworth and the Invention of Tourism*, 70.

57. Wordsworth, *Wordsworth's Guide to the Lakes*, vi.

58. Wordsworth, 1.

59. Buzard, *The Beaten Track*, 80.

60. Seed, "Nineteenth-Century Travel Writing," 2.

61. Buzard, *The Beaten Track*, 81–82.

62. Tuan, "Geography, Phenomenology, and the Study of Human Nature," 181–193; Buzard, *The Beaten Track*, 33.

63. Ozarska, "Grand Tourists or Travellers?" 107.

64. Baines, *A Companion to the Lakes*, 9.

65. Lorimer, "Cultural Geography," 85.

66. Tuan, "Space and Place," 387–427; Berleant, *Aesthetics and Environment*.

67. De Certeau, *The Practice of Everyday Life*, 93.

68. De Selincourt, ed., *The Letters of William and Dorothy Wordsworth*, 31.

69. Wordsworth, *Wordsworth's Guide to the Lakes: The Fifth Edition (1835)*, 27.

70. Wallace, *Walking, Literature and English Culture*, 18.

71. Wordsworth, *Wordsworth's Guide to the Lakes: The Fifth Edition (1835)*, 11.

72. Whyte, "William Wordsworth's Guide to the Lakes," 106.

73. Gold, "Facts, Patterns, Methods, Meaning."

74. Marshall and Walton, *The Lake Counties from 1830 to the Mid-Twentieth Century*, 1.

75. Hess, *William Wordsworth and the Ecology of Authorship*, 13.

76. Gaunt, "Patrician Landscapes," 173.

77. Williams, *The Country and the City*, 165.

78. Di Palma, *Wasteland: A History*, 43–83.

79. Williams, *The Country and the City*, 129.

80. Underwood, *Distant Horizons*, 69.

81. Rebanks, *The Shepherd's Life*, xv–xviii.

82. Rebanks, xix.

83. Wordsworth, *George and Sarah Green*, 52–53.

84. Renouf and David, *Voices of the Lake District*, 8.

85. Hess, *William Wordsworth and the Ecology of Authorship*, 10–11.

86. Huggins, "Popular Culture and Sporting Life," 203.

87. Linton, *The Lake Country*, 53, 102; Linton, *Lizzie Lorton of Greyrigg*, 61, 91.

88. Linton, *The Lake Country*, 199.

89. Linton, *Lizzie Lorton of Greyrigg*, 50.

90. Linton, *The Lake Country*, 186.

91. Anderson, *Woman against Women in Victorian England*, 105.

92. Van Thal, *Eliza Lynn Linton: The Girl of the Period*, 70.

93. Marshall and Walton, *The Lake Counties from 1830 to the Mid-Twentieth Century*, 11–13.

94. Reay, *Rural Englands*; Marshall and Walton, *The Lake Counties from 1830 to the Mid-twentieth Century*.

95. Reay, *Rural Englands*, 15–16.

96. Horn, *The Rural World, 1780–1850*, 254.

97. White, "The Laboring-Class Domestic Sphere," 251.

98. Horn, *The Rural World, 1780–1850*, 33; Menuge, "'Inhabited by Strangers,'" 133–154.

99. Hutton, *Oakwood Hall, a Novel*, vol. I.251.

100. Rollinson, *Life & Tradition*, 17.

101. Budworth, *A Fortnight's Ramble to the Lakes*, 209.

102. Wilson, "Letters from the Lakes," 396.

103. Anon, *The English Lakes*, 27.

104. Walker, *Remarks Made in a Tour from London*, 83.

105. Keats, "Letter to Thomas Keats, 25–27 June 1818," 155.

106. Walker, *Walking North with Keats* (New Haven: Yale University Press, 1992), 12.

107. Ousby, ed., *James Plumptre's Britain*, 139.

108. Yee, *The Silent Traveller*, 7–8.

109. Ritvo, *The Dawn of Green*.

110. Barber, *Beneath Helvellyn's Shade*, 14.

111. Anon, *Keswick and Its Neighbourhood*, 15.

112. Anon, 15.

113. Anon, 15.

114. Anon, 15.

115. Rawlinson, "Report to the General Board of Health," 38.

116. Gray, *Journal of a Visit to the Lake District*, 88.

117. Westover, "William Godwin, Literary Tourism, and the Work of Necromanticism," 304.

118. Wilson, "Letters from the Lakes," 398.

119. Wells-Brown, *Three Years in Europe*, 196.

120. Gilpin, *Observations, Relative Chiefly to Picturesque Beauty*, 230.

121. Blamire, *The Poetical Works of Miss Susanna Blamire*; Blamire, "Stoklewath."

122. Huggins, "Popular Culture and Sporting Life," 194.

123. Marshall and Walton, *The Lake Counties from 1830 to the Mid-twentieth Century*, 1.

124. Wordsworth, *Wordsworth's Guide to the Lakes: The Fifth Edition (1835)*, 32.

125. Wilson, "Letters from the Lakes," 397.

126. Wordsworth, *Wordsworth's Guide to the Lakes: The Fifth Edition (1835)*, 61.

127. Levinson, *Wordsworth's Great Period Poems*, 32.

128. Southey, *Letters from England, by Don Manuel Alvarez Espriella*, 259–260.

129. Southey, 260.

130. Lloyd, "Poverty," 115.

131. Horn, *The Rural World, 1780–1850*, 129.

132. Rowntree and Kendall, *How the Labourer Lives*, 32; Burnett, "Country Diet," in *The Victorian Countryside: Volume Two*, ed. G. E. Mingay (London: Routledge and Kegan Paul, 1981), 565.

133. Williams, *The Country and the City*, 149.

134. Williams, 85.

135. Reay, *Rural Englands*, 12.

136. Winstanley, "Industrialization and the Small Farm," 157–158.

137. Horn, *The Rural World*, 224; Reay, *Rural Englands*, 23.

138. Reay, *Rural Englands*, 23.

139. Horn, *Life and Labour in Rural England*, 1.

140. Horn, *The Rural World*, 129.

141. Ritvo, "Counting Sheep in the English Lake District," 267–268.

142. Horn, *The Rural World*, 30.

143. Young, *Six Months' Tour through the North of England*, vol. III.135.

144. Horn, *The Rural World*, 20.

145. Howkins, *Reshaping Rural England*, 17.

146. Horn, *The Rural World*, 19, 43.

147. Winstanley, "Industrialization and the Small Farm."

148. Reay, *Rural Englands*, 28.

149. Horn, *Life and Labour in Rural England 1760–1850*, 13.

150. Smith., *An Inquiry into the Nature and Causes of the Wealth of Nations*, 127.

151. Baines, *A Companion to the Lakes of Cumberland, Westmoreland, and Lancashire*, 83.

152. Sales, *English Literature in History*, 58.

153. Wordsworth, *Wordsworth's Guide to the Lakes: The Fifth Edition (1835)*, 90.

154. Horn, "Country Children," 526.

155. Reay, *Rural Englands*, 57.

156. Wallace, *Walking, Literature and English Culture*, 11.

157. Wordsworth, *Wordsworth's Guide to the Lakes: The Fifth Edition (1835)*, 68.

158. Mandell, "Gendering Digital Literary History," 511–523.

CHAPTER 4 — WALKING IN THE LITERARY LAKES

1. Wilson, "Letters from the Lakes," 398.

2. Taylor, "Mountain Matter(s)."

3. Palmer, *In Lakeland Dells and Fells*.

4. Lake District National Park Partnership, *Nomination of the English Lake District for Inscription*, 182; McDonagh and Daniels, "Enclosure Stories," 107–121.

5. Williams, *The Country and the City*, 139.

6. Chesnokova et al., "Hearing the Silence."

7. Lake District National Park Partnership, *Nomination of the English Lake District for Inscription*, 140.

8. Lake District National Park Partnership, 564–566.

9. Lake District National Partnership, 182.

10. Leed, *The Mind of the Traveller*, 72.

11. Jarvis, *Romantic Writing*, 37.

12. Wallace, *Walking, Literature and English Culture*, 16.

13. Elder, *Imagining the Earth*, 93.

14. Gros, *A Philosophy of Walking*.

15. Andrews, *Wanderers*.

16. Cadwalladr, "Frédéric Gros: Why Going for a Walk Is the Best Way to Free Your Mind."

17. Sussman and Goode, *The Magic of Walking*, 68–69.

18. Solnit, *Wanderlust*, 232–246.

19. Macfarlane, "Introduction," ix–xxxiv; Macfarlane, *Landmarks*, 55–80.

20. Jamie, "A Lone Enraptured Male."

21. Ross, "Romantic Quest and Conquest," 26–51; Mellor, *Romanticism and Gender*.

22. Bainbridge, *Mountaineering and British Romanticism*; Andrews, *Wanderers*.

23. Pearson and Shanks, *Theatre/Archaeology*, 148.

24. De Certeau, *The Practice of Everyday Life*, 93.

25. Vergunst, "Rhythms of Walking," 381.

26. Stadler, Mitchell, and Carelton, *Imagined Landscapes*, 138.

27. Stadler, Mitchell, and Carelton, 138.

28. Wylie, "Depths and Fold," 533.

29. Murrieta-Flores, Donaldson, and Gregory, "GIS and Literary History."

30. Woolf, *Street Haunting and Other Essays*, 226–227.

31. Forgione, "Everyday Life in Motion, 664–687; O'Byrne, "The Art of Walking in London," 94–107; Brown and Shortell, *Walking in the European City*; Vila-Cabanes, *The Flaneur in Nineteenth-Century British Literary Culture*; Bock and Vila-Cabanes, eds., *Urban Walking*.

32. Langan, *Romantic Vagrancy*.

33. Roe, *The Politics of Nature*, 171.

34. Jarvis, *Romantic Writing and Pedestrian Travel*, 27.

35. Turnbull, "Keswick's Mass Trespass"; Anon, "Mass Trespass on Latrigg Recalled."

36. Lake District National Park Partnership, *Nomination of the English Lake District for Inscription*, 212.

37. Watson, *The Literary Tourist*, 1.

38. Palmer, *Lake Country Rambles*, 1.

39. Baines, *A Companion to the Lakes of Cumberland, Westmoreland, and Lancashire*; Rix, *Down the Duddon*; Coleridge, *The Notebooks of Samuel Taylor Coleridge*; Waugh, *Rambles in the Lake Country*.

40. Keats, "Letter to Thomas Keats, 25–27 June 1818."

41. "scamander, v.," in *OED Online*.

42. "Hike, v.," in *OED Online*.

43. Jennings, *Observations on Some of the Dialects*, 44.

44. Wilkinson, *Tours to the British Mountains*, 170.

45. Waugh, *Rambles in the Lake Country*, 230.

46. Forgione, "Everyday Life in Motion," 668.

47. Walker, *Remarks Made in a Tour from London.*

48. Wallace, *Walking, Literature and English Culture*, 79, 118.

49. Bushell, "Wordsworth's Excursion," 4.

50. Bushell, 4.

51. Rosenberg, "Walking in the City," 131.

52. Liu, *Wordsworth: The Sense of History*, 88.

53. Tuan, "Geography, Phenomenology, and the Study of Human Nature," 190.

54. Martineau, *A Complete Guide to the English Lakes*, 163.

55. Budworth, *A Fortnight's Ramble to the Lakes*, 144.

56. Lake District National Park Partnership, *Nomination of the English Lake District for Inscription*, 566.

57. Palmer, *In Lakeland Dells and Fells*, 62.

58. Murrieta-Flores, Donaldson, and Gregory, "GIS and Literary History."

59. West, *A Guide to the Lakes*, 4–5.

60. Rutherford, "Claife Station and the Picturesque in the Lakes."

61. Palmer, *In Lakeland Dells and Fells*, 61.

62. McGann, *The Scholar's Art*, 161; see also Moretti, *Distant Reading*, 206.

63. Newte, *A Tour in England and Scotland, in 1785*, 54.

64. Budworth, *A Fortnight's Ramble to the Lakes*, 128.

65. Williamson, "The Climbs of the English Lake District," 111.

66. Williamson, 111.

67. Southey, *Letters from England, by Don Manuel Alvarez Espriella*, 240.

68. Gaskell, *The Life of Charlotte Brontë (1857)*, 334.

69. Gaskell, 335.

70. Buzard, *The Beaten Track*, 149.

71. Wallace, *Walking, Literature and English Culture*, 3.

72. Jarvis, *Romantic Writing and Pedestrian Travel*, 9; see also Jones, "John 'Walking' Stewart, and the Ethics of Motion," 119–131.

73. Holt, "Historical Landscape and the Moving Image," 190–191.

74. Jarvis, *Romantic Writing and Pedestrian Travel*, 30.

75. Ruskin, *Iteriad*, v. V.197–220.

76. Frith, *Wanderings in Wordsworthshire*, 421.

77. Budworth, *A Fortnight's Ramble to the Lakes*; Gibson, *The Old Man*; Thorne, *Rambles by Rivers*; Anon, *Gleanings of a Wanderer.*

78. Ramsay, "In Praise of Pattern," 180.

79. Houghton Walker, *Representations of the Gypsy.*

80. Hartman, "Romanticism and 'Anti-Self-Consciousness,'" 553–565; Hasan-Rokem and Dundes, *The Wandering Jew*; Thomson, "Wordsworth's 'song for the Wandering Jew,'" 37–47.

81. Houghton Walker, *Representations of the Gypsy*, 133.

82. Powell, "Johnson and His 'Readers,'" 571.

83. Fussell, *Samuel Johnson and the Life of Writing.*

84. Damrosch, "Johnson's Manner of Proceeding in the Rambler," 70–89.

85. O'Flaherty, "Towards an Understanding of Johnson's Rambler," 527; Robbins, "Victorian Cosmopolitanism, Interrupted," 421.

86. Van Tassel, "Johnson's Elephant," 462.

87. Waugh, *Rambles in the Lake Country and Its Borders*, 87.

88. Waugh, 88.

89. Jarvis, *Romantic Writing and Pedestrian Travel*, 32.

90. Piatti et al., "Mapping Literature," 177–183.

91. Wallace, *Walking, Literature and English Culture*, 120.

92. Drayton, *Poly-Olbion: A Chorographicall Description*, 136.

93. Combe, *The Tour of Doctor Syntax*, 77.

94. Abrams, *Natural Supernaturalism*, 193.

95. Houghton Walker, *Representations of the Gypsy*, 133.

96. Wallace, *Walking, Literature and English Culture*, 118.

97. Simpson, *Wordsworth's Historical Imagination*, 48.

98. Wallace, *Walking, Literature and English Culture*, 118.

99. Wordsworth, *Cornell Edition: The Excursion*, vol. I.132–39.

100. Wallace, *Walking, Literature and English Culture*, 122.

101. Gill, *Wordsworth and the Victorians*; Bushell, *Re-reading the Excursion*.

102. Baines, *A Companion to the Lakes of Cumberland, Westmoreland, and Lancashire*, 95.

103. Yarnall, *Walks and Visits in Wordsworth Country [1876]*, 98–99.

104. Easley, "The Woman of Letters at Home," 291.

105. Andrews, *Wanderers*, 139–145.

106. Todd, *Harriet Martineau at Ambleside*, 159 [original emphasis].

107. Andrews, *Wanderers*, 14.

108. Easley, "The Woman of Letters at Home," 297.

109. Wells-Brown, *Three Years in Europe*, 199–200.

CHAPTER 5 — SEEING SOUND

1. Bicknell, *The Illustrated Wordsworth's Guide to the Lakes*, 192.

2. Bicknell, 192.

3. Coates, "The Strange Stillness of the Past," 641.

4. Rosenfeld, "On Being Heard," 318.

5. Taylor, "Echoes in the Mountains," 383–406.

6. Kaltenecker, "The Discourse of Sound," 9.

7. Wolfson, "Sounding Romantic."

8. Hamilton et al., "Phenomenology in Practice," 31–71; Lindquist, Lange, and Kang, "From 3D Landscape Visualization to Environmental Simulation," 216–231.

9. Kuduk Weiner, "Listening with John Clare," 377.

10. Rowney, "Music in the Noise," 25.

11. Thompson, *The Soundscape of Modernity*, 1.

12. Lefebvre, *The Production of Space*, 47–48.

13. Smith, ed., *Hearing History*, ix.

14. Schafer, *The Soundscape*, 9–10.

15. Schafer, 11.

16. Truax, "The Handbook for Acoustic Ecology."

17. Morton, *Ecology without Nature*, 42.

18. Szendy, *Listen: A History of Our Ears*, 15.

19. Pijanowski et al., "Soundscape Ecology," 203.

20. Pijanowski et al., 204; Krause, "Bioacoustics," 14–18.

21. Schönherr, "Topophony of Fascism," 328–348; Fox, "Topophony."

22. Smith, "Soundscape," 233.

23. Agnew, "Hearing Things," 67–84.

24. Febvre, *The Problem of Unbelief*, 424–437; Corbin, *Village Bells*; Smith, *The Acoustic World of Early Modern England*; Rosenfeld, "On Being Heard."

25. Fisher, "The Value of Natural Sounds," 488.

26. Picker, *Victorian Soundscapes*.

27. Lefebvre, *Rhythmanalysis*, 37.

28. Leigh, *Leigh's Guide to the Lakes and Mountains*, 54.

29. Cohen, *Sensible Words*.

30. Agnew, "Hearing Things"; Dubois, "The Impossible Temptation of Noise," 29; Joy, "Relative Obscurity," 644–661.

31. Beattie, *Essays: On Poetry & Music*, 142.

32. Burke, *A Philosophical Enquiry into the Origin of Our Ideas*, 66.

33. Duff, *An Essay on Original Genius*, 251–253.

34. Wordsworth, *The Major Works*, 611.

35. Wordsworth, *The Thirteen-Book "Prelude,"* bk. II.324–325.

36. Wordsworth, bk. II.322–323.

37. Lefebvre, *Rhythmanalysis*, 37.

38. George, *Notes to William Wordsworth*, 291.

39. Fulford, *The Late Poetry of the Lake Poets*, 235.

40. Wordsworth, *The Major Works*, lines 37–40 [original emphasis].

41. Fulford, *The Late Poetry of the Lake Poets*, 235.

42. Chandler, "The 'Power of Sound' and the Great Scheme of Things."

43. Wordsworth, *The Thirteen-Book "Prelude,"* bk. VIII.10–52.

44. Wordsworth, bk. VIII.13.

45. Wordsworth, bk. VIII.1–4.

46. Wolfson, "Sounding Romantic."

47. Cooke, *The Tourist's and Traveller's Companion*, 95–96.

48. Upton, "Sound as Landscape," 26.

49. Cates, "The Strange Stillness of the Past," 643.

50. Rosenfeld, "On Being Heard," 323; Chesnokova et al., "Hearing the Silence."

51. Bachelard, *The Poetics of Space*, 43.

52. Cage, *Experimental Music*, 13–14.

53. Coates, "The Strange Stillness of the Past," 642.

54. Fisher, "What the Hills Are Alive With," 170.

55. Prynne, *Field Notes*, 28–29.

56. Wordsworth, *The Thirteen-Book "Prelude,"* bk. II.326–330.

57. Jacobus, *Romantic Things*, 150.

58. Anon, *Rambling Notes of a Rambling Tour*, 89.

59. Levinson, *Wordsworth's Great Period Poems: Four Essays*, 32.

60. Rowney, "Music in the Noise," 24.

61. Denney et al., eds., *Sound, Space and Civility*, 3.

62. Anon, *Rambling Notes of a Rambling Tour*, 36.

63. Anon, 88.

64. Wordsworth, *Wordsworth's Guide to the Lakes: The Fifth Edition (1835)*, 45.

65. "sonorous, Adj.," in *OED Online*.

66. Thoreau, *The Correspondence of Henry David Thoreau*, 79.

67. Fisher, "The Value of Natural Sounds," 28.

68. Coleridge, *Letters of Samuel Taylor Coleridge*, 844.

69. Fulford, *The Late Poetry of the Lake Poets*, 55.

70. Terry, "'The Sound Must Seem an Eccho to the Sense,'" 940.

71. Anon, *Keswick and Its Neighbourhood*, 28.

72. Wolfson, "Sounding Romantic."

73. Taylor, "Settling at Keswick," 68–69.

74. Fulford, *The Late Poetry of the Lake Poets*, 52.

75. Hollander, "Wordsworth and the Music of Sound," 44; Téchené, "On the Use and Representations of Sound," 29.

76. Baillie, *Collection of Poems*, 283.

77. Fulford, "The Materialization of the Lyric," 15.

78. Baillie, *Further Letters of Joanna Baillie*, 27.

79. Fulford, *The Late Poetry of the Lake Poets*, 54.

80. Baillie, 282.

81. Baillie, *Collection of Poems*, 280.

82. Baillie, 283.

83. Anon, *Keswick and Its Neighbourhood*, 29.

84. Anon, *The English Lakes*, 23.

85. Hainton and Hainton, *The Unknown Coleridge*, 228.

86. Fisher, "The Value of Natural Sounds," 27.

87. Rosenfeld, "On Being Heard," 323.

88. Street, *The Memory of Sound*, 3.

89. Revill, "How Is Space Made in Sound?" 267.

90. Hollander, *The Figure of Echo*, 3.

91. Rossetti, *The Poetical Works of Christina Georgina Rossetti*, 314.

92. Wordsworth, *The Major Works*, lines 33–36.

93. Klett, "Sound on Sound," 150.

94. Cooke, *The Tourist's and Traveller's Companion*, 76.

95. Coleridge, *Letters of Samuel Taylor Coleridge*, II:844.

96. Baines, *A Companion to the Lakes*, 134.

97. Wordsworth, *The River Duddon*, 34.

98. Corbin, *Village Bells*, 5 [original emphasis].

99. Corbin, 97.

100. Cullen Rath, *How Early America Sounded*.

101. Bour, "Foreword: Noise and Sound,"

102. Block, "Modalities of Sound, Light, and Color," 230.

103. Block, 228–230.

104. Agnew, "Hearing Things."

105. Fisher, "The Value of Natural Sounds," 28.

106. Fisher, "What the Hills Are Alive With," 172.

107. Gilpin, *Observations, Relative Chiefly to Picturesque Beauty*, 60.

108. Gilpin, 60.

109. Wordsworth, *Wordsworth's Guide to the Lakes: The Fifth Edition (1835)*, 22.

110. Hutchinson, *An Excursion to the Lakes*, 68–69.

111. Hutchinson, 68–69.

112. Fisher, "The Value of Natural Sounds," 30.

113. Klett, "Sound on Sound," 151.

114. Fulford, *The Late Poetry of the Lake Poets*, 218.

115. Southey, *Letters from England, by Don Manuel Alvarez Espriella*, 302.

116. Southey, 66.

117. Street, *The Memory of Sound*, 3.

118. Baines, *A Companion to the Lakes*, 210.

119. Morton, *Ecology without Nature*, 43.

CHAPTER 6 — DIGITAL CARTOGRAPHIES AND PERSONAL GEOGRAPHIES

1. Carlson, *Romantic Marks and Measures*; Hall, *Romantic Naturalists, Early Environmentalists*; Hewitt, *Map of a Nation*; Wiley, *Romantic Geography*.
2. Abend and Harvey, "Maps as Geomedial Action Spaces," 172.
3. Gilge, "Google Street View and the Image as Experience," 270.
4. Scott, "Colonialism, Landscape and the Subterranean," 1858.
5. Huggan, "Decolonizing the Map," 115–131; Howard, *Cartographies and Visualization*.
6. Edwards, "How to Read an Early Modern Map," 56.
7. Adey, Whitehead, and Williams, "Introduction: Air-Target Distance," 176.
8. Graham and Hewitt, "Getting Off the Ground," 72–92.
9. Weizman, "Maps of Israeli Settlements," 3.
10. O'Neill and Fogarty-Valenzuela, "Verticality," 383–384.
11. Eve, "Augmenting Phenomenology," 585.
12. Cooper and Priestnall, "The Processual Intertextuality of Literary Cartographies," 250.
13. Ogburn, "Assessing the Level of Visibility of Cultural Objects," 405–413.
14. Eve, "Augmenting Phenomenology," 586.
15. Gillings, "Landscape Phenomenology," 609.
16. Macfarlane, *The Wild Places*, 218.
17. Wilkinson, *Tours to the British Mountains*, 228.
18. Leigh, *Leigh's Guide to the Lakes and Mountains*, 102.
19. Hewitt, *Map of a Nation*.
20. "The Database of British and Irish Hills."
21. Wilkinson, *Tours to the British Mountains*, 228.
22. "The Database of British and Irish Hills."
23. Anon, *Black's Shilling Guide to the English Lakes*, 46.
24. Otley, *A Concise Description of the English Lakes and Adjacent Mountains*, 64.
25. Anon, *Black's Shilling Guide to the English Lakes*, 47.
26. Anon, 47.
27. Anon, 46.
28. Baddeley, *Black's Shilling Guide to the English Lakes*, 109.
29. Baddeley, 109.
30. Colley, *Victorians in the Mountains*; Bainbridge, "Romantic Writers and Mountaineering," 1–15; Bainbridge, *Mountaineering and British Romanticism*; Hansen, *The Summits of Modern Man*; Westaway, "Mountains of Memory, Landscapes of Loss," 174–193; Musa, Higham, and Thompson-Carr, *Mountaineering Tourism*; McNee, *The New Mountaineer in Late Victorian Britain*.
31. Wordsworth, "Letter to William Johnson."
32. Hewitt, "Mapping and Romanticism," 161.
33. Wordsworth, *A Description of the Scenery of the Lakes*, 3.
34. Speich, "Mountains Made in Switzerland," 395.
35. Carlson, *Romantic Marks and Measures*, 60.
36. Nicolson, *Mountain Gloom and Mountain Glory*; Macfarlane, *Mountains of the Mind*.
37. Wilkinson, *Tours to the British Mountains*, v, 229.
38. Wilkinson, *Tours to the British Mountains*, vi [original emphasis].
39. Anon, "Works Preparing for Publication," 474.
40. Linton, *The Lake Country*, 210.
41. Linton, 210.
42. Linton, 210.
43. Colley, "John Ruskin: Climbing and the Vulnerable Eye," 48.

44. Linton, *The Lake Country*, 210.

45. Linton, 210.

46. Wilberforce, *Journey to the Lake District from Cambridge*, 73.

47. Radcliffe, *A Journey Made in the Summer of 1791*, 455.

48. Donaldson, Gregory, and Taylor, "Locating the Beautiful," 53.

49. Ayto, Crofton, and Cavill, eds., "Scafell Pike."

50. Ousby, *James Plumptre's Britain*, 139.

51. Wilkinson, *Tours to the British Mountains*, 228.

52. Ousby, *James Plumptre's Britain*, 139.

53. Wilkinson, *Tours to the British Mountains*, 227.

54. Wordsworth, *The Letters of William and Dorothy Wordsworth*, 507.

55. Westaway, "Mountains of Memory, Landscapes of Loss," 179.

56. Wilkinson, *Tours to the British Mountains*, 225.

57. Green, "The Tourist's New Guide."

58. O'Neill and Fogarty-Valenzuela, "Verticality," 388.

59. Dennis, "'Babylonian Flats' in Victorian and Edwardian London," 233–247.

60. Westaway, "Mountains of Memory, Landscapes of Loss," 175.

61. Leigh, *Leigh's Guide to the Lakes and Mountains of Cumberland*, 103.

62. Coleridge, *Letters of Samuel Taylor Coleridge*, II:844.

63. Anon, *Rambling Notes of a Rambling Tour*, 6–8.

64. Taylor, "Mountain Matter(s)."

65. Holmes, *Coleridge: Early Visions*, 328.

66. Austin, ed., *Characteristics of Goethe*.

67. Modiano, *Coleridge and the Concept of Nature*.

68. Donaldson, Gregory, and Murrieta-Flores, "Mapping 'Wordsworthshire,'" 287–307.

69. Cooper and Gregory, "Mapping the English Lake District."

70. Cooper, Gregory, and Bushell, *Coleridge's "Circumcursion": Mappings*.

71. Coleridge, *The Notebooks of Samuel Taylor Coleridge*, vol. 1, vol. I.1206n.

72. Coleridge, vol. 1, sec. 1205.

73. Taylor, "Mountain Matter(s)," 29.

74. Baker, "Landscape as Textual Practice," 667.

75. Coleridge, *Letters of Samuel Taylor Coleridge*, II:846.

76. Coleridge, II:840.

77. Coleridge, II:840.

78. Coleridge, II:841.

79. Wilkinson, *Tours to the British Mountains*, 226–227.

80. Bainbridge, "Romantic Writers and Mountaineering," 10.

81. Westaway, "The Origins and Development of Mountaineering," 173.

82. Williamson, "The Climbs of the English Lake District," Part 2, 112.

83. Ingold, "Earth, Sky, Wind, and Weather," 19.

84. Bainbridge, "Romantic Writers and Mountaineering," 9.

85. Coleridge, *Letters of Samuel Taylor Coleridge*, II:841–842.

86. Vardy, "Coleridge on Broad Stand."

87. Westaway, "The Origins and Development of Mountaineering," 179.

88. Carlson, *Romantic Marks and Measures*, 60.

89. Coleridge, *The Notebooks of Samuel Taylor Coleridge*, vol. 1, sec. 1675.

90. Bainbridge, "Romantic Writers and Mountaineering," 5.

91. Mackay, *The Scenery and Poetry of the English Lakes*, 146.

92. Wilkinson, *Tours to the British Mountains*, 226.

93. Wilkinson, 228.

94. Wilkinson, 227.

95. Broglio, "Mapping British Earth and Sky," 72.

96. Southey, "The Collected Letters of Robert Southey, Part Five: 1816–1818," 2016, sec. 2849.

97. Wordsworth, "Letter to William Johnson."

98. Martineau, *A Complete Guide to the English Lakes*, 158.

99. Bellanca, "After-Life-Writing," 212.

100. Wordsworth, "Letter to William Johnson."

101. Wordsworth.

102. Wordsworth.

103. Levin, *Dorothy Wordsworth and Romanticism*, 66.

104. Stewart, "'The Eye It Cannot Choose but See.'"

105. Stewart, 418.

106. Boden, "Introduction," xiii.

107. Wordsworth, "Letter to William Johnson."

108. Wordsworth.

109. Bainbridge, "Romantic Writers and Mountaineering," 6.

110. Van Renen, "Decomposing the Picturesque," 166.

111. Wordsworth, "Letter to William Johnson."

112. Bellanca, "After-Life-Writing," 211.

113. Wordsworth, "Letter to William Johnson."

114. Feder, "The Experimental Dorothy Wordsworth," 543.

115. Wordsworth, "Letter to William Johnson."

116. Anon, *Black's Shilling Guide to the English Lakes*, 47.

117. Bainbridge, "Writing 'from the Perilous Ridge,'" 252.

118. Otley, *A Concise Description of the English Lakes*.

119. Williamson, "The Climbs of the English Lake District," Part 2," 110.

CONCLUSION

1. Hammond, Brooke, and Hirst, "Modeling Modernist Dialogism," 50.

2. Kwan, "Visualization"; Kwan, "Is GIS for Women?"

3. Taylor, "Editorial comment: GKS."

4. Bartholl, *Map*, 2006, Sculpture in steel, aluminum mesh, steel cables; Guffey, "The Virtual Paintout"; Southern, "Reflective Assemblages," 15–25; Mennis, "Geographic Representation in GIS and Art," 178–195.

5. Gregory and Cooper, "Thomas Gray, Samuel Taylor Coleridge and Geographical Information Systems," 61–84; Cooper and Gregory, "Mapping the English Lake District."

6. Rupp et al., "Dealing with Heterogeneous Big Data"; Gregory et al., "Geoparsing, GIS and Textual Analysis"; Gregory and Hardie, "Visual GISting," 297–314.

7. Murrieta-Flores et al., "Automatically Analysing Large Texts in a GIS Environment"; Donaldson, Gregory, and Murrieta-Flores, "Mapping 'Wordsworthshire'"; Porter, Atkinson, and Gregory, "Geographical Text Analysis."

8. Donaldson, Gregory, and Taylor, "Locating the Beautiful, Picturesque, Sublime and Majestic"; Taylor, Gregory, and Donaldson, "Combining Close and Distant Reading."

9. For more information about Duncan Hay's Python workshop, visit his GitHub page, https://ddunc23.github.io/.

10. Miller, "God Is in the Machine."

11. McCarty, *Humanities Computing*.

12. McGonigal, "Gaming Can Make a Better World"; Sandbrook, Adams, and Monteferri, "Digital Games and Biodiversity Conservation," 118–124; Reinhold, Gregory, and Rayson, "Deep Mapping Tarn Hows"; Butler and Bushell, *Chronotopic Cartographies: Litcraft.*

13. Taylor and Donaldson, "Footprints in Spatial Narratives."

14. Gaio and Moncla, "Extended Name Entity Recognition"; Karimzadeh et al., "GeoTxt," 118–136.

15. Bushell, *Reading and Mapping Fiction.*

16. Stell, "Qualitative Spatial Reasoning for the Humanities."

Bibliography

Abend, Pablo, and Francis Harvey. "Maps as Geomedial Action Spaces: Considering the Shift from Logocentric to Egocentric Engagements." *GeoJournal*, 82 (2017): 171–183.

Abrams, M. H. *Natural Supernaturalism: Tradition and Revolution in Romantic Literature*. London: W.W. Norton, 1971.

Ackerman, James S. "The Photographic Picturesque." *Artibus et Historiae* 24, no. 48 (2003): 73–94.

Adey, Peter, Mark Whitehead, and Alison J. Williams. "Introduction: Air-Target Distance, Reach and the Politics of Verticality." *Theory, Culture & Society* 28, no. 7–8 (2011): 173–187.

Adolphs, Svenja. *Introducing Electronic Text Analysis*. London: Routledge, 2006.

Agnew, Vanessa. "Hearing Things: Music and Sounds the Traveller Heard and Didn't Hear on the Grand Tour." *Cultural Studies Review* 18, no. 3 (2012): 67–84.

Allison, Sarah. *Reductive Reading: A Syntax of Victorian Moralizing*. Baltimore: Johns Hopkins University Press, 2018.

Anderson, Benedict. *Imagined Communities: Reflections on the Origins and Spread of Nationalism*. London: Verso, 1983.

Anderson, Nancy Fix. *Woman against Women in Victorian England: A Life of Eliza Lynn Linton*. Bloomington: Indiana University Press, 1987.

Andrews, Kerri. *Wanderers: A History of Women Walking*. London: Reaktion Books, 2020.

Andrews, Malcolm. *The Search for the Picturesque: Landscape Aesthetics and Tourism in Britain, 1760–1800*. Palo Alto, CA: Stanford University Press, 1989.

Anon. *Black's Shilling Guide to the English Lakes*. Edinburgh: A. and C. Black, 1853.

———. *Nelson's Handbooks for Tourists: The English Lakes*. London: Thomas Nelson & Sons, 1857.

———. *Gleanings of a Wanderer, in Various Parts of England, Scotland, & North Wales, Made during an Excursion in the Year 1804*. London: Richard Phillips, 1805.

———. *Keswick and Its Neighbourhood: A Hand-Book for the Use of Visitors*. Windermere and London: J. Garnett, and Whittaker and Co., 1852.

———. "Mass Trespass on Latrigg Recalled." *Cumberland & Westmorland Herald*, April 2, 2015. http://www.cwherald.com/a/archive/mass-trespass-on-latrigg-recalled.440708.html.

———. *Rambling Notes of a Rambling Tour, through Some of the English Lake Scenery, by a Volunteer Rifleman*. Sunderland and Windermere: William Henry Hills and J. Garnett, 1861.

————. "Works Preparing for Publication." *Blackwood's Edinburgh Magazine*, July 1818, 474.

Anthony, Laurence. "AntConc: A Learner and Classroom Friendly, Multi-platform Corpus Analysis Toolkit." In *Proceedings of IWLeL 2004: An Interactive Workshop on Language e-Learning*, 2005, 7–13.

Arts, Koen, René Wal, and William M. Adams. "Digital Technology and the Conservation of Nature." *Ambio* 44, no. 4 (2015): 661–673.

Ascari, Maurizio. "The Dangers of Distant Reading: Reassessing Moretti's Approach to Literary Genres." *Genre* 47, no. 1 (2014): 1–19.

Atkinson, Paul, and Ian N. Gregory. "Finding Child Welfare in Victorian Newspapers: An Exercise in Corpus-Based Discourse Analysis." *Journal of Interdisciplinary History*, 48 (2017): 159–186.

Auerbach, Jeffrey. "The Picturesque and the Homogenisation of Empire." *British Art Journal* 5, no. 1 (2004): 47–54.

Austin, Linda Marilyn. "Aesthetic Embarrassment: The Reversion to the Picturesque in Nineteenth-Century English Tourism." *ELH* 74, no. 3 (2007): 629–653.

————. *Automatism and Creative Acts in the Age of New Psychology*. Cambridge: Cambridge University Press, 2018.

Austin, Sarah, ed. *Characteristics of Goethe from the German of Falk, Von Müller, &c.* Vol. 3. London: Effingham Wilson, 1833.

Ayto, John, Ian Crofton, and Paul Cavill, eds. "Scafell Pike." In *Brewer's Britain and Ireland*. Edinburgh: Chambers Harrap, 2005. Accessed November 3, 2021. http://ezproxy .lancs.ac.uk/login?url=https://search.credoreference.com/content/entry /orionbritainireland/scafell_pike/0?institutionId=3497.

Bachelard, Gaston. *The Poetics of Space*. Translated by Maria Jolas. Boston, MA: Beacon Press, 1994.

Baddeley, M.J.B. *Black's Shilling Guide to the English Lakes*. Edinburgh: A. and C. Black, 1900.

Baillie, Joanna. *Collection of Poems, Chiefly Manuscript, and from Living Authors*. London: Longman, 1823.

————. *Further Letters of Joanna Baillie*. Edited by Thomas McLean. Madison, NJ: Fairleigh Dickinson University Press, 2010.

Bainbridge, Simon. *Mountaineering and British Romanticism: The Literary Cultures of Climbing, 1770–1836*. Oxford: Oxford University Press, 2020.

————. "Romantic Writers and Mountaineering." *Romanticism* 18, no. 1 (2012): 1–15.

————. "Writing 'from the Perilous Ridge': Romanticism and the Invention of Rock Climbing." *Romanticism* 19, no. 3 (2013): 246–260.

Baines, Edward. *A Companion to the Lakes of Cumberland, Westmoreland, and Lancashire: In a Descriptive Account of a Family Tour and Excursions on Horseback and on Foot*. London: Simpkin and Marshall, 1829.

Baker, Harold D. "Landscape as Textual Practice in Coleridge's Notebooks." *ELH* 59, no. 3 (1992): 651–670.

Barber, Samuel. *Beneath Helvellyn's Shade: Notes and Sketches in the Valley of Wythburn*. London: E. Stock, 1892.

Barbier, Carl P. *Samuel Rogers and William Gilpin: Their Friendship and Correspondence*. London: Oxford University Press, 1959.

Barnbrook, Geoff, Oliver Mason, and Ramesh Krishnamurthy. *Collocation: Applications and Implications*. Basingstoke, UK: Palgrave Macmillan, 2013.

Barrell, John. *The Dark Side of the Landscape: The Rural Poor in English Painting, 1730–1840*. Cambridge: Cambridge University Press, 1980.

Bartholl, Aram. *Map*. 2006. Sculpture in steel, aluminum mesh, steel cables, 900 × 520 × 20 cm. https://arambartholl.com/map/.

Bate, Jonathan. *Romantic Ecology: Wordsworth and the Environmental Tradition*. London: Routledge, 1991.

———. *The Song of the Earth*. Boston: Harvard University Press, 2000.

Beattie, James. *Essays: On Poetry & Music as They Affect the Mind; on Laughter, and Ludicrous Composition; on the Utility of Classical Learning*. Edinburgh: William Creech, 1778.

Bellanca, Mary Ellen. "After-Life-Writing: Dorothy Wordsworth's Journals in the Memoirs of William Wordsworth." *European Romantic Review* 25, no. 2 (2014): 201–218.

Berleant, Arnold. *Aesthetics and Environment: Theme and Variations on Art and Culture*. Burlington, VT: Ashgate, 2005.

Berman, Merrick Lex, Ruth Mostern, and Humphrey Southall. *Placing Names: Enriching and Integrating Gazetteers*. Bloomington: Indiana University Press, 2016.

Bicknell, Peter, ed. *The Illustrated Wordsworth's Guide to the Lakes*. Hong Kong: St. Martin's Press, 1984.

Blamire, Susanna. *The Poetical Works of Miss Susanna Blamire*. Edinburgh: John Menzies, 1842.

———. "Stoklewath; or, The Cumbrian Village." Eighteenth-Century Poetry Archive. Accessed March 4, 2021. https://www.eighteenthcenturypoetry.org/works/bsb18-w0010.shtml.

Blaxill, Luke. "The Language of Imperialism in British Electoral Politics, 1880–1910." *Journal of Imperial and Commonwealth History* 45 (2017): 416–448.

Block, Ed. "Modalities of Sound, Light, and Color: An Interface of Science, Technology, and Art in the Late Nineteenth Century." *Symposium: A Quarterly Journal in Modern Literatures* 43, no. 4 (December 1989): 227–247. https://doi.org/10.1080/00397709.1990.10733688.

Bock, Oliver, and Isabel Vila-Cabanes, eds. *Urban Walking—the Flâneur as an Icon of Metropolitan Culture in Literature and Film*. Wilmington, DE: Vernon Press, 2020.

Bode, Katherine. *A World of Fiction: Digital Collections and the Future of Literary History*. Ann Arbor: University of Michigan Press, 2018.

Boden, Helen. "Introduction." In *Dorothy Wordsworth, The Continental Journals 1798–1820*. London: Thoemmes Press, 1995: v–xliv.

Bodenhamer, David. "Making the Invisible Visible: Place, Spatial Stories and Deep Maps." In *Literary Mapping in the Digital Age*, edited by David Cooper, Christopher Donaldson, and Patricia Murrieta-Flores, 207–220. London: Routledge, 2016.

Bodenhamer, David, John Corrigan, and Trevor Harris. "Introduction: Deep Maps and the Spatial Humanities." In *Deep Maps and Spatial Narratives*, edited by David Bodenhamer, John Corrigan, and Trevor Harris, 1–6. Bloomington: Indiana University Press, 2015.

Bohls, Elizabeth A. *Romantic Literature and Postcolonial Studies*. Edinburgh: Edinburgh University Press, 2013.

———. *Women Travel Writers and the Language of Aesthetics*. Cambridge: Cambridge University Press, 1995.

Bour, Isabelle. "Foreword: Noise and Sound in the Eighteenth Century." *Etudes Epistémè: Revue de Littérature et de Civilisation*, 29 (2016). http://episteme.revues.org/1136.

Bourrit, Théodore. *Description des glacières de Savoye*. Geneva: Bonnant au Molard, 1773.

Brendon, Piers. *Thomas Cook: 150 Years of Popular Tourism*. London: Secker and Warburg, 1991.

Broglio, Ron. "Mapping British Earth and Sky." *The Wordsworth Circle* 33, no. 2 (2002): 70–76.

———. *Technologies of the Picturesque: British Art, Poetry, and Instruments 1750–1830.* Lewisburg, PA: Bucknell University Press, 2008.

Brown, Evrick, and Timothy Shortell. *Walking in the European City: Quotidian Mobility and Urban Ethnography.* Farnham, UK: Ashgate, 2014.

Budworth, Joseph. *A Fortnight's Ramble to the Lakes in Westmorland, Lancashire, and Cumberland.* London: Hookham and Carpenter, 1792.

Bui, Huong Thanh, Lee Jolliffe, and Anh Minh Nguyen. "Heritage and Aspects of Nation: Vietnam's Ho Chi Minh Museum." In *Tourism and National Identities: An International Perspective,* edited by Elspeth Frew and Leanne White, 151–175. Abingdon, UK: Routledge, 2011.

Burke, Edmund. *A Philosophical Enquiry into the Origin of Our Ideas of the Sublime and Beautiful (1757).* Edited by Adam Phillips. Oxford: Oxford University Press, 1990.

Burnet, Thomas. *Telluris Theoria Sacra, or Sacred Theory of the Earth.* London: H. Lintot, 1734, 1681–1690.

Burnett, John. "Country Diet." In *The Victorian Countryside: Volume Two,* edited by G. E. Mingay, 554–565. London: Routledge and Kegan Paul, 1981.

Bushell, Sally. *Reading and Mapping Fiction: Spatialising the Literary Text.* Cambridge: Cambridge University Press, 2020.

———. *Re-reading The Excursion: Narrative, Response, and the Wordsworthian Dramatic Voice.* Farnham, UK: Ashgate, 2002.

———. "The Slipperiness of Literary Maps: Critical Cartography and Literary Cartography." *Cartographica* 47, no. 3 (2012): 149–160.

———. "Wordsworth's Excursion: Narrative Memory and the 'Minds of Men.'" *Literature Compass,* 1 (2004): 1–12.

Butler, James O., and Sally Bushell. *Chronotopic Cartographies: Litcraft.* 2019. https://www.lancaster.ac.uk/chronotopic—cartographies/litcraft/.

Butler, James O., Christopher E. Donaldson, Joanna E. Taylor, and Ian N. Gregory. "Alts, Abbreviations, and AKAs: Historical Onomastic Variation and Automated Named Entity Recognition." *Journal of Map & Geography Libraries* 13, no. 1 (2017): 58–81.

Buzard, James. *The Beaten Track: European Tourism, Literature, and the Ways to "Culture" 1800–1918.* Oxford: Oxford University Press, 1993.

Byerly, Alison. "The Uses of Landscape: The Picturesque Aesthetic and the National Park System." In *The Ecocriticism Reader: Landmarks in Literary Ecology,* edited by Cheryll Glotfelty and Harold Fromm, 52–68. Athens: University of Georgia Press, 1996.

Cadwalladr, Carole. "Frédéric Gros: Why Going for a Walk Is the Best Way to Free Your Mind." *The Guardian,* April 19, 2014, sec. Books. http://www.theguardian.com/books/2014/apr/20/frederic-gros-walk-nietzsche-kant.

Cage, John. *Experimental Music: Doctrine.* Middletown, CT: Wesleyan University Press, 1957.

Campelo, Adriana, and Robert Aitken. "Travelling to the Past: Narratives of Place and National Identity on the Chatham Islands." In *Tourism and National Identities: An International Perspective,* edited by Elspeth Frew and Leanne White, 190–201. Abingdon, UK: Routledge, 2011.

Carlson, Julia S. *Romantic Marks and Measures: Wordsworth's Poetry in Fields of Print.* Philadelphia: University of Pennsylvania Press, 2016.

Carpenter, J. R. *An Ocean of Static.* London: Penned in the Margins, 2018.

Carter, Nathaniel Hazeltine. *Letters from Europe: Comprising the Journal of a Tour through Ireland, England, France, Italy, and Switzerland.* New York: G. and C. Carvill, 1827.

Carter, Paul. *The Road to Botany Bay: An Exploration of Landscape and History.* Minneapolis: University of Minnesota Press, 1987.

Chainey, Spencer, and Jerry Ratcliffe. *GIS and Crime Mapping.* London: Wiley-Blackwell, 2005.

Chandler, James. "'The "Power of Sound' and the Great Scheme of Things: Wordsworth Listens to Wordsworth." In *"Soundings of Things Done": The Poetry and Poetics of Sound in the Romantic Ear and Era,* edited by Susan J. Wolfson. Boulder, CO: Romantic Circles, 2008. https://www.rc.umd.edu/praxis/soundings/chandler/chandler.html.

Chard, Chloe. "Introduction." In *Transports: Travel, Pleasure, and Imaginative Geography, 1600–1830,* edited by Chloe Chard and Helen Landon. New Haven, CT: Yale University Press, 1996: 1–29.

Chesnokova, Olga, Joanna Taylor, Ian N. Gregory, and Ross S. Purves. "Hearing the Silence: Finding the Middle Ground in the Spatial Humanities? Extracting and Comparing Perceived Silence and Tranquility in the English Lake District." *International Journal of Geographical Information Science,* 2018. https://doi.org/10.1080/13658816.2018.1552789.

Clement, Tanya. *Text Analysis, Data Mining, and Visualizations in Literary Scholarship; MLA Commons,* 2013. https://dlsanthology.mla.hcommons.org/text-analysis-data-mining-and-visualizations-in-literary-scholarship/.

Coates, Peter A. "The Strange Stillness of the Past: Toward an Environmental History of Sound and Noise." *Environmental History* 10, no. 4 (2005): 636–665.

Cockin, William. *Ode to the Genius of the Lakes in the North of England.* London: W. Cockin, 1780.

Cohen, Murray. *Sensible Words: Linguistic Practice in England 1640–1785.* Baltimore: Johns Hopkins University Press, 1979.

Coleridge, Samuel Taylor. *Letters of Samuel Taylor Coleridge.* Edited by Earl Leslie Griggs. Vol. II. Oxford: Clarendon Press, 1956.

———. *The Collected Works of Samuel Taylor Coleridge: Poetical Works.* Edited by J.C.C. Mays. 3 vols. Princeton, NJ: Princeton University Press, 2001.

———. *The Notebooks of Samuel Taylor Coleridge.* Edited by Kathleen Coburn. Vol. 1. London: Routledge and Kegan Paul, 1957.

Colley, Ann C. "John Ruskin: Climbing and the Vulnerable Eye." *Victorian Literature and Culture* 37 (2009): 43–66.

———. *Victorians in the Mountains: Sinking the Sublime.* Farnham: Ashgate, 2010.

Combe, William. *The Tour of Doctor Syntax in Search of the Picturesque.* London: R. Ackermann, 1812.

Cooke, Charles. *The Tourist's and Traveller's Companion to the Lakes of Cumberland, Westmoreland, and Lancashire.* London: Sherwood, Jones and Co, 1827.

Cooper, David. "The Poetics of Place and Space: Wordsworth, Norman Nicholson and the Lake District." *Literature Compass* 5, no. 4 (2008): 807–21.

Cooper, David, and Ian N. Gregory. "Mapping the English Lake District: A Literary GIS." *Transactions of the Institute of British Geographers* 36 (2010): 89–108.

Cooper, David, Ian N. Gregory, and Sally Bushell. *Coleridge's "Circumcursion": Mappings,* 2008. http://www.lancaster.ac.uk/mappingthelakes/Coleridge%20Mapping.htm.

Cooper, David, and Gary Priestnall. "The Processual Intertextuality of Literary Cartographies: Critical and Digital Practices." *Cartographic Journal* 48, no. 4 (2011): 250–262.

Coppock, J. Terry, and David Rhind. "The History of GIS." In *Geographical Information Systems: Principles and Applications. Volume I: Principles,* edited by David J. Maguire., Michael F. Goodchild, and David Rhind, 21–43. London: Longman Scientific and Technical, 1991.

Corbin, Alain. *Village Bells: Sound and Meaning in the Nineteenth-Century French Countryside*. Translated by Martin Thorn. New York: Columbia University Press, 1999.

Cosgrove, Denis E. "Seminar Discussion." In *Landscape Theory*, edited by Rachael Ziady Delue and James Elkins, 128. New York: Routledge, 2008.

Cross, A. "Using a Geographic Information System to Explore the Spatial Incidence of Childhood Cancer in Northern England." In *Proceedings EGIS '90*, 1 (1990): 218–229.

Cullen Rath, Richard. *How Early America Sounded*. Ithaca, NY: Cornell University Press, 2003.

Damrosch Jr., Leopold. "Johnson's Manner of Proceeding in the Rambler." *ELH* 40 (1973): 70–89.

"The Database of British and Irish Hills." 2018. http://www.hills—database.co.uk/downloads.html.

De Certeau, Michel. *The Practice of Everyday Life*. Translated by Stephen Rendall. Berkeley: University of California Press, 1984.

De Selincourt, Ernest, ed. *The Letters of William and Dorothy Wordsworth: The Early Years 1787–1805*. Oxford: Clarendon Press, 1935.

Denney, Peter, Bruce Buchan, David Ellison, and Karen Crawley, eds. *Sound, Space and Civility in the British World, 1700–1850*. Abingdon: Routledge, 2018.

Dennis, Richard. "'Babylonian Flats' in Victorian and Edwardian London." *London Journal* 33, no. 3 (2008): 233–247.

Denyer, Susan. "The Lake District Landscape: Cultural or Natural?" In *The Making of a Cultural Landscape: The English Lake District as Tourist Destination, 1750–2010*, edited by John K. Walton and Jason Wood, 3–30. Farnham, UK: Ashgate, 2013.

Di Palma, Vittoria. *Wasteland: A History*. New Haven, CT: Yale University Press, 2014.

Dixon Hunt, John. *Gardens and the Picturesque: Studies in the History of Landscape Architecture*. Cambridge, MA: The MIT Press, 1994.

———. *The Figure in the Landscape: Poetry, Painting, and Gardening during the Eighteenth Century*. Baltimore: The Johns Hopkins University Press, 1976.

Donaldson, Christopher. "Deep Mapping and Romanticism: 'Practical' Geography in the Poetry of Sir Walter Scott." In *Romantic Cartographies*, edited by Sally Bushell, Julia S. Carlson, and Damian Walford Davies. Cambridge University Press, 2020: 211–231.

———. "'The Travelling Carriage in Old Times': John Ruskin and the Lakes Tour in the Age of William IV." *Yearbook of English Studies* 48 (2018): 101–123.

Donaldson, Christopher, Ian N. Gregory, and Patricia Murrieta-Flores. "Mapping 'Wordsworthshire': A GIS Study of Literary Tourism in Victorian Lakeland." *Journal of Victorian Culture* 20, no. 3 (2015): 287–307.

Donaldson, Christopher, Ian N. Gregory, and Joanna E. Taylor. "Locating the Beautiful, Picturesque, Sublime and Majestic: Spatially Analysing the Application of Aesthetic Terminology in Descriptions of the English Lake District." *Journal of Historical Geography* 56 (April 2017): 43–60. https://doi.org/10.1016/j.jhg.2017.01.006.

Drayton, Michael. *Poly-Olbion: A Chorographicall Description of All the Tracts, Rivers, Mountains, Forests, and Other Parts of This Renowned Isle of Great Britain*. London: A. Mathews, J. Marriott, J. Grismand, and T. Dewe, 1622.

Drucker, Johanna. "Humanities Approaches to Graphical Display." *Digital Humanities Quarterly* 5, no. 1 (2011). http://www.digitalhumanities.org/dhq/vol/5/1/000091/000091.html.

Dubois, Pierre. "The Impossible Temptation of Noise in Late Eighteenth-Century English Music." *Etudes Epistémè: Revue de Littérature et de Civilisation* 29 (2016). https://doi.org/10.4000/episteme.1122.

Duff, William. *An Essay on Original Genius and Its Various Modes of Exertion in Philosophy and the Fine Arts, Particularly in Poetry*. London: Edward and Charles Dilly, 1767.

Easley, Alexis. "The Woman of Letters at Home: Harriet Martineau and the Lake District." *Victorian Literature and Culture* 34 (2006): 291–310.

Edwards, Jess. "How to Read an Early Modern Map: Between the Particular and the General, the Material and the Abstract, Words and Mathematics." *Early Modern Literary Studies* 9, no. 1 (2003): 6, 1–58.

Elder, John. *Imagining the Earth: Poetry and the Vision of Nature.* 2nd ed. Athens: The University of Georgia Press, 1996.

Ellison, Aaron M. "The Suffocating Embrace of Landscape and the Picturesque Conditioning of Ecology." *Landscape Journal: Design, Planning, and Management of the Land* 32, no. 1 (2013): 79–94.

Eve, Martin Paul. *Close Reading with Computers: Textual Scholarship, Computational Formalism, and David Mitchell's Cloud Atlas.* Palo Alto, CA: Stanford University Press, 2019. doi: 10.21627/9781503609372.

Eve, Stuart. "Augmenting Phenomenology: Using Augmented Reality to Aid Archaeological Phenomenology in the Landscape." *Journal of Archaeological Method and Theory* 19, no. 4 (2012): 582–600.

Fairclough, Mary. *John Thelwall and the Politics of the Picturesque.* Edited by Yasmin Solomonescu. Boulder, CO: Romantic Circles, 2013. https://www.rc.umd.edu/praxis/thelwall/HTML/praxis.2011.fairclough.html.

Febvre, Lucien. *The Problem of Unbelief in the Sixteenth Century: The Religion of Rabelais.* Translated by Beatrice Gottlieb. Cambridge, MA: Harvard University Press, 1942.

Feder, Rachel. "The Experimental Dorothy Wordsworth." *Studies in Romanticism* 53, no. 4 (2014): 541–559.

Felluga, Dino Franco, and David Rettenmaier. "Can Victorian Studies Reclaim the Means of Production? Saving the (Digital) Humanities." *Journal of Victorian Culture* 24, no. 3 (2019): 331–343.

Ferri, Sabrina. "Time in Ruins: Melancholy and Modernity in the Pre-Romantic Natural Picturesque." *Italian Studies* 69, no. 2 (2014): 204–230.

Fisher, John Andrew. "The Value of Natural Sounds." *Journal of Aesthetic Education* 33, no. 3 (1999): 26–42.

———. "What the Hills Are Alive With: In Defense of the Sounds of Nature." *Journal of Aesthetics and Art Criticism* 56, no. 2 (1998): 167–179.

Forgione, Nancy. "Everyday Life in Motion: The Art of Walking in Late-Nineteenth-Century Paris." *Art Bulletin* 87, no. 4 (2005): 664–687.

Fotheringham, A. Stewart. "Trends in Quantitative Methods I: Stressing the Local." *Progress in Human Geography* 21 (1997): 88–96.

Fotheringham, A. Stewart, Chris Brunsdon, and Martin Charlton. *Quantitative Geography: Perspectives on Spatial Data Analysis.* New York: Sage, 2000.

Fox, Christopher. "Topophony." *Orchestral Piece,* 2014.

Frith, Henry. *Wanderings in Wordsworthshire.* London: W. Poole, 1881.

Fulford, Tim. *Landscape, Liberty and Authority: Poetry, Criticism and Politics from Thomson to Wordsworth.* Cambridge: Cambridge University Press, 1996.

———. *The Late Poetry of the Lake Poets: Romanticism Revised.* Cambridge: Cambridge University Press, 2013.

———. "The Materialization of the Lyric and the Romantic Construction of Place: Bards and Beats on Dartmoor." *Romanticism* 22, no. 1 (2016): 15–32.

Fussell, Paul. *Abroad: British Literary Travelling between the Wars.* Oxford: Oxford University Press, 1980.

———, ed. *The Norton Book of Travel.* London: W. W. Norton, 1987.

———. *Samuel Johnson and the Life of Writing.* London: W. W. Norton, 1971.

Gage, John. "The Distinctness of Turner." *Journal of the Royal Society of Arts* 123, no. 5228 (1975): 448–458.

Gaio, Mauro, and Ludovic Moncla. "Extended Name Entity Recognition Using Finite—State Transducers: An Application to Place Names." In *The Ninth International Conference on Advanced Geographic Information Systems, Applications, and Services, Mar 2017.* Nice, France, 2017: 15–20.

Gaskell, Elizabeth. *The Life of Charlotte Brontë (1857).* London: Penguin, 1997.

Gaunt, Richard A. "Patrician Landscapes and the Picturesque in Nottinghamshire c.1750–c.1850." *Rural History* 26, no. 2 (2015): 161–180.

George, A. J. *Notes to William Wordsworth, The Prelude, or Growth of a Poet's Mind.* Boston: D. C. Heath, 1888.

Gibson, Alexander Craig. *The Old Man; or Ravings and Ramblings Round Conistone.* London: J. Whittaker, and J. Garnett, 1849.

Gilge, Cheryl. "Google Street View and the Image as Experience." *GeoHumanities* 2, no. 2 (2016): 469–484.

Gill, Stephen. *Wordsworth and the Victorians.* Oxford: Oxford University Press, 2001.

Gillings, Mark. "Landscape Phenomenology, GIS and the Role of Affordance." *Journal of Archaeological Method and Theory* 19, no. 4 (2012): 601–611.

Gilpin, William. *Observations on the River Wye, and Several Parts of South Wales, &c: Relative Chiefly to Picturesque Beauty: Made in the Summer of the Year 1770.* London: A. Strahan, 1800.

———. *Observations, Relative Chiefly to Picturesque Beauty, Made in the Year 1772, on Several Parts of England; Particularly the Mountains, and Lakes of Cumberland, and Westmoreland.* London: R. Blamire, 1786.

Glickman, Susan. *The Picturesque and the Sublime: A Poetics of the Canadian Landscape.* Montreal & Kingston, CA: McGill-Queen's University Press, 1998.

Gold, Matthew K. "Facts, Patterns, Methods, Meaning: Public Knowledge Building in the Digital Humanities," 2015. http://blog.mkgold.net/2015/04/20/facts-patterns-methods-meaning-public-knowledge-building-in-the-digital-humanities.

Goldstone, Andrew. "The Doxa of Reading." *PMLA* 132, no. 3 (May 2017): 636–642. https://doi.org/10.1632/pmla.2017.132.3.636.

Goodchild, Michael F. "Geographical Information Science." *International Journal of Geographical Information Systems* 6 (1992): 31–45.

Graham, Stephen, and Lucy Hewitt. "Getting Off the Ground: On the Politics of Urban Verticality." *Progress in Human Geography* 37, no. 1 (2012): 72–92.

Gray, Thomas. *Journal of a Visit to the Lake District in October 1769.* Edited by William Roberts. Liverpool: Liverpool University Press, 2001.

Green, William. *The Tourist's New Guide, Containing a Description of the Lakes, Mountains and Scenery.* 2 vols. Ambleside, UK: Lough & Co, 1819.

Gregory, Ian, Sally Bushell, Christopher E. Donaldson, and Paul Rayson. "Geospatial Innovation in the Digital Humanities." Accessed September 2, 2017. wp.lancs.ac.uk/lakesdeepmap.

Gregory, Ian N., and David Cooper. "Thomas Gray, Samuel Taylor Coleridge and Geographical Information Systems: A Literary GIS of Two Lake District Tours." *International Journal of Arts and Humanities Computing,* 3 (2009): 61–84.

Gregory, Ian, and Christopher Donaldson. "Geographical Text Analysis: Digital Cartographies of Lake District Literature." In *Literary Mapping in the Digital Age,* edited by David Cooper, Christopher Donaldson and Patricia Murieta-Flores, 67–87. London: Routledge, 2016.

Gregory, Ian N., Christopher Donaldson, Patricia Murrieta-Flores, and Paul Rayson. "Geoparsing, GIS and Textual Analysis: Current Developments in Spatial Humanities Research." *International Journal of Humanities and Arts Computing*, 9 (2015): 1–14.

Gregory, Ian N., and Paul Ell. *Historical GIS: Technologies, Methodologies, Scholarship.* Cambridge: Cambridge University Press, 2007.

Gregory, Ian N., and Alistair Geddes. *Toward Spatial Humanities: Historical GIS & Spatial History.* Bloomington: Indiana University Press, 2014.

Gregory, Ian N., and Andrew Hardie. "Visual GISting: Bringing Together Corpus Linguistics and Geographical Information Systems." *Literary and Linguistic Computing* 26 (2011): 297–314.

Gregory, Ian N., Karen K. Kemp, and Ruth Mostern. "Geographical Information and Historical Research: Current Progress and Future Directions." *History and Computing* 13, no. 1 (2001): 7–23.

Gros, Frédéric. *A Philosophy of Walking.* Translated by John Howe. London: Verso, 2011.

Groth, Alexander J. "Major Ideologies: An Interpretative Survey of Democracy." In *Socialism and Nationalism.* New York: Wiley-Interscience, 1971.

Grover, Claire, Richard Tobin, Kate Byrne, Matthew Woollard, James Reid, Stuart Dunn, and Julian Ball. "Use of the Edinburgh Geoparser for Georeferencing Digitized Historical Collections." *Philosophical Transactions of the Royal Society A* 368 (2010): 3875–3889.

Guffey, Bill. "The Virtual Paintout," 2009–2018. http://virtualpaintout.blogspot.com/

Hainton, Raymonde, and Godfrey Hainton. *The Unknown Coleridge: The Life and Times of Derwent Coleridge, 1800–1883.* London: Janus, 1996.

Hall, Dewey W. *Romantic Naturalists, Early Environmentalists: An Ecocritical Study, 1789–1912.* Farnham, UK: Ashgate, 2014.

Hall, Stephen S. "I, Mercator." In *You Are Here: Personal Geographies and Other Maps of the Imagination,* edited by Katharine Harmon, 15–19. New York: Princeton Architectural Press, 2004.

Hamilton, Sue, Ruth Whitehouse, Ken Brown, Pamela Combes, Edward Herring, and Mike Seager Thomas. "Phenomenology in Practice: Towards a Methodology for a "subjective" Approach." *European Journal of Archaeology* 9, no. 1 (2006): 31–71.

Hammond, Adam, Julian Brooke, and Graeme Hirst. "Modeling Modernist Dialogism: Close Reading with Big Data." In *Reading Modernism with Machines: Digital Humanities and Modernist Literature,* edited by Shawna Ross and James O'Sullivan, 49–78. Basingstoke, UK: Palgrave Macmillan, 2016.

Hanley, Keith, and John K. Walton. *Constructing Cultural Tourism: John Ruskin and the Tourist Gaze.* Bristol, UK: Channel View Publications, 2000.

Hansen, Peter H. *The Summits of Modern Man: Mountaineering after the Enlightenment.* Cambridge, MA: Harvard University Press, 2013.

Hardie, Andrew. "Modest XML for Corpora: Not a Standard, but a Suggestion." *ICAME Journal* 38, no. 1 (2014): 73–103.

Harris, Trevor M. "Deep Geography—Deep Mapping: Spatial Storytelling and a Sense of Place." In *Deep Maps and Spatial Narratives,* edited by David Bodenhamer, John Corrigan, and Trevor Harris, 28–53. Bloomington: Indiana University Press, 2015. https://doi.org/10.2307/j.ctt1zxxzr2.6.

Hartman, Geoffrey H. "Romanticism and 'Anti—Self—Consciousness.'" *Centennial Review* 6, no. 4 (1962): 553–565.

Hasan-Rokem, Galit, and Alan Dundes. *The Wandering Jew: Essays in the Interpretation of a Christian Legend.* Bloomington: Indiana University Press, 1986.

Hembry, Phyllis. *The English Spa 1560–1815: A Social History.* London: The Athlone Press, 1990.

Heringman, Noah. "Romantic Antiquarianism: Introduction." *Romantic Antiquarianism*, 2014.   https://www.rc.umd.edu/praxis/antiquarianism/praxis.antiquarianism.2014 .heringman_lake.html.

———. *Romantic Rocks, Aesthetic Geology*. Ithaca, NY: Cornell University Press, 2004.

Hess, Scott. *William Wordsworth and the Ecology of Authorship: The Roots of Environmentalism in Nineteenth-Century Culture*. Charlottesville: University of Virginia Press, 2012.

Heuser, Ryan, Franco Moretti, and Erik Steiner. *The Emotions of London*. Literary Lab, 13, October 2016. https://litlab.stanford.edu/LiteraryLabPamphlet13.pdf.

Hewitt, Rachel. *Map of a Nation: A Biography of the Ordnance Survey*. London: Granta, 2010.

———. "Mapping and Romanticism." *Wordsworth Circle* 42, no. 2 (2011): 157–165.

Hill, Rosemary. "Keats, Antiquarianism, and the Picturesque." *Essays in Criticism* 64, no. 2 (2014): 119–137.

Hipple Jr., Walter John. *The Beautiful, the Sublime and the Picturesque in Eighteenth—Century British Aesthetic Theory*. Carbondale: The Southern Illinois University Press, 1957.

Hitchcock, Tim. "Confronting the Digital: Or How Academic History Writing Lost the Plot." *Cultural and Social History*, 10 (2013): 9–23.

Hollander, John. *The Figure of Echo: A Mode of Allusion in Milton and After*. Berkeley: University of California Press, 1981.

———. "Wordsworth and the Music of Sound." In *New Perspectives on Coleridge and Wordsworth: Selected Papers from the English Institute*, edited by Geoffrey Hartman, 41–84. New York: Columbia University Press, 1972.

Holmes, Richard. *Coleridge: Early Visions*. London: Harper Collins, 1989.

Holt, Jenny. "Historical Landscape and the Moving Image." *Cultural History* 2, no. 2 (2013): 182–198.

Horn, Pamela. "Country Children." In *The Victorian Countryside: Volume Two*, edited by G. E. Mingay, 521–530. London: Routledge and Kegan Paul, 1981.

———. *Life and Labour in Rural England 1760–1850*. Basingstoke, UK: Macmillan, 1987.

———. *The Rural World, 1780–1850: Social Change in the English Countryside*. London: Hutchinson, 1980.

Houghton Walker, Sarah. *Representations of the Gypsy in the Romantic Period*. Oxford: Oxford University Press, 2014.

Housman, John. *A Topographical Description of Cumberland, Westmoreland, Lancashire, and a Part of the West Riding of Yorkshire*. London: F. Jollie, 1800.

Howard, David. "Cartographies and Visualization." *A Concise Companion to Postcolonial Literature*. Edited by Shirley Chew and David Richards. London: Blackwell, 2010.

Howkins, Alun. *Reshaping Rural England: A Social History 1850–1925*. London: Harper Collins Academic, 1991.

Huggan, Graham. "Decolonizing the Map: Post-colonialism, Post-structuralism and the Cartographic Connection." *Ariel* 20, no. 4 (1989): 115–131.

Huggins, Mike. "Popular Culture and Sporting Life in the Rural Margins of Late Eighteenth-Century England: The World of Robert Anderson, 'The Cumberland Bard.'" *Eighteenth-Century Studies* 45, no. 2 (2012): 189–205.

Hunston, Susan. *Corpora in Applied Linguistics*. Cambridge: Cambridge University Press, 2002.

Hutchinson, William. *An Excursion to the Lakes in Westmoreland and Cumberland*. London: J. Wilkie, 1776.

———. *The History of the County of Cumberland*. Carlisle: F. Jollie, 1794.

Hutton, Catherine. *Oakwood Hall, a Novel, Including a Description of the Lakes of Cumberland and Westmoreland, and a Part of South Wales*. London: Longman, 1819.

Inaki, Akiko, and Tomoko Okita. "A Small-Corpus-Based Approach to Alice's Roles." *Literary and Linguistic Computing* 21, no. 3 (2006): 283–294.

Ingold, Tim. "Earth, Sky, Wind, and Weather." *Journal of the Royal Anthropological Institute*, 13 (2007): 19–38.

Ives, Christopher D., David J. Abson, Henrik Wehrden, Christian Dorninger, Kathleen Klaniecki, and Joern Fisher. "Reconnecting with Nature for Sustainability." *Sustainability Science* 13, no. 5 (2018): 1389–1897.

Jacobus, Mary. *Romantic Things: A Rock, a Tree, a Cloud*. Chicago: University of Chicago Press, 2012.

Jamie, Kathleen. "A Lone Enraptured Male." *London Review of Books* 30, no. 5 (March 6, 2008).

Jarvis, Robin. *Romantic Writing and Pedestrian Travel*. London: Macmillan, 1997.

Jennings, James. *Observations on Some of the Dialects in the West of England*. London: John Russell Smith, 1825.

Jockers, Matthew. *Macroanalysis: Digital Methods & Literary History*. Champaign: University of Illinois Press, 2013.

Jones, Ewan. "John 'Walking' Stewart, and the Ethics of Motion." *Romanticism* 21, no. 2 (July 2015): 119–131.

Joy, Louise. "Relative Obscurity: The Emotions of Words, Paint and Sound in Eighteenth—Century Literary Criticism." *History of European Ideas* 40, no. 5 (2014): 644–661.

Juvan, Marko. "From Spatial Turn to GIS-Mapping of Literary Cultures." *European Review* 23, no. 1 (2015): 81–96.

Kaltenecker, Martin. "The Discourse of Sound." *Tempo* 70 (2016): 5–15.

Karimzadeh, Morteza, Scott Pezanowski, Alan M. MacEachren, and Jan O. Wallgrün. "GeoTxt: A Scalable Geoparsing System for Unstructured Text Geolocation." *Transactions in GIS* 23 (2019): 118–136.

Keats, John. "Letter to Thomas Keats, 25–27 June 1818." In *The Letters of John Keats*, edited by Maurice Buxton Forman, 154–157. Oxford: Oxford University Press, 1947.

Kesebir, Selin, and Pelin Kesebir. "A Growing Disconnect from Nature Is Evident in Cultural Products." *Perspectives on Psychological Science* 12, no. 2 (2017): 258–269.

Kirschenbaum, Matthew G. "What Is Digital Humanities and What's It Doing in English Departments?" In *Defining Digital Humanities: A Reader*, edited by Melissa Terras, Julianne Nyhan, and Edward Vanhoutte, 195–204. Farnham, UK: Ashgate, 2013.

Klein, Lauren F. "Distant Reading after Moretti." *ARCADE* (blog), 2018. https://arcade.stanford.edu/blogs/distant-reading-after-moretti.

Klett, Joseph. "Sound on Sound: Situating Interaction in Sonic Object Settings." *Sociological Theory* 32, no. 2 (2014): 147–161.

Knowles, Anne Kelly, Levi Westerveld, and Laura Strom. "Inductive Visualization: A Humanistic Alternative to GIS." *GeoHumanities* 1, no. 2 (2015): 233–265.

Kostelnick, Charles. "Wordsworth, Ruins, and the Aesthetics of Decay: From Surface to Noble Picturesque." *Wordsworth Circle* 19, no. 1 (1998): 20–28.

Krause, B. L. "Bioacoustics: Habitat Ambience in Ecological Balance." *Whole Earth Review* 57 (1987): 14–18.

Kretzschmar, Jr., William A. "GIS for Language and Literary Study." *Literary Studies in the Digital Age: An Evolving Anthology*. MLA Commons, 2013. https://dlsanthology.mla.hcommons.org/gis-for-language-and-literary-study/

Kuduk Weiner, Stephanie. "Listening with John Clare." *Studies in Romanticism* 48, no. 3 (2009): 371–390.

Kulldorff, Martin. "A Spatial Scan Statistic." *Communications in Statistics: Theory and Methods*, 26 (1997): 1481–1496.

Kwan, Mei-Po. "Is GIS for Women? Reflections on the Critical Discourse in the 1990s." *Gender, Place and Culture* 9 (2002): 271–279.

———. "Visualization: Re-envisioning GIS as a Method in Feminist Geographic Research." *Annals of the Association of American Geographers* 92 (2002): 645–661.

Labbe, Jacqueline. *Romantic Visualities: Landscape, Gender and Romanticism*. London: Palgrave Macmillan, 1998.

Lake District National Park Partnership. *Nomination of the English Lake District for Inscription on the World Heritage List*, 2015.

Langan, Celeste. *Romantic Vagrancy: Wordsworth and the Simulation of Freedom*. Cambridge: Cambridge University Press, 1995.

Leed, Eric J. *The Mind of the Traveller: From Gilgamesh to Global Tourism*. New York: Basic Books, 1991.

Leetaru, Kalev. "In Machines We Trust: Algorithms Are Getting Too Complex to Understand." *Forbes*, 2016. https://www.forbes.com/sites/kalevleetaru/2016/01/04/in-machines-we-trust-algorithms-are-getting-too-complex-to-understand/#734bb72033a5.

Lefebvre, Henri. *Rhythmanalysis: Space, Time and Everyday Life*. Translated by Stuart Elden and Gerald Moore. London: Bloomsbury, 2014.

———. *The Production of Space*. Translated by Donald Nicolson-Smith. Oxford: Blackwell, 1991.

Leigh, Samuel. *Leigh's Guide to the Lakes and Mountains of Cumberland*. London: Samuel Leigh, 1830.

Levin, Susan M. *Dorothy Wordsworth and Romanticism*, rev. ed. Jefferson, NC: McFarland, 2009.

Levinson, Marjorie. *Wordsworth's Great Period Poems: Four Essays*. Cambridge: Cambridge University Press, 1986.

Lindquist, Mark, Eckart Lange, and Jian Kang. "From 3D Landscape Visualization to Environmental Simulation: The Contribution of Sound to the Perception of Virtual Environments." *Landscape and Urban Planning* 148 (2016): 216–231.

Linley, Margaret. "Lake District Online: Studies in Book Ecology and Digital Migration." *Victorian Studies* 58, no. 2 (2016): 258–271.

Linton, Eliza Lynn. *Lizzie Lorton of Greyrigg*. London: Tinsley Brothers, 1866.

———. *The Girl of the Period and Other Social Essays*. London: Richard Bentley & Son, 1883.

———. *The Lake Country*. London: Smith, Elder & Co, 1864.

Liu, Alan. "Transcendental Data: Toward a Cultural History and Aesthetics of the New Encoded Discourse." *Critical Inquiry* 31, no. 1 (2004): 49–84.

———. *Wordsworth: The Sense of History*. Palo Alto, CA: Stanford University Press, 1989.

Livesey, Ruth. *Writing the Stage Coach Nation: Locality on the Move in Nineteenth-Century British Literature*. Oxford: Oxford University Press, 2016.

Lloyd, Sarah. "Poverty." In *An Oxford Companion to the Romantic Age: British Culture 1776–1832*, edited by Iain McCalman Jon Mee, Gillian Russell, Clara Tuite, Kate Fullagar, and Patsy Hardy, 114–125. Oxford: Oxford University Press, 1999.

Lorimer, Hayden. "Cultural Geography: The Busyness of Being 'More-than-Representational.'" *Progress in Human Geography* 29 (2005): 83–94.

Louv, Richard. *The Nature Principle: Reconnecting with Life in a Virtual Age*. Chapel Hill, NC: Algonquin, 2011.

Lynch, Tom, Cheryl Glotfelty, and Karla Armbruster. "Introduction." In *The Bioregional Imagination: Literature, Ecology and Place*, edited by Karla Armbruster, Ezra J. Zeitler, Tom Lynch, and Cheryll Glotfelty. Athens: University of Georgia Press, 2012.

Macarthur, John. *The Picturesque: Architecture, Disgust and Other Irregularities*. London: Routledge, 2007.

MacCannell, Dean. *The Tourist: A New Theory of the Leisure Class*. Berkeley: University of California Press, 1979.

Macfarlane, Robert. "Introduction." In *Nan Shepherd, The Living Mountain*. Edinburgh: Canongate, 2011.

———. *Landmarks*. London: Penguin, 2016.

———. *Mountains of the Mind: A History of a Fascination*. London: Granta, 2003.

———. *The Wild Places*. London: Granta, 2008.

Mackay, Charles. *The Scenery and Poetry of the English Lakes: A Summer Ramble*. London: Longman, 1846.

Macpherson, Hannah. "Walkers with Visual-Impairments in the British Countryside: Picturesque Legacies, Collective Enjoyments and Well-Being Benefits." *Journal of Rural Studies* 51 (2017): 251–258.

Mailing, D. H. *Coordinate Systems and Map Projections*. 2nd ed. Oxford: Pergamon, 1992.

Mandell, Laura. "Gendering Digital Literary History: What Counts for Digital Humanities." In *A New Companion to Digital Humanities*, edited by S. Schreibman, R. Siemens, and J. Unsworth, 511–523. Hoboken, NJ: John Wiley & Sons, 2016.

Marr, J. E. *The Geology of the Lake District and the Scenery as Influenced by Geological Structure*. Cambridge: Cambridge University Press, 1916.

Marshall, J. D., and John K. Walton. *The Lake Counties from 1830 to the Mid-Twentieth Century: A Study in Regional Change*. Manchester: Manchester University Press, 1981.

Martineau, Harriet. *A Complete Guide to the English Lakes*. Windermere, UK: J. Garnett, and Whittaker and Co, 1855.

———. *Harriet Martineau's Autobiography*. Edited by Maria Weston Chapman. Boston: James R. Osgood & Co., 1877.

Mason, Nicholas, Paul Westover, and Shannon Stimpson. "Introduction." *Second Edition of Romantic Circles Guide to the Lakes*. Boulder, CO: Romantic Circles, 2020. https://romantic-circles.org/editions/guide_lakes/editions.2020.guide_lakes.introduction.html.

McCarty, Willard. *Humanities Computing*. Basingstoke, UK: Palgrave Macmillan, 2005.

McDonagh, Briony, and Stephen Daniels. "Enclosure Stories: Narratives from Northamptonshire." *Cultural Geographies* 19, no. 1 (2012): 107–121.

McDonough, Katherine, Ludovic Moncla, and Matje van de Camp. "Named Entity Recognition Goes to Old Regime France: Geographic Text Analysis for Early Modern French Corpora." *International Journal of Geographical Information Science* (2019). https://doi.org/10.1080/13658816.2019.1620235.

McEnery, Anthony, and Helen Baker. *Corpus Linguistics and 17th-Century Prostitution: Computational Linguistics and History*. London: Bloomsbury, 2016.

McEnery, Anthony, and Andrew Hardie. *Corpus Linguistics: Method, Theory and Practice*. Cambridge: Cambridge University Press, 2012.

McGann, Jerome. *The Scholar's Art: Literary Studies in a Managed World*. Chicago: University of Chicago Press, 2006.

McGillivray, Glen. "The Picturesque World Stage." *Performance Research* 13, no. 4 (2008): 127–139.

McGonigal, Jane. "Gaming Can Make a Better World." *TEDTalk*, 2010. https://www.ted.com/talks/jane_mcgonigal_gaming_can_make_a_better_world.

McNee, Alan. *The New Mountaineer in Late Victorian Britain: Materiality, Modernity, and the Haptic Sublime*. Basingstoke, Uk: Palgrave Macmillan, 2016.

Mellor, Anne K. *Romanticism and Gender*. Abingdon, UK: Routledge, 1993.

Mennis, Jeremy. "Geographic Representation in GIS and Art: Common Threads as Exemplified in Paintings by Seurat, Signac, Mondrian, and Diebenkorn." *GeoHumanities* 4, no. 1 (2018): 178–195.

Menuge, Adam. "'Inhabited by Strangers': Tourism and the Lake District Villa." In *The Making of a Cultural Landscape: The English Lake District as Tourist Destination, 1750–2010*, edited by Jason Wood and John K. Walton, 133–154. Farnham, UK: Ashgate, 2013.

Miller, Carl. "God Is in the Machine." *The TLS*, 2018. https://www.the-tls.co.uk/articles/public/ridiculously-complicated-algorithms/.

Modiano, Raimonda. *Coleridge and the Concept of Nature*. London: Macmillan, 1985.

Moretti, Franco. *Atlas of the European Novel, 1800–1900*. London: Verso, 1997.

———. *Graphs, Maps, Trees: Abstract Models for a Literary History*. London: Verso, 2005.

———. *Distant Reading*. London: Verso, 2013.

Morton, Timothy. *Ecology without Nature: Rethinking Environmental Aesthetics*. Cambridge, MA: Harvard University Press, 2007.

Murrieta-Flores, Patricia, Alistair Baron, Ian Gregory, Andrew Hardie, and Paul Rayson. "Automatically Analysing Large Texts in a GIS Environment: The Registrar General's Reports and Cholera in the Nineteenth Century." *Transactions in GIS* 19 (2015): 296–320.

Murrieta-Flores, Patricia, Christopher Donaldson, and Ian Gregory. "GIS and Literary History: Advancing Digital Humanities Research through the Spatial Analysis of Historical Travel Writing and Topographical Literature." *Digital Humanities Quarterly* 11, no. 1 (2017). http://digitalhumanities.org/dhq/vol/11/1/index.html

Musa, Ghazali, James Higham, and Anna Thompson-Carr. *Mountaineering Tourism*. Abingdon: Routledge, 2015.

Newte, Thomas. *A Tour in England and Scotland, in 1785*. London: G.G.J. and J. Robinson, 1788.

Nicholson, Catherine. "Algorithm and Analogy: Distant Reading in 1598." *PMLA* 132, no. 3 (2017): 643–650.

Nicolson, Marjorie Hope. *Mountain Gloom and Mountain Glory: The Development of the Aesthetics of the Infinite*. Seattle: University of Washington Press, 1959.

Noggle, James. *The Temporality of Taste in Eighteenth-Century British Writing*. Oxford: Oxford University Press, 2012.

O'Byrne, Alison. "The Art of Walking in London: Representing Urban Pedestrianism in the Early Nineteenth Century." *Romanticism* 14, no. 2 (July 1, 2008): 94–107. https://doi.org/10.3366/E1354991X08000214.

O'Connor, Ralph. *The Earth on Show: Fossils and the Poetics of Popular Science, 1802–1856*. Chicago: University of Chicago Press, 2007.

OED Online. "Hike, v." Accessed March 16, 2016. http://www.oed.com/view/Entry/86975?rskey=NK7usl&result=2#eid.

OED Online. "Scamander, v." Accessed December 20, 2016. http://www.oed.com/view/Entry/171833?rskey=zi3t51&result=1&isAdvanced=false#eid.

OED Online. "Sonorous, Adj." Oxford University Press, December 2016. http://www.oed.com/view/Entry/184658?redirectedFrom=sonorous&.

OED Online. "Tourist, n." Accessed October 14, 2016. https://www.oed.com/view/Entry/203937?rskey=9jR3eF.

O'Flaherty, Patrick. "Towards an Understanding of Johnson's Rambler." *Studies in English Literature* 18, no. 3 (1500): 523–536.

Ogburn, Dennis E. "Assessing the Level of Visibility of Cultural Objects in Past Landscapes." *Journal of Archaeological Science* 33 (2006): 405–413.

Oldroyd, David R. *Earth, Water, Ice and Fire: Two Hundred Years of Geological Research in the English Lake District.* London: The Geological Society, 2002.

O'Neill, Kevin Lewis, and Benjamin Fogarty-Valenzuela. "Verticality." *Journal of the Royal Anthropological Institute, N.S.* 19 (2013): 378–389.

Openshaw, Stan, Martin Charlton, Colin Wymer, and Alan Craft. "A Mark 1 Geographic Analysis Machine for the Automated Analysis of Point Data Sets." *International Journal of Geographical Information Systems* 1, no. 4 (1987): 335–358.

Otley, Jonathan. *A Concise Description of the English Lakes and Adjacent Mountains.* 4th ed. Keswick: J. Otley, 1830.

———. *A Concise Description of the English Lakes and Adjacent Mountains: With General Directions to Tourists, Notices of the Botany, Mineralogy, and Geology of the District, Observations on Meteorology, the Floating Island in Derwent Lake, and the Black-Lead Mine in Borrowdale.* Keswick: J. Otley and J. Richardson, 1823.

Ottum, Lisa. "Discriminating Vision: Rereading Place in Wordsworth's Guide to the Lakes." *Prose Studies* 34, no. 3 (2013): 167–184.

Ousby, Ian, ed. *James Plumptre's Britain: The Journals of a Tourist in the 1790s.* London: Hutchinson, 1992.

Owens, Trevor. "Defining Data for Humanists: Text, Artifact, Information or Evidence?" *Journal of Digital Humanities* 1, no. 1 (2011). http://journalofdigitalhumanities.org/1-1/defining-data-for-humanists-by-trevor-owens/.

Ozarska, Magdalena. "Grand Tourists or Travellers? Dorothy Wordsworth's and Mary Shelley's Travel Journals." *Zeitschrift für Anglistik und Amerikanistik* 61, no. 2 (2013): 107–120.

Palmer, William T. *In Lakeland Dells and Fells.* London: Chatto & Windus, 1903.

———. *Lake Country Rambles.* London: Chatto & Windus, 1902.

Paterson, Laura L., and Ian N. Gregory. *Representations of Poverty and Place: Using Geographical Text Analysis to Understand Discourse.* Basingstoke, UK: Palgrave Macmillan, 2019.

Pavlovskaya, Marianna, and Kevin St. Martin. "Feminism and Geographic Information Systems: From a Missing Object to a Mapping Subject." *Geography Compass* 1, no. 3 (2007): 583–606.

Pearson, Mike, and Michael Shanks. *Theatre/Archaeology.* Abingdon. UK: Routledge, 2001.

Pennant, Thomas. *A Tour in Scotland. 1769.* Chester, UK: John Monk, 1771.

———. *A Tour in Scotland, and Voyage to the Hebrides, 1772.* Chester, UK: John Monk, 1774.

Pergams, Oliver R. W., and Patricia A. Zaradic. "Evidence for a Fundamental and Pervasive Shift Away from Nature-Based Recreation." *Proceedings of the National Academy of Sciences of the United States of America* 105, no. 7 (2008): 2295–2300.

Pfau, Thomas. *Wordsworth's Profession: Form, Class and the Logic of Early Romantic Cultural Production.* Palo Alto, CA: Stanford University Press, 1997.

Piatti, Barbara, Hans Rudolf Bär, Anne-Kathrin Reuschel, Lorenz Hurni, and William Cartwright. "Mapping Literature: Towards a Geography of Fiction." In *Cartography and Art,* edited by William Cartwright, Georg Gartner, and Antje Leh, 177–183. Berlin: Springer, 2009.

Picker, John M. *Victorian Soundscapes.* Oxford: Oxford University Press, 2003.

Pijanowski, Bryan C., Luis J. Villanueva-Rivera, Sarah L. Dumyahn, Almo Farina, Bernie L. Krause, Brian M. Napoletano, Stuart H. Gage, and Nadia Pieretti. "Soundscape Ecology: The Science of Sound in the Landscape." *BioScience* 61, no. 3 (2011): 203–216.

Piper, Andrew. *Enumerations: Data and Literary Study.* Chicago: University of Chicago Press, 2018.

Plumptre, James. *The Lakers: A Comic Opera in Three Acts.* London: W. Clarke, 1798.

Porter, Catherine. "Introduction: The Importance of Place and Openness in Spatial Humanities Research." *International Journal of Arts and Humanities Computing* 12, no. 2 (2018): 91–101.

Porter, Catherine, Paul Atkinson, and Ian Gregory. "Geographical Text Analysis: A New Key to Nineteenth-Century Mortality." *Health and Place* 36 (2015): 25–34.

Porter, Dahlia. "Maps, Lists, Views: How the Picturesque Wye Transformed Topography." *Romanticism* 19, no. 2 (2013): 163–178.

Powell, Cecilia, ed. *Excursion to Wordsworthshire: A Victorian Family in the Lakes.* Grasmere, UK: Wordsworth Trust, 2015.

Powell, Manushag N. "Johnson and His 'Readers' in the Epistolary Rambler Essays." *Studies in English Literature* 44, no. 3 (2004): 571–594.

Pressman, Jessica, and Lisa Swanstrom. "The Literary And/As the Digital Humanities." *Digital Humanities Quarterly* 7, no. 1 (2013). http://digitalhumanities.org:8081/dhq/vol/7/1/000154/000154.html.

Prynne, J. H. *Field Notes: "The Solitary Reaper" and Others.* Cambridge: Cambridge Printers, 2007.

Radcliffe, Ann. *A Journey Made in the Summer of 1791.* London: G.G.J. and J. Robinson, 1795.

Ramsay, Stephen. "In Praise of Pattern." *TEXT Technology: The Journal of Computer Text Processing* 14, no. 2 (2005): 177–190.

Rarey, Matthew Francis. "Camera Lucida Mexicana: Travel, Visual Technologies, and Contested Objectivities." In *Visuality's Romantic Genealogies.* Boulder, CO: Romantic Circles, 2014. https://www.rc.umd.edu/praxis/visualities/praxis.visualities.2014.rarey.html.

Rawlinson, Robert. *Report to the General Board of Health on a Preliminary Inquiry into the Sewerage, Drainage, and Supply of Water, and the Sanitary Condition of the Inhabitants of the Township of Alnwick and Canongate in the County of Northumberland.* London: W. Clowes & Sons, 1850.

Raymond, Joad, and Noah Moxham, eds. *News Networks in Early Modern Europe.* Leiden: Brill, 2016.

Rayson, Paul, Alexander Reinhold, James Butler, Christopher Donaldson, Ian N. Gregory, and Joanna E. Taylor. "A Deeply Annotated Testbed for Geographical Text Analysis: The Corpus of Lake District Writing." In *GeoHumanities '17: 1st ACM SIGSPATIAL Workshop on Geospatial Humanities.* Association for Computing Machinery, 2017. https://doi.org/10.1145/3149858.3149865.

Reay, Barry. *Rural Englands: Labouring Lives in the Nineteenth Century.* Basingstoke, NY: Palgrave Macmillan, 2004.

Rebanks, James. *The Shepherd's Life: A Tale of the Lake District.* London: Penguin, 2015.

Reinhold, Alexander, Ian N. Gregory, and Paul Rayson. "Deep Mapping Tarn Hows: Automated Generation of 3D Historic Landscapes." In *Eurographics Workshop on Graphics and Cultural Heritage. The Eurographics Association, Congress Visual Heritage,* edited by R. Sablatnig and M. Wimmer. Vienna, Austria: The Eurographics Association, 2018. https://doi.org/10.2312/gch.20181366

Renouf, Jane, and Rob David. *Voices of the Lake District.* Stroud, UK: The History Press, 2011.

Reuschel, Anne-Kathrin, and Barbara Piatti. "Ein Literarischer Atlas Europas." In *Geoinformationssysteme, Beiträge zum 16. Münchner Fortbildungsseminar,* edited by M. Schilcher, 254–272. Heidelberg: ABC Verlag, 2011.

Revill, George. "How Is Space Made in Sound? Spatial Mediation, Critical Phenomenology and the Political Agency of Sound." *Progress in Human Geography* 40, no. 2 (2016): 240–256.

Rezaeian, Mohsen, Graham Dunn, Selwyn St. Leger, and Louis Appleby. "Geographical Epidemiology, Spatial Analysis and Geographical Information Systems: A Multidisciplinary Glossary." *Journal of Epidemiology & Community Health* 61, no. 2 (2007): 98–102.

Risen, James, and Eric Lichtblau. "How the U.S. Uses Technology to Mine More Data More Quickly." *New York Times*, June 2013. https://www.nytimes.com/2013/06/09/us /revelations-give-look-at-spy-agencys-wider-reach.html

Ritvo, Harriet. "Counting Sheep in the English Lake District: Rare Breeds, Local Knowledge and Environmental History." In *Beastly Natures: Animals, Humans, and the Study of History*, edited by Dorothee Brantz, 264–279. Richmond: University of Virginia Press, 2010.

——. *The Dawn of Green: Manchester, Thirlmere, and Modern Environmentalism*. Chicago: Chicago University Press, 2009.

Rix, Herbert. *Down the Duddon with Wordsworth [1883–1893]*. London: Bouverie, 1893.

Robbins, Bruce. "Victorian Cosmopolitanism, Interrupted." *Victorian Literature and Culture*, 38 (2010): 421–425.

Robinson, John. "A Guide to the Lakes." In *Cumberland, Westmorland, and Lancashire*. London: Lackington and Co, 1819.

Roe, Nicholas. *The Politics of Nature: William Wordsworth and Some Contemporaries*. Basingstoke, UK: Palgrave Macmillan, 2002.

Rollinson, William. *Life & Tradition in the Lake District*. Lancaster, UK: Dalesman Books, 1981.

Rosenberg, Elissa. "Walking in the City: Memory and Place." *Journal of Architecture* 17, no. 1 (2012): 131–149.

Rosenfeld, Sophia. "On Being Heard: A Case for Paying Attention to the Historical Ear." *American Historical Review* 16, no. 2 (2011): 316–334.

Ross, Marlon B. "Romantic Quest and Conquest: Troping Masculine Power in the Crisis of Poetic Identity." In *Romanticism and Feminism*, edited by Anne K. Mellor, 26–51. Bloomington: Indiana University Press, 1988.

Rossetti, Christina. *The Poetical Works of Christina Georgina Rossetti with Memoir and Notes &c by William Michael Rossetti*. London: Macmillan, 1935.

Rossetto, Tania. "Theorizing Maps with Literature." *Progress in Human Geography* 38, no. 4 (2014): 513–530.

Rowney, Matthew. "Music in the Noise: The Acoustic Ecology of John Clare." *Journal of Interdisciplinary Voice Studies* 1, no. 1 (2016): 23–40.

Rowntree, Benjamin Seebohm, and May Kendall. *How the Labourer Lives: A Study of the Rural Labour Problem*. London: Thomas Nelson and Sons, 1917.

Rupp, C. J., Paul Rayson, Ian Gregory, Andrew Hardie, Amelia Joulain, and Daniel Hartmann. "Dealing with Heterogeneous Big Data When Geoparsing Historical Corpora." In *Proceedings of the 2014 IEEE Conference on Big Data*, 80–83, 2014. https://ieeexplore .ieee.org/document/7004457

Ruskin, John. *Iteriad; or, Three Weeks among the Lakes [1830–32]*. Newcastle, UK: Frank Graham, 1969.

——. "Modern Painters." In *The Complete Works of John Ruskin Vols.III—VII*, edited by E.T. Cook and Alexander Wedderburn. London: George Allen, 1903.

——. *Sesame and Lilies, The Ethics of Dust and The Crown of Wild Olive with Letters on Public Affairs 1859–1866*. In *The Complete Works of John Ruskin*, edited by E. T. Cook and Alexander Wedderburn, Vol. XVIII. London: George Allen, 1905.

———. *The Seven Lamps of Architecture.* In *The Complete Works of John Ruskin*, edited by E. T. Cook and Alexander Wedderburn, Vol. VIII. London: George Allen, 1903.

Rutherford, Sarah. "Claife Station and the Picturesque in the Lakes." In *The Making of a Cultural Landscape: The English Lake District as Tourist Destination, 1750–2010*, edited by John K. Walton and Jason Wood, 201–218. Farnham, UK: Ashgate, 2013.

Sales, Roger. *English Literature in History: Pastoral and Politics 1780–1830.* London: St. Martin's Press, 1983.

Samsung Galaxy S8 Commercial, 2017. https://www.youtube.com/watch?v=yRmIKHhCejo.

Sandbrook, Chris, William M. Adams, and Bruno Monteferri. "Digital Games and Biodiversity Conservation." *Conservation Letters* 8, no. 2 (2014): 118–124.

Santesso, Aaron. "The Birth of the Birthplace: Bread Street and Literary Tourism Before Stratford." *ELH*, 71 (2004): 377–403.

Schafer, R. Murray. *The Soundscape: Our Sonic Environment and the Tuning of the World.* Rochester, VT: Destiny Books, 1993.

Schöch, Christof. "Big? Smart? Clean? Messy? Data in the Humanities." *Journal of Digital Humanities* 2, no. 3 (2013). http://journalofdigitalhumanities.org/2-3/big-smart-clean-messy-data-in-the-humanities/.

Schönherr, Ulrich. "Topophony of Fascism: On Marcel Beyer's The Karnau Tapes." *Germanic Review: Literature, Culture, Theory* 73, no. 4 (1998): 328–348.

Scott, Allen J. "The Cultural Economy of Landscape and Prospects for Peripheral Development in the Twenty-First Century: The Case of the English Lake District." *European Planning Studies* 18, no. 10 (2010): 1567–1589.

Scott, Heidi. "Colonialism, Landscape and the Subterranean." *Geography Compass* 2 (2008): 1853–1869.

Seed, David. "Nineteenth-Century Travel Writing: An Introduction." *Yearbook of English Studies*, 34 (2004): 1–5.

Simpson, David. *Wordsworth's Historical Imagination: The Poetry of Displacement.* London: Methuen, 1987.

Smith, Adam. *An Inquiry into the Nature and Causes of the Wealth of Nations.* Edited by Edwin Cannan. New York: The Modern Library, 1776.

Smith, Bruce R. *The Acoustic World of Early Modern England: Attending to the O-Factor.* Chicago: University of Chicago Press, 1999.

Smith, Lindsay. *Victorian Photography, Painting and Poetry: The Enigma of Visibility in Ruskin, Morris and the Pre-Raphaelites.* Cambridge: Cambridge University Press, 1995.

Smith, Mark M., ed. *Hearing History: A Reader.* Athens: University of Georgia Press, 2004.

Smith, Susan J. "Soundscape." *Area* 26, no. 3 (1994): 232–240.

Snyder, John P. *Flattening the Earth: Two Thousand Years of Map Projections.* Chicago: University of Chicago Press, 1997.

Solnit, Rebecca. *Wanderlust: A History of Walking.* London: Verso, 2001.

Southall, Humphrey, Ruth Mostern, and Merrick Lex Berman. "On Historical Gazetteers." *International Journal of Humanities and Arts Computing* 5 (2011): 127–145.

Southern, Jennifer Ann. "Reflective Assemblages: Real and Imagined Mobilities in Locative Media Art." In *Envisioning Networked Mobilities: Art Creativity, Performance*, 15–25. New York: Routledge, 2017.

Southey, Robert. *The Collected Letters of Robert Southey, Part Three: 1804–1809.* Edited by Carol Bolton and Tim Fulford. Boulder, CO: Romantic Circles, 2013. https://romantic-circles.org/editions/southey_letters/Part_Three/index.html.

———. *The Collected Letters of Robert Southey, Part Five: 1816–1818.* Edited by Tim Fulford, Ian Packer, and Linda Pratt. Boulder, CO: Romantic Circles, 2016. https://romantic-circles.org/editions/southey_letters/Part_Five/index.html.

———. *Letters from England, by Don Manuel Alvarez Espriella*. Edited by Carol Bolton. Abingdon. UK: Routledge, 2016.

Speich, Daniel. "Mountains Made in Switzerland: Facts and Concerns in Nineteenth-Century Cartography." *Science in Context* 22, no. 3 (2009): 387–408.

St. Clair, William. *The Reading Nation in the Romantic Period*. Cambridge: Cambridge University Press, 2004.

Stadler, Jane, Peta Mitchell, and Stephen Carelton. *Imagined Landscapes: Geovisualizing Australian Spatial Narratives*. Bloomington: Indiana University Press, 2016.

Stell, John G. "Qualitative Spatial Reasoning for the Humanities." *International Journal of Humanities and Arts Computing* 13 (2019): 2–27.

Stewart, Suzanne. "'The Eye It Cannot Choose but See': Dorothy Wordsworth, John Constable, and the Plein-Air Sketch." *English Studies* 92, no. 4 (2011): 405–431.

Street, Sean. *The Memory of Sound: Preserving the Sonic Past*. Abingdon: Routledge, 2015.

Sussman, Aaron, and Ruth Goode. *The Magic of Walking*. New York: Simon & Schuster, 1980.

Svensson, Patrick. "Humanities Computing as Digital Humanities." In *Defining Digital Humanities: A Reader*, edited by Melissa Terras, Julianne Nyhan, and Edward Vanhoutte, 159–186. Farnham, UK: Ashgate, 2013.

Szendy, Peter. *Listen: A History of Our Ears*. Translated by Charlotte Mandell. New York: Fordham University Press, 2008.

Tavel Clark, Michael, and David Wittenberg, eds. *Scale in Literature and Culture*. Basingstoke: Palgrave Macmillan, 2017.

Taylor, Joanna E. "Echoes in the Mountains: The Romantic Lake District's Soundscape." *Studies in Romanticism* 57, no. 3 (2018): 383–406.

———. "Mountain Matter(s): Anticipatory Cartography in Nineteenth-Century Mountain Literature." In *Anticipatory Materialisms in Literature and Philosophy, 1790–1930*. Basingstoke: Palgrave Macmillan, 2019.

———. "Settling at Keswick: Affective Bioregionalism in Southey Country." In *Romanticism on the Net*, 68–69, 2017. https://ronjournal.org/s/3412.

Taylor, Joanna E., and Christopher E. Donaldson. "Footprints in Spatial Narratives: Wearable Technology, Active Reading, and a New Digital Literary Mapping of Dorothy Wordsworth's Scafell Pike Excursion." In *Spatial Narratives*, edited by Dan Punday. Abingdon: Routledge, 2022: 124–141.

Taylor, Joanna E., Christopher Donaldson, Ian N. Gregory, and James O. Butler. "Mapping Digitally, Mapping Deep: Exploring Digital Literary Geographies." *Literary Geographies* 4, no. 1 (2018): 10–19.

Taylor, Joanna E., Ian N. Gregory, and Christopher Donaldson. "Combining Close and Distant Reading: A Multiscalar Analysis of the English Lake District's Historical Soundscape." *International Journal of Humanities and Arts Computing* 12, no. 2 (2018): 163–182.

Taylor, P. J. "Editorial comment: GKS." *Political Geography Quarterly* 9 (1990): 211–212.

Téchené, Claire. "On the Use and Representations of Sound in British Pre-Romantic and Romantic Poetry, or 'On The Power of Sound.'" *Etudes Epistémè: Revue de Littérature et de Civilisation* 29 (2016). https://doi.org/10.4000/episteme.1032.

Terry, Richard. "'The Sound Must Seem an Eccho to the Sense': An Eighteenth-Century Controversy Revisited." *Modern Language Review* 94, no. 4 (1999): 940–954.

Thompson, Emily. *The Soundscape of Modernity: Architectural Acoustics and the Culture of Listening in America, 1900–1933*. Cambridge, MA: Harvard University Press, 2002.

Thomson, Heidi. "Wordsworth's 'Song for the Wandering Jew' as a Poem for Coleridge." *Romanticism* 21, no. 1 (March 17, 2015): 37–47. https://doi.org/10.3366/rom.2015.0209.

Thoreau, Henry David. *The Correspondence of Henry David Thoreau: Volume 1: 1834–1848.* Edited by Robert N. Hudspeth. Vol. 1. Princeton, NJ: Princeton University Press, 2013.

Thorne, James. *Rambles by Rivers.* London: Charles Knight, 1844.

Todd, Barbara. *Harriet Martineau at Ambleside.* Carlisle, UK: Bookcase, 2002.

Toner, Anne. "Landscape as Literary Criticism: Jane Austen, Anna Barbauld and the Narratological Application of the Picturesque." *Critical Survey* 26, no. 1 (2014): 3–19.

Townsend, Dabney. "The Picturesque." *Journal of Aesthetics and Art Criticism* 55, no. 4 (1997): 365–376.

Truax, Barry. "The Handbook for Acoustic Ecology," 2nd ed. 1999. https://www.sfu.ca /sonic-studio-webdav/handbook/index.html.

Tuan, Yi Fu. "Geography, Phenomenology, and the Study of Human Nature." *Canadian Geographer* 15, no. 3 (1971): 181–193.

———. "Space and Place: Humanistic Perspective." In *Philosophy in Geography*, edited by Stephen Gale and Gunnar Olsson, 387–427. Boston, MA: D. Reidel Publishing, 1979.

Turnbull, Belinda. "Keswick's Mass Trespass." *Lake District National Park Blog* (blog), October 2, 2014. https://www.lakedistrict.gov.uk/the-blog/blog-posts/keswicks-mass-trespass.

Tyndall, John. *Sound.* London: Longman, Greens, & Co., 1867.

Underwood, Ted. *Distant Horizons: Digital Evidence and Literary Change.* Chicago: University of Chicago Press, 2019.

———. "Distant Reading and Recent Intellectual History." In *Debates in the Digital Humanities*, edited by Matthew K. Gold and Lauren F. Klein: 530–533. Minneapolis: University of Minnesota Press, 2016. http://dhdebates.gc.cuny.edu/debates/part/14.

Upton, Dell. "Sound as Landscape." *Landscape Journal* 26, no. 1 (2007): 24–35.

Urry, John. *The Tourist Gaze.* 2nd ed. London: SAGE, 2002.

Urry, John, and Jonas Larson. *The Tourist Gaze 3.0.* London: SAGE, 2011.

Van Renen, Denys. "Decomposing the Picturesque and Re-collecting Nature in Dorothy Wordsworth's Scotland." *Journal of Narrative Theory* 45, no. 2 (2015): 165–192.

Van Tassel, Mary. "Johnson's Elephant: The Reader of *The Rambler.*" *Studies in English Literature* 28, no. 3 (1988): 461–469.

Van Thal, Herbert. *Eliza Lynn Linton: The Girl of the Period: A Biography.* London: Allen and Unwin, 1979.

Vardy, Alan. "Coleridge on Broad Stand." *Romanticism and Victorianism on the Net* 61 (2012). https://doi.org/10.7202/1018600ar.

Vergunst, Jo. "Rhythms of Walking: History and Presence in a City Street." *Space and Culture* 13, no. 4 (2010): 376–388.

Vila-Cabanes, Isabel. *The Flaneur in Nineteenth-Century British Literary Culture: "The Worlds of London Unknown."* Newcastle-on-Tyne, UK: Cambridge Scholars Publishing, 2018.

Wainwright, Alfred. *The Outlying Fells of Lakeland.* Kendal, UK: Westmorland Gazette, 1974.

Wakeford, Richard, Keith Binks, and David Wilkie. "Childhood Leukaemia and Nuclear Installations." *Journal of the Royal Statistical Society Series A* 152, no. 1 (1989): 1–26.

Walker, Adam. *Remarks Made in a Tour from London to the Lakes of Westmoreland and Cumberland, in the Summer of 1791.* London: G. Nicol and C. Dilly, 1792.

Walker, Carol Kyros. *Walking North with Keats.* New Haven: Yale University Press, 1992.

Wallace, Anne D. *Walking, Literature and English Culture: The Origins and Uses of Peripatetic in the Nineteenth Century.* Oxford: Oxford University Press, 1993.

Walton, John K. "Setting the Scene." In *The Making of a Cultural Landscape: The English Lake District as Tourist Destination, 1750–2010*, edited by John K. Walton and Jason Wood, 31–48. Farnham, UK: Ashgate, 2013.

Walton, John K., and Jason Wood, eds. *The Making of a Cultural Landscape: The English Lake District as Tourist Destination, 1750–2010*. Farnham, UK: Ashgate, 2013.

Watson, Nicola J. *The Literary Tourist: Readers and Places in Romantic and Victorian Britain*. Basingstoke, UK: Palgrave Macmillan, 2006.

Waugh, Edwin. *Rambles in the Lake Country and Its Borders*. Manchester: John Heywood, and Simpkin, Marshall and Co, 1861.

Weingart, Scott. *The Moral Role of DH in a Data-Driven World*, 2014. http://www .digitalhumanities.org/dhq/vol/5/1/000091/000091.html.

Weizman, Eyal. "Maps of Israeli Settlements." *Open Democracy*, April 24, 2002. https:// www.opendemocracy.net/ecology—politicsverticality/article_631.jsp.

Wells, Amy. "La cartographie comme outil d'analyse litteraire: Des cartes metaphoriques aux cartes SIG." In *Geographie poetique et cartographie litteraire*. Edited by Véronique Maleval, Marion Picker, and Florent Gabaude, 169–186. Limoges, France: Pulim, 2012.

Wells-Brown, William. *Three Years in Europe: Or, Places I Have Seen and People I Have Met*. London: Charles Gilpin, 1852.

West, Thomas. *A Guide to the Lakes: Dedicated to the Lovers of Landscape Studies, Etc.* London: Richardson and Urquhart, and W. Pennington, 1778.

Westaway, Jonathan. "Mountains of Memory, Landscapes of Loss: Scafell Pike and Great Gable as War Memorials, 1919–24." *Landscapes* 14, no. 2 (2013):,174–193.

———. "The Origins and Development of Mountaineering and Rock Climbing Tourism in the Lake District, c.1800–1914." In *The Making of a Cultural Landscape: The English Lake District as Tourist Destination, 1750–2010*, edited by John K. Walton and Jason Wood, 155–180. Abingdon, UK: Routledge, 2013.

Westover, Paul. "William Godwin, Literary Tourism, and the Work of Necromanticism." *Studies in Romanticism* 48, no. 2 (2009): 299–319.

White, Jonathan. "The Laboring-Class Domestic Sphere in Eighteenth-Century British Social Thought." In *Gender, Taste, and Material Culture in Britain and North America, 1700–1830*, edited by John Styles and Amanda Vickery, 247–263. New Haven, CT: Yale University Press, 2006.

White, Leanne, and Elspeth Frew. "Tourism and National Identities: Connections and Conceptualisations." In *Tourism and National Identities: An International Perspective*, edited by Elspeth Frew and Leanne White, 1–10. Abingdon, UK: Routledge, 2011.

Whitson, Roger. *Steampunk and Nineteenth-Century Digital Humanities: Literary Retrofuturisms*. Media Archaeologies, Alternate Histories. Abingdon: Routledge, 2017.

Whyte, Ian. "William Wordsworth's Guide to the Lakes and the Geographical Tradition." *Area* 32, no. 1 (2000): 101–106.

Wickman, Matthew. "Travel Writing and the Picturesque." In *The Edinburgh Companion to Scottish Romanticism*, edited by Murray Pittock, Ian Brown, and Thomas Owen Clancy, 61–71. Edinburgh: Edinburgh University Press, 2011.

Wilberforce, William. *Journey to the Lake District from Cambridge*. Stocksfield, UK: Oriel Press, 1983.

Wiley, Michael. *Romantic Geography: Wordsworth and Anglo-European Spaces*. Basingstoke, UK: Palgrave Macmillan, 1998.

Wilkens, Matthew. "Canons, Close Reading, and the Evolution of Method." In *Debates in the Digital Humanities*, edited by Matthew K. Gold, 249–258. Minneapolis: University of Minnesota Press, 2012.

———. "The Geographic Imagination of Civil War–Era American Fiction." *American Literary History* 25, no. 4 (2013): 803–840.

Wilkinson, Thomas. *Tours to the British Mountains, with the Descriptive Poems of Lowther.* London: Taylor and Hessey, 1824.

Williams, Raymond. *Problems in Materialism and Culture.* London: Verso, 1980.

——. *The Country and the City.* London: Vintage, 1973.

Williamson, C. N. "The Climbs of the English Lake District," Part 2. *All the Year Round,* November 8, 1884.

Wilson, John. "Letters from the Lakes. Translated from the German of Philip Kempferhausen— Written in the Summer of 1818." *Blackwood's Edinburgh Magazine,* January 1819, 396–398.

Winstanley, Michael. "Industrialization and the Small Farm: Family and Household Economy in Nineteenth-Century Lancashire." *Past & Present,* 152 (1996): 157–195.

Wolfson, Susan J. "Sounding Romantic: The Sound of Sound." In *"Soundings of Things Done": The Poetry and Poetics of Sound in the Romantic Ear and Era.* Edited by Susan J. Wolfson. Boulder, CO: Romantic Circles, 2008. https://www.rc.umd.edu/praxis/.

Woolf, Virginia. *Street Haunting and Other Essays.* London: Vintage, 2014.

Wordsworth, Dorothy. *George and Sarah Green: A Narrative.* Edited by Ernest De Sélincourt. Oxford: Clarendon Press, 1936.

——. "Letter to William Johnson." Wordsworth Trust, October 1818. WLL / Wordsworth, W and D / 4 / 326.

Wordsworth, William. *A Description of the Scenery of the Lakes in the North of England.* London: Longman, 1822.

——. *The Excursion.* Edited by Sally Bushell, James A. Butler, and Michael C. Jaye. Ithaca, NY: Cornell University Press, 2007.

——. *Last Poems, 1821–1850.* Edited by Jared Curtis. Ithaca, NY: Cornell University Press, 1999.

——. *The Letters of William and Dorothy Wordsworth: The Middle Years: Pt. 2, 1812–1820.* Oxford: Clarendon Press, 1967.

——. *Lyrical Ballads and Other Poems, 1797–1800.* Edited by James Butler and Karen Green. Ithaca, NY: Cornell University Press, 1993.

——. *The Major Works.* Edited by Stephen Gill. Revised. Oxford: Oxford University Press, 1984.

——. *The River Duddon: A Series of Sonnets.* London: Longman, 1820.

——. *The Thirteen-Book "Prelude."* Edited by Mark L. Reed. Ithaca, NY: Cornell University Press, 1992.

——. *Wordsworth's Guide through the District of the Lakes: The Fifth Edition (1835).* Edited by Ernest De Selincourt. Oxford: Oxford University Press, 1906.

Wyatt, John. *Wordsworth and the Geologists.* Cambridge: Cambridge University Press, 1995.

Wylie, John. "Depths and Fold: On Landscape and the Gazing Subject." *Environment and Planning D: Society and Space* 24 (2006): 519–535.

Yarnall, Ellis. *Walks and Visits in Wordsworth Country [1876].* New York: Macmillan, 1899.

Yee, Chiang. *The Silent Traveller: A Chinese Artist in Lakeland.* London: Country Life Ltd, 1937.

Yoshikawa, Saeko. *William Wordsworth and the Invention of Tourism, 1820–1900.* Farnham, UK: Ashgate, 2014.

Young, Arthur. *Six Months' Tour through the North of England.* London: W. Strahan, W. Nicoll, B. Collins, J. Balfour, 1770.

Index

Page references to figures and tables in italics.

Paintings, key primary texts, and works from the CLDW included in the index are referenced under both title and name of author, where applicable.

About the Authors

Joanna E. Taylor is a presidential fellow in digital humanities at the University of Manchester in the UK. Her research explores the uses of digital technologies at the intersection between literary geographies, cultural heritage, and environmental studies. She has published on these topics in leading journals across literary studies, digital humanities, and geographical information science.

Ian N. Gregory is a professor of digital humanities at Lancaster University in the UK. He is particularly interested in using geographical information systems (GIS) with texts as well as the more traditional quantitative sources. He has used these approaches to study a range of topics from historical demography to Lake District literature. This research has been the subject of a number of major projects, including the European Research Council-funded Spatial Humanities: Texts, GIS, Places project and the Leverhulme Trust-funded Geospatial Innovation in the Digital Humanities.